INSIGHT GUIDE
THE NETHERLANDS

APA PUBLICATIONS
Part of the Langenscheidt Publishing Group

Editorial

Editor
Teresa Machan
Editorial Director
Brian Bell

Distribution

UK & Ireland
GeoCenter International Ltd
The Viables Centre , Harrow Way
Basingstoke, Hants RG22 4BJ
Fax: (44) 1256-817988

United States
Langenscheidt Publishers, Inc.
46–35 54th Road, Maspeth, NY 11378
Fax: (718) 784-0640

Canada
Prologue Inc.
1650 Lionel Bertrand Blvd., Boisbriand
Québec, Canada J7H 1N7
Tel: (450) 434-0306. Fax: (450) 434-2627

Worldwide
Apa Publications GmbH & Co.
Verlag KG (Singapore branch)
38 Joo Koon Road, Singapore 628990
Tel: (65) 865-1600. Fax: (65) 861-6438

Printing

Insight Print Services (Pte) Ltd
38 Joo Koon Road, Singapore 628990
Tel: (65) 865-1600. Fax: (65) 861-6438

CONTACTING THE EDITORS
Although every effort is made to
provide accurate information, we
live in a fast-changing world and
would appreciate it if readers
would call our attention to any
errors or outdated information
that may occur by writing to:
**Insight Guides, P.O. Box 7910,
London SE1 1WE, England.
Fax: (44 20) 7403-0290.**
e-mail:
insight@apaguide.demon.co.uk

This guidebook combines the
interests and enthusiasms of
two of the world's best known information providers: Insight Guides,
whose titles have set the standard
for visual travel guides since 1970,
and Discovery Channel, the world's
premier source of nonfiction television programming.

The editors of Insight Guides provide practical advice and general
understanding about a destination's
history, culture and people. Discovery Channel and its
popular Web site,
www.discovery.com,
help millions of viewers
explore their world from
the comfort of their
own home and also en-
courage them to ex-
plore it first hand.

This updated edition

of *Insight: The Netherlands* is carefully structured to convey an understanding of The Netherlands and its
culture as well as to guide readers
through its sights and activities:

◆ The **Features** section, indicated
by a yellow bar at the top of each
page, covers history and culture in a
series of informative essays.

◆ The main **Places** section, indicated by a blue bar, is a complete
guide to all the sights and areas
worth visiting. Places of special
interest are coordinated by
number with the maps.

◆ The **Travel Tips** listings
section, with an orange bar,
provides a handy point of
reference for information
on travel, hotels, shops,
restaurants. An index to
the section can be found
on the back flap.

EXPLORE YOUR WORLD

The contributors

This latest edition of *Insight: The Netherlands* was built on the previous edition edited by **Christopher Catling**, and based on the excellent research done by Catling and the original contributors, much of whose text remains in this edition. These were writers **Derek Blyth**, **Michael Gray**, **Lisa Gerard-Sharp**, **Tim Harper**, and **Joan Corcoran-Lonis**.

This edition has been completely revised with the invaluable help of three dedicated updaters: Joan Gannij, Frank Balleny and George McDonald.

Joan Gannij was responsible for updating the Amsterdam, The Hague, Rotterdam and Gelderland chapters, and she also contributed a number of the book's new feature essays, including those on Modern Art and Architecture. Gannij also

wrote the special features on Cafés and Festivals. Joan Gannij moved to Amsterdam in 1987 as editor of *Master Chef*, an international food, wine and travel magazine. She has worked with Insight Guides for five years and has also contributed to books on Finland, Oslo and Bergen.

The feature on Nature Reserves was written by **George McDonald**, who also updated the chapters on Zeeland, Noord Brabant, Limburg and IJsselmeer and re-vamped parts of the History section. George McDonald is a Brussels-based journalist who lived in Amsterdam as deputy editor of the KLM in-flight magazine, *Holland Herald*, before becoming editor of Sabena's in-flight magazine, *Sphere*. Brussels is close to the Dutch province of Zeeland, which McDonald visits whenever he needs a breath of fresh air to remind him of his native Scotland.

Amsterdam Environs, Utrecht, Flevoland, Overijssel, Drenthe and Friesland were updated by **Frank Balleny**, who also wrote the special feature on Boat Trips. Of English and Dutch parentage, Balleny's poetry has been published in both languages.

As in all Insight Guides, photography plays a major part. The difficult task of bringing the largely uniform landscape of the Netherlands to life fell to *Insight* veteran **Bill Wassman**. Another major contributor, **Eddy Posthuma de Boer**, lives and exhibits his work in his native Amsterdam.

Thanks also go to **Tim Harrison** and **Cathy Muscat** for their copyediting contributions, and finally to **Penny Phenix**, who proofread and indexed the book.

Map Legend

▬ ▬	International Boundary
▬ ▬ ▬	Province Boundary
▬ • ▬	National Park/Reserve
▬ ▬ ▬	Ferry Route
Ⓜ	Metro
✈ ✈	Airport: International/Regional
🚍	Bus Station
🅿	Parking
❶	Tourist Information
✉	Post Office
✝ ✝ ✝	Church/Ruins
✝	Monastery
☾	Mosque
✡	Synagogue
🏰	Castle/Ruins
∴	Archaeological Site
∩	Cave
🗽	Statue/Monument
★	Place of Interest

The main places of interest in the Places section are coordinated by number with a full-colour map (e.g. ❶), and a symbol at the top of every right-hand page tells you where to find the map.

INSIGHT GUIDE
The NETHERLANDS

CONTENTS

Maps

Inside front cover:
Netherlands
Inside back cover:
Amsterdam

Hoorn harbour,
west Friesland

Information panels

Travel Tips

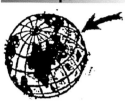

♦ **Full Travel Tips index
is on page 321**

Places

DUTCH TREATS

*They conquered the sea, championed the tulip, and gave birth
to Rembrandt and Mata Hari. The Dutch are worth visiting*

The Dutch appear on first acquaintance an enigmatic people, full of apparent contradictions, which they either reconcile with a shrug or not at all. Beyond what may seem to be an exterior gruffness, though, most Dutch are cordial and frank-speaking. Direct as they are in communicating, however, they tend to encourage interested travellers to discover their country and its inhabitants for themselves. Indeed, it is part of the Dutch character to let people go their own way and draw their own conclusions.

The Dutch are also self-effacing, but the Netherlands has a long and varied history, and the people are proud of it. Few other countries, let alone such a small one, can claim a period comparable to the 17th-century Golden Age, when Holland and its allied provinces dominated European culture and commerce. Along the way, the Dutch created many of the concepts of modern humanism, including freedom of religion and freedom of the press – concepts that remain the ideals for modern democratic society.

In addition, the Dutch have made their country one of the most accommodating for foreigners. Almost everyone speaks English, along with several other languages. These days, with its large immigrant population, the Netherlands is a melting pot of almost daunting proportion. Accommodation – from camp sites to hotels – is abundant in every price range. The lager is cold, the coffee is always "klaar", or freshly brewed, and the apple pie is irresistible.

For travellers who enjoy meeting people and absorbing different ways of life, this culturally and geographically diverse country will have an instant appeal. Contrasts abound, from the modern cities of Rotterdam and Eindhoven to the ancient towns of Haarlem and Delft and the wild landscapes of the islands of Friesland.

Most visitors tend to stop off in Amsterdam before making their way through an itinerary of other European capitals. But, just as Paris does not represent all things French, so too Amsterdam is not typical of the Netherlands, and to understand the Dutch mentality, one should explore the rural, relaxed provinces. Here, windmills are not just props in a landscape, and the "Afsluitdijk" is a phenomenon of human endeavour that can be explored by walking along the man-made polders. There are 16th-century castles to visit, royal woods to wander, and romantic windswept dunes to stroll. Outside the large cities are intimate hotels with excellent kitchens, antiquarian bookstores, museums of every type and, of course, those spectacular Dutch skies – Delft blue with huge puffy clouds. Even the climate is varied: as the saying goes: "If you don't like the weather, just wait a minute." ❑

PRECEDING PAGES: North Holland trawler; Beemster Canal; Begijnhof, Amsterdam; a cosy brown café – a traditional neighbourhood pub.
LEFT: traditional costume.

RECLAIMED FROM THE SEA

The Netherlands is one of Europe's smaller nations. But if nature had been left to take its course, the country wouldn't be even half its present size

The pagan settlers who first colonised the western shores of the Netherlands must have eked out a wretched existence – even by Dark Age standards. If they escaped starvation or drowning – both caused by frequent floods – marauding Vikings would pack their slave holds with them.

A thousand years earlier, inhabitants of the inland dunes and bogs had survived through marginal arable farming and raising livestock. Tribal warfare following the collapse of the Roman Empire forced many to move seaward for a more peaceful existence.

Pushed to what are now Groningen and Friesland provinces in the north, these people had to find a way to live with the tides. As they could not stop the sea, their only choice was to raise the land. They constructed mounds anchored by long stakes driven into the mud flats, surrounded by seaweed and tidal debris, and covered with layers of muddy clay. Finally, they built huts on top of the hillocks, called *terpen*, many of which are still visible today.

New lands

Until the early 11th century, the amount of farming land in the Netherlands was little more than half its current area. Over the centuries, dykes, canals, polders, windmills and, ultimately, monstrous tidal barriers have been used to reclaim thousands of square kilometres. Without them, waves would be lapping at Utrecht and half the country – 18,000 sq. km (7,000 sq. miles) and the habitat of more than 60 percent of the population – would either be underwater or subject to frequent flooding.

People began building small dykes (embankments) to protect their homes and farms as early as AD 700. As competition for farmland intensified, they surrounded marshes and swampy lakes with dykes and canals to drain the ground. In those times, drainage was often a simple matter of opening a canal sluice gate at low

tide, letting water flow out into the river or sea.

The first major sea dyke was constructed in 1320, when residents of Schardam, northwest of Amsterdam, built an embankment across the Beemster basin to prevent the Zuiderzee (today's IJsselmeer) from flooding their land. Again in 1380, in the same region, farmers built

a dyke to separate the Purmer lake from the Zuiderzee at Monnickendam. Without the dykes, the soft, marshy land sank below sea level when it was drained. Seawater swallowed the freshwater lake and large bog northeast of Amsterdam, turning the entire area into a shallow, southern bay of the North Sea.

Protecting low-lying areas created polders – a word stemming from the old Germanic *pol*, referring to the stakes used to hold together dykes, dams and mounds. Now the term is used for reclaimed land.

Land reclamation methods have changed little in 600 years. Even using 20th-century drainage and pumping technology, and after the

LEFT: flooding of the River Ijssel, near Doesburg.
RIGHT: Beemster polder road.

construction of dykes and drainage canals, the land that emerges a year or so later is still a swampy morass. The next stage is the digging of many shallow run-off ditches. The land is then seeded with grass to help it dry, as well as to prevent the growth of persistent weeds and to gradually draw the salt out of the soil.

Drying takes about five years, and today, when this process is complete, roads, water, electricity and other infrastructure have to be provided. During this period the government controls the agricultural conversion process before turning the land over to selected farmers a few years later.

high tides, and were frequently breached by the surge of an angry sea. They gave some protection, though, and a measure of how important they were to the community can be seen from the cruel and unusual penalty for damaging a dyke: the guilty person had their right hand amputated before being banished.

Centuries of disasters

Records from as far back as 1287 indicate that great floods occurred practically every century. An estimated 50,000 people drowned in 1404, and on All Hallow's Eve, 1570, granite blocks protecting dykes were tossed aside like drift-

Slow progress

Land reclamation gathered pace during the 14th and 15th centuries, when many towns, such as Amsterdam, began to expand. Despite their engineering expertise, the Dutch still faced an uphill battle against the forces of nature. This was exacerbated by the effects of peat extraction in more inland areas. With such a watery landscape, few trees were available for fuel, and peat was the common alternative. But as this was dug from the earth, it left a wake of sterile, sandy deserts.

Despite great efforts, flooding was never completely controlled. Dykes and canals merely provided a breathing space between seasonal

wood and entire houses swept out to sea. The worst 20th-century flood occurred in 1953, when more than 1,800 people lost their lives and nearly 100,000 people were left homeless.

Such disastrous inundations created a rich folklore of stories involving heroic deeds accomplished against all the odds. Sadly, there is no truth to the tale about Hans Brinker, the boy who saved all of Holland by sticking his finger in a leaky dyke, even though there is a symbolic statue of him at Spaarndam. There was, however, a ship's captain who saw a dyke near Rotterdam about to be breached during the severe storm of 1953. At great risk to himself, and the ruin of his boat, he steered the vessel into the waters rushing over the dam, turning his vessel sideways so that the waters swept him broadside to plug the fast-growing gap. The dyke was saved and, in probablility, so were hundreds of people.

Permanent, substantial land reclamation did not emerge in the Netherlands until the late 16th century, when windmills were converted into wind-pumps. This allowed them to drive scoop-wheels, fitted with buckets for raising water from the drainage ditches.

DEEP DARK DAYS

The All Hallows Eve flood of 1570 was the worst in the Netherlands' history; some estimates place the level of the floodwaters at more than 5 metres (16½ ft).

higher up. To be effective on large polders, windmills are used in series, each one raising the water to a higher level. Every polder has a network of drainage ditches that flow into progressively wider and deeper canals, and ultimately into the ring canal that surrounds the polder. From the ring canal, water drains either into the sea or into a freshwater reservoir. There are many such reservoirs around Amsterdam, which are used for recreation and irrigation during sustained periods of drought.

A great leap forward came with the invention of a windmill with a top that could be rotated to face the wind. Water could then be scooped out constantly and more efficiently. Around the year 1620, using some 20 windmills, the Beemster, Purmer and Wormer polders, created over three centuries earlier, were finally drained sufficiently enough to allow arable farming.

Mills, then and now, work by scooping water from the drainage ditch, raising it, and emptying the water into a larger canal several feet

LEFT: canal building in the 1930s.
ABOVE: dyke construction in progress.

Menace from the sea

Around 1700, another disaster threatened, potentially as devastating as any flood. Wooden dykes became infested with shipworm, an aquatic termite. Foreign newspapers solemnly forecast Amsterdam's doom. Begged, borrowed and imported stone was the initial solution and new materials, including metal, concrete and plastic, were gradually developed.

Land reclamation ceased during the early 18th century, when the Netherlands was continuously at war with England and France, and did not begin again in earnest until the mid-1850s when steam – and later diesel – engines were used to power the pumps.

The first major area to be reclaimed using steam-powered pumps, beginning in 1852, was the Haarlemmermeer. The rehabilitation of this huge swamp west of Amsterdam created new road and rail connections and more farmland. Today, Schiphol airport and its surrounding high-tech distribution and printing businesses are located on the former marsh, some 4.5 metres (13 ft) below sea level.

Zuiderzee dam

Plans for protecting Amsterdam by enclosing and draining parts of the Zuiderzee had been around since engineer Hendrik Stevin first pro-

could proceed from both directions. Huge willow "mattresses" were first laid down so that subsequent layers of stone and pilings would not sink into the sea bed.

At first, building in the shallow water went smoothly. But, as the gap between the two arms was reduced, the seemingly calm tidal pond began to cut a deep channel in the sea bed as water rushed through the narrowing gap. By the time the opening was just 14 metres (45 ft) across, the engineers began to have serious doubts about the project's feasibility.

In the end, they completed the final section in a matter of hours, racing against time, an

posed a scheme in 1667. Others flirted with the notion in subsequent centuries, but it wasn't until 1916 that work actually began.

This monumental project began by draining the 20,000-hectare (50,000-acre) Wieringermeer polder and constructing the *Afsluitdijk*, a 32-km (20-mile) long, 90-metre (300-ft) wide dyke across the Zuiderzee, which cuts off the tidal basin from the sea. It was completed in 1932, and the old sea, now a freshwater lake, has been known as the IJsselmeer ever since.

An artificial island and harbour, built from concrete caissons and dredgings, was created at the halfway point so that construction, involving 500 boats and more than 80 tugboats,

incoming tide and an approaching storm. A barrier of sorts was quickly built in front of the opening to slow the rushing water. This enabled willow mattresses and stones to be positioned properly to complete the dyke. Now, at the barrier's central point, large sluice gates and locks allow the passage of ships and marine life, in particular young migratory eels.

More than 1,800 sq. km (700 sq. miles) of polders were subsequently developed, with some reaching completion only in the 1980s. Two of the largest are the Noordoostpolder and Flevoland province, east of Amsterdam. The new town of Lelystad, Flevoland's provincial capital, is named after the engineer I. C. Lely, who designed the Zuiderzee reclamation project at the beginning of the 20th century.

After the devastating 1953 storm, which flooded 185,000 hectares (460,000 acres) in the southwest, the government embarked on another massive scheme: the Delta Plan. It took some 32 years and 12 billion guilders (£4 billion/US$6.5 billion) to complete this massive tidal barrier sealing off 700 km (430 miles) of tidal flats and flood-prone estuaries where the Rhine, Maas, Waal and Scheldt rivers empty into the North Sea.

> **LAND OF WINDMILLS**
>
> Despite their previous ubiquity, only about 1,000 windmills remain today – mostly as private homes or museums. Not more than a handful are still in working order.

When the project began, few could have imagined the scale of the problems that would be encountered. Artificial islands had to be built; rivers diverted or dammed. The project dwarfed all previous flood control efforts. A short stretch of dam at Haringvliet needed 65 massive pilings, some driven as much as 53 metres (175 ft) deep. The steel sluice gates are 12 metres (40 ft) high and wide, and weigh 543 tonnes (535 tons); huge engines are needed to open and close them.

Ecology and environment

Concerns about the environment soon became a serious and unforeseen stumbling block, particularly in the estuary between Noord-Beveland and Schouwen-Duiveland where a solid dam had been planned. Fishermen, backed up by Holland's formidable environmental lobby, warned against the loss of commercial oyster and mussel beds and the consequences of swamping miles of ecologically rich salt marshes. After an eight-year delay, the government eventually agreed on a smaller, movable barrier with gates that would permit a degree of tidal flow. As a result, although the marshes shrunk in extent from 16,200 hectares (40,000 acres) to 600 hectares (1,500 acres), the mudflats, crucial for birds and fish, diminished by just one-third.

A potential super project for the 21st century remains on the drawing board: to provide further protection for the IJsselmeer and its many polder farms and communities, not to mention Amsterdam. The government hopes to link up the Frisian Islands in the northeastern tip of the country by means of a series of dykes. The project would cut off the Waddenzee (the waters that separate the islands from the mainland) from the North Sea, creating recreational freshwater areas whilst preventing further saltwater infiltration into groundwater and polders. But, for the time being, this project is being kept on ice.

Another major reclamation project – building a new Schiphol airport off the coast – is being

considered. The cost would be formidable, but Amsterdam's existing airport will reach its growth limit around 2020 and, as it is a vital component of the Dutch economy, new room for expansion will have to be found.

Some lobbyists question whether new land is needed at all. Why trouble to create new polders when simple flood protection might be enough? The answer cuts to the heart of the economy. Whilst some oil reserves have been discovered offshore, the Netherlands has little in the way of natural resources. This small country – Europe's most densely populated – has no choice but to make increased use of all the land available for agriculture. ❏

LEFT: the construction of the Oosterschelde storm surge barrier.
RIGHT: visitors at the Delta Expo, in Zeeland.

JAARLYKSE OMMEGANK DER LEPROOZEN. OP

OPPERTIES MAANDAC OPGEHOUDE int JAAR 1005

Decisive Dates

EARLY DAYS (150 BC–AD 1220)

circa **150 BC** Romans establish a fort at Noviomagus (Nijmegen) and use baths at Maastricht and Heerlen for recreation.

AD 69 Batavi rebel against Roman rule; they are defeated, but remain a thorn in Rome's flesh.

circa **700** Following the Frankish King Pepin II's defeat of the Frisian Radboud, Utrecht becomes a bishopric under the English monk Willibrord, and establishes itself as a power centre.

12th century The first communities of herring

fishermen settle on the banks of the Amstel.
circa **1220** First Dam, or sluice, is built to hold back the tidal waters of the Zuiderzee.

THE GROWTH OF NATIONHOOD (1275–1568)

1275 Floris V, Count of Holland, grants the people of "Amestelledamme" freedom from tolls on goods passing through the county; first documentary record of Amsterdam.

1300 Bishop of Utrecht grants Amsterdam official city status.

1350 Amsterdam becomes the export centre for local beers and an entrepôt for Baltic grain.

1452 Fire destroys much of Amsterdam's timber-and-thatch buildings. New laws ordain that new buildings be constructed using brick and tile.

1519 Spain's Charles V is crowned Holy Roman Emperor. Amsterdam, as a result of war, treaties and marriage alliances, is part of the Spanish Empire and Catholic, but remains tolerant of Protestant minorities.

1535 Anabaptists invade Amsterdam's Town Hall and proclaim the Second Coming. The occupiers are executed and strict Catholicism is reimposed.

1566 Calvinists protesting the lack of religious freedom storm many of Amsterdam's churches. They are given a church of their own.

1567 Philip II of Spain sends the tyrannical Duke of Alva to restore Catholic control. Many Protestants are executed; and others flee to England.

WAR AND PEACE (1568–80)

1568 Low countries revolt against Spanish rule, launching 80 Years' War.

1572 Dutch Revolt against Spanish rule, led by William of Orange, begins in earnest.

1574 Relief of Leiden by Dutch troops following a 131-day siege by the Spanish.

1576 Amsterdam, loyal to Philip II, is besieged by Prince William's troops.

1578 Amsterdam capitulates to Prince William. Protestant exiles return to the city. Calvinists take over the churches and reins of government.

1579 The seven northern provinces of the Netherlands sign the Treaty of Utrecht. The southern provinces remain under Spanish Catholic control. Protestant refugees from Antwerp seek asylum in Amsterdam, laying the foundations for the city's Golden Age.

THE GOLDEN AGE (1580–1660)

1595–97 Dutch ships sail east via the Cape of Good Hope and reach Indonesia.

1602 Dutch East India Company founded.

1609 Bank of Amsterdam formed.

1618–19 Catholicism is outlawed.

1626 Peter Minuit "purchases" Manhattan island and founds the colony of Nieuw Amsterdam.

1642 Rembrandt paints *The Night Watch*.

1648 Under the Treaty of Münster the northern provinces are recognised as a republic.

1650 Amsterdam's population reaches 220,000.

1652 First of numerous wars with the English for maritime supremacy.

A NEW CONSCIOUSNESS (1660–1810)

1688 William III of Holland is crowned King of the United Kingdom. William's wars with France strain the economy of the Netherlands and the republic begins to decline as a trading nation.

1702 William III dies without heir. The northern provinces suffer further inroads to their trade when Austrian Emperor Charles VI sets up a rival East Indies Company in Ostend.

1744 France invades the southern provinces.

1747 William IV is elected hereditary head of state of the seven northern provinces ("the United Provinces"), now unified under one leader.

1751–88 United Provinces torn by civil strife between conservative supporters of the House of Orange and liberal reformers, called Patriots, demanding greater democracy.

1795 France invades the north and, in alliance with the Patriots, sets up a National Assembly. United Provinces renamed the Batavian Republic after the Batavi tribe that rebelled against Roman rule in AD 69.

1808 Napoleon reverses the constitutional reforms and establishes his brother, Louis Napoleon, as King of the Netherlands.

A PERIOD OF TRANSITION (1810–50)

1813 After the Napoleons' defeat, William VI is welcomed back from exile.

1814 William VI crowned King of the Netherlands. Austrians give up their claim to the southern provinces and north and south are united under one monarch.

1831 After years of unrest against rule from The Hague, the southern provinces win independence and are renamed the Kingdom of Belgium.

1845 Amsterdam Riots call for democratic reform.

1848 A new Dutch constitution comes into force.

EUROPE IN TURMOIL (1850–1945)

1870–76 Railways are established; the new North Sea Canal revives Amsterdam's position as an important port.

1914–20 The Netherlands remain neutral during World War I, but food shortages lead to strikes, riots and support for the Communist Party.

1928 Amsterdam hosts the Olympic Games.

1930s The Great Depression.

1932 Closing of the Zuiderzee and creating the freshwater IJsselmeer.

1940 Germany invades on 10 May.

PRECEDING PAGES: 17th-century Amsterdam, by A. van Nieulandt.
LEFT: *The Cannon Shot*, W. Van de Velde de Jonge.
RIGHT: The Noorderkerk, 1644, A. Beerstraten.

1942 Anne Frank and family go into hiding.

1945 After a bitter winter, Amsterdam is liberated on 5 May.

THE MODERN WORLD (POST-1945)

1949 Indonesia wins independence, first of the Dutch colonies to do so.

1953 Catastrophic flood in southwest; government response is the Delta Plan, a 20-year project to strengthen sea defences.

1963 Amsterdam's population reaches 868,000. Squatters protest over housing shortages.

1966 Protesters disrupt the wedding of Princess Beatrix and Claus von Amsberg.

1975 Protests in Amsterdam reach a peak as police battle with demonstrators over demolition and redevelopment policies.

1989 The government is brought down because its proposed anti-vehicle laws are not considered tough enough.

1990 Vincent van Gogh centenary; major exhibition at Amsterdam's Van Gogh Museum.

1992 The proposed Maastricht Treaty rocks the European Union, but is ratified by all member states in 1993.

1998 Amsterdam's Gay Games attract thousands of visitors.

1999 European Monetary Union; The Netherlands is one of 11 countries to establish the euro. ❑

EARLY HISTORY

The story of the country's early development is a tale of hardship, war and religious strife, enlivened by the whims of dynastic empire-builders

Traces of human habitation dating back more than 30,000 years have been found in the Netherlands, though it is not until around 4500 BC and the paleolithic farming communities of Limburg that a picture emerges of the prevailing culture and lifestyle.

Between around 3000 and 2000 BC, construction of megalithic funerary monuments called *hunebedden* flourished in Drenthe – 53 can still be seen along the *Hondsrug* (Dog's Back) north of Emmen. Each *hunebed* must have required considerable effort to build, using giant stones deposited by a glacier that had reached its endpoint in this area and then receded. The megaliths and distinctive bell-beaker pottery found in the graves connect their neolithic makers with the predominant cultural trend in western Europe at that time.

A new dawn

From about 2000 BC onwards, the megalith builders' civilisation disappeared. From the onset of the Bronze Age, human settlers began to spread westwards towards the North Sea and the low-lying deltas of the rivers Scheldt, Waal, Maas, Rhine, IJssel and Ems, burying their dead in funeral mounds, individual graves and urns containing ashes. Around 500 BC, settlers in coastal Friesland and Groningen began to give themselves some protection from the tides by constructing *terpen*, low earthen mounds on which they built their huts and animal enclosures. More than a thousand *terpen* have been identified, and some of them form the origins of contemporary towns and villages.

At about the same time as the Celts were taking over further south, Germanic tribes, including the Batavians and Frisians, occupied the area of the present-day Netherlands and were firmly established by 50 BC, when the Romans appeared on the scene. Julius Caesar credited the Batavians with making a spirited and fierce defence of their swampy homeland.

LEFT: Karl Der Grosse. **RIGHT:** Philip the Fair, who ruled the Low Countries in the 15th century.

In AD 12, the Roman general Drusus Germanicus brought the Batavians into the imperial fold in the role of an auxiliary cavalry to support the legions. But, in AD 69 the Batavian leader Claudius Civilis led an uprising. He was ultimately defeated, although he did manage to secure concessions for his people.

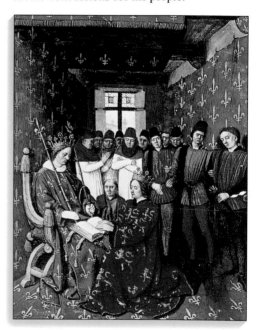

Frisian resistance

The Romans could make no headway against the Frisians, however, and were content to hold the line of the River Rhine. They established a legionary base at Ulpia Noviomagus (Nijmegen), a crossing of the Maas (Meuse) at Mosae Trajectum (Maastricht) and built baths at Coriovallum (Heerlen).

In 382, St Servaas (Servatius) became the Netherlands' first bishop, when he moved the seat of his bishopric from Tongeren to Maastricht. The Germanic peoples erupted across the Rhine during the 5th century to tear the Western Roman Empire apart. The Franks, led by Clovis (466–511), defeated and absorbed the Batavians, but the Frisians were again too hot to handle. Not until 689 did the Franks, under Pepin, defeat the still-pagan Frisians.

Insurrection continued amongst the feisty Frisians, as attempts were made to convert them to Christianity. It took the heavy broadsword of Charlemagne during the late 8th century to finally subdue these proud and independent people, and thus integrate the Low Countries (the present-day Netherlands, Belgium and Luxembourg) into his wider European empire.

After Charlemagne's death in 814, the Frankish Empire was divided among his sons, and

The birth of Amsterdam

Born amid water, Amsterdam is surrounded by it still. The fishermen who built the first huts at the mouth of the River Amstel around 1200 must have earned a good living for that period from the rich Zuiderzee fishing grounds. Yet they and their families were at the mercy of wind and sea in that swampy delta, and many must have lost their lives when storm surges washed their dwellings away. Yet the community flourished, particularly when, around 1220, a dam was built to hold the Zuiderzee at bay. As a byproduct, it also created a good anchorage at the point where Centraal Station now stands.

most of the Low Countries passed to the Middle Kingdom (Lotharingia/Lorraine), which later became a duchy of the Germanic Holy Roman Empire. As Frankish rule weakened during the 10th century, Vikings took the opportunity to invade and ravage the land.

Although nominally owing allegiance to the empire, from the 10th century to the 14th century, the Low Countries comprised a number of feudal states. The rulers of these states enjoyed many privileges and, in practice, were semiautonomous. Among the feudal rulers were the bishops of Utrecht, the dukes of Brabant, the counts of Zeeland and the increasingly powerful counts of Holland.

Named Amstelledamme, the settlement expanded as a commodities market, helped by an influx of Flemish weavers and Jewish merchants. In 1275, the year that is considered the city's official foundation date, Count Floris V of Holland granted the people of Amstelledamme toll-free passage on the waterways – a sign of its growing importance and a move that spurred further growth in trade. Ships unloaded cargoes of Baltic timber, salt and spices on what is now the Dam, and sailed away laden with cloth, furnishings and grain.

In 1300 the Bishop of Utrecht gave Amstelledamme its town charter, and in 1317 Count Willem III of Holland took over the town from the bishops, who at that time controlled it. Another link in the commercial chain was forged in 1323, when Count Floris VI named Amsterdam as a toll-point for the import of beer, which was an essential alternative to tainted water supplies. Amsterdam joined the trade-centred Hanseatic League in 1369, and by 1414 was Holland's biggest town, with a population of around 12,000.

> **STRIKE ACTION**
>
> Industrial relations were often fraught in 15th-century Amsterdam. Sometimes, entire groups of labourers would protest by simply leaving town *en masse*.

While its trading status became firmly established, Amsterdam itself remained on less secure ground, and, although built on swampy land, the town's buildings proved susceptible to the ravages of fire. Indeed, in 1452 most of them were burnt to a crisp. Following this catastrophe, the City Fathers ordained that all new buildings would be made from stone. Only two wooden houses remain today.

The Good, the Mad and the Bold

In 1384 Count Lodewijk of Flanders died and was succeeded by his daughter Margaret, the wife of Duke Philip the Bold of Burgundy, beginning the Low Countries' dazzling Burgundian period. Over the next century or so the dukes of Burgundy gained possession of most of the Low Countries, partly through dynastic marriages and partly by conquest.

Duke Philip the Good was the family's top hand at acquisitions, taking over Limburg in 1430 and Holland and Zeeland in 1433. By 1473 his successor, Charles the Bold, controlled all of the present-day Netherlands except Friesland, in addition to Belgium, Luxembourg and territories in France. On his death in battle in 1477, he was succeeded by his daughter Mary, wife of the Habsburg Empire's Crown Prince Maximilian of Austria. Mary died aged 25 in a horse-riding accident in 1482, pitching the Burgundian Empire – and the Netherlands along with it – into Habsburg hands.

One of Maximilian's enduring acts was, in 1489, to grant Amsterdam the right to use the imperial crown on its coat of arms, a symbol you can see most prominently today gracing the summit of the city's Westerkerk tower.

LEFT: Cornelius Anthoniszoon's 1538 map of Amsterdam.
RIGHT: Charles the Bold, Duke of Burgundy.

Maximilian's son, Philip the Fair, succeeded to the rule of the Low Countries when his father stepped up to become Holy Roman Emperor. He later married Joan the Mad of Spain, thereby retaining the family penchant for bizarre monikers and bringing Spain into the Habsburg fold – a development that in due course would have grim repercussions for the Low Countries. The high tide of Netherlandic influence would seem to have come when Charles V, born in Ghent, inherited the Low Countries in 1515, Spain in

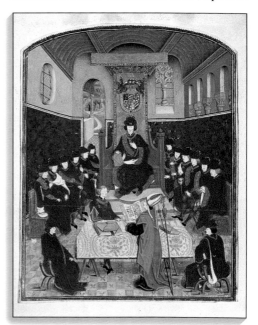

1516, and the Holy Roman Empire in 1519. But Charles was forced to engage in relentless warfare to preserve his unwieldy and scattered realm and used the Low Countries as a reservoir of money and soldiers, at the same time shifting the empire's centre of gravity to Spain.

While blue-bloods and their dynasties came and went, a more fundamental change was brewing. Martin Luther's 1517 condemnation of the Catholic Church provoked the rise of Protestantism, a development that was reaching crisis proportions in the Low Countries by 1555, when Philip II, a fanatical Catholic, began to inherit the empire from the failing hands of Charles V. ❑

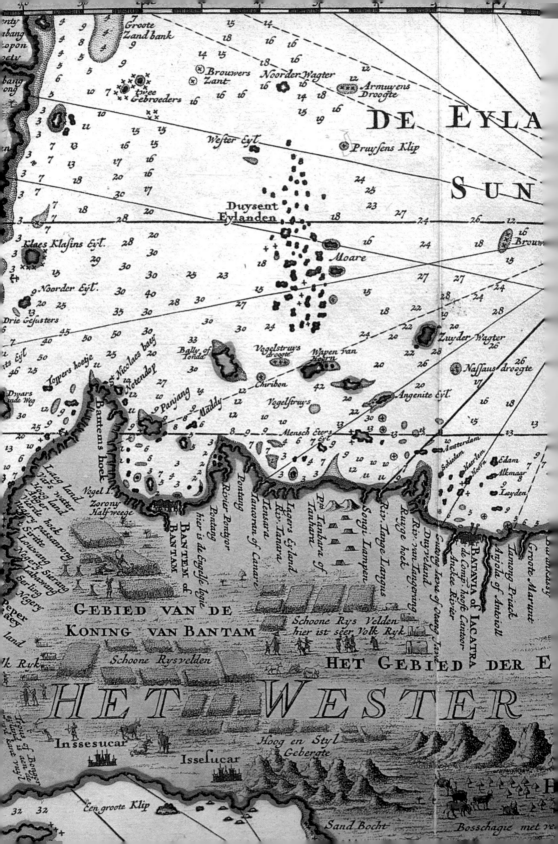

THE GOLDEN AGE

The Netherlands' Golden Age of the 17th century was the zenith of its power –

a glittering period of empire, enormous wealth and remarkable art

One of the best ways to gauge the impact of the Dutch Empire is to walk into an antique map store almost anywhere in the world. Ask to see 17th-century Dutch world maps and watch the proprietor's eyes light up at the prospect of dealing with a connoisseur.

For much of the 17th century, when Dutch ships and banks ruled the commercial world, maps made in Amsterdam were regarded as the best, both for accuracy – Dutch ships sailed to more places and brought back more reliable geographic information than those of any other country – and beauty. Dutch 17th-century cartographers, artists, engravers and printers were to mapmaking what Dutch Masters were to 17th-century painting – perhaps the greatest collection of talent ever working at one time in a single country. Even today, many map collectors and dealers believe that Dutch Golden Age maps have never been surpassed for quality. So, if you visit an antique map shop, and don't plan to spend a fortune on an authentic Blaeu or Janszoon, dampen the proprietor's enthusiasm by adding, "I'm just looking."

Art flourishes

The growth of empire and the prosperity it brought spawned an extraordinary period of artistic and cultural production. The Golden Age, noteworthy by any nation's standards, was especially remarkable in that it occurred in a small, waterlogged land of stubborn people.

Many believe the Golden Age is unparalleled in world history. "There is perhaps no other example of a complete and highly original civilisation springing up in so short a time in so small a territory," wrote the modern historian Simon Schama.

This was not due solely to the ambition and acumen of the merchant middle class that provided the empire's driving force. Those important qualities were there in abundance in the

late 16th century, for the Dutch had already developed a thriving Baltic-based commodities trade in salt, herring, wine, bricks, cereal, wood, iron and copper.

Equal in importance to the merchant-trader's desire to get rich was an external event that triggered their determination to succeed – the 80

years of struggle against Spain that began in 1568. The conflict began with the anti-heresy campaign of the Spanish king, Philip II, who saw it as his duty to wipe out the Calvinist movement that had taken root in the northern Netherlands. When Philip outlawed Calvinism, the northern provinces rebelled under the leadership of William the Silent, whom the Dutch regard as the father of their country.

Decades of strife with Spain were the result of religious differences, but there were also economic factors. Spain not only wanted to control religion, but also to restrain the Dutch economy. The Dutch reacted in typical hardheaded fashion, outlawing Catholicism and

LEFT: Golden Age map of the Dutch East Indies (Indonesia).

RIGHT: *Man Writing a Letter*, G. Metsu.

doing all they could to expand their economy, including setting up in trade competition with Spain across the globe.

The 1579 Treaty of Utrecht created the United Provinces and provided the foundation of the modern Netherlands through the alliance of seven northern provinces – the southern provinces remained subject to Spain and eventually became Belgium and Luxembourg. More significantly for the development of a Dutch Empire, the treaty gave the United Provinces shipping con-

LITTLE AND LARGE

Unlike any other great artistic period in Europe, the big-name Dutch Masters were surrounded by many "Little Masters", whose paintings are still in demand.

France continued, more Dutch ships undertook ambitious voyages with little fear of reprisal, and set about opening new routes, establishing colonies and plundering other countries' trade.

At home, the Dutch were fast becoming the bankers of Europe. The Bank of Amsterdam was formed in 1609, and the Amsterdam Stock Exchange began trading in 1611. Favourable interest rates, reliable foreign currency exchanges and the willingness of Dutch bankers to loan money attracted investors and

trol of the lower Rhine, and allowed Amsterdam to eclipse rival Antwerp, as the region's principal commercial centre.

Trading advantage

Dutch sailors and merchants of the late 16th century were skilled, but they were also lucky that their enemies and competitors were distracted by other wars. England's destruction of the Spanish Armada in 1588 is an example. The Dutch were emboldened by knowing that many of the cannon that might have challenged them on the other side of the world were now rusting in galleons at the bottom of Plymouth Sound. As Spain's entanglements with England and

financiers from across Europe – and greatly spurred on the ventures of Dutch entrepreneurs.

Born out of religious repression, the United Provinces of the north provided freedom of conscience to all citizens. Protestants, Jews and other religious refugees poured in from France, Spain, Portugal and elsewhere. Anyone could emigrate to the United Provinces for 8 guilders – a year's pay for a Dutch sailor. The entry fee was often waived for refugees with a valuable skill or craft. In addition, the United Provinces boasted a free press – a rarity in those days – that attracted writers, thinkers and academics. The result was an infusion of the best and brightest talent from across Europe.

There were some constraints. Speaking Yiddish was illegal and Catholicism was formally banned, although the authorities allowed Catholics to worship as long as they didn't hold public services. The result was dozens of small private "churches", often hidden in secret rooms in homes and warehouses. A fine surviving example can be seen at Amsterdam's Amstelkring Museum, a refurbished 17th-century merchant's home known as "Our Lord in the Attic" because of its Catholic chapel under the roof. Later, the existence of so many hidden rooms would enable Jewish refugees to hide from the Nazis in Dutch homes.

both the wealth with which Dutch citizens patronised the arts, and the artistic stimulus for new designs. In the early 1600s, a Dutch merchant ship returned from a voyage to China with a hold packed with late Ming Dynasty porcelain, which proved so popular that it inspired the beginning of the national pottery industry, based in Delft.

The finer things

Material prosperity meant that ordinary citizens could afford the finer things in life, such as silver salt shakers and original paintings that they themselves had commissioned. Such paintings

Today, the Golden Age is best remembered for paintings by the three greatest Dutch Masters – Vermeer, Frans Hals and, of course, Rembrandt, whose work has probably enjoyed a longer period of sustained popularity than that of any other painter. But as well as painting, numerous other artistic disciplines – such as architecture, sculpture, furniture-making, silver working and porcelain production – all flourished during the Golden Age of the 17th century. The country's success in trade was the great enabler, providing

LEFT: *Battle of Gibraltar*, Hendrick Cornelisz Vroom.
ABOVE: *De Veepont 1653*, Salomon J. van Ruysdael.

A CLASSLESS SOCIETY

The Golden Age was a time of great prosperity enjoyed by all – not merely ruling classes. Openness and market competition existed in all spheres of life, not just in art, and attracted an exceptional number of skilled, ambitious citizens able to use their talent and determination to improve their lot in life.

Unlike many other European countries at that time, it was possible for people to move from class to class. Members of the middle, and even lower, classes could become clergymen, artists, craftsmen, traders and merchants. They could get rich, and have an influence in provincial affairs.

Sailors' Talk

A lthough the Dutch language is similar to German, it can sound strange and alien. Not for nothing was the term "double Dutch" coined in the 18th century to describe someone whose speech was incoherent or impenetrable.

Even words you might think you know turn out very different when spoken by a native. Gouda, the town and the world-famous cheese, is pronounced something like "chowda" – the *ch* sound being hard and guttural, as in the Scottish pronunciation of loch.

Vincent van Gogh, known to the English as Van Goff, and to Americans as Van Go, is an almost unpronounceable Van Choch in his native tongue. Again, the *ch* sounds as if the speaker were clearing his throat – perhaps it is the phlegmatic effects of living with cold, damp air rising from a watery polder landscape that has resulted in such a guttural consonant.

On the other hand, written Dutch can be deceptively easy. Sue Limb weaves real Dutch words into her entertaining autobiography, *Love Forty*, as in this conversation: *"Uur klogs aar bei de bakdor,"* called his wife as he went. *"Ij moovd dem uit ov de utilijtij-roem bekos ov de stink." "Ja, dat wwas de pijg-schijt vrom de manuur-heep. Sorrij."*

Many Dutch words – most of them earthy and verging on the unprintable – have been assimilated into English. Robert McCrum, author of *The Story of English*, catalogues *fokkinge, kunte* and *krappe* as words that we euphemistically call Anglo-Saxon but which are, in fact, Low Dutch.

Poppycock, which has become an acceptable expletive, derives from the Dutch *pappekak* (literally, soft dung). Sailors from the Low Countries probably introduced these words to England and the Americas, along with purely nautical terms like smuggler (from *smuckeln*) and keelhaul (from *kielhalen*).

Dutch territorial influence in North America ceased when British settlers seized Nieuw Amsterdam and renamed it New York. But the Dutch linguistic contribution to American English lingers on in place names like Harlem and Brooklyn (originally called Haarlem and Breukelyn).

Contemporary American English contains many words derived from Dutch. To quote McCrum: "If you have a *waffle* for brunch, or *coleslaw* with your dinner, or a *cookie* with your coffee, you are using Dutch American. If you ride through the *landscape* in a *caboose* or on a *sleigh*, if you find your *boss* or neighbour *snooping* and accuse him of being a *spook*, you are also using words that come to America from the Netherlands."

Pessimists are concerned for the language's very survival. English (or its American variant) is widely understood and spoken and has become the language of pop, video, satellite TV and advertising. The Netherlands is one of the world's biggest markets for English-language publications. In the past, Dutch absorbed many foreign words yet remained a distinctive tongue, despite Oliver Goldsmith's dismissive comment in 1759 that the Dutch were "destitute of what may be properly called a language of their own."

Today, some alarmists fear that without a determined effort to keep the language alive, Dutch could die, leaving a handful of (English) four-letter words as its only legacy. Sporadic outbursts against the inroads English has made seem to confirm this concern. However, most Dutch people – young and old – are proud of their language; giving it up would be tantamount to surrendering part of themselves. Despite their fluency in English, there is no sign that they are willing to take this ultimate step, or even let it happen by default. Cosmopolitanism has its limits. ❑

LEFT: nautical reminders in a wall plaque, Friesland.

represented something new – non-classical art. The Dutch School launched realism in painting. Instead of merely forming the background, landscapes and seascapes became the central subject matter of paintings. And individuals and families posed, and were painted, as themselves instead of in the guise of Biblical or mythological figures.

The love of art was universal; visitors to the Netherlands during the Golden Age routinely remarked on how everyone, from blacksmith to baker to burgher, seemed to have original art, often personally commissioned, hanging prominently at home and in their business

mere reportage. A sensitive feeling for the painterly view of everyday life and nature not infrequently raised their production to the level of great art."

Golden city

Amsterdam, which dominated Holland province, the richest and most important of the seven, is one of the most striking legacies of the Golden Age. In 1607, when the Singel canal was no more than a ditch around the 15th-century city walls, the council approved a plan for three new canals: Herengracht, Keizersgracht and Prinsengracht. Fine houses, built to strict

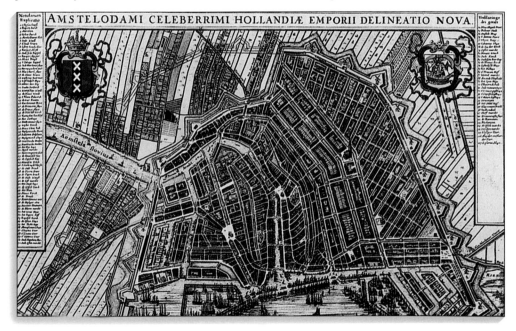

premises. Merchants commissioned paintings of their trade ships, and farmers of their prize cows – the scene often completed by an artistically rendered cowpat on the ground. Realism extended to street scenes and facial expressions that captured a moment or an emotion of everyday life. A modern critic sums it up: "The Dutch described their life and their environment, their country and their city sights so thoroughly that their paintings provide a nearly complete pictorial record of their culture. However, it was more than

ABOVE: Amsterdam in 1640 showing the first stage of canal construction.

requirements, were built along the main canals, with shops along interlinking side canals. The Jordaan was added in 1612 as a self-contained community of artists and craftsmen.

The plan of central Amsterdam, which was completed in the late 17th century, remains one of the most successful examples of forward-looking town planning in history. One modern critic notes: "It is not often that a town has been enlarged so sensitively as to increase its characteristic beauty. Its great claim is in the noble dimensions of the canals, in the wonderfully successful relation between the breadth of the water and of the quays on either side, and the height of the buildings."

For a glimpse of how Golden Age merchants lived, visit the Willet-Holthuysen Museum, a refurbished canal house at 605 Herengracht. Originally built as a wealthy family's gift to a pampered eight-year-old son, the museum displays furniture, glass, silver and Golden Age ceramics.

Many houses on Herengracht show how merchants, though constrained by strict building requirements and zoning laws, quietly tried to outdo each other with fancy gables and flourished façades. Other examples of the way that comfortable Dutch lived in 17th-century Amsterdam can be seen at Rembrandt's former house, 4–6 Jodenbreestraat, which has a collection of the artist's drawings and rooms furnished in period style. Perhaps the grandest of all the architecture of the period can be seen in the Town Hall, now the Royal Palace in Amsterdam, and the Mauritshuis in The Hague, both designed by Haarlem-born painter and architect Jacob van Campen.

An empire in decline

At the empire's height, Dutch holdings encompassed parts of Brazil, Dutch Guyana (now Surinam) on the northeast coast of South America, a fistful of tiny but productive Caribbean

t' Fort nieüw Amsterdam op de Manhatans

islands, Manhattan Island, African outposts that provided slaves for Caribbean sugar plantations, parts of Sri Lanka, South Africa, Tasmania, and – the jewel of the realm – most of present-day Indonesia.

Little remains. Much of the empire was lost – even during the Golden Age. As traders, the Dutch were among the best; as colonists, they were among the worst. More interested in trade than migration, they exploited the people and resources of their colonies and returned home with wealth instead of putting down roots.

The end of the Thirty Years' War, in 1648, allowed England, Spain and France to turn their attention to the marauding Dutch. Colonies stolen from the Spanish and Portuguese were taken back again. Neglect by the States General, the United Provinces' ruling body, as much as English aggression, was to blame for the loss in 1664 of Nieuw Amsterdam – renamed New York.

Other factors at home added to the empire's decline. The Zuiderzee was silting up, making it difficult for ships to reach Amsterdam docks. This did not matter to many descendants of the original merchants, traders and bankers who had been

SHREWD INVESTMENT

There had been a practical side to the Dutch devotion to the arts: with the economy expanding as rapidly as the empire, work by well-known artists was a sound hedge against inflation.

Golden Age is that during the late 17th century and well into the 18th – a period known as the *Pruikentijd*, or "age of wigs" – everything French became all the rage and French was spoken instead of Dutch in the finer salons.

Francophilia failed to diminish – even after France had conquered the Netherlands in the late 18th century. French rule was maintained until the point of Napoleon's abdication in 1815, after which the Netherlands gradually evolved into a constitutional monarchy.

responsible for building the empire. New generations seemed more interested in spending than making money, leading one Dutch historian to suggest that the 17th century should be called the Age of Wood and Steel because of its commodity trading and shipbuilding, and the 18th century the Golden Age because of all the gold the Dutch locked away in strongboxes instead of investing in new ventures.

A curious historical footnote to the decline of the Dutch Empire and the fading of the

LEFT: New York, 1614, then called "neu-Amsterdam."
ABOVE: view of Amsterdam in a plaque on Oude Schans canal, Amsterdam.

The end of empire

In shops and museums displaying Dutch maps, the decline of the Golden Age is very easy to see. By the turn of the 18th century, many Dutch maps were little more than plagiarised copies of French and English maps that were by then leading the way.

Despite contrary evidence, many Dutch cartographers copying earlier maps continued to show California as a separate island up to the 18th century. It wasn't until 1704, when the French government formally declared California part of the American mainland, that Dutch mapmakers at last fell into line. The Golden Age was indeed over. ❑

THE ART OF THE GOLDEN AGE

*The most glittering period in The Netherlands' history is also
one of the most culturally rich the world has ever seen*

The 17th-century Golden Age was a time of excellence in politics and economics as well as in the arts. The Dutch Republic ruled the seas and was one of the most powerful countries in Europe. The Treaty of Westphalia (also known as the Treaty of Münster), concluded with Spain in 1648, merely sealed

the formal independence that the seven northern provinces of the Netherlands had won almost a century earlier.

Painting exhibited a distinctive national character and many artists took their subjects from their own experiences and the environment that surrounded them, athough generally they confined themselves to a single type of subject matter, such as portraiture, still lifes, landscapes or domestic scenes of everyday life.

Many 17th-century Dutch and Flemish painters improved on the techniques of their predecessors, painting on skilfully cut thin oak panels which rarely warp or crack. Besides wood, other materials such as copper were used,

though canvas predominated as it was better for large paintings, allowing a freer and bolder style – even if the weave occasionally showed through. The different surfaces and their preparation had an important influence on the techniques and styles of the artists of the Golden Age. Wooden panels with a white chalk ground gave a smoothness that was conducive to minute detail and the meticulous finish that led Gerard Dou (1613–75) to found the important school of genre painting at Leiden known as the Fijnschilders.

Dou painted *Young Mother* (now in the Mauritshuis, The Hague) "so finely as hardly to be distinguish'd from enamail." The Rijksmuseum in Amsterdam has fine examples of most of the painters of that splendid era, and all the works mentioned here are in that museum, unless otherwise noted.

The greatest of the era

Though Rembrandt is today regarded as the most outstanding 17th-century painter, Frans van Mieris and Adriaen van der Werff were considered the greatest painters of the day by their contemporaries. Others, such as Cesar van Everdingen, Honthorst and Brugghen, were equally talented and highly regarded. But unlike the prolific painters whose work is on public view, such artists have been more or less forgotten, their paintings either lost or destroyed, or held in private collections.

The still-life painting of the Golden Age was initially very sober, as the works of Pieter Claes (1597/8–1661) and Willem Heda (1594–1680) demonstrate. Their work is characterised by the rendering of a combination of objects carefully chosen for their symbolism. Gold and silver cups and fragile glasses and jugs often feature, serving as a warning against excess and acting as a reminder of the transitory nature of life – a favourite theme of the still life genre.

As the century progressed, the Eighty Years' War came to an end, prosperity increased and Calvinism turned away from depictions of religious themes. More elaborate fruit bowls and flower vases, ever more splendid gold and silver cups and rich tapestries appear in portraits and sumptuous still lifes, such as those by Willem Kalf (1619–93) and Abraham van Beyeren (1620/1–90).

Institutional patronage

It was also customary to paint group portraits of the regents and regentesses of institutions, *hofjes* (almshouses for the elderly), orphanages and hospitals. Frans Hals (1581/5–1666) was a masterly portrait painter who captured the essence of his models as shown in his famous *Merry Drinker*. The Frans Hals Museum, in a

paintings of his early period, such as *The Musical Company* and *Tobias Accusing Anna of Stealing the Kid*, are very colourful. Later on, Rembrandt's preference for strong contrasts between light and shade becomes apparent, as in his *Old Woman Reading* and *Jeremiah Lamenting the Destruction of Jerusalem.*

Rembrandt left Leiden in 1631 to move to Amsterdam, where he worked until his death in 1667. There he abandoned the meticulous style of his Leiden period for a broader manner, in which light and shadow merge into each other and his greys and browns have a deep warm glow about them.

17th-century (men's) almshouse in Haarlem, the town in which he lived, exhibits most of his group portraits, which are also known as Corporation Pieces.

Rembrandt van Rijn (1606–69) is undoubtedly one of the world's greatest artists. He can certainly be called the painter of humanity, since he always emphasised the human element, not only in his portraits, but also in his Biblical and history paintings. Until 1631, he worked in Leiden, his birthplace. The first

LEFT: Rembrandt self portrait.
ABOVE: symbols of life's transience –
Still Life, P. Claesz.

COLOURS OF THE AGE

The Dutch artist of the 17th century suffered a fairly limited palette. Certain colours like blue and green were difficult and expensive to get hold of, and were therefore used sparingly and to dramatic effect. Natural ultramarine (lapis lazuli) was the most expensive and azurite, a blue copper carbonate mineral, very scarce. Poor-quality artificial azurite, indigo for underpainting and smalt (ground-up blue cobalt glass) were often used instead. Green was obtained from a mixture of blue and a lead-tin oxide or vegetable-dye yellow. The yellow has often faded, leaving some Dutch paintings of this era with blue foliage and grass in woods and fields.

A world-famous work of his Amsterdam period, which Rembrandt completed in 1642, was originally called *The Company of Captain Frans Banning Cocq and Lieutenant Willem van Ruytenburch*, and depicts the moment when the captain gives his lieutenant the order for the guards to march out. The painting was given the title *The Night Watch* in the 19th century. This large work, originally installed in the Arquebusiers' Guildhall, now hangs in the Rijksmuseum.

AGEING GRACEFULLY

Restored Dutch paintings look clean and crisp – even when dark colours were used – because they were covered with a turpentine-based varnish which can be easily removed by restorers.

Duurstede and his grand *View of Haarlem*, van Ruisdael presented the impressive expanse of the flat Dutch countryside under enormous cloudy skies. Other landscape painters worth looking out for are Adriaen van de Velde (1636–72), Aert van der Neer (1603/4–77) and Paulus Potter (1625–54) who painted animals in extensive landscapes.

The painters' decision to concentrate on their own surroundings was particularly well suited to the rendering of church interiors. The impressive

Dutch landscapes

It is understandable that at a time when the country was fighting for its independence, painters would choose that land, their own immediate environment, as a subject for their pictures. A good example of this genre is the large *Winter Landscape with Ice-Skaters* by Hendrick Avercamp (1585–1634). Other good examples are Jan van Goyen's (1596–1656) majestic *Landscape with Two Oaks* and Esaias van de Velde's (*circa* 1591–1630) sombre *Cattle Ferry*.

Landscape painting reached its zenith in the 17th century in the work of Jacob van Ruisdael (1628/9–82). *In The Windmill at Wijk bij*

Interior of St Mary's Church at Utrecht by Pieter Saenredamis (1597–1665) is one of many fine examples.

Merry company

Another favourite subject matter were Dutch scenes from daily life, divided by subject matter into groups: what we know as "merry company" scenes (*gheselschapjes*), outdoor scenes (*buitenpartij*) and brothel scenes (*bordeeltjen*), most containing a hidden moral. These subjects are characteristic of Dutch genre painting, yet there is no Dutch word – past or present – that directly corresponds to the present-day English sense of the word "genre".

Dutch genre painting originated in the 16th century with Patenir and his Flemish followers, the greatest of whom was Pieter Brueghel the Elder who developed landscape into a subject of its own rather than using it merely as a background to religious, mythological or historical scenes. Brueghel left Antwerp during the Spanish occupation and moved to Amsterdam, where his work gave impetus to the development of new forms of Dutch painting.

Although Brueghel's paintings retained a moralistic tone, he depicted scenes from peasant life, *kermisses* (fairs and carnivals) and weddings. By contrast, other early "merry

for example, the typically Dutch Feast of St Nicholas and that of adults at a fair or an inn. Adriaen van Ostade (1610–85), from Haarlem, specialised mainly in scenes taken from peasant life.

The public were well aware of how to "read" these paintings: a map frequently indicated the absence of the head of the household, gone travelling overseas on trade; a dog in inns and brothels pointed to gluttony and licentiousness; a cat and a mouse reinforced the sense of the transience and uncertainty of human existence, while the ploy of a painting within a painting often pointed out a moral or a warning.

company" paintings showed elegantly dressed and cosmopolitan young men and women eating, drinking, playing music and embracing in taverns or in landscape settings; Dirck Hals, the lesser known younger brother of Frans, was a great exponent of these "merry company" scenes until the 1630s. His contemporary, Jan Miense Molenaer (1609/10–1668), painted children, often in theatrical settings, symbolising freedom from care.

The witty and perceptive Jan Steen (1626–79) also depicts the behaviour of children in,

Left: *The Syndics of the Cloth Hall*, by Rembrandt.
Above: *Winter Scene*, by H. Avercamp.

Canvas nasties

Amsterdam was a vigorous centre of genre painting in the first three decades of the 17th century. Particularly popular were barrack-room scenes and tavern interiors with soldiers drinking, fighting and womanising. It is curious that Amsterdam merchants should have chosen to hang scenes of brawling soldiery on their walls. Perhaps they wanted a contrast to their relatively peaceful lives (after all, very little fighting ever took place in Amsterdam) – or perhaps they enjoyed these pictures for much the same reasons that people today like to watch action movies or the portrayal of violence on television – the vicarious thrill.

The talented Willem Duyster (*circa* 1599–1635) specialised in these active, yet delicately painted, scenes and Gerard ter Borch (1617–81), considered by some to be as great as Rembrandt, began his career as a painter of barrack-room scenes. His later, more refined art, of which his *Gallant Conversation* and *Seated Girl* are remarkable examples, represents a distinct departure and stands in a class of its own.

It goes without saying that painters in Holland – a country wrested from the sea – found

water a natural subject for their pictures. Willem van de Velde the Younger (1633–1707), of *The Cannon Shot*, is the best known Dutch marine painter, but another master of the genre, Jan van de Capelle (1626–79), was by no means his inferior.

Light plays a crucial part in the work of the Delft Master Johannes Vermeer (1632–75), and, because he is sparing in his use of shadow, he achieves a great translucency of colour. Despite their small size, his paintings belong among the most monumental works in Dutch art. You'll find four in the Rijksmuseum – *The Kitchen Maid, Woman Reading a Letter, The Love Letter* and *The Little Street*.

QUALITY CONTROL

Despite being one of the most celebrated of all Dutch painters, Vermeer was far from prolific; only 30 works by him are known.

Painters often chose a townscape or a single street as a subject, as did Gerrit Berckheyde (1636–98) and Jan van der Heyden (1637–1712). The domestic interiors of Pieter de Hooch (1628–*circa* 1683) were similar to those of Vermeer, though less serious and less strong in form. *Woman with a Child in a Pantry* and *Courtyard Behind a House* are among his best works.

The explosion of artistic talent in the 17th century is truly remarkable, yet the popularity of painting in the Golden Age did not obscure other forms of achievement – architecture, sculpture, silver, porcelain and furniture – which demonstrated a high standard of individual craftsmanship. Beautiful objects then being created were integrated into the houses of the wealthy. Chairs, tables and cabinets, even bird cages and doll's houses, were as much on display as the works of art.

Imitation and flattery

Delft is now known for the blue and white painted pottery which Italian potters introduced to the region, although early production centred on Antwerp. In the 17th century the descendants of these potters, now Protestant refugees, moved from Antwerp into the northern provinces where they made Rotterdam and Haarlem their main centres. Not long after, the city of Delft began producing its characteristic tin-glazed tiles, plates and panels, painted with blue decoration copied from Chinese wares imported by the East Indies Company. By the mid-17th century, Delft jars, vases and bowls, and even door portals and lintels, were everywhere, ornamented with landscapes, portraits and Biblical or genre scenes.

During the 17th century large quantities of silver were also made – not only in cities such as Amsterdam and Rotterdam but also in the smaller towns where traditional forms were kept. One such was the characteristic Friesland marriage casket or *knottekistje*, shaped like a knotted handkerchief.

From the first decade of the 17th century silver drinking horns used on ceremonial occasions, as well as vessels, basins, urns and salt cellars, began to be decorated with a new ear-shaped form. This "auricular" design, created by Paulus van Vianen of Utrecht, was soon joined by flowing patterns of sea creatures and molluscs developed by van Vianen's brother Adam and his nephew Christian. Later in the century, a profusion of flowers found their way into the decorative armoury, including the newly imported and highly prized tulip. Adam and Paulus both excelled in the production of representational scenes. The German painter Sandrart said of Paulus that "with the hammer alone he could make whole pictures... with animals and landscapes, all perfect in their decoration, design and elegance."

The Dutch Renaissance

Innovation in architecture and sculpture was largely due to the influence of one stonemason employed by the city of Amsterdam – Hendrick de Keyser. He developed his own characteristic style, freeing Dutch sculpture from its former rigidity and symbolic quality, which resulted in a softer, anatomic style full of movement and became known as "Dutch Renaissance".

Moving on to be an architect, he related the interior spaces of buildings to the exteriors, integrating the ornament to the structure rather than applying it superficially. His masterpiece is the mausoleum of William the Silent, Prince of Orange, built on the site of the former high altar of the New Church in Delft (1614–21). The bronze figure of William the Silent is surrounded by tall obelisks, linking it to the High Gothic interior of the New Church. Two of his most impressive and characteristic buildings that survive in Amsterdam are the Zuiderkerk (1603) and the Westerkerk (1620), where Rembrandt is buried. With an imposing build-up of Dorian, Ionic and Corinthian columns, and imperial crown of the Holy Roman Emperor Maximilian I adorning the 85-metre (280-ft) high steeple, the Westerkerk is the most monumental example of Dutch Renaissance architecture.

The architect Jacob van Campen designed the Mauritshuis and the Huis ten Bosch in The Hague, and the New Church at Haarlem in the spirit of "Dutch Classicism", but his major project of the century was the construction of a new Town Hall for Amsterdam.

This imposing building, now the Koninklijk Paleis (Royal Palace) was built on a massive

LEFT: Vermeer's *Head of a Girl*.
RIGHT: Amsterdam's Dam Square and the new town hall, painted by G. A. Berckheyde in 1673.

scale and is one of the few classical buildings in the Netherlands. Solid and rational, it seems the ultimate expression of the values of the Golden Age. Built when the Netherlands was at the height of its powers, the new city hall reflected the wealth of the city. The first foundation stone was laid in 1648 and by 1655 part of the building was put into use. The artist Artus Quellien of Antwerp was appointed as sculptor and, together with other skilled craftsmen, they executed the designs of van Campen. Artists such as Ferdinand Bol and Govert Flinck, both pupils of Rembrandt, painted large chimney pieces for the major rooms.

In 1808, Louis Napoleon, King of Holland and brother of the French Emperor Napoleon Bonaparte, took over the building and converted it into a royal palace, furnishing it with a valuable and extensive collection of Empire (or Napoleonic-style) furniture. Eventually King William I returned the building to the city government and it still remains in use as a royal palace, which the Queen uses for special ceremonial occasions. With its painted wall reliefs, sculptures, Empire-style furniture, chimney pieces and marble inlaid map of the world, it is no wonder that the 17th-century poet Constantin Huygens described the building as "the eighth wonder of the world." ❑

FROM COLONISTS TO CONQUERED

The Golden Age was all but over, and the Netherlands was to see peace and prosperity fade in a gradual but distinct turnaround in fortune

You can still see and touch the Golden Age legacy all around you in Amsterdam and other Dutch towns. Even though the lustre has been dulled by the passage of four centuries, its glint is firmly embedded. But by the start of the 18th century, the reservoir of inspiration, confidence and wealth that was its wellspring had run dry. The Zuiderzee had begun silting up, making it difficult for ships to reach Amsterdam. But, perhaps more significantly, many wealthy citizens of the town living in their fancy new canalside houses no longer wanted ships sailing up to their front doors and disgorging cargoes into the attic.

The second and third generations of the merchant families did not share their ancestors' zest for chasing the guilder to the ends of the earth; they were more interested in spending money than in garnering it. The merchant fleet was depleted, the national debt grew, and peasants who had been wearing leather shoes went back to making wooden ones. The United Provinces went into a period of decline, losing commercial pre-eminence to England and France.

William and Mary

In 1688, in what Protestants called the "Glorious Revolution", England's Catholic monarch, James II, was deposed. In his place, William of Oranje-Nassau, stadholder of Holland and Zeeland, and his wife, the English princess Mary Stuart – daughter of James II – were jointly crowned as William III and Mary II of England. William's wars against France in opposition to Louis XIV's expansionist policies strained the economy of the United Provinces, and the republic went into steep decline as a trading nation.

William III died without an heir in 1702 and the stadholdership was left vacant until 1747, when William IV inherited it, for the first time unifying the republic under one leader. But

between 1751 and 1788, the United Provinces were torn by civil strife between conservative supporters of the House of Orange and liberal reformers, called Patriots, demanding greater democracy and combining republicanism with the new ideas of the Enlightenment.

A side effect of this struggle was that in

LEFT: Neptune, Netherlands Scheepvaart Museum (Dutch Maritime Museum). **RIGHT:** Tsar Peter the Great studied ship-building methods in 1697.

1782, the Dutch were the first to recognise the United States and grant loans to the new democracy. The Patriots aimed to replace the United Provinces' patrician plutocracy and its Orangist traditionalism with a much wider democracy. What they did, however, was unite these former ruling class foes, in particular after the Patriots seized power in 1785, and provoke a pro-monarchy Prussian invasion two years later that sent the Patriots packing, mostly to France.

They returned in 1795 when a French revolutionary army invaded and replaced the antiquated political institutions of the United

resources and the Dutch lost most of their overseas trade because of the British blockade. Napoleon's failed 1812 invasion of Russia and his crushing defeat at Leipzig in 1813 spelled the end of the Napoleonic adventure. Prince William VI of Orange, son of William V, returned from exile and was crowned King William I of the Netherlands in 1814.

A new nation, a new voice

Dutch troops played a prominent part in the Duke of Wellington's decisive Allied victory over Napoleon at Waterloo in June 1815, earning the country a voice at the Congress of

Provinces with the French-sponsored Batavian Republic, a unitary state with its own National Assembly, named after the Batavi tribe that rebelled against Roman rule in AD 69. Stadholder William V fled to England.

In 1806, Napoleon Bonaparte took over the republic and proclaimed his brother Louis Napoleon King of the Netherlands, with Amsterdam as his capital. Rather unexpectedly, Louis proved too sympathetic to his new subjects, and in 1810 Napoleon forced him to abdicate and incorporated the country into the French Empire. Throughout this period economic activity declined on a disastrous scale. The French requisitioned men and

Vienna that same year. Austria renounced its claim to the southern provinces of the Low Countries – Belgium and Luxembourg – and the congress attached both regions to the Kingdom of the Netherlands. North and south were united again under one monarch for the first time in more than two centuries.

The Dutch managed to hold on to a good part of their empire when the Netherlands emerged from French rule at the end of the Napoleonic era. Trade in colonial products remained an integral part of the economy until World War II. William ruled as a constitutional monarch, though parliament's role was limited. His efforts to unify the two halves of the country, and the 1830 Belgian Revolution that followed years of unrest, gave the southern provinces independence as the Kingdom of Belgium. William recognised Belgian independence in 1839, and abdicated the following year. Pro-democracy riots that took place in 1845 led to a constitutional convention under J. R. Thorbecke, and in 1848 William II accepted reforms that provided for a directly elected parliament; thus the Netherlands became a constitutional monarchy.

> ### GOLDEN TREASURY
>
> You get a good idea of the style in which wealthy Amsterdammers of the fading Golden Age lived at the city's Museum Willet-Holthuysen and Museum Van Loon, both well-preserved patrician houses.

their northern neighbours, and among them waschoirmaster Lieven Defosel of Brussels, whose efforts at Haarlem's Concertgebouw concert hall helped raise funds to care for the dispossessed.

Conditions slowly improved during the 1920s, and in 1928 Amsterdam proudly hosted the Olympic Games. This all too brief post-war high was then followed by the Great Depression of the 1930s, during which many thousands of unemployed people worked on job creation schemes, such as the

Prosperous ports

A period of rapid development, beginning in 1870, saw improvements in education and public health provision. The economy received a boost when in 1872 the Nieuwe Waterweg opened, strengthening Rotterdam's position as a port; in 1876 the Noordzee Kanal (North Sea Canal) opened, reviving Amsterdam's port and bringing freshprosperity. Bicycles appeared in 1880 – the start of a passionate romance that continues unabated to this day. The first car put in an appearance in Amsterdam on 21 July 1897; a century later cars were guests who had overstayed their welcome in the city of Golden Age canals and narrow streets, and tough measures were put in force to control, and ultimately, to banish them.

Economically, the Netherlands concentrated on trade and agriculture well into the 20th century, then developed a large-scale industrial base. Politically, parliamentary authority was supreme and the electorate was expanded when universal male suffrage was introduced in 1917 and women's suffrage after World War II.

The country remained neutral during World War I, but the combined effect of the blockade of Germany imposed by the Allied nations and the operation of German U-boats in the area choked off trade and caused food shortages that led to strikes, riots and support for the Communist Party. Most of Belgium had been occupied by the Germans, and Belgians fled in large numbers to the safety of the Netherlands. As many as a million refugees sheltered with

construction of the Amsterdamse Bos recreation park, to the south of the capital. Amid chronic shortages and massive riots, the government used the army to maintain public order. In 1932 the *Afsluitdijk* (Enclosing Dyke) was completed, closing off the Zuiderzee and creating the freshwater IJsselmeer.

The Netherlands had hoped to remain neutral once more at the outset of World War II, which began with Germany's invasion of Poland in September 1939. Hitler had little time for the Netherland's neutrality, however, and on 10 May 1940 German air and ground units crossed the Dutch border, plunging the nation into the darkest chapter in its history. ❑

LEFT: Ludwig Napoleon Bonaparte.
RIGHT: J. R. Thorbecke (1796–1872), father of the modern Dutch constitution.

Amsterdam: An Historical Portrait

"**T**he pungent salt smell, the northern, maritime keynotes of seagull and herring, the pointed brick buildings, tall and narrow, with their mosaic of parti-coloured shutters, eaves, sills, that give the landscapes their stiff, heraldic look." Nicolas Freeling, the Dutch crime-writer, presents this romantic view of the city in his novel, *A Long Silence*. By contrast, the historian Simon Schama smells the underbelly of the beast: "In

high summer, Amsterdam smells of frying oil, shag tobacco and unwashed beer glasses. In narrow streets, these vapours stand in the air like an aromatic heat mist."

The reality

Amsterdam's elegance lies in its ingenious use of space. As Schama says: "In Amsterdam, alleys attract, avenues repel. The Kalverstraat's din and cheerful vulgarity are the authentic Dutch response to the alienating breadth of a boulevard."

Indeed, every inch of space seems to be accounted for. Statistics show that in terms of people per square metre, Amsterdam is as crowded as Hong Kong or Sri Lanka.

The sense of homogeneity suggested by the concentric canals is countered by the individuality of each neighbourhood, from the raffish waterfront district to the bohemian yet understated Jordaan, the melancholy (though in transition) Jodenbuurt (Jewish quarter) to the gentrified Museum District, the schizophrenic Oude Zijds (Old Side) to the sleazy red-light Wallen (literally quays).

The most appealing districts are, almost by definition, those with peculiar geography and the most chequered history. A patriotic 18th-century city burgomaster once presented his guests with a banquet celebrating the "courses" of the city's history. Hors d'oeuvres of red herring and cheese (representing early trade commodities) were followed by heavy puddings and roasts (the apogee of the Golden Age) and, for dessert, French wines and delicacies (representing decadence). The guests' reactions to this exercise in patriotic nostalgia are not recorded. Today the final course would be a hearty Indonesian *rijsttaffel*.

The birth of a city

By the 13th century a flourishing community had built a dam across the Amstel River and settled on the land around the marshy mouth. Named Amstelledamme, the medieval town soon prospered as a commodities market, helped by an influx of Flemish weavers and Jewish merchants. Ships unloaded precious wood, wool, salt and spices on Dam square and sailed away with fine cloth, furnishings and grain.

As the town expanded, the 14th-century city walls, built along Oudezijds and Nieuwezijds Voorburgwal, outlived their usefulness and placed constraints on Amsterdam's growth. In 1452, after a series of disastrous fires, the City Council decreed that all houses should henceforth be built of slate and stone rather than of wood.

Amsterdam prospered quietly under Burgundian and Habsburg domination but was politically marginalised until the end of the 16th century. The turning point in Amsterdam's fortunes came in 1578 when the city changed sides and supported the Dutch Calvinist, William of Orange, against Philip II and the Spanish Catholics.

This event, known as the "Alteration", made Amsterdam a natural home for Huguenot refugees and Flemish Protestants. After the declaration of the United Provinces in 1581, religious tolerance fostered the establishment of "clandestine"

LEFT: *The Munttoren* (1751), by J. ten Compe.

Catholic churches such as the Amstelkring on Oudezijds Voorburgwal. Although Catholic worship was officially illegal, the authorities tolerated discreet observance.

Dutch maritime superiority and mercantile success helped usher in the Republic's Golden Age, and Amsterdam enjoyed unrivalled prosperity as a banking centre and the hub of a burgeoning Dutch Empire. During the 17th century, Amsterdam perfected its burgerlijk culture, an aspiration to the highest civic and moral values rather than a mere embodiment of bourgeois taste. The Republic saw itself as "an island of plenty in a sea of want."

In 1613, Amsterdam's wealthy ruling class embarked on an ambitious foray into town planning with the building of the city's three greatest canals, the crescent-shaped Herengracht, Keizersgracht and Prinsengracht. These canals (*grachtengordel*) were soon adorned with magnificent gabled warehouses and patrician town houses.

The 18th century saw Amsterdam's gradual economic decline, coinciding with a conservative reaction against the perceived excesses of the previous century. The decline was only reversed when the creation of the Noordzee Kanaal in 1876 engendered a shadow "Golden Age", with an architectural revival and population growth. The wealthy built neoclassical mansions while the poor made do with good low-cost housing schemes in the De Pijp and Old South districts.

As a result of enlightened Dutch social policies, Amsterdam embarked on new low-cost housing schemes between the wars. The Jordaan was already well established as a working-class district, but the city's housing shortage was alleviated by the creation of garden suburbs in Amsterdam's Old South. Designed by architects of the Amsterdam School, these quirky yet utilitarian estates are characterised by multi-coloured bricks, bulging façades and bizarre windows.

Young and old

More recently, the city has bucked the Dutch trend towards *cityvorming*, the clinical planning ethos that has blighted Rotterdam, The Hague and Utrecht. By contrast, conservation and anti-development measures are generally favoured by Amsterdam's left-wing City Council and supported by the city's predominantly young population. Even so, cherished landmarks have been demolished. In the 1970s, Nieuwmarkt and a section of the Jodenbu-

urt were sacrificed to make way for a metro system. As for the completion of the Muziektheater and Stadhuis (City Hall) complex on Waterlooplein in 1987, the controversy lingers on.

Resistance to *cityvorming* is particularly strong in Amsterdam's most closely-knit neighbourhoods. The Nieuwmarkt, Jordaan, Western Islands and De Pijp districts are not about to be re-designed in a bland new international style. The Nieuwmarkt's cultural identity is not cast in stone: the buildings have been altered frequently since the 16th century, but the neighbourhood's resilience and its mercantile spirit remain intact. The district has traditionally welcomed refugees, from the Jews of the

17th century to today's Chinese, Indonesian and Surinamese immigrants.

Elsewhere, Amsterdam's best-loved district, the Jordaan, is immune to outside pressure. Its rebellious identity was forged in early industrial disputes and this closely packed quarter has been home to Huguenots, craftsmen, almshouse-dwellers, hippies, students and yuppies. This strangely harmonious community lives in a network of narrow streets which, tucked in between the grander canals, is little changed despite its gentrification. It is such neighbourhood identities which provide the key to Amsterdam's architectural integrity – and maintain its position as one of the most distinctive of European cities. ❏

RIGHT: Beurs van Berlage building, Amsterdam.

THE WAR YEARS

*The Dutch thought they had little to fear from Hitler's Germany, but nothing
could prepare them for the terrible consequences of Nazi ambition*

World War II began for the Dutch in the early hours of a beautiful Friday morning – 10 May 1940. As dawn broke over the flat, peaceful landscape, Junkers-Ju 52 transport planes flew in from the east carrying parachute troops, while ground forces, including an SS motorised regiment, swarmed over the German/Dutch frontier, dispelling any lingering hopes that the Netherlands could remain neutral. Later that same morning, Germany's Ambassador to The Hague, Count Von Zech Von Burckersroda, wept as he handed over the official declaration of war to the Dutch Foreign Minister.

Hitler had pencilled in a one-day schedule for the complete occupation of the Netherlands, one of the important first stages of his master plan to overrun Europe. There was a slight hitch; the Dutch Davids, confronted with the Teutonic Goliath, dared to fight back. The Dutch armed forces were hastily trained and poorly equipped. Many soldiers were still getting used to their army boots, and almost all of them were pacifists at heart and had no enthusiasm for war. Despite such circumstances, they kept their country out of German hands for five days – four more than Hitler had calculated

The masterplan

The Führer planned to launch his main offensive against Britain and France from Dutch and Belgian bases, after he had subdued the population, occupied France and taken care of what he euphemistacally dubbed "the Jewish problem." While, tragically, he succeeded only too well with certain parts of his plan, he never quite managed to subdue the Dutch.

The combined Dutch forces of 350,000 men bought enough time to enable Princess Juliana, accompanied by Prince Bernhard and their two children, to escape to Canada, and for Queen Wilhelmina, together with her cabinet, to reach the safety of British shores.

LEFT: Liberation Day, Dam Square, Amsterdam.
RIGHT: the bombardment of Rotterdam.

Dutch losses during those first days of confrontation hardly mean much when set against the backdrop of the millions of Allied troops who lost their lives defending democracy during the struggle against the Nazis. But the five-day battle took its toll, leaving 2,200 soldiers and 2,159 civilians dead, and 2,700 wounded.

It is difficult to calculate the exact number of Germans who died; many lost their lives when the defenders blew up vital bridges, and others were shot down in the Ju 52s. Official records show that 1,600 Germans were taken prisoner. For 1,200 of them, shipped to Britain just before the capitulation, the combat years of World War II were very short.

The Dutch had been well aware of the developments in Germany in the 1930s that brought Hitler to power and, ultimately, devastation to Europe. But the people of the Netherlands hoped that, as long as they did not catch their neighbour's eye, like the playground bully he would go away, or at least leave them alone.

Wall Street and the guilder

They had their own problems to contend with. The same economic shock waves that reached Germany from America in 1929 also reached the Low Country. The Wall Street crash had just as devastating an effect on the Dutch guilder as it had on sterling and the German mark. But the Dutch thought that stoicism in the face of adversity would win the day. The Prime Minister implemented belt-tightening measures and curbed spending in order to maintain the strength of the guilder.

Neighbouring Britain devalued sterling, but the guilder held while unemployment soared.

People concentrated on having a good time to avoid the economic issues and they blocked their ears to the echoes of Hitler's ranting and to the sound of marching jackboots drawing uncomfortably close across the frontier.

Royal wedding

First came the World Jamboree Celebrations, then the marriage of shy young Princess Juliana to the German Prince Bernhard. The 24-year-old Princess had met the young German Prince in 1935. He was invited to lunch with the Royal Family at their Austrian ski resort, and, while Queen Wilhelmina did most of the talking, the two were busy falling in love. "She struck me," he said later, "as immensely lovable, with a touching innocence."

Her innocence and euphoria could not have lasted long. Soon the young couple were confronted with Dutch reservations about the Prince's nationality, together with a Nazi witch-hunt against Prince Bernhard, who let it be known he would have no truck with the Nazis. In fact, three years after his wedding he would be found crouching on the roof of Soestdijk Palace, defiantly machine-gunning low-flying German planes.

The Dutch, who had previously avoided disturbing the enemy at the gate, finally showed their feelings on the day that the royal engagement was announced. Some Germans living in the Netherlands flew the swastika. In The Hague, seat of government and home to the country's reticent and well-behaved army of civil servants, people tore down the hated and feared insignia.

The German press blamed Prince Bernhard for the insult and started a campaign against him, and the German government withdrew the passports of nationals who had been invited to attend the wedding. The Dutch government opened talks and a compromise was reached, by which German nationals living in the Netherlands were advised not to display the swastika, while the Dutch agreed that Germany's national anthem and the "Horst Wessel" song could be sung at the gala wedding evening. During the singing, some German guests gave the Hitler salute. Dutch and other guests responded by singing *Rule Britannia*. It was a tense situation.

Dutch fascism

The early years of the 1930s had seen the emergence of Dutch fascism. The leader of the Dutch NSB (National Socialist Movement), whose members liked to strut around in black shirts and call themselves Nazis, was a short, vain man called Anton Mussert. A great admirer of Mussolini, he set himself up as the voice of order and solidarity which would unite the Dutch Aryan race and get rid of the enemy (Jews and any other undesirable foreigners), bringing the country back to prosperity.

Mussert hoped for power once the Germans occupied the Netherlands. He liked to quote Mussolini: "The people are like a woman, they will go with the strongest." He never tired of telling people that the Italian dictator was, "like Hitler and I, not very tall." Mussert faced a Dutch firing squad on 7 May 1946. He had not grown much in the interim and never achieved the position of power for which he yearned.

Rotterdam burns

At 10.30 on the morning of 14 May 1940, four days after the invasion, three German soldiers waving a white flag picked their way through the smoke-filled city streets of Rotterdam, heading towards the headquarters of the leader

ARMY IN EXILE

Despite fleeing Holland, fervent Nazi-hater Prince Bernhard did not sit out the war; after leaving his family safely in Canada he led the Dutch free forces from Britain.

planes and was now heading for the city. Rotterdam port was one of the Germans' main objectives and it was taking too long to conquer. General Schmidt, commanding German troops at Rotterdam, Moerdijk and Dordrecht, sent Colonel Scharroo an uncompromising message. The city was to be surrendered or face a heavy infantry attack starting at 1pm on the same day, followed 20 minutes later by heavy bombardment from the air. Colonel Scharroo was given two hours to think it over.

213Ton RDAM

of the Dutch troops, Colonel Pieter Scharroo. They came to deliver an ultimatum.

After smashing Waalhaven airport, where eight Fokker G-I fighters managed to shoot down two enemy bombers, the Germans met with fiercer opposition in Rotterdam itself. The city had a defence force of only 1,400 soldiers armed with just 24 light and nine heavy machine guns between them.

Fuelled by desperation, anger and courage, these men fought the German infantry force, which had landed on the river Maas in sea-

LEFT: trench warfare.
ABOVE: Rotterdam burns.

Stay of execution

Neither Scharroo, nor the city's mayor, needed two hours. Their minds were made up: there would be no surrender. A quick call was made to a senior Dutch officer, General Winkelman. He contacted the Queen's commissioner and Colonel Scharroo was ordered to send a message to General Schmidt stating that any ultimatum must be officially signed, giving the signatory's identity and rank. Meanwhile, General Schmidt sent a message back to Germany saying that the bombardment should be delayed while negotiations took place.

It was noon and Rotterdammers, taking advantage of the lull in fighting, were shopping

for food amid general relief that the shooting had stopped. Trams were running, children were on the streets. Meanwhile in Germany, the first squadrons of heavily loaded bombers were already moving down the runway at bases in Bremen and Westphalen on their way to their target – Rotterdam.

Hundreds of Rotterdammers had 90 minutes left to live – the time it would take to fly from Bremen and Westphalen on a clear day – and 14 May was another clear spring day. General Schmidt wrote and signedhis latest ultimatum. The answer was to be in his hands by 4.20 pm. The Dutch messenger, Captain Backer, accom-

panied by two German soldiers, set off again with a white flag. They may have exchanged remarks; certainly they looked up when they heard a deep sonorous sound in the air coming from the south and east. The German planes had arrived. The raid commander had been told that if red flares were set off Rotterdam was to be spared. Red flares went up – it appeared that the Rotterdammers had been given a reprieve.

Death from the air

The first group of planes changed course and flew off, their bombs still in their holds. However, a second wave remained on course, and dropped their bombs on thousands of screaming, panicked people who had never really believed the Germans would actually do this. It was 1.30 pm. and many children were back at their school desks.

The Germans sent a message to Dutch headquarters in The Hague. Utrecht, a historic and beautiful city of many thousand inhabitants, would be next. All other Dutch cities would be bombed in turn. General Winkelman reluctantly decided to give in.

A message of surrender was sent to German headquarters at the Hotel des Indes in The Hague; it was a lovely old building, where Pavlova had died and Mata Hari used to meet her consorts. Word was sent to Dutch troops to destroy their weapons. Unwilling to believe the battle was lost and their country was now in German hands, they did not start to do so until the next day, Wednesday, 15 May.

At the time, Queen Wilhelmina was staying in London, as a guest of George VI at Buckingham Palace. She was about to sit down to

---

THE DOCKWORKERS' STRIKE

A statue of a burly docker stands in Amsterdam's Jonas Daniël Meijerplein, commemorating the general strike of 25 and 26 February 1941, mobilised in protest at the Nazi deportation of the Jewish population.

Led by the city's dockers, it was Amsterdam's first open gesture of rebellion, as revulsion for the occupiers began to conquer collective fear. The strike has gone down in Dutch history as the "day beyond praise".

The Germans, who at first were taken aback by this brazen show of defiance, then moved quickly to stamp out what they saw as a dangerous undermining of their authority. Police patrolled the streets, shooting at passers-by, and

notices were posted ordering the people to return to work immediately. Their message was unequivocal: "There will be no meetings or gatherings of any kind, nor any political party activity. Anyone disobeying will be proceeded against under German military law. Hereafter, anyone who strikes, or who agitates for strikes will receive up to 15 years and, if the defence industry is involved, death."

People slowly went back to work, but morale had been temporarily boosted by the fact that Amsterdammers had dared to resist the tyranny under which they laboured. There were no more posters urging the Dutch to trust their German friends. The kid glove was shown to cover a steel fist.

supper with the King when the terrible details reached her. That night, 125 Amsterdam Jews took their own lives.

Ten weeks later, the shattered ruins of Rotterdam were still smouldering. The death toll was recorded at 800, while some 80,000 people had been made homeless. Around 24,000 houses had been destroyed, along with 2,500 shops, 1,200 factories, 500 cafés, 70 schools, 21 churches, 20 banks, 12 cinemas and two theatres. The Nazis had truly arrived.

CRUEL COLLABORATION

Though few in number, Dutch Nazis played a prominent role in occupied Holland by betraying Resistance members and rounding up Jews for the death camps.

in occupied Europe, never gave up hope. As time went on, acts of resistance grew in number and by the end of the war, the Dutch Resistance was one of the most effective of any occupied country.

The Biesbosch marshes, a hard-to-penetrate area near Dordrecht, became a relatively safe haven for Resistance fighters and, by 1944, a transit route for Allied agents, downed airmen, refugees and arms between the occupied and liberated parts of Holland. The Germans tried to root the Resistance fighters from their

LEFT AND ABOVE: refugees flee the war-torn cities by whatever means they can.

Dark days

Four years of misery descended upon the Netherlands. Each day brought new deprivations, degradations and sources of fear: shortage of food, lack of freedom, curfews, media censorship, death. Long cold winters had to be endured with no fuel for heating. In sudden *razzias* (round-ups), thousands of men were herded off to work in forced labour camps. For the country's Jewish population, it was a period of absolute and unadulterated terror.

But the Dutch, like so many others elsewhere

hiding-holes among the reeds and marshes, but failed. Captured German soldiers were held as prisoners-of-war in the Biesbosch, under the occupiers' noses.

False dawn

September 1944 was a cruel month, marked by two particularly black dates. The first was *Dolle Dinsdag*, "Mad Tuesday", which took place on 5 September. The German army had been routed in France and was fleeing in confusion through the Netherlands towards the German frontier. The Dutch thought freedom was at hand, their jubilation countered by the panic which broke out among collaborators, who joined the retreating Germans. Desperate people who had worked with the occupiers thronged train stations. Hundreds left their luggage on the platforms in their rush to get on trains heading East.

Dutch citizens thronged the streets in Arnhem and surrounding villages, jeering the departing German troops and the flotilla of dispossessed traitors scurrying along behind. People started to wave anything they could find that was coloured orange – the Dutch Royal Family's

> ### BRAVERY IN DEFEAT
>
> A force of 10,000 Allied airborne troops was due to hold the bridge at Arnhem for just two days; in the event, against overwhelming odds, a mere 600 men held it for four.

down in history as the Battle of Arnhem, or Operation Market Garden.

The Allied offensive, which began on 17 September 1944, was meant to open a corridor in central Holland from Eindhoven to Arnhem through which troops and tanks would sprint, and crossing the Rhine, head into the heart of Germany. Had it succeeded, the daring plan devised by Britain's Field Marshal Montgomery might possibly have brought the war to an end within weeks.

colour – and rumours were rife: Rotterdam had already been liberated, the Queen was returning, the British were on their way.

Freedom at last?

Then, almost as suddenly as the flow of troops had started, it stopped. The next day the streets of Arnhem were still. A horrible realisation began to sink in. The British were not coming and the Germans were not going. They were recovering, regrouping and preparing to fight another battle, one of the most important of World War II, during which more Allied troops would die than in the Normandy landings. The tragic events that were to follow would go

The plan was breathtaking in its simplicity. The Allied airborne operation involved flying in men, artillery and equipment of the First Allied Airborne Army. There were to be 5,000 fighters, bombers, transports and more than 2,500 gliders. On the ground, the British Second Army's massed tank columns were poised along the Dutch/Belgian border.

Five major river and canal bridges and other minor crossings were to be seized by the airborne troops, opening up a long narrow corridor, with Arnhem the last gateway to the final

ABOVE: still from Richard Attenborough's 1977 movie version of *A Bridge Too Far*. **RIGHT:** war-time rations.

goal, the Rhine, and Germany's heartland. The Third Reich would be toppled, bringing an end to the war in 1944.

A bridge too far

During the last conference at Montgomery's headquarters, Lt-General Frederick "Boy" Browning, the British Deputy Commander of the First Allied Airborne Army, made the memorable remark: "I think we may be going a bridge too far." He was proved tragically right. When the Allied paratroopers arrived, the Germans, who were not supposed to be in the area in such strength, were waiting to meet them.

The elite Second SS Panzer Corps had been quartered near Arnhem in the quiet, green area around Oosterbeek to rest and recuperate from recent combat.

While the US 101st and 82nd Airborne divisions succeeded in capturing Eindhoven and Nijmegen, when the battle for Arnhem began, the British First Airborne Division found itself cut off from help along the corridor: they fought bravely and desperately, but many were killed or captured. Dutch families around the area opened their doors and hearts to the wounded and dying. Many acts of individual heroism that day are recorded for history. But

THE ANATOMY OF BATTLE FAILURE

There are many theories as to exactly why Operation Market Garden failed. Was it a breakdown in communications? Overconfidence? Or the weather? A combination of all these reasons is probably the answer. Recriminations were thrown about, with each party blaming the other.

Cornelius Ryan, former war correspondent and author of *A Bridge Too Far*, which records every detail of the battle, once interviewed General Eisenhower, commander of Allied forces in Europe. Eisenhower, who insisted the interview should not be published until after his death, described Montgomery as "a psychopath", "egocentric" and "a man trying to prove that he was somebody."

Ryan also interviewed Montgomery. The Irishman was himself "difficult" and admitted he did not suffer fools at all. But he did not think Montgomery a fool.

In an interview given at the launch of *A Bridge Too Far*, Ryan had this to say of General Montgomery: "He was a vain, arrogant man. Ambitious as hell, popular with his men, a great publicist and highly intelligent, but Montgomery can never be forgiven for one act. This man knew that the Second SS Panzer Corps was in the Arnhem area yet still he sent his airborne troops in on top of them, and, for that matter, so did Eisenhower. They both overruled the Dutch intelligence reports."

the saddest reminder of the battle must be the rows of simple white crosses in Oosterbeek War Graves Cemetery. Operation Market Garden left 17,000 Allied soldiers, British, American and Polish, killed, wounded or missing.

The failure of Operation Market Garden had a further terrible legacy; thousands of people in industrial areas around Amsterdam, The Hague and Rotterdam died of hunger, while, in the death camps of Central Europe, hundreds of thousands of Jews died, as the Nazis, aware of

> **TERRIBLE TOLL**
>
> The Battle of Arnhem left over 10,000 Dutch dead, most of them civilians, victims of the campaign itself or of the terrible "hunger winter" that followed.

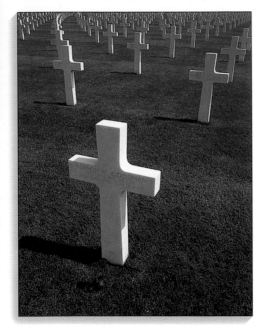

the Allies' imminent arrival, tried to destroy evidence of the policy that would come to be called the Holocaust.

Freedom at last

Finally, on 5 May 1945, Germany capitulated and the Netherlands was liberated. The official document was signed in Wageningen. A jubilant Prince Bernhard was present, together with General Blaskowitz, Commander of the German troops in the Netherlands, and the Canadian General Faulkes.

There were scenes of ecstatic joy in Amsterdam, The Hague, Delft and Rotterdam (most of the south of the country had already been liberated before the winter). But there was a marked difference in the appearance of the cheering crowds to those, say, of Paris. The faces of many were grey and hollow; some people could hardly stand on their pathetically thin legs. Children were weak and had to be held. Many were suffering from tuberculosis.

After the Allied attack on Arnhem, the Germans had deliberately slowed down vital transport carrying food to the industrial areas of the Netherlands. Food and fuel supplies ran out during the winter. Many people were so desperate that they resorted to eating tulip bulbs. While the relief drops of Operation Manna (*see facing page*) did much to alleviate suffering, thousands died before spring finally arrived, bringing with it the long-awaited liberation.

Revenge and recrimination

On the evening of Liberation Day ugly scenes took place as terrified women and girls who had "fraternised" with German soldiers were rounded up and had their heads shaved. Dutch Nazis, and other collaborators who had not already fled, were arrested as the euphoria led to an explosion of bitter anger amongst the recently liberated. But the Dutch are a reticent people. There were no public lynchings. Of 154 death sentences passed only 42 were carried out. Practical as ever, the Dutch set most of the collaborators to work rebuilding damaged roads and buildings.

As the country slowly started to heal, a tally was made of the ravages caused by the war; hundreds of thousands were dead or missing, and the bill for damaged property reached billions of guilders. The list of destruction included 70,000 houses, 8,360 farms, 10,000 factories and 200 churches.

There was a special figure for the Jewish population. In 1940, 140,000 Jews lived in the Netherlands – mostly in Amsterdam. At the end of the war less than a third of that number remained alive. Of those who survived, most had lost everything – family, home, friends, possessions. Then the struggle began to understand it all and learn the lessons. ❑

LEFT: Margraten War Cemetery.

Operation Manna

The bitterest months of the Occupation began for the Dutch after the failure of Arnhem; life under the desperate and revengeful enemy was to prove horrific. Several thousand Dutch men, women and children died as a result of German reprisals, many killed in retaliation for kidnappings carried out by the Resistance. But the most atrocious figure was the 15,000 who died from hunger, in the last year of the war.

By October 1944, the war's front line ran right through the Netherlands; the northern part of the country was still in German hands and cut off from food supplies. Food was failing to get through because of rail strikes, and the Germans had blocked the waterways in retaliation for the strikes.

The whole country suffered, but cities were the worst hit: The Hague, Rotterdam and Amsterdam. Pathetic streams of people made their way out of the cities to the countryside, pushing wheelbarrows laden with personal possessions to barter for food. They often returned empty-handed. Most heart-rending of all were the children, many of whom dropped dead from exhaustion on the streets. To compound the misery, it was a bitterly cold winter, and fuel had run out. People cut down trees in the cities' parks for firewood; the wooden blocks between the train rails disappeared overnight. By midwinter the death toll was high.

In December 1944, Minister Gerbrandy, head of the Dutch government in London, wrote to General Eisenhower: "The Dutch government cannot accept that eventual liberators will be liberating dead bodies." The letter pressed for an offensive to begin to free the north of the Netherlands.

But on the day Mr Gerbrandy wrote his letter the Germans started their own desperate offensive in the Ardennes. Every available German soldier was needed for battle, so, to release them from internal duties in Holland, Dutchmen were despatched in their thousands to labour camps in Germany.

In January 1945, the death rate in Amsterdam was 500 a week; as there was no wood for the luxury of a coffin, most bodies were buried in paper or rolled in a sheet.

That spring, the first weak sun shone on some very pathetic faces: some were green-tinged from eating too many tulip bulbs; infectious diseases, including typhoid and diptheria, were rampant.

RIGHT: food parcels dropped during Operation Manna.

Then, on 25 April, posters appeared promising relief from the months of relentless misery. The Allies were to start air-drops of food.

This risky exercise was called Operation Manna. On 29 April the skies above the north of Holland were suddenly filled with the deep sound of low-flying Lancaster bombers; this time when their shutters opened it was to release crates of food rather than bombs. Pilots and crews risked their lives as they flew as low as 60 metres (200 ft) above the dropping areas. People filled the streets waving to the planes; many were crying and waving sheets, shirts, anything that would flap in the wind.

Some crews emptied their pockets, throwing out chocolate and cigarettes. When the second wave of planes came, people had messages ready. Sheets were spread out reading "God Bless You" or, in some cases, "Cigarettes here please."

From the first of May, American B-17 "flying fortresses" joined the exercise. To many Dutch, "Operation Manna" was the final dramatic sign that the misery was over. "It was a wonderful sight, the great billowing parachutes, crates of food attached. It was 'Manna from Heaven' for us, the survivors," said one Dutch woman who, at the age of five, tasted her first chocolate bar thrown from the cockpit of a Lancaster. "I've never tasted anything as good since, and I still have the wrapping." ❏

MODERN HISTORY

At the end of World War II, the future of The Netherlands appeared bleak.

Instead, the country has emerged as the very model of a modern European nation

As was the case elsewhere in newly liberated Europe – indeed, in many countries throughout the world – the immediate post-war period was difficult for the Netherlands. The priorities were reconstruction, in particular of war-shattered cities such as Rotterdam, Arnhem, Eindhoven and Nijmegen, and

repairing the widespread damage done by flooding when dykes had been damaged. As the economy slowly recovered, the foundations were laid for the country's cradle-to-grave welfare system, which, financed by high taxation, would become one of the most generous and comprehensive in the world.

Benelux, a customs union with Belgium and Luxembourg, came into force in 1947, followed by Dutch membership of the European Coal and Steel Community in 1952, and the European Economic Community (now the European Union) in 1958. Queen Wilhelmina abdicated in 1948 in favour of her daughter, Juliana. The following year, with the Soviet Union present-

ing the latest security threat to western Europe, the Netherlands joined NATO.

In 1953, disaster struck. A devastating North Sea storm broke through the dykes in the southwest, causing catastrophic flooding, accompanied by substantial loss of life and property, in parts of Zeeland, Noord-Brabant and Zuid-Holland provinces. The Dutch government's response was the Delta Project, a 30-year engineering effort begun in 1958 to strengthen sea defences by sealing off river estuaries and coastal inlets and raising dykes throughout the southwest. It reached its climax in 1987, with the opening of the colossal *Oosterschelde Stormvloedkering* (Eastern Scheldt Storm Surge Barrier). Land has continued to be reclaimed from the sea, especially around the freshwater IJsselmeer lake that replaced the Zuiderzee after 1932, when the *Afsluitdijk* (Enclosing Dyke) was completed. In 1986 Flevoland became the country's 12th province.

End of the colonial era

After World War II, the East Indies emerged from Japanese occupation with a new determination to seek independence. The Dutch fought desperately to restore colonial rule but yielded in the face of an insurrection led by General Sukarno, whose aims were supported by the United States and most of Europe. Independence was granted in 1949 and the Dutch East Indies became Indonesia, with Sukarno as its first president. Visitors to the Netherlands today can't fail to see an influence, from the many citizens of ethnic Indonesian origin (there have been hundreds of thousands of Indonesian immigrants) to the Indonesian restaurants that serve some of the best food in the country.

A few small Caribbean islands of the Netherlands Antilles, among them Aruba, Bonaire and Curaçao, remain part of the Dutch realm, but the western colonies have had far less cultural impact on the Netherlands – perhaps because of slavery, lower profits and relatively disinterested rule. By the time Dutch Guyana gained independence as Surinam in 1975, its Dutch roots were so shallow that many of the former colony's educated and professional classes were Javanese, trained in the East Indies and brought in by the Dutch to help run the place. At independence, 150,000 of Surinam's 400,000 population exercised their right of immigration to the Netherlands. Though many of them represented the educated middle class – and the majority have become valued Dutch society members – Surinamese immigrants are frequently blamed for involvement in criminal activity, and have generally not assimilated as well as Indonesian immigrants.

PROFIT & LOSS

Surinam's Independence in 1975 had a poignant significance for the new, post-colonial Holland; it was the same year that Amsterdam celebrated its 700th anniversary.

The rise and fall of the empire helps put the modern country and its ethnic and cultural diversity into perspective, and goes a long way towards explaining how Amsterdam in particular has become the distinctive city it is today.

During the 1960s Amsterdam was a hotbed of radical political activity, led by the anti-establishment "Provos" (a term derived from provocateurs), dedicated to shaking Dutch complacency. The Provos won seats on the city council in 1965, and the following year led demonstrations that disrupted the wedding of Princess Beatrix to German Claus von Amsberg. The Provos disbanded in 1967.

Fighting in the streets

Protests in Amsterdam reached a violent peak in 1975, as police confronted "Stop the Stopera" demonstrators over plans to demolish housing in the old Jewish Quarter around Nieuwmarkt to build a new metro system. Similar battles broke out in the adjacent Waterlooplein neighbourhood in an attempt to prevent construction of a new Opera/Dance venue and Town Hall complex. Despite such strong opposition, the metro opened in 1980, followed by the Muziektheater/Stadhuis in 1986 – the Opera House is now one of the city's foremost cultural attractions.

Throughout the 1970s and 1980s, and even into the 1990s, a severe shortage of decent quality, affordable housing fuelled the activities of a well-organised movement of squatters, called "crackers" in Dutch. The government's prioritisation of hotel construction – along with the

aforementioned new Town Hall and Muziektheater – rubbed salt in the crackers' perceived wounds and provoked many homeless people into taking over unoccupied houses.

In 1980, violent disturbances rocked the city as 500 police, using armoured vehicles and CS gas, evicted crackers from properties in the heart of the museum quarter. That same year, the celebrations for Queen Beatrix's coronation were disrupted in a major way, with protesters and police once again slugging it out in

Amsterdam's streets amid clouds of tear-gas.

Such epic events are now little more than memories. In recent years the city's political and business leaders have tried to promote an image – and a reality – more in tune with the needs of commerce. Amsterdam has consolidated its position as an international business centre, the European headquarters of multinational corporations, and a transport and distribution hub.

Politics today

Holland remains a constitutional monarchy, with a parliament of two houses, an Upper Chamber and a Lower Chamber. Queen Beatrix's eldest

LEFT: the Dutch army in Indonesia before independence.
RIGHT: Queen Beatrix.

son, Prins Willem-Alexander, is heir to the throne and to the House of Oranje-Nassau's long-running legacy.

In 1981 the Dutch vigorously opposed NATO's planned deployment of US nuclear-tipped cruise missiles on their soil. Prime Minister Van Agt's government supported the deployment, a policy that contributed to his defeat in the 1982 general election. He was replaced by the business-friendly coalition government of Ruud Lubbers, in turn replaced as Prime Minister by Wim

RADICALISM REDONE

As a fading echo of the "cracker" radicalism of the 1970s and 1980s, environmentally-minded Amsterdammers voted in 1992 to drastically cut car use in the city.

million inhabitants in its 34,000 sq. km (13,000 sq. miles), the Netherlands probably needs every centimetre of sea floor it can lay its hands on. But statistics can be deceptive. Two-thirds of the population live in one-fifth of the country, the western "Randstad" area that includes Rotterdam, The Hague, Amsterdam and Utrecht.

In the remainder, population pressures are far less apparent. Farmland and national parks take up much of the available space, and cities like Maastricht, Eindhoven

Kok, who was re-elected to a second term in 1998. During the 1990s, the Netherlands has been the setting for two far-reaching European Union treaties: the 1992 Maastricht Treaty that created the Single European Market; and the 1997 Treaty of Amsterdam, which confirmed the course of European Monetary Union (EMU) and the creation of the euro as the Single European Curency. When the first EMU deadline arrived in 1999, the Netherlands was one of 11 countries to establish the euro.

State of the Nation

A small, densely populated country (the population has tripled during this century), with 16

and Groningen are fewer and further between. Landscapes vary from flat polders, through heaths and lakes, even hills, while cultural differences ensure that the languages of Friesland and Zeeland co-exist with Dutch and a gaggle of local dialects. In place of the stress and aggression which might normally result, the Dutch have developed a tolerant, live-and-let-live attitude that has coloured their politics and culture.

In some countries, certain social groups or classes are described as the "pillars of society", be it the middle class, the judiciary, or religious institutions. The Netherlands took this idea a stage further by making all groups the *zuilen* (pillars) of society, any one of which could survive perfectly happily without reference to the others, yet which generally chose mutual co-operation over confrontation as a way of achieving goals.

Divisions in society

Today it remains true that the media, education, trade unions, hospitals and cultural organisations are divided according to religious and political groupings. That the system has worked owes much to the celebrated contradictions of Dutch

> ### MONEY MAGNET
>
> Holland's "offshore" tax laws and stable economic and political climate attracts a great number of overseas companies, as well as highly paid entertainers such as the Rolling Stones.

lished significant operations here, while a number of liberalisation measures have spurred a reduction in unemployment, which had stubbornly remained until recently at around the 10 percent mark.

The great middleman

"Gateway to Europe" and "Holland Distribution Land" are slogans often used to underline the country's geographical advantages. Positioned at the transport hub of western Europe, and possessed of such important

society, where unity and diversity, conservatism and liberalism, stuffiness and adventure, are easy bedfellows. The Dutch are renowned the world over for their tolerance.

A lack of political angst has enabled the Dutch to concentrate on creating and sharing prosperity. In the decades since the war, the economy, motivated by a lack of raw materials and the loss of Indonesia, has been transformed from one based on agriculture to one where high-tech industries and trade predominate. Many multinational companies have estab-

assets as Schiphol Airport and the port of Rotterdam, the Netherlands are considered the middleman par excellence.

But a simpler, more human concept underlines everyday life. When all the grand ideas of tolerance, Golden Ages and commercial acumen have been weighed in the scales of a nation's worth, you may still be struck more forcefully by the constant Dutch search for *gezelligheid*. This is an enigmatic word for that special something that makes a country friendly, cosy, comfortable, familiar, welcoming and memorable. Dutch, in fact. *Gezelligheid* may turn out to be the country's most important commodity. ❑

LEFT: Prince Willem Alexander.
ABOVE: Dutch Prime Minister Wim Kok.

THE EVOLUTION OF A NATION

Religious freedom, coupled with a hatred of being told what to do, has in many ways moulded the Dutch into a cosmopolitan and relatively classless society

Many elements of Dutch society, like the Dutch themselves, are a study in contradictions. The Netherlands is a nation devoted to tidiness and a strong sense of order, yet its capital is known for pavements slippery with dog droppings, graffiti-scarred walls and dishevelled drug addicts. The Dutch hate taking orders and gleefully jeer the self-important, yet they revere their monarchy. It is a nation founded on religious tolerance, yet features a powerful religious lobby. The people fiercely guard their privacy, yet leave their living-room curtains open all evening, maintaining that they have nothing to hide.

The Dutch rarely try to explain; to them, the contradictions are simply part of being Dutch. Like their sense of humour: the Dutch revel in hearing or telling a good joke, yet they also admit they are a stolid, dull people ("but not as dull as the Belgians," they quickly point out). They are not prone to apologies, (though they are not beyond a simple "sorry" if they bump into you on the street). This remains a source of frustration to foreign visitors used to having their own "space".

But in such a crowded country, visitors are expected to go with the flow. And in anarchic cities like Amsterdam, that means dealing with cyclists racing through red lights and taxis permitted to drive along the tram tracks.

The break with Spain

The emergence of the Netherlands as a nation can be traced back to the late 16th century. The whole of the Netherlands was then under Spanish rule, but already divided by religion. The southern provinces (modern Belgium and Luxembourg) were staunchly Catholic and accepted Spanish sovereignty, unlike the Dutch in the northern provinces who rebelled against Philip II's efforts to impose Catholicism on them and-stamp out the Calvinist movement.

PRECEEDING PAGES: traditional Friesland pottery; IJsselmeer fishermen. **LEFT:** traditional Dutch costume. **RIGHT:** bridal flourish.

The northern Protestant-dominated region came to be known as the United Provinces after the seven member provinces signed the Treaty of Utrecht in 1579. From that time onwards, the United Provinces acted as a separate nation, though not one recognised by the Spanish. The alliance, which left each of the seven provinces

with considerable independence, served as a model for the federalism that evolved in later nations, including the United States.

Then, as now, the Dutch hated being told what to do, whether by a foreign king or by one of their own dukes. As a result, the seven provinces were run in much the same manner as the medieval city-states of Europe: each province made its own laws and other states had little or no say in a province's internal affairs. The only real influence of the States General, the assembly to which each province sent representatives to discuss issues of common importance, came in military affairs and in drawing up economic policy when that was considered an integral part of military strategy. The United Provinces rarely recognised a national leader, except in dire necessity such as times of war.

Wealth creation

There was another critical element in the way the United Provinces were run. Instead of allegiance to a king or prince or a set of ruling families, power rested with the commercial classes – the merchants, traders and bankers who created the wealth. And they did create wealth. The 17th century, despite continuing conflict with Spain, has become known as the Golden Age of the Netherlands; in that century the Dutch carved out a trading empire around the world and used their prosperity at home to create an era of achievement in fields as disparate as art, architecture and town planning.

Many believe that the Golden Age would have had no lustre if the United Provinces had not been founded on the principle of freedom of conscience. In one of the earliest examples of Dutch contrariness, Calvinism was the official religion and Catholicism was formally outlawed, but the United Provinces allowed anyone to practise any religion they wished in private, Catholics included.

This religious freedom, along with the then rare freedom of the press, drew refugees to the United Provinces from all over Europe – many of them the richest, most ambitious and best skilled in their own countries. Later, as the empire grew, many natives of the Dutch colonies, particularly from what is now Indonesia, came to settle in the Netherlands, often through intermarriage with the Dutch or working for Dutch companies. Consequently, the Netherlands has always had a cosmopolitan flair, mixing races and religions and a more or less equal chance of exploiting individual talents. One legacy of the Golden Age is that anyone could become a member of the clergy, an artist or an entrepreneur. Although not a completely classless society, most Dutch belong to one large, dominant middle class.

Social structure

For centuries Dutch society was built on *zuilen*, or "columns", representing different components of the population. The members of each group kept to themselves but nonetheless held up the ideals of the nation. The two main columns consisted of Protestants and Catholics. They not only had their own churches, but their own schools, civic organisations and political parties. Parts of some towns would be Catholic, other parts Protestant, while some towns were completely one or the other.

Since World War II, the distinctions have faded. Some historians give Hitler the credit: the Nazi Occupation forced Dutch who had never mingled – Calvinists and Catholics, city dwellers and villagers, northerners and southerners – to work together. Today, the *zuilen* are still there but they are ineffective and many Dutch are members of more than one column.

CREATION OF THE WELFARE STATE

Some believe that the Netherlands transformed itself into a welfare state in the 1960s, but the roots go far deeper. Virtually every town has surviving examples of *hofjes*, the small houses often set around garden squares that were built by religious organisations and family trusts for the poor and elderly. In Amsterdam an example is the Begijnhof, a square just off the Kalverstraat. Just as the unemployed, disabled and aged of the late 20th century find succour in the welfare state, the poor of the 16th and 17th centuries were looked after by charities. About two-thirds of today's gross national product is redistributed by the government.

Perhaps the biggest change has taken place in religious attitudes. Church attendance has fallen dramatically, and polls indicate that many Dutch are now agnostics or atheists. Many only set foot in a church for one of the non-religious talks, concerts or regular exhibitions that take place.

Religion and politics

In politics, the Protestant and Catholic parties merged in the 1960s, creating the Christian Democratic Appeal (CDA), which became the dominant centrist party. Significantly, in this

ANYTHING GOES

Despite a surface control by Calvinist ideals, the Dutch largely retain a live-and-let-live attitude to foibles in their society.

His successor, Wim Kok of the Worker's Party (PvdA), received his political grounding in the hierarchy of trade unions, hence his Socialist view, and has taken a completely different approach.

Yet the Calvinists remain influential, using their powerful lobby to restrict aspects of everyday life such as drinking laws and opening hours. Dutch television features some of the most biting satire in the world, which pokes fun at all aspects of the Establishment – except God and religion – which are still largely taboo.

mostly Protestant country, the charismatic Ruud Lubbers, a Catholic, became the leading Dutch politician of the late 20th century, with a series of Christian Democrat election victories that gave him repeated terms as Prime Minister. When protesters marched on Pope John Paul II chanting "Kill the Pope!" during a 1985 visit to the Netherlands, Lubbers was reluctant to criticise those who took part in the demonstration. "We do not believe in holy men," he told one interviewer. "The Pope came here as a man higher than others. That is not the Dutch way."

LEFT: carnival in the Catholic province of Limburg.
ABOVE: Catholic church service.

When laws are elastic

The role of religion and the Calvinist lobby may be partly responsible for the continuing contradictions – some might say hypocrisy, others just typical Dutch pragmatism – that continue to exist between Netherlands' law and day-to-day practice. To visitors, prostitution and drug use are obvious examples. In theory, drugs are illegal, though you wouldn't know it from the way police calmly stroll past marijuana cafés. Brothels were only legalised in the 1990s, although they have been flourishing in many Dutch cities for centuries. A less well known example is the general attitude towards euthanasia, however. Though technically illegal, it is practised by doctors with the tacit approval of the authorities.

Prostitution, soft drugs and euthanasia remain illegal because any attempts to change the legal status quo would be strongly opposed by the Calvinist lobby. But such practices go on openly because the Dutch people, with their legendary tolerance, don't really care whether they're illegal or not. The café owners and prostitutes are even invited to become members of the local Chamber of Commerce.

This remarkable ability to look the other way can sometimes embarrass the Dutch. In recent years, for example, the Netherlands has been

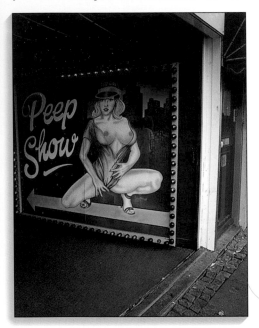

forced by pressure from other countries to act against its child pornography industry, which was supplying much of the rest of the world with explicit magazines and videos of youngsters in acts of sex and violence involving adults, other children and animals. "People, normal people, did not realise how nasty or extensive this stuff is," one Member of Parliament admitted. However, after the infamous Dutroux child abuse scandal that rocked the people of Belgium in the late 1990s, closer attention is being paid on this subject.

At the same time, the Calvinist traditions of the Netherlands can be viewed as a contributing factor in some of the country's most pro-

gressive programmes, including a long-term National Environment Plan, which calls for water, air and soil pollution to be reduced by up to 90 percent before 2010 – a goal that would consume up to 3.5 percent of the gross national product. It is a programme and a cost that few other countries would dare undertake, but as one financial analyst concluded: "Gripped by Calvinistic guilt over lapsed stewardship of the earth, the Dutch are convinced that their country is the sink of Europe. They point out that it is a small, densely populated land, a third of which is covered with water, and close to what they regard as pollution-spewing Britain and western Germany."

No doubt the Calvinist traditions also have played a role in the leadership the Dutch have assumed in the world peace movement since it began in the Netherlands at the end of the 19th century.

Order and respectability

The liberal attitudes of the Dutch – perhaps "libertarian" would be a better word, though some critics might prefer "libertine" – are one of the country's biggest contradictions. Despite a long history of religious intolerance, the Dutch willingness to let anyone do anything provided it doesn't hurt other people seems at odds with other basic elements of the Dutch character. They are a people in many ways obsessed with respectability and with a strong sense of order.

Some of the most interesting, and indeed most appealing traits of the Dutch people have emerged from this particular contradiction between tolerance and respectability. A good example is the way a Dutch family on holiday will gather up everyone, from grandparents to teens to small children, and head for the nearest brown café (traditional and cosy neighbourhood pub) so that dad doesn't have to drink beer by himself.

Another example is the story of a prominent journalist, a husband and father, from The Hague. For years he has been telephoning a woman from Friesland whom he met on a business trip. He always invites her to meet him for a tryst, and after her routine refusal he settles for telling her the latest dirty jokes. He makes these calls only from hotel rooms when he's travelling on business. And while the woman has no intention of ever meeting the man again, she admits that she enjoys the slightly naughty, forbidden aspect of their telephone relationship. "He makes me laugh," she says, and in the Netherlands that can cover a multitude of sins, whether real or imagined.

Women and family

Dutch feminism presents a number of other contradictions. At first glance, women in the Netherlands seem to be among the most broad-minded and outspoken anywhere in the world. Is there any other society

> ### NOTHING TO HIDE
>
> Some believe one reason the Dutch keep their curtains open is that they want their neighbours to know that their homes are clean and that they have no reason to hide anything going on inside.

than in hospital. Several weeks before any scheduled birth, a midwife is sent to inspect the mother-to-be's home to make sure the parents (or parent) are prepared. Midwives generally supervise the birth. On the day after the birth, the government sends a young woman to the home. For the next eight days, from 7am to 6pm she acts as a mother's helper: cleaning up, washing, taking care of the other children, shopping, making meals, receiving visitors, and so on.

where so many women roll their own cigarettes? Yet, until quite recently, relatively few Dutch women went out to work, compared with other industrialised western countries.

Formerly, Dutch women worked only until they got married and became housewives and mothers. Today, increasing numbers of married women go out to work, although most wait until their children are at school. It is interesting to note that the majority of children in The Netherlands are born at home, rather

LEFT: pornographic cinema in Amsterdam.
ABOVE: another, tamer face of Holland – traditional folk dancing in Friesland.

Attitudes to royalty

The Dutch may occasionally joke about their monarchy, but in fact the royal family is extremely popular. In typical Dutch fashion they live in much less ostentation than say, the British royals, and treat the accident of birth as a lifelong job that fate has assigned to them. In Britain, abdication would probably be viewed as an earthshaking event; in The Netherlands abdication is routine.

The last two queens have retired in great dignity to let their younger heirs carry on, and it is likely that Queen Beatrix will do the same for Crown Prince Willem Alexander. One of the reasons the Dutch royals are so popular is that they behave just like a modern family and the Dutch people can therefore relate closely to their problems. Prince Claus, husband of Queen Beatrix, has been widely praised for his courage in discussing publicly his battles, over a number of years, with depression. "We like him for it. By discussing it, he's helped lots of other people with the same problems," one Dutch academic said.

Family life

The Dutch are very orientated towards family life and visitors from other countries often remark on the healthy, friendly relationship that

exists between Dutch parents and their children. The common emphasis, if there is one, seems to be on avoiding the sort of conflicts that can create a permanent rift and issues are often approached from the child's perspective.

Golden Age values

Dutch home life encompasses several values that seem to date back to the Golden Age. The television age has inevitably changed traditional trends as it has elsewhere in the world, but it is still not unusual for a Dutch family to turn off the television and spend an evening together making conversation or playing music.

Still important is the concept of *deftig*, which doesn't translate directly but can be described as "dignity, respectability, stateliness" (*see page 84*). Visitors express surprise that most Dutch homes have no curtains in the front room, but the Dutch do not feel the need to hide the way they live. At the same time they attach importance to the concept of *gezellig*, or "cosiness, conviviality," as represented by the *schemerlampen*, the soft-shaded "twilight lamps" still found in many Dutch homes. There's even a word in Dutch for sitting up late and watching the fire die down.

The Dutch also have a reputation for hard-headed shrewdness in business (in the 17th and 18th centuries they sold weapons to, and even underwrote the ship insurance of their enemies). Yet quality of life is not equated with prosperity, and the gap between the highest and lowest incomes is much less than in most other developed nations.

The Dutch may at first may seem a little stand-offish or even gruff to outsiders but this is a misleading impression. In fact, they love to go out to eat in large, noisy groups, following the Dutch adage, "Pleasure shared is pleasure doubled." The Dutch generally like to make friends and look for any excuse to chat: over coffee in the morning, tea in the afternoon and beer or *jenever* (gin) in the evening. A Dutch person who is dining alone in a restaurant is unlikely to be offended at an invitation to join someone else who is also seated alone. As a result, there is often ample opportunity for the solitary visitor with the appetite – or the thirst – to learn first-hand about Dutch society and its many contradictions. ❏

LIBERAL PARENTING

One Dutch mother interviewed says she did not try to discourage her two daughters from teenage sex; she advised them on birth control. When the daughters dabbled in marijuana, the mother didn't harangue them; she had smoked pot herself. The junkies on the streets sent a stronger anti-drug message to the girls. When one daughter went through a punk phase, the mother agreed that it was ridiculous for people to be afraid of green hair. When the other daughter had her fourth bicycle stolen in one year, the mother didn't question her when she arrived home with another days later. "I suppose she stole it, but who can blame her?"

LEFT: mussel-eating festival at Yerseke, in Zeeland.

The House of Orange

It is not easy trying to fathom the monarchy's appeal to Dutch citizens. Queen Beatrix is the most improbable of monarchs, a high-spirited, apple-cheeked queen who wore a polo-necked pullover for the commemorative photograph of her investiture, and is happiest cycling around the Dutch countryside.

The appeal of the House of Orange remains linked to its role as a unifying force during the struggle for independence. The Oranje-Nassau dynasty dates back to medieval times, when the German Count of Nassau was granted estates in the Low Countries, but the dynasty only came of age in the late 16th century when William of Orange inherited these estates along with the southern French principality of Orange. The colour orange is displayed on all ceremonial occasions.

In 1966, amidst social unrest, Princess Beatrix married German diplomat Claus von Amsberg, previously a member of the Hitler Youth and the German army. The wedding, in Amsterdam, was the occasion for smoke bombs, tear gas and violent demonstrations. A decade later, Queen Juliana's consort, Prince Bernhard, was found guilty of being "open to favours" and accepting a million dollars from Lockheed in connection with defence contracts. Even so, tolerance and esteem for the royal family ensured that a constitutional crisis was avoided.

In 1980 rioting disrupted Queen Beatrix's investiture in Amsterdam. The city was in the throes of a housing crisis, while 84 million guilders was being spent on the royal residence in The Hague. The protesters' slogan was *Geen woning, geen kroning* (No home, no coronation).

The royal role, enshrined in the Constitution, is "above politics" and the monarch is the only fixed factor in a fast-changing, pluralist political scene. But the monarchy can be abolished at any time by Act of Parliament. The Dutch are no blind loyalists and should the Orange dynasty die out, would not hesitate to proclaim a republic.

Despite loyalty to the House of Orange, much credit is due to the influence of recent monarchs. During Queen Wilhelmina's 50-year reign (from 1898 to 1948), moral leadership was the keynote. She was a member of the Reformed Movement and, as a pious Calvinist, encouraged the Church

RIGHT: Queen Beatrix.

to resist secularisation. In true Dutch fashion, Queen Juliana rebelled against her mother's imperiousness. During her reign, from 1948 to 1980, she proved a natural communicator with a common touch. Irene, one of four daughters, caused her mother anguish by falling in love with a pretender to the Spanish throne, converting to Catholicism and renouncing her rights of succession. None of this, however, dented Irene's popularity in the public's eyes.

Juliana's youngest daughter, Christina, married a Cuban-born social worker – Beatrix often said that if she hadn't been Queen, she too would have been a social worker. Although marriage to a Ger-

man was not popular, Beatrix endeared herself to the public with her egalitarianism, low profile and conscientiousness. The second richest woman in Europe, she shows social restraint bordering on parsimony. The royal family resists ostentatious limousines and will drink cheap Luxemburg sparkling wine rather than fine French Champagne.

Likewise, Beatrix is careful not to inflate her role in the public's eye. In return for toeing the line, the royal family expects a level of privacy envied by members of other European royal families. Today's House of Orange offers the nation a peaceful continuity, symbolic unity, moral leadership and, in a country of faceless governments, a professional and identifiable brand name. ❑

PROVINCIAL LIFE

At first glance, the Netherlands may seem like a nation divided between town and country, but at heart the population's values are closely linked

The Netherlands is not where I want to live,
you always have to keep your urges in check
for the sake of good neighbours,
who peer eagerly through every crack.
You always have to be striving for something,
thinking of the well-being of your fellow man.
Only on the sly may you give offence.

In his famous poem *In Nederland*, J. Slauerhoff presents the typical metropolitan view of provincial life. Such disparaging sentiments are probably endorsed by many wouldbe sophisticates in Amsterdam or Rotterdam, but the poet's criticism is clearly the view of a privileged outsider from Randstad Holland.

The Randstad

Best translated as the Western Conurbation, the Randstad is the crescent-shaped area embracing Amsterdam, Utrecht, Dordrecht, Rotterdam, The Hague, Leiden and Haarlem. Although it is not a geographical region and has no official status, the term encompasses the Netherlands' most powerful urban centres in North and South Holland and Utrecht. This is the hub of the country; elsewhere tends to be dismissed as "the provinces".

This Randstad bias emerged with the mighty Dutch Republic in the 17th century. Before then, the distinction was between town and country: an inhabitant's sense of identity was bound up in the municipality; and, unlike today, the southern cities were more powerful than those in the west. Towns relegated to provincial obscurity today were then in the ascendancy. In the south, Middelburg, Maastricht and the old Flemish towns were important dukedoms, trading or religious centres. Nijmegen, in the heart of the country, was an important member of the medieval Hanseatic League while Groningen and Leeuwarden, in the north, were prosperous merchant cities trading in spices, tobacco and cloth.

LEFT: Durgerdam on the IJseelmeer.
RIGHT: festive costume.

With the creation of the Dutch Empire, metropolitan Amsterdam and South Holland province acquired a disproportionate weight that it still retains today. Despite modern government's attempts at decentralisation, the Randstad reigns supreme economically. However, unlike the provinces, the Randstad is vul-

nerable to encroaching internationalism. The small-town flavour of the region is endangered by silicon flatlands, dormitory suburbs, chain hotels, cosmopolitan culture and fast food outlets. Of course, this pessimistic view ignores the concentration of cultural riches in the Randstad, from Rembrandts to Delftware, gables to Van Goghs, international ballet to experimental jazz – the provinces can rarely compete on this scale. Even so, in looking at the glittering shop window of the Randstad, it is all too easy to miss the more old-fashioned goods in the stockroom. Despite the surface gloss of metropolitan culture, the provinces offer a truer picture of traditional Dutch culture and values.

There is, then, a strong case for seeing the Netherlands as two separate nations: the Randstad and the rest. In broad brushstrokes, the distinction is between modernity and authenticity.

Compared with the hectic metropolis, the southern and eastern provinces and the islands are more traditional, insular and agricultural. Stepping outside the Randstad enables one to peer through the curtains into the world of small-town Holland, where the pace of life is much slower.

The provinces

Starting in the north of the country, on the remote Wadden Islands, one might encounter Texel boat repairers, conservationists or fishermen. In rural Friesland, dairy farmers can be spotted chatting outside huge pyramid-shaped farmhouses. Their obscure language, Fries, bears relation to both English and German. In the capital of Groningen, the neighbouring province, university students can be seen gossiping in trendy chrome-clad cafés.

To the west, in Flevoland province, Urk is a poignant reminder of the price traditional fishing villages have had to pay for the damming of the old Zuiderzee (now called the IJsselmeer).

LOCAL TRANSPORT

In summer on the Wadden Islands there may be sightings of locals practising the odd sport of *wadlopen*, "mud-walking" across the tidal mudflats of the Wadden Sea.

Since the building of the *Afsluitdijk* and the ban on trawling in the IJsselmeer, local fishermen have had to sail further for their catch. Recently introduced EC quotas have made life even more difficult, yet old values, including the wearing of traditional costumes, are still prevalent.

Just east, in Overijssel province, the lake district based on the water-locked village of Giethoorn has been developed as a boating centre. Giethoorn's relative openness to outsiders contrasts with the insularity of the farming communities located to the south of the lakes. Staphorst, for instance, has a strict church-going community, whose members discourage the use of cars on Sunday and reject many aspects of modern life.

Negative impacts

The eastern part of the province, known as Twente, is another casualty of Randstad economics. The old textile towns have declined pitifully, deprived of re-investment and commercially marooned. West of Overijssel, the inhabitants of Flevoland could also be viewed as Randstad victims. The new polder landscape was intended to provide housing for the adjoining metropolis, but commuters have proved reluctant inhabitants to places such as Emmeloord, which is little more than an overgrown housing estate.

Just west of Flevoland, North Holland embraces the Randstad with happier results. Despite bordering the metropolis, the cluster of former fishing villages has a clear sense of identity. Volendam, for instance, has exploited its picturesque past as a modern-day tourist trap, while Marken remains a traditional fishing village to all appearances – the only element it lacks is the fish.

South of the former Zuiderzee, most of Utrecht province falls into the urban Randstad, but lesser-known Gelderland is a snapshot of suburban Holland. Apeldoorn advertises itself as "the biggest garden city in the Netherlands" but is in reality a collection of gentrified garden suburbs, the slightly snobbish inhabitants forming the last vestiges of empire.

South of Gelderland lie Noord-Brabant and Limburg, the Catholic southern provinces. These regions differ from the north in religion, temperament and economic success. Breda and Bergen op Zoom are hearty commercial towns with lively carnivals and a Burgundian flavour. As for the Brabant countryside, Van Gogh's village of Nuenen and its surrounding heathland and peat bogs are still recognisable from many of the painter's early landscapes.

Although both provinces are dotted with unspoilt villages, the region proves that international business can succeed outside the metropolis: Eindhoven, for instance, is home to the giant Philips electrical company; while Limburg has benefited from the relocation of government departments – a move that has

Provincial architecture

Building up the provinces has not always been successful. Lelystad was built in the 1960s as a dormitory town for Amsterdam and Utrecht and as a recreation centre for city-dwellers. Lelystad followed what was then known as "the mathematics of space", the obsessively geometrical lines of De Stijl architecture (*see page 93*). Although it was heavily criticised in its early years for lacking character, this experiment is getting renewed attention from innovative young architects intent on making it more livable. In nearby Almere, built on the edge of the Randstad in the 1970s, architects attempted to

transformed the former coal-mining town of Heerlen. Zeeland, just south of the Randstad, has elements of both the north and south provinces. Its proximity to old Flanders has given the region more exuberance than its northern neighbours, while the watery isolation has helped preserve intact its Protestant idiosyncrasies.

Contradictory Zeeland is home to costumed farmers' wives in Middelburg, struggling fishermen on the coast and prosperous yacht-owners at Veere.

LEFT: rural retirement.
ABOVE: IJsselmeer eel auction.

counter the anonymity of high-rise blocks with a construction resembling an open chest of drawers, intended to create the feeling of an old Dutch *buurt* (neighbourhood). Although Almere was dismissed as a "modern ghost town" and an impersonal, characterless suburb, it too is receiving renewed attention, largely due to its proximity to Amsterdam.

Dutch planners have since realised that provincials prefer vernacular architecture to mono-functional creations. In this vein, there has been an interesting development on the Oosterlijke Islands just east of the Amsterdam Maritime Museum, called the "New East". The Java, Borneo and KNSM islands have architecture that offers residents a waterfront view just a few minutes by bike or ferryboat from the city centre. In the near future, an area called Ijburg, further southeast, will also contribute to solving housing problems. In particular, the Dutch dislike tower blocks: over 70 percent of the population live in family houses and reject the credo of the De Stijl movement: "No more masterpieces for the individual... but mass production and standardisation with a view to providing decent housing for the masses".

Elsewhere in the provinces, new bourgeois garden suburbs are popular, as are well-restored traditional gabled townhouses. Because of the high cost of land, houses tend to be small and rather minimalist in style, almost regardless of the relative wealth of their inhabitants. Certainly there are differences in social status between a modest fisherman's cottage in the Biesbos marshes and a grand villa on the wooded outskirts of The Hague, but extremes of affluence are less visible in the Netherlands than they would be elsewhere in Europe.

This was even the case with Amsterdam's 17th-century architecture: the gabled working-class houses in the Jordaan are almost as impressive as the prosperous merchants' houses that line Herengracht.

RURAL ARCHITECTURE

In the countryside residents favour neat, barn-like farmhouses adorned with mottoes or decorative gables. Any comparison between the Randstad and the provinces must take account of the importance of land to the provinces – farming is the one occupation that the provinces have in common. The fact that the Netherlands is the world's third largest agricultural producer is, with the exception of bulb growing, thanks to provincial efforts.

Although specialisation is increasing, most farms are still family-run and passed down the generations. The type of farming varies regionally: horticulture on the polderland; cattle and dairy farming in Friesland; fruit farming in Gelderland and mixed farming in Noord-Brabant and Limburg. The farm buildings also differ: T-shaped farms in Gelderland and Overijssel while Noord-Brabant favours farms with long, low façades. Limburg boasts white half-timbered farmhouses and fortified farms built around a courtyard. Friesland has long, pyramid-shaped or granary-style barns, raised on *terpen* (artificial mounds).

All Dutch farmhouses exude an air of security and dependability, the epitome of Dutch rural values. Old farms in Flevoland often have mottoes adorning the façade. One typical motto, *Werklust* (joy in work) makes the point that this is serious hard-working countryside.

Domestic life

The provinces have long been a shrine to family values and it can be argued that, since the 17th century at least, the Dutch have worshipped domestic culture. As historian Simon Schama says: "The predominant perception among Dutch people is that for all their international orientation and progressiveness, there is still something of the mentality of the village or the small town: one's image is important, an eye must always be kept on what the neighbours are doing, what they think, and anything that breaks out of the comfortable small-scale pattern is to be treated with suspicion."

home is a fortress against the world. As befits the methodical humanity of the Dutch caretaker state, sick or elderly family members are well-cared for. The elderly receive the largest state pension in Europe, and such economic power means that not only do they they rarely burden their family, but also have the opportunity to spoil their grandchildren.

Provincial family life is essentially low key, comforting, conservative and conformist. The domestic cocoon is easily mocked but seldom pierced by outsiders. In fact, a predilection for cosy domesticity is often cited as the fundamental flaw in Dutch literature.

The Dutch adore their children but, in return for the attention lavished upon them, children are expected to be both polite and respectful. Critics claim that far too much emphasis is placed upon being "*normaal*" – conforming to parental expectations. A common expression is "Act normally and you're conspicuous enough," an indication of the level of decorum expected.

Psychologists characterise the Dutch as an introverted family culture, one in which the well being of the family is paramount and the

LEFT: Netherlands Open-Air Museum, Arnhem.
ABOVE: horse market in the province of Drenthe.

THE WOMAN'S ROLE

Most provincial housewives believe that cherishing the home is a virtue that outweighs a second wage. As a result, fewer women go out to work here than in any other European Union country, although the disparity started to narrow during the 1990s.

Feminists point out that the Dutch government was the last to sign an EU directive granting equal pay and rights to women and that legislation discriminates against women. Moreover, Dutch social services assign benefits on a family basis. Although these criticisms are well founded, it is still a fact that the home remains the cornerstone of Dutch life for many provincial women.

Provincial culture

Visitors who restrict their travels to Amsterdam could be excused for thinking that the Dutch spend their leisure time at the National Ballet, fringe theatres and night clubs. But this is not true of provincial culture, and in a small village in Friesland, entertainment is more likely to involve singing in a local choir, skating or fishing.

> ### GAMBLING SOCIETY
>
> Gambling is popular in the provinces. A visit to one of Heerlen's casinos shows that the old Dutch dictum remains true : "I invest, you speculate, they gamble."

A mirror of provincial culture is presented by Heerlen, an unexceptional commercial town in Limburg. On a typical day, an amateur group

will be performing a play in local dialect, various brass bands will be rehearsing for the Carnival and an experimental ballet will be on at the Stadschouwburg. For those in need of a simple night out, there are bowling clubs, multiplex cinemas, pancake houses and rustic-style bars. There, the regulars smoke, drink, socialise or just read the evening newspaper.

Provincial culture is essentially populist and, in this, is heir to the hearty alehouse scenes painted by Jan Steen. Burghers in the 17th century used to claim that: "the first little glass is for health, the second for a toast, the third for a nightcap and the next can only be for pleasure." Smoking, then as now, remains a popular pas-

time. Although there are some non-smoking areas in Dutch cafés and restaurants, smoking, like coffee drinking, seems to be the national pastime. And the traditional way of rolling one's own cigarette continues.

Outside the Randstad, the survival of regional dialects, costumes, folkloric festivals and traditional sports indicates the diversity and depth of provincial culture. Even though there are few remote areas in the Netherlands, regional accents are proudly retained. Dialects are spoken in the Veluwe, Groningen, Drenthe and Gelderland. Frankish is spoken on the German border while dialects of Vlaams (Flemish) survive in Brabant and Limburg. Guessing where someone comes from is a popular game. In the case of Friesland, however, there is little room for doubt. The province has its own language, quite distinct from Dutch.

Costumes

Regional costumes are another sign of local identity preservation. Costumes are most common on the shores of the IJsselmeer, in Overijssel and on the islands of Zeeland. However, even within the Randstad costumes have not disappeared completely. In Scheveningen, formerly a small fishing village near The Hague but now a popular holiday resort, matronly fishwives still wear their black costumes with pride; by contrast, young locals refer to their elders with embarrassment as "the black stockings." In touristy Volendam, men pose for pictures in baggy trousers and women wear black striped or pleated skirts. In neighbouring Marken, once an island, the costumes are entirely different and worn more naturally. Women's dress includes bonnets, long-sleeved blouses, cotton waistcoats and embroidered bodices while men wear a red sash and a blue smock over their baggy black trousers.

Sport and festivals

Traditional sports and regional festivals continue to draw enthusiasts. Many activities such as skating, walking, fishing and sailing arose naturally from the landscape. In Friesland, duck-trapping, once the "poor person's hunting" is widely enjoyed, and in Middelburg (Zeeland), a curious form of bowling called *krulbollen* is still played. Friesland boasts the greatest variety of quaint sports, including *fierl-jeppen* (pole-vaulting over a canal) and *sktje-silen* (races in flat-bottomed sailing boats). Even within the Randstad, traditional pursuits remain. Every year, in the North Sea near Scheveningen, a five-day pole-sitting marathon takes place: the winner is the last person left sitting on the pole.

Ordinary sports are popular throughout the provinces and the emphasis is always upon group involvement. Soccer (*voetbal*), the country's biggest spectator sport, is worshipped nationally, as is the case across most of Europe.

based. Gardening is so popular that even families without gardens attentively cultivate allotments. Even the smallest community has a music group or choir with its own banner, motto and public performances. On a daily basis, the streets of many provincial Dutch towns (and even those of Amsterdam) are filled with music, ranging from muzak to Flemish carillons and street organs.

Folklore fairs, cheese markets, herring festivals and carnivals have survived all over the provinces. In the time of the Republic, the *Middenstand* ("bourgeoisie") had a taste for public festivities and little has changed today.

Cycling is another common pursuit, particularly on the polderland or in the Gelderland national parks.

Walking events, such as the four-day Nijmegen marathon, are professionally organised but it is generally felt that community spirit is more important than competition.

Leisure

Given the importance of domestic values, leisure is often family-orientated or home-

LEFT: the costume of the Marken islanders.
ABOVE: the Elfstedentocht (11-cities skating competition) can attract over 18,000 competitors.

THE ELFSTEDENTOCHT

The *Elfstedentocht* (11-cities race) is a marathon skating competition. The race begins in Leeuwarden and covers 200 km (125 miles) and 10 other cities before ending in national exhaustion, watched on television by the whole population. There are about 300 serious competitors but over 18,000 skaters try to complete the gruelling eight-hour course. The ritual begins and ends in darkness and skaters endure harsh winter conditions.

The competition is only held in severe winters but its infrequency alone cannot explain its cathartic effect on the nation. Perhaps it reminds the Dutch that they have forged their identity from struggles against ice and water.

Morality and class

The Dutch are a relentlessly moral people, in their aspirations at least. The 17th-century battle to put "honour before gold" continues, as does the struggle between puritanism and sensuousness. New moral dilemmas seek out the balance between individuality and conformity, tolerance and righteousness, merit and grace.

There are, however, significant differences between the moral values of the Randstad and the provinces. In practice, the Randstad weights the balance in favour of tolerance and individuality rather than conformity. Metropolitan intellectuals have even coined the term "Hollanditis" to describe the "Dutch disease" of excessive liberality. In The Hague and Amsterdam new protest groups emerge daily to challenge the authorities on the housing crisis, environmental issues or unemployment. The provinces are far less confrontational and view situations with classic Dutch earnestness.

The provinces think of themselves as holding the moral high ground, usually supported by their religious faith and old-fashioned domestic virtues. The cornerstone is the belief in *deftigheid* (decorum) which masks the provincial yearning for respectability. The younger generation, however, even in the provinces,

LOVE OF THE LANDSCAPE

A deep appreciation of Dutch landscape unites painters as various as Brueghel, Hieronymous Bosch, Ruysdael and, in more recent times, Mesdag and the Dutch Post-Impressionists. It is best expressed in Ruysdael's moody paintings: he places the horizon so low that cities and human life appear submerged in the cloudy skies.

This attachment is both proud and sentimental, but hard to fathom since nature dealt the Dutch an indifferent hand. The puritanical reply is that through God-given grace they have redesigned the watery landscape: having valiantly fought against countless floods, they have a right to feel proprietorial about their achievement.

often equates the term with excessive civility, stiffness and even hypocrisy.

For the older generation, *deftigheid* can take the form of an obsession with propriety. Some "rules" of etiquette include not laughing too heartily and making as few gestures as possible. Greeting with a big hug is not done. Certainly, provincials attach great importance to manners: there are set times when coffee should be served to guests; when coming into a room, the newcomer must greet the others who are present by turn; and at a birthday party or some other social function, one must ensure that they shake hands with everyone and introduce themselves formally.

In business letters, men and women often use only their initials in order to protect their privacy. Such propriety and reserve can expose the provincial to the charge of a rather mindless conformity, but luckily individuals have their ways of escaping this straitjacket – often by way of a broken outburst of bluntness. *Nivellering*, the trend towards equality, has helped blur class barriers, particularly in the larger cities. However, in the north of the country and out on the islands, social hierarchy is noticeably more

> **SABBATH DAY**
>
> A Dutch Sunday is still sacrosanct. There are no Sunday papers, and in rural communities, costumed farmers and their families walk to church in silent files.

not always hold true when they are abroad. Then the Rolex watches are worn with pride and the expensive sports cars are driven to impress. It is a strange paradox. The Dutch are a nation often accused of having the good life – but of not knowing how to enjoy it.

Certainly, the old battle between puritanism and sensuousness still rages in the provinces, while the struggle between godliness and greed remains as fraught in the countryside as it is in the midst of the city.

LEFT: Bunschoten people.
ABOVE: traditions thrive in Bunschoten-Spakenburg.

rigid. In Friesland, Overijssel and Zeeland, for instance, social cachet still belongs to the bigger farmers, landowners and wealthy shopkeepers. The term *Boerenslim* (farmer's intuition) is used as a compliment.

As if to counteract differences in wealth and status, there is little display of affluence or conspicuous achievement. Although in the 1990s the presence of the Yuppie with mobile phone and flash car became more apparent, because of their Calvinist roots wealthier citizens still tend to play their status down, although this does

Religion

Although Randstad residents are not as churchgoing as in the past, provincial Dutch remain tied to their religious landscape as a matter of course: religion is a key pillar in the traditional Dutch scheme of compartmentalising society.

Known as *verzuiling*, the practice of dividing society into denominational groups still pervades the provinces, influencing the choice of school, newspaper, leisure pursuits, political party, hospital and pension scheme. It is still common for, say, a young Catholic teacher living in Noord-Brabant to be educated at a denominational college, join a Catholic brass band or chess club, listen to a Catholic radio station, read a Catholic newspaper, and go on a holiday organised by a Catholic club. By the same token, it is quite common for a Protestant member of the Reformed Church (Hervormde Kerk) or Orthodox Reformed Church (Gereformeerde Kerk) to follow a completely separate yet parallel path. A farmer from Zwolle in Overijssel might typically subscribe to a Protestant weekly, shop at a Protestant grocers, be innoculated at a Protestant hospital, meet his future wife at a church dance and end his days in a Protestant old people's home.

Given the importance of these religious distinctions, people are skilled at reading the vis-

ible clues of affiliation. Catholics, for instance, distinguish themselves from Protestants by wearing their wedding ring on the third finger of the left hand instead of on their right hand.

Church services vary considerably in both style and content. Compared wih the sober tone of Protestant services, the services of the catholic church have much more ritual and Catholics also favour melodic hyms over more sombre psalms.

Protestant distinctions

Although the Netherland's two main Protestant parties are merging, the distinction between them is still important. Approximately 32 per-

cent of the Dutch population are Calvinists; and of this number 22 percent are Reformed and 10 percent Orthodox Reformed.

Out in the countryside the smaller and stricter Orthodox Reformed Church has greater power. It is more cohesive and conservative than its big sister, and its power base comes more from the working class. By contrast, the Reformed Church is perceived as being more liberal on social issues, but is also seen as being more vulnerable to the modern trend, leaning towards secularisation.

Catholicism

While Protestants dominate the northern provinces, the Catholics are in the majority in the south and form a narrow majority nationally (38 percent). In Catholic terms, the Dutch are most liberal, favouring contraception and women priests, as well as attending to Third World issues.

Dutch Catholic opinion often conflicts with Rome's, and it is little wonder that Ruud Lubbers' Christian Democratic Party enjoyed so much power during the 1980–90s. A public protest during one of the pope's last visits proclaimed: "The church, once built on a rock, is slowly sinking into the marshy soil of the provincial Netherlands."

Even though atheists account for 40 percent of the population, 70 percent of Dutch schools are religiously segregated, though this paradox has more to do with academic achievement than anything else. In Amsterdam and other major cities, churches are being turned into exhibition centres but a Dutch Sunday is still sacrosanct. There are no Sunday newspapers; no television commercials; most shops and petrol stations are closed. A Sunday visit to any rural community presents a scene little changed for decades.

But attachment to place, God, domestic virtues and a moral code are not uniquely provincial. Most Dutch subscribe to these values in part, and difference is more in emphasis than essence: the Randstad presents an international face but retains a provincial heart. In a Dutch home, you may notice the family Bible, piano, home-made *appeltaart* and handmade toys – all clues to the fact that few nations are more domesticated than the Dutch.   ❑

LEFT: Alkmaar street performer.

A Scenic Cycle

Whatever it is that makes the Netherlands tick, the bicycle must be a vital part of the mechanism, for there are 11 million bikes in this country of 15 million people. Most are humble *stadfietsen* (city bikes), and many of them will have been stolen any number of times, and then put back into circulation again. Despite the absence of any mountains, Dutch cyclists generally have a second bike in their locker, a smart racer, touring bike or even a mountain bike for heading out into the wide green yonder at the weekend or on holidays.

The bicycle might have been invented with the Netherlands in mind. Not only is there a vast network of bicycle paths and signposted cycling routes, but myriad tiny roads lead into the heart of polders, farming country, forests and heathland.

Cycling in the Netherlands is a sociable business, not least because so many people do it. Not a few are of an age at which they might ordinarily be thinking of slippers, warm fires and quiet evenings in. Don't underestimate these older riders, who are willing and able to keep going in all weather; often long after the young hotshots have hung up their Lycra racing suits for the day.

If you've resisted the temptation to join the legions of cyclists in towns and cities for fear of swirling traffic, head out into the countryside. Hire a bike in town then take a train to almost anywhere you fancy; or hire a bike from the railway station at your destination – most main stations and many small ones have hire facilities. Flopping aboard a train at the end of the day is also a good way to get you, your bike and your weary legs back to base.

Once aboard your trusty steed, watch for blustery winds threatening to separate you from the saddle. Wind is a fact of life on the spirit-level-flat polders near the coast and anyone not up to the challenge is advised to seek a more sheltered experience on inland forest trails. Take heart, though: even if you set off into the teeth of a strong wind, you may find that on the way back it is now behind you, allowing you to fly with the wind in your sails.

In places where inhabitants and tourists are thin on the ground, and the pace of life slackens off a gear or two, you may be the only thing moving in the landscape – apart from whirling windmill blades. There is an exhilarating sense of freedom and mobility on a bike. From your saddle, the countryside drifts past at a pace you can absorb. You feel like part of the process, instead of a four-wheel interloper.

Cycling Excursions from Amsterdam

For an easy, 4-hour round-trip avoiding most of the city traffic, cycle southwards along the banks of the River Amstel. After a half-hour or so, you emerge suddenly into the countryside on the way to the pretty village of Ouderkerk aan de Amstel.

A far tougher proposition is cycling round the

IJsselmeer. Until the 1930s, this big lake on Amsterdam's doorstep was not a lake but a sea, the Zuiderzee, which the Dutch penchant for reshaping their country has transformed. Who can resist cycling round a sea? For a cyclist, it is the perfect Dutch experience, immersed in wind, sun or rain, following a narrow track between the polders and the lake.

Experienced racing cyclists can do the 400-km (250-mile) round-trip in a day. If you're not getting as many miles to the gallon as you used to, set yourself a more modest target of four to six days. The IJsselmeer is one of the most beautiful areas in the country, and there is more to cycling it than counting kilometres per hour. ❑

RIGHT: a familiar sight on Netherlands streets.

A FEAST OF FESTIVALS

There's plenty of opportunity to enjoy the spectacle of local festivals, and if going to the provinces, it's worth timing a visit to see one

The Dutch enjoy a celebration and love to sing, dance, make music and dress up in costume. Thanks to its rich history and multicultural population there are hundreds of festivals held throughout the year in the Netherlands. These celebrate everything from film and music to sports, poetry, tall ships, flowers, and plenty more besides.

In March, the extremely festive Pre-Lent Carnival in the provinces of Noord Brabant and Limburg celebrates the arrival of spring. Three days of organised anarchy reigns with a spectacular parade plus plenty of dancing, eating, and drinking. The Summer Carnival Street Parade in Rotterdam snakes its way through the city at the end of July. In August, Sail Amsterdam hosts thousands of ocean-going vessels from around the world in a celebration that occurs every five years. The annual Bloemen Corso (August 31 & September 1-3) is a colourful parade of flowers and music that makes its way from Aalsmeer to Amsterdam and should not be missed. Contact the local VVV tourist office for further details.

▷ **BRIGHT SPARK**
Vividly coloured and exotic costumes are the highlight of the joyful and ethnic Caribbean Festival.

◁ HIT PARADE
The Pre-Lent Carnival dates back to 1100 BC, when the Athenians celebrated this three-day event. People proclaimed their joy of living and wine flowed freely.

△ CHILL-OUT ZONE
On Queen's Day, the Vondelpark in Amsterdam offers families a slightly more relaxed way to enjoy the festivities; away from the thronging crowds.

◁ FLOWER FESTIVAL
The hundreds of varieties of flowers on parade during the Flower Festival include tulips, roses, hyacinths, narcissi, orchids, irises, carnations and lilies.

▷ COME SAIL WITH ME
Sail Amsterdam's opening parade through the North Sea Canal is truly a sight to behold. Sail 2000 (August) will also host the trans-Atlantic Tall Ships event.

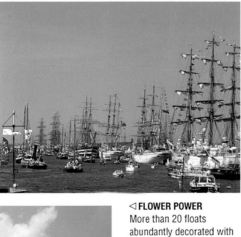

◁ FLOWER POWER
More than 20 floats abundantly decorated with flowers make their way through Amsterdam's streets for the annual Bloemen Corso.

▷ LITTLE BUDDHAS
Amsterdam's Leidseplein is where the crowds gather to hear opera singers performing at the Buddhist Festival.

A RIGHT ROYAL CELEBRATION

Queen's Day should certainly be experienced at least once. For those who unknowingly arrive in Amsterdam on 30 April, it could be quite a shock to discover thousands of people swarming into the city from Centraal Station and heading towards the city centre.

Although every city and village has a Queen's Day celebration, the Dutch capital is the place to be. There is music in the air with bands at nearly every major intersection, and food vendors offering a range of international snacks. In honour of the House of Orange, people adorn themselves with orange scarves, lapels and often paint their faces, too. Even the red, white and blue Dutch flags are decorated with orange pennants.

The canals play host to an unofficial boat parade which is a show within a show. And there is a so-called free market, a tradition that allows people to set up vending stands. The Queen's Day event ends in the evening with a fireworks display.

MODERN ART

It's not easy to follow in the footsteps of Rembrandt, Vermeer and Van Gogh.

But today's artists have defined their own standards of excellence

When one thinks of Dutch art, the great masters of the 17th century come to mind: Rembrandt, Ruisdael, De Hooch, Steen, Cuyp, Hals and Vermeer, among others. The quiet strength of serene, detailed works; the powerful *chiaroscuro* portraits; the cluttered naturalism of rustic still lifes; intense raging seas and pastoral Dutch landscapes. The 18th century reflected earlier achievements in art, with no new directions taken. It was a time of contentment and the good life *à la Française*. Rather than the grand imagery of the past, a lighter attitude prevailed in the 18th century, with anecdotal portraits by painters like Troost and De Lelie. In the 19th century, Van Gogh's expressionism contrasted with Breitner's visual realism and, in retrospect, can be seen as one of the many starting points of modern art.

However, if the importance of Van Gogh seems assured now, it certainly wasn't during his lifetime. He famously sold just one painting and led an impoverished life that is still seen as the epitome of what it means to be an entirely and hopelessly impassioned artist. It is staggering to think that his entire output – around 800 paintings – was completed in just ten years, from first taking up the brush at 27 to ending his life with a bullet at 37. It is no exaggeration to say that the instability of Van Gogh's mind is reflected in his visceral canvases, which swirl with thick brushstrokes. Such works can never be adequately reproduced, and so the Van Gogh Museum is the perfect place to get closer to his work.

Mondrian and De Stijl

Although the preceding centuries were a tough act to follow, there was no turning back for 20th-century art. In 1917 the artists of the De Stijl movement emerged, intent on seeking a new and contemporary tradition, staking new territory, making new visual statements. Piet

PRECEDING PAGES: Groninger museum, Groningen.
LEFT: images of Van Gogh.
RIGHT: *Composition in Oval* by Piet Mondrian.

Mondrian was its most prominent member. But it was Theo van Doesburg, founder of a dogmatic and polemical magazine called *De Stijl* (*The Style*) who would start rumblings toward the subsequent development of modern art in The Netherlands. Its purpose was "to state the logical principles of a style now ripening, based

on a pure equivalence between the age and its means of expression..."

The basic problem being addressed by individual painters throughout Europe was what to paint and how to paint. This was the problem that De Stijl intended to address, based on a coherent theory that if the individual was the measure of all things, then anything could be art if the artist presented it as such.

Mondrian's œuvre would mark him as one of the greatest of the 20th-century Modernist painters. Although his early work portrayed a romantic symbolism, his canvases made a radical shift over the next few years until he reached the easily identifiable "contra-compositions" in red, yellow and blue. In those classic paintings produced during the 1920s and 1930s, space is evoked and structured with the use of black lines and small blocks of primary colour. Mondrian's well-known *Victory Boogie Woogie* painting, which dates from 1943, can be seen in the Gemeente Museum in The Hague, along with five other canvasses.

In his book *Dutch Painting* (1978), Rudi Fuchs, states that with the exception of Van Gogh, Expressionism never really caught on in The Netherlands. "Whether that is because the Dutch character is not given to the display of strong emotion (Van Gogh after all found his own style in France) is difficult to decide. In fact, Dutch art between the two wars, with the exception of De Stijl, found itself curiously apart from international developments. The Dutch either did not know about them or rejected them."

The COBRA Movement

After World War II, greater social involvement seemed to be an essential requirement for the newly evolving art. Socialism brought together a group of free-wheeling personalities intent on creating a fresh, vivid style of painting. Exhibitions of 20th-century masters such as

MAGIC REALISM

A group of original artists who painted in a cold, precise, realist style labelled "Magic Realist" were Carel Willink, Pyke Kock and Raoul Hynckes. Similar in style were painters Charley Toorop and Dick Ket.

Carel Willink's description of their work is perhaps the most insightful of this brief fling with expressionism: "Our vision is the confrontation with the never re-assuring, never completely comprehensible world of phenomena in which the smallest and most familiar object can suddenly turn into something frightening; a world stranger and more dreadful in its haughty impenetrability than the most terrifying nightmare."

Picasso, Braque, Léger and Chagall served as inspiration to these young, creatively restless artists. Constant, Corneille and Karel Appel joined forces with their Belgian and Danish counterparts Christian Dotremont, Joseph Noiret and Asger Jorn in 1948 to form an international group which took its name, COBRA, from the first letters of their three European capitals (Copenhagen, Brusssels, Amsterdam).

The movement's artists experimented – playfully at times – drawing on the influence of folk art, primitivism, naïve painting and the drawings of children and the mentally ill. As Constant summarised COBRA: "A painting is no longer a construction of colours and lines, but an animal, a night, a cry, a man, or all of these together. Suggestion is boundless, and that is why we can say that, after a period in which art represented nothing, art has now entered a period in which it represents everything."

In 1995, the COBRA Museum opened its doors in Amstelveen, a suburb of Amsterdam. The main focus of the collection is modern art from 1945 onwards and it features leading works from the short-lived COBRA movement. There is also a collection of abstract and semi-abstract Netherlandish art from the 1940s and 1950s.

> ### ART OF THE TIMES
>
> Karel Appel said of his work within the COBRA Movement:
> "I paint like a barbarian in a barbarous age."

Challenging art-making

In the early 1960s other artists emerged like Jan Schoonhoven, influenced by Duchamp and the emerging Tachism movement in Paris – a variation on post-war abstract expressionism.

The Pop Art movement was another influence for Schoonhoven and others such as Armando, Daan van Golden and J. C. J. van der Heyden, who, according to Rudi Fuchs, would "come to terms with the fact that they were producing simple visual objects, the artistic importance of which did not reside in a 'content' but an ideological position. In an extremely and even disturbingly off-hand manner, their works questioned the nature of art, and the nature of art-making."

Other artists such as Peter Struycken, Ad Dekkers and Bonies "sought a way out of the deadlock by going back to Mondrian's claim that art should not be based on private intuition, but that art-making required continuous and strict analysis of one's procedures." They maintained the position that "everything could be art, that art was in the mind of the beholder... Continuing Mondrian's search, in a sense, they proposed that a painting should be analysed and broken down into its basic elements – such as colour, form, scale, surface and so on."

Co Westerik is more of a realist painter with quite a large following, and Reinier Lucassen's highly imaginative work has many recognisable visual elements. Jan Dibbets and Ger van Elk have included photography and photomontage

LEFT: typical style of Theo van Doesburg, Haags Gemeentmuseum.
RIGHT: COBRA Museum, Amsterdam.

in their paintings. Stanley Brouwn and Rene Daniels are other important contemporary artists with an international following.

On a more "commercial" note, Jan Cremer, a 1970s' writer of the Henry Miller ilk, who added painting to his colourful achievements, has had his share of successful one-man shows in recent years, as has the Dutch rock musician Herman Brood. On the distaff side, Marlene Dumas' provocative paintings and drawings are often included in major international exhibitions in Venice and

Kassel and she has managed to be accepted into the "boy's club" in terms of her work being purchased by museums. Although she was born in Capetown, South Africa, she adopted Holland as her home in 1976. Marijke van Warmerdam has also been invited to exhibit her work at the Venice Biennale.

Today a new (and slightly younger) generation of artists is emerging whose work is being taken seriously by collectors: among them, Winneke Dijkstra, Arnold Mik, Liza May Post, Joep van Lieshout, Sylvie Fleurie, Job Koelerij, Gerald van der Kaap and Ronald Ophuis. These days, when it comes to art in The Netherlands, there is much to discover. ❑

DE OUDE KARREMAN
1885

ARCHITECTURE

The architectural heritage of The Netherlands is not restricted to antiquity.

In fact, the country was at the vanguard of the modern movement

When one thinks of architecture in The Netherlands, it is the timeless buildings of the 17th century which spring most readily to mind: Amsterdam's patrician canal houses and stately churches with their crown-bearing towers, which are also found in many of the country's larger cities. But there are other important architectural periods in The Netherlands – and examples are not only to be found in its capital.

Over the ages, there have actually been three periods of serious growth in architecture: The Middle Ages; the Golden Age between 1550 and 1700; and the first half of the 20th century. The latter, in fact, enjoyed two peak periods; in the first three decades, and during the major building activity after World War II with its massive housing projects designed on a human scale by socially committed architects like Aldo van Eyck and Herman Hertzberger.

Contemporary architecture

In looking at Amsterdam's architectural tradition, it's hard to imagine that not all that much has changed since P. J. H. Cuypers (1827–1921) built his monumental neo-Gothic churches and other grand landmarks. Centraal train station and the Rijksmuseum are two buildings of huge national significance.

Fin de Siècle architecture in The Netherlands was not based on the same motifs as seen in the more organic Art Nouveau creations in Belgium and France. The Dutch "New Art" was influenced more by geometric, abstract motifs with a Far-Eastern bias. Many artists and architects became attracted to the socialist and anarchist movements as well as to the esoteric approach of theosophy, and the distinction between art and life was getting blurred.

It was a time to return to craftsmanship and innovation. Architects were at the helm of new design, not only in their buildings, but in the creation of furniture, ceramics, glassware and the graphic arts which were often integrated into their projects. The Amsterdam Stock Exchange (or the Beurs van Berlage) is a good example of architectural design, with its striking red brick exterior, imposing clock tower and skylit interior with built-in and carved wood elements.

Modern master

H. P. Berlage (1856–1934) is regarded as the father of modern Dutch architecture. A visionary who managed to break from the past and approach architecture more rationally, Berlage's craft finds its purest manifestation in his Gemeentehuis (Municipal Museum) and First Church of Christ, Scientist, both in the Hague. His Stock Exchange building has additional elements of Cuypers' Dutch Renaissance influence, while a trip to America also acquainted him further with the work of Frank Lloyd Wright. Even more important are his contributions to Dutch urban design, in Amsterdam, the Hague, Rotterdam and Utrecht.

LEFT: The Ceramic Tile Museum, Otterlo, Gelderland.
RIGHT: Berlage Stock Exchange.

The Housing Act of 1901 was a pivotal point in Dutch architecture, which opened up the possibility of subsidised housing to meet the needs of the working class. This found its conduit in Berlage's ambitious development plan in Amsterdam South, notable for its decorative use of brickwork with detailing in wood, sculpture, iron and distinctive window shapes, doors and even mail boxes.

> **BIG IDEAS**
>
> The most important thing about the influential De Stijl group was exactly that: their influence. Few of their designs were actually built.

This form of craftsmanship, or façade architecture became officially known as the "Amsterdam School" in 1916, and would alter the

appearance of the city quite dramatically. Defined by its elegance and creativity of design, local variants on this theme soon appeared elsewhere in The Netherlands, from churches to bridges and railway stations, post offices to schools. Each project gave the architect – Berlage, De Klerk, Kramer, Staal and many others – the opportunity to explore ideas that added novelty and a sense of playful wonder to constructed forms.

The Dada-inspired De Stijl movement (Dutch for "The Style"), founded in the early 1920s, had more of a utopian approach toward a unity of the arts: to create a balanced environment that would dominate all aspects of life. The group's leader, architect Theo van Doesburg, spoke of creating a new consciousness of beauty aimed at the universal. Painters Piet Mondrian and B. van der Leck were other proponents of the movement, along with mathematicians, poets and sculptors. Influenced mainly by Berlage and Wright, the De Stijl architects were joined by Gerrit Rietveld (1888-1964), a cabinet-maker known for his red-blue wooden chair, whose design was years ahead of its time. Resembling a toy construction, it is actually quite comfortable. After World War II, De Stijl continued to be an inspiration for architects who aspired more to the avant-garde direction of modernism.

The Nieuwe Bouwen (New Building) movement, or Dutch functionalism, developed during the 1920s, and was based on rational and economic considerations rather than the craftsmanship approach of the "Amsterdam School". Architects Mart Stam, J. Duiker and J.B. van Loghem (among others) were inspired by Berlage's ideas on normalisation in housing and were vehement proponents for an industrialised system of building affordable housing in large quantities. Their ground and first-floor housing projects in Haarlem and The Hague proved that their functionalist principles could be put into practice.

The new century

The 21st century is already witness to another boom in architecture in the Netherlands. The Hague is being re-invented with its revitalised city centre, while Rotterdam is a city literally on the rise with development in both its "downtown" and harbour areas. Many of the buildings have been designed by leading Dutch talents such as Rem Koolhaas and Jo Coenen, as well as architects of international repute like Sir Norman Foster and Frank Gehry.

However, no matter how much land has been – and continues to be – reclaimed, housing remains a problem in The Netherlands. The VINEX project was launched in 1992 by the Minister for Housing to create a million new homes in The Netherlands over the following 25 years. Another architectural golden age may well be around the corner. ❑

LEFT: modernity and architecture go hand in hand.

Inside Story

In the Golden Age, Dutch canal-side mansions were very different from Venetian palazzi: the grandest Dutch rooms were always on the ground floor while the depth of the building was always greater than its breadth.

Inside a gabled mansion in Amsterdam, Delft or Leiden lay a cornucopia of treasures. Marble fireplaces would be surrounded by Delftware tiles, while heavily embossed sideboards indicated the burghers' taste for exuberant Flemish design. Oriental porcelain, Venetian glassware and mirrors shone brightly – despite the clergy's denunciation of such "devilish vanity".

Superficially, the modern Dutch home would appear to be a complete break with the past. However, despite the love of order, there are occasional sentimental lapses into houses of cloying sweetness and Hansel and Gretel tweeness. An immaculate front garden is often complemented by well-trained hanging baskets, matching window boxes and topped, perhaps, by a mail-box masquerading as a bird-house or dolls' house. There is often a plaster replica of a *kabouter*, or gnome, or an eerily authentic-looking heron.

The house itself is also left open to inspection, as passers-by will note from the only partly-drawn frilly lace curtains. This goes along with the ideology that the Dutch have nothing to hide. The provincial Dutch home often treads a fine line between sweetness and kitsch – before accidentally crossing it. Closer examination, however, reveals shades of 17th-century values and tastes in the solid furniture, soft lighting and cut flowers, not to mention the orderliness, cleanliness and propriety. Sir William Temple, the British ambassador to the Netherlands during the Republic, was puzzled to find that spitting at banquets was frowned upon. Thomas Nugent, a 17th-century traveller, agreed, reporting that the Dutch were "perfect slaves to cleanliness... for the streets are paved with brick and as clean as any chamber floor." There is still a low shame threshold as far as cleanliness is concerned: until about 10 years ago, it was common to see doorsteps scrubbed daily.

As for interior design, furniture is generally solid, imposing and, although shunning flamboyance, contains intricate details. Flowers are essential to the Dutch concept of homeliness. In provincial

RIGHT: interior at the Arnhem Open-Air Museum.

homes you will find a far greater variety and profusion of pot plants and cut flowers than in the more contemporary environs of the Randstad. Most guests still visit with flowers, rather than wine. Contrary to expectation, the most popular flowers are not tulips or sunflowers, but a mixed bouquet.

Comfort is the main factor in a Dutch home, although Dutch interiors began a transition after World War II from a pseudo-Bauhaus period with ultra modern elements to the "*Goede Wonen*" concept of the 1960s and early 1970s. This was spearheaded by a group of designers and furniture companies who promoted pure, airy and light interiors with no-frills.

As Dutch design continued to develop with more emphasis on style, function and aesthetics, interiors became more unique. Beauty and simple elegance are more important to a Dutch household than glitzy objects.

And it is no surprise that the Dutch have a great affinity for colour which they often use in subtle and original combinations. Flea market finds sit quite comfortably next to a designer chair. A collection of Tiffany glass is placed above a 16th-century marble fireplace.

Because of the variety of old and unusual buildings, often with minimal space, the Dutch are masters at improvising and also at accommodating the smallest of spaces creatively. ❑

FLOWERS – A WAY OF LIFE

The tulip is perhaps the most definitive image of The Netherlands, alongside
cheese and clogs, and Dutch horticulturalists work hard to retain this reputation

In a country where land is precious, the majority of city dwellers take great pride in their interior gardens. Rare is a Dutch house or apartment that doesn't have flowers on the table, an array of pot plants or window boxes in constant bloom. In rural areas, a house isn't a home without a garden. Only the Japanese buy more flowers per annum than the Dutch. In the Netherlands, people spend an average of 120 guilders a year (about £45/US$60) on cut flowers alone, whereas in the United Kingdom and the United States the average is around 50 percent less.

Bouquets are bought and presented for almost any occasion, often complete with their own mythology and hidden meaning, depending on flower type, colour and presentation. A bouquet of fewer than 10 flowers is always a social blunder in Holland – in spring, when tulips are plentiful, they are sold in groups of 50. Yellow tulips, for example, are the specified flower on birthdays that occur on 21 May. Legend has it that on this day yellow flowers also signal unrequited love. If presented upside down, however, this unhappy situation may well be remedied.

The flower industry

Today the specially cultivated flowers, bulbs, fruits and vegetables that comprise Dutch horticulture bring in more than 20 billion guilders a year (£6 billion/US$10 billion) as an export. Horticulture accounts for more than 25 percent of the revenue from all Dutch agricultural exports. With this boost, the Netherlands is the third largest agricultural exporter in the world after the United States and France, with most of its production going to European Union nations.

The Netherlands and, in particular, the Westland area between Amsterdam and Rotterdam, exports more cut flowers than the rest of

LEFT: Keukenhof gardens in bulb season.
RIGHT: preparing for the flower show
at Eelde, in Drenthe province.

the world combined (75 percent global market share). In potted plants, the market domination is the same, but the competition is tighter among its geographical neighbours. The Dutch also sell more than 51 percent of the world's pot-plants; Denmark is next in line, but way down with 18 percent.

Cultivating the landscape

In the Netherlands, more than 10,400 hectares (33,000 acres) are under glass in modern greenhouse production. About half of this area is devoted to flowers and plants, the rest to hydroponic fruits and vegetables. The Dutch were quick to take advantage of this modern method of growing tropical or seasonal produce year-round. It works without soil by anchoring the plants in porous gravel and flooding them frequently with highly enriched, inorganic nutrients. Dutch hydroponically grown tomatoes, cucumbers, red, green and yellow peppers, aubergines, lettuces and strawberries end up in supermarkets the world over.

More than 60 percent of available land in the Netherlands – 2 million hectares (5 million acres) – is used for agriculture. The specific activity is dictated by soil type. The abundance of sandy soil means that over 60 percent of this agricultural land is used as pasture for feeding livestock to support the enormous Dutch dairy industry. Another 35 percent is rich enough for arable farming.

Outdoor production of flowers and house plants occupies the rest: about 2,000 hectares (5,000 acres) in total. With so much space for livestock available, it is not surprising that the Netherlands has more pigs than people. The nation's 50,000 livestock and poultry farmers between them keep more than 14 million pigs, 5 million cattle and some 90 million chickens.

However, what is also not surprising for this small, densely populated country with a very high water table, is its monumental manure problem. These animals produce more than 90 million tonnes of waste annually, about twice as much as is needed for fertiliser. Unfortunately, all of it has been going back on to the ground. The result is diminishing soil fertility, nitrate poisoning of the ground water and even acid rain as a result of the gases given off by the manure.

CAROLUS CLUSIUS

From the 1570s a Flemish botanist called Carolus Clusius (or L'Ecluse in French) was advising gardeners all over Europe on the care, cultivation and scientific aspects of gardening and flower care, with special attention to the newly imported tulip. In 1587, Dutch enthusiasm for flowers combined with their appreciation of scientific study led to the foundation in Leiden of one of the first European institutes for botanical study. Clusius was its second director and went on to lead the institute into the successful propagation of many new plant varieties, including tulips, crocuses and irises, thereby laying the foundation for the horticulture industry that we see today.

For the moment the government has restricted the wholesale spreading of manure, set herd limits and established "manure banks" for farmers to deposit their excess while scientists search for alternative uses for the unavoidable by-product.

Landscape gardening

As far back as the late 1500s, Dutch gardeners and botanists were setting European standards for horticulture and the design of stately gardens. As Dutch merchant vessels began to sail the world's oceans in search of tradeable goods, they regularly brought back new species and varieties of plants never seen before in northern Europe. The Dutch reputation for horticulture spread internationally and, in particular, to England.

During this period, and for centuries to come, Dutch and French garden styles set the standard for the rest of Europe. This was especially true for the English where, during and after the Civil War, Royalists and Catholic sympathisers favoured the French garden style, while Parliamentarians and Protestants leaned toward the Dutch .

In Britain, the reign of the Dutch Protestant King William of Orange and his wife Mary (1688–1702) also had a large influence on

Tulip development

The roots of Dutch horticulture and garden influence can equally be traced back to the import and development of the tulip, the Netherlands' most famous flower.

The tulip originated in the Caucasus and spread as far as present-day China. In the wild, the flower grows along a corridor on either side of the 40th Parallel. Explorers were sending back new varieties from this area until the beginning of World War II.

The first recorded instance of the tulip being successfully cultivated for garden use was in Turkey. By the 18th century, Turkish growers

English and European garden styles. Their royal gardener, a Dutchman named Bentinck, designed one of the best surviving examples of a Dutch-style enclosed garden at the magnificent Hampton Court near Richmond. Dutch gardens (ironically called English gardens in the Netherlands) were typically enclosed by a wall and divided internally by hedges. Brilliant and colourful floral patterns, topiary designs, tightly ordered and decoratively trimmed trees as well as ornamental hedges have always been considered typical Dutch features.

LEFT: maze garden at Het Loo Palace, Apeldoorn.
ABOVE: bike riding among the tulip fields.

had registered more than 1,500 different tulip varieties and were the undisputed masters of tulip growing in the world. Strict standards for shape, colour and production were maintained and Constantinople was the only place where Turks could legally sell their tulip bulbs. For several Turkish sultans, this precious flower held a position of courtly honour, and festivals involving at least 500,000 tulips were spectacular annual events.

Tulips came to Europe in the middle of the 16th century through trade and diplomatic channels, which is how Clusius obtained his first bulbs. With the growth of the East Indies Company, trade and prosperity increased in the

Amsterdam area. The bulbs travelled easily and the rare and colourful flowers became a natural way for the increasingly wealthy merchants and nouveaux riches to flaunt their wealth. A garden full of expensive tulips was a sure sign of prestige and social standing.

Mysterious petals

During this period and long after, the most valued tulip had petals that were known as "feathered" for their broken or striated colour patterns. For centuries no one could determine what made the unusual and beautiful petals. Botanists were especially confounded because

the patterns of one generation of bulbs would produce seedlings whose flowers often did not resemble their parental generation at all. Only much later did scientists discover that the breakage in colouring was due to insect-borne viruses attacking the bulbs. Experts also say that the tulips of this period did not resemble the familiar shape we know today. Paintings of the time depict them with larger, often ragged heads with more petals, less graceful leaves and overall a less streamlined look.

Growers in the Netherlands now produce more than nine billion bulbs annually, two-thirds of them grown for export. Export bulbs are split into two markets: dry sales and the forcing market. Dry sales are simply propagated bulbs harvested from the fields. For the forcing market, bulbs are sold to greenhouses for year-round cultivation to produce cut flowers.

Flower auctions

Hundreds of different species of flowers are sold daily at the Aalsmeer Flower Auction (informally known as the VBA, the initials of the old name *Verenigde Bloemenveilingen Aaslmeer*) in the Netherlands.

Visitors are welcome at this open auction from Monday to Friday from 7.30 to 11am. (For more information, contact: Legmeerdijk 312, Aalsmeer, tel: 0297 392 185.) Here, the vast majority of produce – 90 percent of all bulbs and flowers and 85 percent of other fruits and vegetables – are sold through the unique Dutch "clock" auction system.

There are five auction halls with a total of 14 clocks. The buyers are exporters, wholesalers,

---

TULIPMANIA

Because of the unpredictability from one crop to the next and the rising demands, rabid speculation on bulb prices took hold in the 1630s. The craze became known as "tulipomania" or "the wind trade" by Dutch florists, satirists and historians alike – nothing in the market reflected any true value of the bulbs; hence, trading the wind.

As wealth trickled down to the middle classes the speculative frenzy in the bulb trade increased. Family fortunes were made and eventually wiped out in the bidding fever that gripped Amsterdam and the western Netherlands. At one point, one white flamed Semper Augustus bulb reportedly sold for at least 10,000 guilders

(£3,600/US$5,600). Churches echoed with sermons on the evils of bulb gambling and politicians tried to prohibit it, no doubt fuelling prices even more.

Eventually, prices returned to more reasonable levels, and other bulb and corm flowers, such as daffodils, lilies, crocuses, irises and hyacinths, dahlias and gladioli, became popular, though none rivalled the tulip. Greenhouses, which began to multiply rapidly at the turn of the 20th century, changed the nature of the industry. In due course the rose displaced the tulip as the best-selling flower, a trend that continues, with the tulip relegated to fourth on the sales charts, behind roses, chrysanthemums and carnations.

shopkeepers and street traders who are seated on benches and can purchase via all the clocks in their halls by pressing a switch. Under this system, the pointer turns round a large dial indicating the price of a lot.

The clock starts at "noon", which represents the highest prices and sweeps downward. The auctioneer calls out which flowers are on offer, specifying their grower and the minimum quantity which the buyer must purchase. Prices start high and decrease as the pointer turns. Bidders can stop the clock at the price which they are willing to pay.

Across the country 41 separate auctions use this system for selling flowers, fruit and vegetables, including the world's largest, located at Aalsmeer, near Schiphol airport in Amsterdam. Each year on the first weekend of September, the *Bloemencorso* (parade) takes place from the centre of Aalsmeer via Amstelveen to Amsterdam and Zaandam with festive, colourful floats that delight the thousands of spectators who throng the route. In Aalsmeer, the celebration continues with a range of activities and flower exhibitions.

In the old days, buyers used to gather in the growers' fields to inspect the crop in the ground before the bidding would start. Today these so-called "green" auctions have become exceedingly rare. With the technical precision and predictability of greenhouse growing, produce and bulbs are now "sold forward," meaning that the bulbs are still in the ground or the produce still on the vine at the time of purchase. At the auctions today, brokers acting for buyers and sellers from around the world do all the bidding, while thousands of packers and shipping agents wrestle with the millions of flowers in other parts of the auction hall.

New techniques

Most plants are still cultivated vegetatively, by sowing or striking off young buds from the more mature and strongest plants. But tissue culture and meri-stem culture are used increasingly as methods of ensuring quick, identical and disease-free flowers.

Under a microscope, laboratory technicians cut tiny stems from selected young plants. The cuttings are then grown in test tubes for a set number of weeks depending on the plant. The process then starts all over again, with the best samples used for breeding, and the rest sold. These plants have not seen a rainy day for dozens of generations and black dirt, to them, is ancient history.

Growers prefer test tube methods because they increase productivity and speed up the search for new colours, qualities and varieties of plant. Methods are now so well developed that one million seedlings per year can be produced from a single plant. This method also guarantees that the plants are bred disease-free, which opens up new export markets, such as

Australia and New Zealand, for example, both of which have strict import regulations.

With the rising cost of natural gas needed to heat the greenhouses and of electricity to run every other automated and computer-controlled climatological aspect, growers are now hunting for plant strains that can be grown without the consumption of so much heat and light. Many Dutch laboratories are also working hard to produce infertile plants so that competitors cannot profit from their research and produce new generations of flowers virtually identical to the seedlings they have purchased. One can only imagine what these vegetative eunuchs might be called. ❏

LEFT: tulip and spider, Balthasar Assteyn.
RIGHT: flower market at Aalsmeer.

FOOD AND DRINK

You won't go hungry in Holland. As well as hearty traditional dishes, you can enjoy more recent imports like the delicious cuisine of its former colonies

In years gone by, Dutch cuisine was synonymous with potatoes, cabbage, bread, cheese, potatoes, herring, endive and more potatoes – with some sausage thrown in for good measure. To bear this out, you only have to look at Dutch still life paintings, with their bountiful buffets, any number of Old Master paintings with the family gathered round a sumptuous meal and, of course, Van Gogh's celebrated portrait of the *Potato Eaters*.

Because the Dutch prefer to eat their national dishes in their own homes, restaurants offering Dutch specialities are often hard to track down. However, Amsterdam favourites like Dorrius, Haesje Claes, De Blauwe Hollander and the Hotel Port van Cleve take pride in serving traditional food; dishes like *hutspot met klapstuk* (hotchpotch of meat, carrots and potatoes), *stamppot van zuurkool en worst* (sauerkraut mashed with potatoes and sausage) and *bruine bonen* (brown bean) soup. And at the renowned Five Flies restaurant, the diverse menu is based on the "new Dutch cuisine", which features fresh local produce prepared seasonally from traditional recipes, but cooked with a light touch in terms of fat content.

Eating out

Happily, when dining out in The Netherlands these days, there is plenty of variety. In Amsterdam and a few of the larger cities, it is possible to dine in almost any language thanks to the proliferation of ethnic restaurants – from Vietnamese to Ethiopian. And just as the Dutch explorers once brought back spices from around the world, innovative chefs are combining east with west to create unique and delicious "fusion" dishes. In other cities, the choice is more limited to the local pancake house, the ubiquitous pizzeria or Chinese and Indonesian restaurants. Food from Surinam, the former Dutch colony near South America, offers a spicy mixture of Creole and Indian, a kind of

soul food, with hearty curries and roti bread, peanut soup, and *pom*, a type of sweet potato. But there is also a lot to enjoy about hearty Dutch cuisine, especially in winter months.

Severe winter weather and travel by foot, on skates or by boat necessitated large, hearty meals rich in fats and carbohydrates to provide

energy and retain body heat. But vast meals are a thing of the past and thick soups and mashed vegetable dishes omit the extra fat in deference to the health-conscious. The most traditional winter dish, and still popular among the older generation, is *boerenkool – stamppot met worst* (cabbage mashed with potatoes and served with smoked sausage or *rookworst*). There is a Dutch saying that *boerenkool* ("farmer's cabbage", which we know as kale) is best when taken from the ground after the first frost. But young people tend to prefer McDonald's, which has in recent years, along with other American fast food chain restaurants, become a very visible part of the national foodscape.

LEFT: cheese at the Leidseplein market, Amsterdam.
RIGHT: a herring stall in Albert Cuypmarkt, Amsterdam.

Other specialities of the Dutch kitchen include white asparagus served with ham and chopped egg (in May and June), smoked eel, special puddings with whipped cream, pancakes and the famous herring, known as "the poor man's oyster". Herrings are eaten as a snack, raw or salted, with plenty of chopped onion, either picked up by the tail and dropped whole into the mouth, or, more often, eaten with a fork from a small plate. Herring stalls are a feature of Dutch life, especially in May when everyone wants to try the mild *nieuwe* (or *groene*) *haring* – the first green herring of the season. These stalls or wagons attract a vari-

ety of clients, many of whom eat it the traditional way, holding it expertly aloft by the tail between thumb and forefinger of the right hand, head lifted, mouth open and then swallow! Others may prefer a *broodje haring*, slices of herring in a soft roll or just slices of herring. Whatever way you choose, chopped onions are *de rigueur*. If you prefer another sort of fish, the stalls also sell smoked salmon, smoked eel and two varieties of succulent Dutch shrimp, the *Noordse* or *Hollands garnalen*, the North Sea's finest.

Drinking habits

Many people drink beer, especially pils, a light beer, though the favoured drink is *jenever* or Dutch gin, made from distilled malt wine with juniper berries. At about 5pm people drop into their local *caf* for a *borrel*: a small glass of either the colourless *jonge* (young) jenever, less creamy than the *oude* (old), which has a pale yellow colour and a noticeably heavier, muskier flavour. The Dutch are famous for their liqueurs and fruit brandies, although these are now losing popularity to imported drinks. Beer, mineral water and wine are drunk with meals. A favourite New Year drink called *Bisschopswijn* ("Bishop's Wine") may have been named after St Nicholas. This mulled wine is used for a Dutch toast – *Gezondheid* (Your health!) or *Proost*.

If you get hungry while in a *caf* before the dinner hour, try a plate of *borrelhapjes* (snacks) like *kroketten* (meat or shrimp croquettes) or *bitterballen*, meatballs coated with breadcrumbs, deep fried and served with mustard. Make sure to let them cool before taking a bite; the inside is notoriously hot and the Dutch always enjoy a perverse chuckle watching foreign guests innocently tuck into them. Later in the evening, a *tosti*, or grilled cheese sandwich, often combined with a slice of ham, usually hits the spot and helps temper the effects of a potential hangover.

Coffee is the Dutch national drink and "*koffiedrinken*" is the national pasttime. A cup of strong coffee, a *bakkie*, is usually served black. Espresso is a popular alternative and *koffie verkeerd*, or "wrong coffee" is a popular choice, a kind of café au lait, with a lot of steamed milk and a little coffee. Hot chocolate is mostly a winter drink and when people go skating, stands are set up on the ice with large urns on stoves.

FOOD ON THE RUN

If you fancy a quick snack, there are a number of options, from the simple shop selling *broodje* (filled bread rolls), or the Vietnamese *loempia* (spring roll) vendor to the Middle Eastern takeaway stand that sells *shoarma* (roast pork or lamb) in a pitta or falafel. However, the most popular Dutch snack is Belgian-style *patat* chips (or *frites*). Instead of eating them smothered in the usual tomato ketchup, the Dutch dip them into mayonnaise or other types of exotic sauces – a habit satirised by John Travolta's character in the film *Pulp Fiction*. They have little to do with their fast-food counterparts, so make sure you try them. And don't skimp on the mayo.

Breads and pastries

The bread basket on a breakfast table holds a varied selection of bread, from pre-cut white to heavy, black rye, and perhaps wholewheat, raisin and seed bread. A spiced cake, known as *ontbijtkoek* or *peperkoek*, and often eaten just with butter, varies according to each province. Some towns have their own special recipes for *peperkoek* which are closely guarded by local bakers.

In larger towns croissants are overtaking the *broodje* as a snack food, and are sold filled with combinations of cheese, ham, liver, shrimp, smoked eel, steak tartare, salad or herring. The *koffietafel* (coffee table) lunch which is served in homes and in office canteens includes a variety of breads, cheeses and meats. The drink of choice is usually milk or *karnemelk* (buttermilk).

Pastries are light and inventive and not too heavy on the sugar, although the *boterkoek*, Dutch pound cake, is quite rich in butter. On St Nicholas' Eve (5 December) chocolate-covered alphabet letters are made to be given to friends and family. The *boterletter*, made from old-fashioned puff pastry and almond paste filling served hot, is still a traditional part of the festivities. For a Christmas wreath (*kerstkrans*) the Dutch shape the *boterletter* into a ring instead of a letter. It is then spread with icing and decorated with candied cherries, orange and lemon peel and a red bow.

Sweets and biscuits

The Dutch are also fond of sweets and biscuits. *Stroopwafel* consists of two thin wafers sandwiched together with syrup, best eaten when warm and traditionally served with afternoon tea. Spiced cookies, *speculaas*, often windmill-shaped, are sold in packets or by weight and usually eaten with coffee. In the past they were made on *koekplanken* ("cookie planks"), moulds hollowed out into the shapes of windmills, mermaids, elephants or whatever; today, genuine *koekplanken* are sold in antiques shops and modern copies, made as souvenirs, are widely available.

LEFT: a typical Dutch dish of herring salad.
RIGHT: exotic fruit for sale at the annual Indonesian Market, The Hague.

The classic *appeltaart* (apple pie), made with special rum-soaked raisins and apples, is generally served in the afternoon rather than after an evening meal. *Oliebollen*, spicy doughnuts sprinkled with powdered sugar, were traditionally made to eat around Christmas time and on New Year's Eve, but are now a popular street food all year round.

Although vegetarianism has been on the increase in recent decades, meat is still a basic staple in the daily diet, supplemented in winter by potatoes, red and white cabbage, kale and

zuurkool (saurkraut). In spring, there is an abundance of asparagus, fennel and various green beans, peas, courgettes, aubergines, artichokes, carrots, onions, spinach and many salad foods, many of which are produced in quantity by the hothouse horticulturalists of the Netherlands. In the 17th century the Dutch, inspired by their East Indies Company, began to cultivate as many exotic fruits as they could induce to grow. In 1636 the great still-life artist Jan Davidsz de Heem even chose to live in Antwerp (now part of Belgium) because, Sandrart recorded, "there one could have rare fruits of all kinds, large plums, peaches, cherries, oranges, lemons, grapes, and others, in finer

Drinking

Drinking in Amsterdam should always be a pleasurable experience, but before embarking on a big night out, it's advisable to be acquainted with the beverages available. Beer is invariably served in glasses of 25cl. called an Amsterdammer or *vaas* (vase). A smaller glass of 20cl. is known as a *fluitje* (pronounced floutcha, meaning whistle – its shape is akin to that of a steam whistle). Finally, anything resembling a pint is politely known as a *pul* (50cl.), but locals humourously refer to it as an *emmer* (bucket).

Most cafés serve Heineken or Amstel, however Grolsch, Brand and Oranjeboom have made their presence felt in recent years. The beer drinking public favours these lagers, all of which are around 5% volume. Traditionally lager is served with froth, so don't be offended; locals would not consider the beer fresh any other way. There are many other beers available, *witbier* (white beer), a cloudy concoction usually served with a slice of lemon, is made from wheat and has a bitter-sweet taste. Other alternatives include darker, sweeter beers, often on draught and served in semi-spherical glasses. De, Koninck and Palm are the most famous. At this juncture it's worth bearing in mind the importance of measuring beer strength in percentage alcohol by volume: an extremely reliable indicator of price and potency. The more adventurous drinker will be easily seduced by the superbly rich and diverse amount of Belgian beers, often brewed in monasteries, the effects and flavours of which may be as celestial as the price after too many temptations.

Jenever (pronounced yurnayver), and commonly known as Dutch gin to English speakers, is a beautifully subtle spirit often called a *borrel*. There are three sorts; *jonge* (pronounced yonger) young jenever, *oude* (pronounced owd) old jenever, and *korenwijn* (pronounced corenvain). Ironically, the difference between old and young jenever is not age. Jenever is distilled from grain (usually barley and rye) and malt, the resultant distillate being malt wine (50 percent alcohol by volume). The law stipulates that young jenever contains no more than 15 percent malt wine, old jenever no less than 15 percent and *korenwijn* no less than 40 percent.

Traditionally the young jenever's strength is raised by the addition of molasses alcohol and, unlike the others, is delicately flavoured with juniper berries. Only some old jenevers are aged in vats (*korenwijn* always is) and take on the hue of a distinguished malt whisky. Beer, drunk in combination with a jenever is aptly named a *kopstoot* meaning "headbang".

Concluding our Bacchanal tour is a brief look at liqueurs. About 300 years ago when distilling was developed in The Netherlands, pure alcohol wasn't considered palatable. With the newly arrived choice of spices and other goodies, courtesy of the Dutch East Indies Company, were all sorts of splendid "remedies" with names that still reflect their dubious qualities.

Bruidstranen or "Bride's Tears", for example, served directly after marital vows, is a pure orange liqueur containing 22 carat gold leaf and silver leaf tears. Others include *Naveltje Bloot* or "Naked Navel" to be taken as a salutation to a pregnant damsel's newly rounded belly, and probably the most famous of all *Oranje Bitter* made of steeped Malaga orange peel, an esprit of Valencia peel plus a touch of aniseed esprit served on Queen's Day (30 April), a national holiday of monumental proportions. On this day one could easily consume all of the above and recover with a *Bittere Lijdenstroost* or "Bitter Consolation", a liqueur made of vanilla, cinnamon, Malaga orange and a hint of Amsterdams bitters. *Proost!* ❑

LEFT: what's your tipple?

condition and state of ripeness to draw from life." These days, fresh fruits abound, but are generally imported.

The Netherlands is the only country in Europe where it is legal to shoot wild boar all the year round. The main hunting areas lie in the province of Limburg, particularly the woods between Maastricht and Venlo. However, restaurant customers are used to a distinct game season in the cold months and there is no demand for wild boar in the summer. Quail, partridge, pheasant, hare and rabbit

> ### HAPPY EATING
>
> If a waiter says to you "*Smakelijk eten*", don't worry – he is not being rude. He is simply saying "Enjoy your meal."

A passion for pancakes

Dessert menus in restaurants might well feature the traditional Dutch *flensjes* (thin pancakes) but given a fancy French name – such as *crêpes Suzette* or *crêpes Bresilliennes*, the latter filled with vanilla ice cream coated with a warm sauce made from half chocolate and half coffee. Ordinary plate-sized pancakes of the savoury variety are made with a meat, tomato, cheese or mushroom ragout, or some other such topping and served at dinner. A sweet version may be topped with Grand

are all popular winter dishes, mostly cooked in beer, wine or cognac. Another traditional game recipe is *Jachtschotel* ("Hunter's Dish"), made from stewed venison covered with mashed potatoes and topped with sliced apples and breadcrumbs. It is served with red cabbage.

In all country areas, free-range poultry is plentiful – many families rear their own chickens, guinea-fowl, turkeys, ducks and geese. In restaurants fowl is often accompanied by apple sauce or *stoofpeertjes* (little stewing pears" cooked in red wine and cinnamon), or redcurrant sauce.

ABOVE: Brouwhuis Maximiliaan, Amsterdam.

> ### THE INDONESIAN *RIJSTTAFEL*
>
> The Indonesian *rijsttafel*, or rice table, has anything from 16 to 30 side dishes based around rice. Dishes which might include such favourites as *ayam goreng*, (Indonesian fried chicken), *sambal oedang* (shrimps in a red sauce), and *pisang goreng* (fried bananas) are accompanied by crunchy prawn crackers known as *kroepoek*.
>
> If you prefer to eat less or are watching the budget, order *nasi rames*, a miniature *rijsttafel* with generous spoonfuls of various side dishes. If you prefer noodles instead of rice, order the *bami rames* instead, And be careful with the *sambal*, which is Indonesian chilli sauce – a little goes a long way.

Marnier, strawberries or chocolate sauce and whipped cream, or else served up the no-frills way with maple syrup or *stroop*, a type of treacle. *Poffertjes*, or mini pancakes, are another variation on the same theme.

At home, dessert might consist of a delicious and filling bread pudding made from slices of stale bread, eggs and dried fruit. *Vla* is also a popular country dessert, similar to custard. You'll seldom find it in restaurants but supermarkets sell many different kinds flavoured with vanilla, chocolate or fruits.

Another favourite when dining out is the traditional *Dame Blanche* – vanilla ice cream with

chocolate sauce. Cheese platters are an option as a final course with many cheeses made from sheep and goat's milk.

Local flavours

Each region has its own food specialities. The southern provinces, for instance, are well known for Burgundian pleasures of the table. In Maastricht, in the province of Limburg, the local dish is a stew resembling Hungarian goulash. Raw vegetable salads served with sausages are also popular.

Their local pastry (*vlaai*) is either filled with seasonal fruits (ranging from apricots and cherries to apples or plums) topped with a lattice

pattern or filled with rice and cream. The people of Leiden eat *hutspot* on 3 October to commemorate the town's liberation from the Spanish in 1574.

Leiden had been under siege for several months and the townspeople were starving. Then Prince William of Orange ordered the sluices to be opened to flood the surrounding land and, faced with the prospect of drowning, the invaders retreated. When a Leiden boy climbed up to explore the deserted ramparts he found an iron pot left by the Spanish containing a stew of beef and vegetables. The people of Leiden now make their own commemorative *hutspot* with *klapstuk* (boneless beef short ribs), carrots, potatoes and onions.

In Zeeland, seafood predominates, especially mussels, oysters, sole and turbot. Many local restaurants are built on stilts at the water's edge. There are also a good many glass-fronted restaurants, where you can sit and enjoy the outlook over the beach as you tuck into the delicious seafood on your plate.

In both the polder lands in the north of the country, and in the new province of Flevoland, country dwellers keep their own cattle, pigs and hens. On the whole, these hard-working people eat more meat than city dwellers; a family might, on average, eat more than 2 kg (4 lb) of meat every day. Then again, some farmers might dine exclusively on potatoes, with each family member eating around 1 kg (2 lbs) worth, dipped into an individual bowl of gravy from the meat dish of the previous day.

Colonial legacy

Because of Holland's colonial legacy, Indonesian food is extremely popular. So much so that the cuisine has become entirely integrated into the Dutch way of life. Most restaurants specialise primarily in dishes from the islands of Java and Sumatra, and you'll find the best in the larger cities such as The Hague, Amsterdam and Rotterdam.

Because it is home to the highest population of Indonesians (and Dutch resettled from Indonesia), The Hague justifiably lays claim to the most authentic restaurants, and certainly offers the spiciest food. ❑

LEFT: a tempting bread stall in Amsterdam's Leidseplein. **RIGHT:** small-scale cheese making on display at Woerden, Utrecht.

PLACES

A detailed guide to the entire country, with principal sites clearly cross-referenced by number to the maps

The Netherlands is a small country, approximately 255 km (160 miles) north to south, and 180 km (112 miles) east to west. English speakers habitually refer to the country as "Holland". The Dutch know the country as the Kingdom of the Netherlands. Strictly speaking, Holland refers only to the two provinces of Noord (North) and Zuid (South) Holland. Most of the best-known cities of the Netherlands are located in these two provinces, including the administrative capital The Hague ('s-Gravenhage, or Den Haag, in Dutch), Rotterdam, Amsterdam, Delft, Leiden, Gouda and Haarlem.

This densely populated region appears, from the train at least, to be one unbroken conurbation. The distances separating these cities and towns is small, and the Dutch call the region the Randstad; ring-town, but a better, if less literal translation, is "the big village".

The remainder of the Netherlands comprises 10 provinces: Zeeland, Utrecht, Noord-Brabant, Limburg, Gelderland, Flevoland (created in the 20th century from reclaimed land and declared a province only in 1986), Overijssel, Drenthe, Groningen and Friesland.

The landscape and character of these more rural provinces is surprisingly varied and conforms little to the cliché-ridden image of flat, monotonous polder. Zeeland is a region of islands, peninsulas, sandy coastline and bird-filled marshes. The southern provinces of Noord-Brabant and Limburg have a distinctly Catholic culture, a more flamboyant, Gothic-inspired architecture and wooded hills.

Further north, the great rivers (Rhine, Mass and Waal) cut through the heath and woodland landscape of the central provinces, while Gelderland and Overijssel form a region of meadowlands, orchards and streams, known as the Achterhoek (back corner).

In Drenthe a wilder landscape is dotted with megaliths, marking the giant communal graves of prehistoric settlers; as the province merges into Groningen, man-made hillocks rise from the peat levels as further evidence of early settlement. Finally Friesland, with its thatched barns and farmhouses, gives way to the shallow Waddenzee and a chain of often remote but completely unspoiled islands.

Exploring this varied country is made easier by the network of tourist information centres (known by the initials vvv), which are found in virtually every town. As well as handling bookings for accommodation and entertainments, they are an excellent source of free maps and general information. ❏

PRECEDING PAGES: flower bulb fields near Lisse; windmills lining the Kinderdijk; Amsterdam's Oude Kerk. **LEFT:** the photogenic windmills at Kinderdijk, south of Rotterdam, were once used to pump water from low-lying land.

Netherlands

20 km

20 miles

N

NORTH
SEA

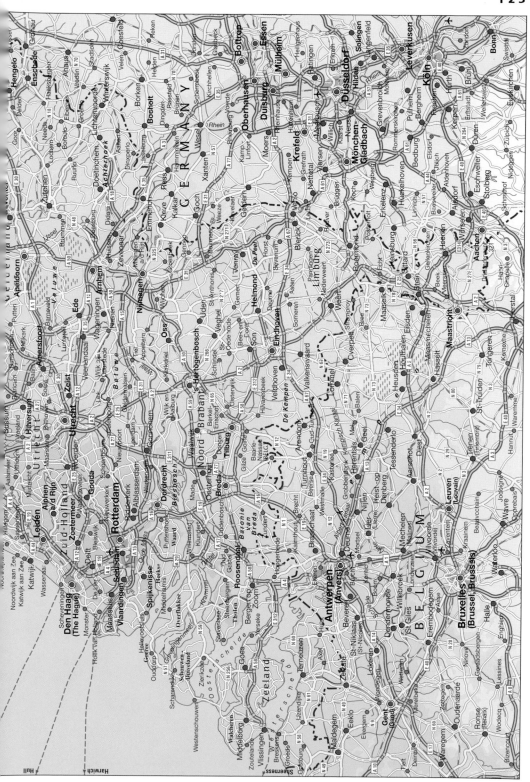

Amsterdam

0 ———— 500 m
0 ———— 500 yds

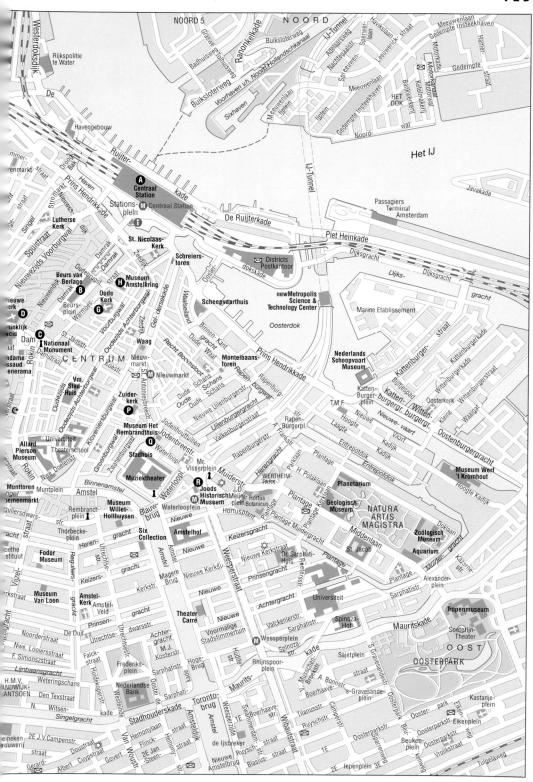

AMSTERDAM

The Netherlands' capital has stood the test of time. Modern Amsterdam offers something for everyone, from world-class art and stunning architecture to colourful streets that hum with life

For most visitors, an encounter with Amsterdam begins among the organ-grinders, street musicians, jugglers, harried commuters and weary travellers on Stationsplein, in front of **Centraal Station** . This is a disconcerting yet appropriate beginning, in keeping with the district's voracious appetite for novelty, trade and travel.

Since 1855, however, the city has been severed from the sea by the Centraal Station and now looks inward for its identity. Built on an artificial island in Het IJ, the city's old inner harbour, the station gives little sense of its watery origins until you cross Prins Hendrikkade towards Damrak. Only then are you aware of the redundant stretch of water (on the left) that was once the cutting edge of the Dutch Empire, its quaysides and warehouses disgorging goods on their way from the East Indies to Germany and the Baltic.

Today, commuters take two different ferries to the other side of the IJ from Amsterdam North, and both of these give tourists the opportunity to enjoy a free sightseeing trip. The area to the east, just a few kilometres further on, known as the Oostelijk Eilanden (or eastern islands), comprising KNSM, Java and Borneo, has undergone extensive development in recent years to provide innovative housing for people wishing to live just outside the city. Further in, a group of islands along the IJsselmeer called the IJjburg development, will provide new housing for at least 20,000 inhabitants by 2002.

Starting point

Just as the city has turned its back on the sea, so too do the visitors who rush down busy **Damrak**. This tawdry thoroughfare, bordered by smoky cafés, tacky souvenir shops, and a fleet of canal boats, pumps tram and taxi traffic south to the heart of Amsterdam. Ignore the "change" shops and cheap fast food storefronts on the right, and focus instead on the stately **Beurs van Berlage** , the former Stock Exchange, on the left. The Dutch have always been a nation of gamblers, and when, in the 17th century, they would lay a wager on anything from the sex of a baby to the profits of a tulip harvest, much of this speculation centred around the Beurs.

The origins of the Beurs lie in informal dealings in neighbouring Warmoesstraat, but in 1608 a Stock Exchange was created on the Rokin and, at the turn of the last century, a new Beurs replaced it on Damrak. The greatest Dutch poet, Vondel, railed against the first Exchange as a "bringer of misery; sunlight never penetrates thy building." Inside the spacious main hall of the Beurs, one can admire plain ironwork, narrow arcades and Romanesque and neo-Renaissance motifs. Designed by architect H. P. Berlage, the

PRECEDING PAGES: Damrak.
LEFT: Herengracht.
BELOW: mime artist.

remarkable Dutch Modernist building is now a unique cultural centre, home to the Netherlands Philharmonic Orchestra and the Berlage Museum; concerts and architectural exhibitions are held throughout the year.

Tulipomania

In 1636, tulip mania was widespread, and bulbs, imported from Turkey and traded on the exchange, were considered more exotic than emeralds, Arab stallions, Ming vases and other less precious commodities. Aristocrats snapped up flowers in rare colours, but even ordinary burghers traded in red or yellow tulips. This widespread preference for flowers over jewels is seen as proof of the essential bourgeois nature of Dutch culture.

It is better to continue along Damrak into Dam square rather than to turn into **Nieuwendijk**, a snaking street of vulgar shops running parallel to Damrak. The **Dam**, the city's only unencumbered square, was long a public and political forum, thanks to the presence of the Royal Palace, once the Town Hall (Stadhuis), and a space large enough for medieval executions, Republican processions and 1980s demonstrations against cruise missiles. Today, demonstrations, carnivals and various cultural and political events are held on the site. The most notable event takes place on 4 May at 8pm, just across the Square at the Dam monument, when two minutes' silence is observed in honour of those who died in World War II. This event, which is televised across the country, is attended by the Queen and many notables, and viewed by thousands who arrive hours ahead to secure a good view of this moving ceremony.

Also on the Dam is the **Nationaal Monument** ⊙. This obelisk is a war memorial containing urns of earth from each of the Netherlands' 11 provinces

Clogs adorn plenty of shops around the more touristy parts of Amsterdam.

BELOW: enjoying Dam Square.

Map
on pages
124–5

(it predates the creation of Flevoland, the 12th province) and from Indonesia. The sculptures of naked war victims surrounding the obelisk bear the message "Never again". Vivid memories and marks of World War II are ever present in Amsterdam, from the excellent Resistance and Jewish Historical Museums to the Anne Frank House (*see page 143*).

Although now sliced by shuttling trams, the Dam has kept some of its public character, although today its political role is marginal. The Koninklijk Paleis, built between 1648 and 1655 by Jacob van Campen, maintains a stately presence on the Dam, opposite the equally impressive **Nieuwe Kerk**. The Queen still welcomes Heads of State and other VIP guests during the year (look for the guards surrounding the palace and the curious crowds of on-lookers. The Palace is open to visitors during summer months, Easter and the October school holiday. A free brochure in several languages is available.

Proud symbol

At its inception the former Stadhuis (town hall) was a celebration of Dutch independence and renewed peace. Poet Constantijn Huygens praised it as "the world's Eighth Wonder. With so much stone raised high and so much timber under," a reference to its creation on 13,659 wooden piles. The Stadhuis's symbolic importance to 17th-century Amsterdam is emphasised by the innumerable paintings of the building that hang on the walls of the Historical Museum.

A distinguished neighbour of the Koninklijk Paleis, the **Nieuwe Kerk ❶**, is new in name only. Built in 1400 after a series of fires, the New Church received grand 17th-century additions to its late Gothic structure. Then, however, it was forbidden from having a tower because the Regents feared competition with the

For a peek into everyday life in Amsterdam, be sure to stop by Dam Square, particularly if you are visiting during May. Medieval executions have now given way to carnivals and cultural and political events.

BELOW:
street art – or a blot
on the landscape?

TIP

After visiting the
Nieuwe Kerk, try De
Drie Fleschjes in
Gravenstraat, for the
atmospheric feel
of a 17th-century
tasting house.

Town Hall. Today, the church's fine interior and importance as a cultural centre have helped it emerge from the Town Hall's shadow. A proliferation of temporary art exhibitions often makes it difficult to see the 17th-century organ, choir rail and pulpit or to admire the marble mausoleum of Admiral de Ruyter, so it is worth trying to attend one of the many concerts which are offered throughout the year. Since 1815, Dutch kings and queens have been invested here, most recently Queen Beatrix in 1980.

Brief interlude

Tacked on to the church are several miniscule shops and a quaint café. However, for the more genuine article, try *De Drie Fleschjes* in Gravenstraat, a 17th-century tasting house tucked behind the church. Known as *proeflokalen*, such atmospheric bars originally allowed customers to sample jenever (Dutch gin), but now serve an extraordinary range of spirits and cocktails.

Wijnand Fockink, innocent despite its name, was the most famous, but it closed in 1990 after failing to compete with the rash of brown cafés and designer bars. On parting, the owner proudly declared: "At least I always considered myself to be a host, not a mere publican." In 1992 it reopened its doors under new ownership and continues to be a stopping point for connoisseurs of Dutch gins and liqueurs. Beer on tap is also available.

Thus rejuvinated, cross the Dam and walk down commercial **Kalverstraat** past countless clothing and snack shops. Avoid the endless stream of pedestrians by turning into a lopsided gateway adorned with the triple-cross arms of Amsterdam. Notice the figures of chubby children dressed in red and black uniforms, a reminder that the gate once led to the **City Orphanage**. Founded in 1578 on the site of St Lucy's, a former convent, the orphanage was a tribute to the enlightened rule of the city fathers. The orphanage board had a seat on the City Council because "the rich need the poor for the quiet of their souls." On reaching adulthood, successful orphans were supposed to show their gratitude by becoming donors to the orphanage, but the majority of would-be entrepreneurs had already been recruited as lowly errand boys by local fishwives. The orphanage was moved out in 1960 and the site was transformed into the **Amsterdams Historisch (Historical) Museum ❸** (359 Nieuwezijds Voorburgwal, tel: 020-523 1822; open Mon–Fri 10am–5pm, Sat and Sun 11am–5pm; entrance fee).

Before entering the museum itself, prolong the sense of solitude by entering the adjoining **Begijnhof ❺**, Amsterdam's finest almshouse court and one of the city's most spiritual enclaves. In the 15th century this religious quarter was literally an island and, although the once-polluted Beguinensloot moats were filled in 1865, the Begijnhof remains a place apart. First recorded in 1389, the almshouses were home to the sisters of St Lucy, a Franciscan order that replaced the once popular lay *beguine* way of life for women. Beguines chose to lead a partial form of convent life, including the vow of chastity. The last beguine died in 1971 but the almshouse continues as a residential sanctuary for "unmarried women of good repute."

BELOW:
the Begijnhof.

Timber house

The Begijnhof, reached through a number of inner courtyards, comprises a series of brick and stone gabled houses built between the 14th and 17th centuries. *Het Houten Huys*, No. 34, was built in 1460, making it the oldest surviving dwelling in Amsterdam. It is one of only two remaining wooden houses, erected before fire regulations forbade such flammable building materials.

Amsterdammers are fondest of the Begijnhof in spring when the lawn becomes a carpet of daffodils and crocuses. No. 26, one of the grandest houses, was the home of Sister Antoine, the last beguine, and has been preserved as she left it. The small church in the square, given to the city's English and Scottish Presbyterians over 300 years ago, hosts intimate concerts.

Opposite the church is one of the city's many clandestine Catholic chapels, a darkly Italianate church, which still smells of hot wax and serious prayers. Do keep in mind that people live in this sacred refuge and show respect for the peaceful ambience. From here, walk back through the courtyards of the former orphanage and through the unique Schuttersgalerij (Civic Guards gallery) which leads to the Historical Museum. Stop for a drink at the David & Goliath café and toast the original residents, the nuns at St Lucy's convent, who brewed and marketed their own beer.

Historical Museum

Inside the Historical Museum itself, the trail through Amsterdam's history is imaginatively presented, running both chronologically and thematically, without restricting viewers to a particular order. The strength of the collection lies not only in its accurate portrayal of social history through paintings, furniture

Map on pages 124–5

Pay attention to detail while walking; there's more to Amsterdam than gabled roofs.

BELOW: one of many city flower markets.

and cleverly juxtaposed artefacts, but in its creative, changing exhibitions which reflect Amsterdam's evolving character.

Highlights of the collection include *het groei carte* ("growth map") tracing Amsterdam's growth over the centuries. Extending to three storeys, is a remarkable exhibition of assorted objects featuring *Het Wapen* (city symbol of Amsterdam) ranging from serious to kitsch. Exhibits were added in 1999 that document historical events of the 19th and 20th centuries.

There are also early works by Jan Luyken, Rembrandt and Van Gogh, and other fascinating tableaux of time past, but the museum is famed for its 16th-, 17th-, and 18th-century group portraits of the civic guards (employed from the 14th century onwards to protect Amsterdam's citizens), which are literally hung on the street inside a glassed-in gallery leading to the Begijnhof. Finally, as in the Resistance Museum, the presentation of Dutch "anti-democratic movements" deals frankly with the existence of Dutch Fascist sympathisers and with the later Jewish deportations.

Contrasting moods

For something completely different, find the doorway between the houses numbered 37 and 38 in the Begijnhof and follow the passageway to **Spui**, the lively university quarter and home to numerous brown cafés. Café Hoppe (Spui 18) is perhaps the city's most celebrated brown café, frequented by artists and writers, with an intimate, slightly louche atmosphere, in tone with the nicotine-stained walls. Opposite is Café Swart, outside which bankers and men in suits stand with their beers in warm weather. For elegance and great people-watching, try Luxembourg (Spui 22–24), but to escape the crowds there is only De

BELOW: B. van der Helst's *The Banquet of the Civic Guard* displayed in the Rijksmuseum.

Stoep (Singel 415). On Fridays, an antiquarian book market offers a good selection of English language books at reasonable prices. Just opposite is the Athenaeum Book Store and News Centrum, which offers a range of books, newspapers and magazines in English.

If you have the energy for extended café crawling or nightclubbing, follow Kalverstraat south to Rembrandtplein, the most frenetic part of town. En route, call in at the **Tuschinski Cinema** in Reguliersbreestraat and admire its splendid art deco interior. Further up on the Reguliersdwarstraat (behind the Flower Market) Amsterdam's predominantly gay quarter, with dining, cruising and clubbing, offers yet another new dimension to city life.

If dinner in a less lively but more stylish district appeals, avoid the tourist-crammed Rembrandtplein and Leidseplein quarters with their piano bars, fast food restaurants and overpriced "tourist traps" and walk down any of the four main canals (Singel, Herengracht, Keizersgracht, Prinsengracht), where you will discover many fine, reasonably priced restaurants along the small streets that crisscross the canals, such as Runstraat, Reestraat, Hartenstraat and Wolvenstraat. There are inexpensive ethnic restaurants, elegant dining establishments with well-known chefs, as well as charming brown cafés inhabited by congenial locals.

Oude Zijde (Old Side)

Affectionately known as "Mokum" (the Yiddish word for "place"), the historic heart of Amsterdam contains the Old Church and the Amstelkring, a "clandestine" church on Oudezijds Voorburgwal. The red light district crowds around the north end of the latter canal. The area also harbours more subtle attractions, including the Waag, or Weigh House and the East Indies House.

After the space of the Dam and Damrak, turning into cramped, dingy Warmoesstraat is a shock. In medieval times, this narrow street (running parallel with, and to the east of, Damrak) was once the centre of the fabric and furnishing trades. The shops stocked Nuremburg porcelain, Lyons silk and Spanish taffeta as well as Delftware and Haarlem linen. Fallen on harder times, the narrowest shopping street in town now relies on cafés and restaurants, but a smattering of traditional trades retain a presence here.

Geels, at No. 67, is a long-established coffee and tea merchant's, whose owner, Piet Hein is a mine of information, and offers more than 25 types of coffee and more than 150 kinds of tea.

Despite these pockets of respectability, **Warmoesstraat** glows, if not red hot, at least a warmish pink hue. At the Condomerie Het Gulden Vlies (The Golden Fleece), a post-Aids boom means that the shop sells nothing but condoms – from run-of-the-mill to novelty wear – with sales assistance from sensitive and helpful staff.

From here, any alley east leads to the heart of the **red light district** in Oudezijds Achterburgwal and Zeedijk. If you want to have an inside look at the *walletjes* (red light area), visit the Prostitutie Informatie Centrum at Engekerksteeg 3.

Map on pages 124–5

TIP

Walk along any of the four main canals to discover reasonably priced restaurants and charming brown cafés away from the busier tourist hubs.

BELOW: Friday's book market in the lively Spui quarter.

Try to hear an author's reading or one of the excellent organ recitals at the Oude Kerk.

BELOW: the Oude Kerk (Old Church).

The Old Church

Although Oude Zijds has been blighted by the sex industry, the district's dilapidated condition should not blind visitors to the wealth of architectural treasures hidden behind uninviting façades. When walking these streets, however, do pay attention to your wallet and bags and avoid deserted side alleys.

At the Damrak end of Warmoesstraat the Wijde Kerksteeg alley leads to the **Oude Kerk** Ⓖ (Old Church), Amsterdam's oldest building, and the original church of the Amestelledamme fishing community. Despite a number of fires, the church's 13th-century tower remains, along with a chapel added in the 15th century. Before the "Alteration" in 1578, many windows and paintings were destroyed by Protestant iconoclasts, but enough treasures remain to make this the best preserved of Amsterdam's churches. In the 17th century, the Oude Kerk was the city's first experiment in transforming churches into community centres, a secular tendency which is most marked in today's Nieuwe Kerk. By contrast, the Oude Kerk continues to attract a congregation, even if many of those who attend services are partly drawn by the excellent organ recitals.

Inside this freezing cold church, the dusty medieval misericords, heavy grey flagstones, half-erased family crests and faded murals give the interior a forsaken feel. This contrasts with many other Dutch churches, which tend to be clinical and over-restored. There is much to admire, from the ornate organ to the wooden vaulted ceiling and cherubic statues. Some of the stained-glass windows, a vivid kaleidoscope of reds, blues and purples, date from the 16th century but others are modern replicas. The best time to see the church is during the winter months, when the light is low and shining through the coloured glass. The church hosts occasional concerts and author's readings.

If you happen to meet the sexton, comments on the number of ominously drawn red curtains in the vicinity of the church are likely to provoke a wave of resentment. "Don't forget that many ordinary working people live in this area. The prostitutes come from elsewhere and are not welcome."

Map on pages 124–5

Hidden church

Lucky visitors may hear the church's 15th-century bells before crossing the smelly Oudekerksbrug to the right bank of the Oudezijds Voorburgwal. Turn left and follow the canal a little way north, then cross the Leidsesluis bridge back to the left bank. Beside the bridge is the **Amstelkring ⓗ**, one of Amsterdam's most charming and least explored museums.

Also known as Ons' Lieve Heer op Solder (Our Lord in the Attic), this 17th-century merchant's house, renovated in 1999, conceals the finest of the city's "clandestine" churches, and offers many other surprises, from the cellar to the attic. The lower part of the house, however, gives an accurate glimpse of its more ordinary past. It was used by Catholics from 1650 until 1795, when the French rulers restored the Catholics' right to worship openly. Jan Hartman, a Catholic sympathiser, linked the top floor of three gabled houses to form two galleries with space for up to 400 worshippers.

Upstairs, a tiny chaplain's room nestles on the landing, but right under the eaves lies the large church itself, a tiered gallery formed by opening up the three attics. The size of the lower gallery, not to mention the creaking floor, makes the secrecy of the services rather fanciful. Apart from the sweet Maria Chapel, decorated with fresh flowers and 18th-century paintings, the charm lies in odd details such as the revolving mahogany pulpit, ready to be hidden at a

BELOW: Amstelkring Museum.

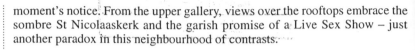

moment's notice. From the upper gallery, views over the rooftops embrace the sombre St Nicolaaskerk and the garish promise of a Live Sex Show – just another paradox in this neighbourhood of contrasts.

Seediness and gentility

From here there is a choice of routes. The faint-hearted can avoid the brashness of the red light area by walking south down Oudezijds Voorburgwal towards **Rokin**. Known in the 16th century as the Velvet Canal, because of its prosperous air, refined traces still remain in the unusual gable stones of houses lining the canal. From Rokin, the red light area can be viewed from the safety of a candle-lit boat cruise.

The fearless, as well as those who are soon offended by the tasteless patter of sex-show hawkers and the line of gawking tourists outside a window displaying scantily dressed woman, can cross to the right bank of the Oudezijds Voorburgwal and brave the junkies or heroin dealers on the **Damstraat** in order to see some more of the city's architectural gems, like the Zeedijk. At No. 2 is a well-restored gabled house, the second of the city's remaining wooden houses. Be careful in this area as pickpockets and purse and camera snatchers are rampant, but this shouldn't spoil your experience.

The Zeedijk ends in **Nieuwmarkt**, an abrasive but interesting area housing **Chinatown** and some prize-winning social housing, but historically it bordered the Jodenbuurt (Jewish quarter). During World War II, Jews were assembled here to await deportation to transit camps.

BELOW: Chinatown has a good choice of restaurants.

Have a look at the imposing **Waag** (weighing house) on the square. In its time, this medieval gatehouse has been a civic weighing house, a guild house for both the militia and the surgeons and the predecessor of today's Jewish Historical Museum. An *eetcafé* on the ground floor is worth a visit. Also along the Zeedijk are several good Chinese restaurants, including Hoi Tin and Nam Kee. There are patrolling police around, but try and steer clear of the ubiquitous junkies and dealers in this area. If you follow the Zeedijk toward Centraal Station, you'll find many high quality restaurants en route, including Japanese, Portuguese and Malaysian.

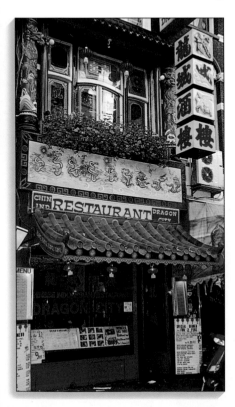

Ruling élite

Nieuwmarkt can also be reached by a less tawdry route via **Koestraat**. In passing, notice the optimistic carvings of Faith, Hope and Charity on Nos. 7 to 11, and the wine-merchants' guild house at No. 10. Koestraat ends in Kloveniersburgwal and the 17th-century mansion (No. 29) known as the **Trippenhuis**. Military insignia on the façade indicate that this was once the home of the Trip family of armament manufacturers. The Trips were powerful members of the "Magnificat", the ruling clique of families who governed the city during the Golden Age. Opposite, at No. 26, is the so-called smallest house in Amsterdam, once owned by the Trip family's coachman. From here, you can turn left into Nieuwmarkt or follow the canal to the right until you reach the imposing red-brick building by the next bridge. This was the headquarters of the **East Indies Company** and, as such, frequently received deliveries of precious commodities, such as spices, coffee, ebony and mahogany.

Further down Klovenicrsburgwal, a small alley lined with bookstalls, Oudemanhuispoort, passes through former almshouses to the photogenic **Huis op de Grachten** (House on the Canals). On the right is the Agnietenkapel, the cradle of the Amsterdam University.

The best way to discover a city is to people-watch, and if you need a break from sightseeing, head for one of the modern "grand cafés". **De Jaren** (Nieuwe Doelenstraat 20), has the most popular outdoor terraces in town. There is a salad bar at lunch, and at dinner a reading table, with English periodicals. But, for more elegance and intimacy, opt for the **Grand Hotel Westin Demeure** (Oudezijds Voorburgwal 197). A century ago it was the City Hall, and a century before that a hostelry for distinguished travellers. Transformed into a five-star hotel in 1992, it's a good spot for lunch or afternoon tea.

The Jordaan

With its bouquet of streets named after flowers and plants, the Jordaan is probably derived from the French word *jardin* (garden). This French connection has been present since Huguenot refugees settled here in 1685, but the Jordaan's history dates back to the preceding century. Then, the city was bounded by the Singel canal and the Jordaan – outside the city walls – was a district inhabited by immigrants and the lower classes. Many of the early residents were employed to dig Amsterdam's great concentric canal system in 1607. As a mere suburb, the Jordaan was outside the city's jurisdiction and prey to property speculators, resulting in diverse architectural styles and standards.

Entertaining street theatre around the city's Rokin district.

BELOW: East Indies Company headquarters.

By the 19th century, the Jordaan housed the city's industrial working class and was a hotbed of political activism. With 83,000 people living in this cramped district, protests and strikes were frequent, provoking the Netherlands' first asphalt road programme – the original cobbles had been thrown at Queen Wilhelmina during an official visit in the 1930s. In the 1970s, the district was given a major face-lift and began to attract professionals as well as arty and "alternative" Amsterdammers. With property prices on the increase and rent control on the decrease, a good portion of the Jordanese population was forced to relocate to newly developed areas outside of Amsterdam, such as Almere. This area to the west of Dam square is a tight grid of narrow streets bounded by Brouwersgracht, Prinsengracht, Rozengracht and Lijnbaansgracht.

Jordaan North, the area above Westerstraat, is a maze of small alleys, quiet restaurants and thriving workshops and retains many of its working-class roots. The North has many "true" Jordaaners, independent-minded students, crafts and trades people born and bred in the quarter. **Jordaan South**, situated below Westerstraat, is more gentrified, with highly individualistic shops on delightful side streets adjacent to the larger canals and a variety of renowned brown cafés. For generations, the Jordaan was a humble, working class neighbourhood, but the now-popular streets surrounding the canals, known as the grachtengordel (canal girdle) have been sadly "yuppified" in recent years, sending property prices sky high. But it still retains much of its atmosphere.

Specific routes through the Jordaan are unnecessary since its appealing canals and geometric alleys entice strollers to abandon fixed plans and instead fall into the nearest brown café, book store, art gallery or trendy shop. Apart from mandatory visits to the Westerkerk and the Anne Frank Huis, which are technically on the edge of the Jordaan, aimless wandering is the order of the day.

Outdoor life

Starting from the hectic Leidseplein, head into central Amsterdam along Leidsestraat and turn left at Prinsengracht. Soon you will cross Leidsegracht and (five streets beyond, on the left) you will reach **Looiersgracht**. At the first sign of sunshine hitting the city's streets, locals bring their chairs out into the roadways or, those lucky enough, sit sunning themselves on balconies. The low-key Café de Chaos (bearing no resemblance to its name) on Looiersgracht typifies the city's laid-back atmosphere.

Just north of Looiersgracht, **Elandsgracht** is best known for its idiosyncratic indoor market (the Looier), a mass of stalls selling anything from 1950s memorabilia to handmade pottery, old dolls and toys; but there are no great bargains to be had here. If you subscribe to the adage "you get what you pay for", however, take a stroll down the Oude Spiegelstraat, Amsterdam's antiques row, where discerning antiquaries do business. (See the Museum District, *page 148*). **Lauriergracht**, the next real canal north, has gabled houses towards the eastern end, but avoid the seedier **Lijnbaansgracht**, at the opposite end, where African music blares out at night from tatty-looking bars well decorated with "no dealing" signs.

TIP

The Jordaan is perfect for meandering around Wander at will, and when you tire of its picturesque streets, drop into one of its many trendy shops, brown cafés or bookshops.

BELOW: shopping for mementoes.

Character traits

Continue along Prinsengracht and across the hectic Rozengracht, with its variety of shops, unique ethnic bakeries and *trâiteurs* (from Turkish to Spanish) and several modern furniture galleries. Look skyward and you will see the familiar spire that is the landmark of the Westerkerk (West Church). The small canals and streets radiating from the Westerkerk are distinctly chic and occasionally over-restored. Even so, the neighbourhood remains eclectic, and attractions around here range from the elegant Christophe restaurant to cosy lunch rooms, minimalist architects' studios and second-hand bookshops.

The **Westerkerk ❶**, which dates back to 1630 and was renovated in 1990, is the city's finest church, a masterpiece in Dutch Renaissance style by the talented father and son, Hendrick and Pieter de Keyser. Its soaring spire, the highest in the city at 85 metres (275 feet), is crowned by a glinting yellow and blue crown, a reminder of former Habsburg rule. The view from the tower stretches to the Rijksmuseum in the south; to the harbour in the north. Anne Frank's house bordered the Prinsengracht and she described Westerkerk's carillon chimes in her diary. Today you can still hear them toll on the hour and there are occasional outbursts of a popular or classic refrain, depending on the occasion.

Compared with the Oude Kerk, the Westerkerk's interior is slightly disappointing, but its popularity with tourists is secured by the fact that Rembrandt's grave was discovered here during excavations. Classical music concerts are held on certain days (Monument Day, for instance). If you are feeling energetic, the view across Amsterdam from the tower is remarkable. Look for the statue of Anne Frank on the square near the entrance to the church and, if you want a snack, there are several stands selling herring and Dutch *frites*, known as *patat*.

Map on pages 124–5

LEFT: converted warehouses.
BELOW: Amsterdam's colourful face.

Anne Frank

On Monday 6 July 1942, Anne Frank accompanied her family into the Achterhuis (the back annexe) of Prinsengracht 263. In February 1941, the Nazis had begun their first round-up of Jews in Amsterdam. Otto Frank was already planning an escape. Forced by the Germans to leave his prosperous business, he was still able to prepare several rooms on the top floors and back of Prinsengracht 263, a combined warehouse and office, as a secret hiding place.

The safety of his family and four other Jews was to hinge on a swinging cupboard concealing the stairs to the back portion of the building. Otto Frank had planned to disappear on 16 July but on 5 July a deportation order for his daughter Margot arrived. At 7.30 am the next day the Frank family made their way to 263 with another family.

Anne Frank's record of life in their secret refuge is remarkable, not just as a diary of a Jewish family in hiding, but as a record of the intellectual growth of a young girl already blessed with obvious literary talents, as she passes through her formative adolescent years under fearful circumstances. As you turn the pages, it is her steadily maturing mind that proves to be the real source of interest behind her narrative.

The second entry of her diary could have been written by any 13-year-old. She writes: "I had my birthday on Sunday afternoon. We showed a film *The Lighthouse Keeper* with *Rin-Tin-Tin*, which my school friends thoroughly enjoyed. We had a lovely time." In July 1944 the same diarist, now 15, wrote: "It is a great wonder that I have not given up all my expectations because they seem absurd and unfeasible. But I still cling to them, despite everything, because I still believe in the inner goodness of humanity. It's absolutely impossible for me to base everything on death, suffering and confusion."

Just 20 days later the refugees in the annexe were discovered by the Gestapo and sent to concentration camps. Only Anne's father Otto returned. Anne Frank died at Bergen-Belsen in March 1945 aged 15, only three weeks before a British battalion arrived to liberate it. Her diary had been left behind among old books, magazines and newspapers lying on the floor and recovered by Miep Gies, one of the family's helpers.

A complete version of the diary was published several years ago. Of the many mature and perceptive passages written during the last weeks she spent in hiding, the most famous quotes come from the final paragraphs of her entry for 15 July. Ironically, three months previously, on 4 April, she had written: "I want to live on after my death." With over 52 translations of her book reaching millions of people, she has achieved the immortality she desired.

Frank's spirit provides the key to the real significance of Prinsengracht 263. The Anne Frank Huis is more than a place where a world-famous diary was penned. It is both a living monument to all those who were victims of racism, fascism and anti-Semitism in World War II and a warning to the modern world that intolerance and racial violence are still with us. ❑

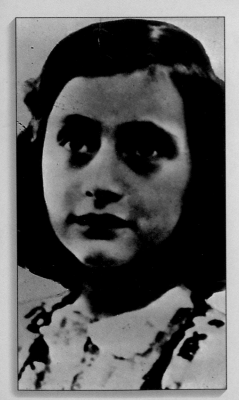

LEFT: Anne Frank.

Map
on pages
124–5

In remembrance

Beside the Westerkerk is the **Homo-Monument**, a sleek flight of marble stairs leading into the canal, although you have to be looking to spot it. This new memorial commemorates homosexuals who died in the Nazi camps, or suffered persecution in the past.

For an insight into life in Amsterdam during the Occupation, visit the **Anne Frank Huis ❶** (263 Prinsengracht, tel: 020-556 7100; open 9am–7pm daily; Apr–Sept: 9am–9pm, closed 1 Jan and Jewish hols; entrance fee). From 1942 to 1944, the Frank family hid in a secret attic annexe and were sustained by helpers who provided them with food bought on the black market. In 1944, German police raided the house and discovered their hideout. They deported the entire Frank family, first to the transit camp at Westerbork, and then to Auschwitz and Bergen-Belsen. The Anne Frank Huis is usually at the top of most visitor lists. After a renovation and expansion in 1999, visiting conditions have been vastly improved, as has the interpretation of Frank's diary. With the addition of an adjacent building, there is now extra space for temporary exhibitions, as well as for the Educational Department, multi-media resource centre, bookstore and café. (See page opposite)

A statue of Anne Frank outside her former house.

Gather your thoughts by crossing Prinsengracht and retreating to the Jordaan proper. Beyond Egelantiersgracht turn left and look for the 17th-century almshouse court in Eerste Egelantiers Dwarsstraat. Known as the **Claes Claesz Anslo Hofje**, these beautifully restored houses offer fine examples of step, spout and neck gables. On neighbouring Egelantiersgracht is the Café't Smalle, a cosy brown café said to be one of Amsterdam's oldest. During summer months many boats pull up to its outdoor landing and join the terrace crowd. Smoking and drinking have been part of the Jordaan's charm since the 17th century. The description of the stereotypical Dutchman at the time, quoted by Simon Schama, could well apply to a dying breed of Jordaaner: "Barrel-shaped in girth, sozzled with gin, he is often seen lighting the next pipe with the smouldering embers of the last." Looking around at some of the café folk and imagining them minus their modern atttire, many could have stepped out of a period painting.

BELOW: perfect for a leisurely stroll.

Quiet courtyards

If hidden almshouses appeal, the Jordaan district is the right place to be, however, due to too many visitors disturbing the peaceful ambience, doors tend to remain locked. If they happen to be open, do tread quietly and respect the inhabitants. From Claes Claesz. Anslo, a short walk northwards along the Prinsengracht takes you to Zon's Hofje at Nos. 157–171 and the Van Bienen Hofje at Nos. 89–133.

Stemming from the early Dutch Republic's belief in the virtue of personal charity, such almshouses nowadays represent the institutionalised form, but nevertheless manage to retain a tangible spirituality. A short walk across Prinsengracht leads to the **Noordermarkt**, and Hendrick de Keyser's last great church, the Noorderkerk, built in 1620 and remodelled in 1998. En route, visitors may be distracted by cafés and stylish shops along the Prinsenstraat.

Health fiends will enjoy the Saturday farmer's market.

Approaching the Noorderkerk the atmosphere becomes more laid-back Jordaan than upmarket chic. In summer, several festivals are held here, and on Mondays and Saturday mornings this friendly square is home to a market. The Monday flea market sells everything from fabric and sewing items to books, toys, tools and ethnic snacks, while Saturdays feature a popular farmer's market which specialises in organic produce, natural breads, grains and other health-oriented products. Adjacent is a small flea market offering second-hand clothes, vinyl records, books and ethnic jewellery. Attracting a lively crowd of shoppers, street musicians and curious tourists, it should not be missed.

On market Mondays and Saturdays the long queue on the corner will doubtless be outside the Winkel lunch café, famed for its apple tart, baked on the premises and served warm with whipped cream. *Ah,wat lekker!*

Peaceful moments

The dignified **Noorderkerk** Ⓚ (North Church) stands aloof from surrounding chaos. Like the Westerkerk, this church is owned by the state and renovations have at last been completed following a fund-raising initiative; the official reopening was honoured by Queen Beatrix. Organ concerts are now held throughout the year. The building itself is notable for its subdued atmosphere and stark statue outside. In keeping with such a radical area, this statue of chained figures is a monument to the Jordaanoproer 1934, the Jordaan unemployment riots during the Depression years. "The strongest chains are those of unity," reads the moving inscription.

BELOW: food finds at Noordermarkt.

Jordaaners still commemorate the uprising every year with poems, posters and floral tributes. On the church itself is a memorial to another significant event in

local history. A sign commemorates the 400 local Jews who were deported as a reprisal for the killing of a single Dutch Nazi-sympathiser during a street battle.

From the Noorderkerk, myriad escapes lead to the measured, bourgeois calm of **Prinsengracht**; the elegant clusters of typical façades range from grey to ice-cream pink. Guessing the meaning of the gable stones provides an interesting game: Jesus and the fishes gives way to the three wise men, two turtle doves and finally to St Paul blowing a trumpet. Note the large hooks placed just below the gable on each and every home. Purely functional, these serve to transport furniture and other household goods by rope to and from the house when the inhabitants are relocating. Most front doors are painted a dark Amsterdam green – a colour chosen long ago (though not 100 percent mandatory) for its compatibility with the colour of the canal water.

Map on pages 124–5

Water walks

From the Prinsengracht, the choice is yours. Walking east leads to **Keizersgracht** and **Herengracht**, the grander grachtengordel canals. Alternatively, continuing north along the Prinsengracht leads to an entirely different cityscape. The **maritime quarter**, beginning at the Haarlemmerstraat, and bordered by the parallel Brouwersgracht (brewer's canal), with its picturesque old converted warehouses (*pakhuizen*), is unquestionably one of Amsterdam's most picturesque canals. The long Haarlemmerstraat is filled with small shops and restaurants, and an intimate cinema, appropriately called The Movies.

But for those who love bohemian Jordaan, the decision is easy: lunch at a popular *eetcafé* like Café de Tuin (Tweede Tuindwaarstraat 13) or Café de Prins (Prinsengracht 124), or dinner in Jordaan North (perhaps near Westerstraat) at a simple ethnic restaurant. Choose from a variety of cuisines, including Spanish tapas, Greek, Italian, Indian or seafood.

It is inexcusable to leave the Jordaan before discovering a final brown café. On Lindengracht, De Kat in de Wijngaert offers classical or blues music from their extensive CD collection. For a more eclectic clientele, the owners of De Doffer on Runstraat promise that "In the Jordaan, we serve tramps as well as lawyers." Here, you can, as the Amsterdammers say, "consume your days in smoke." But as Jacob Cats, the famous poet, used to say, "My kitchen is my pipe; my pouch a well-stocked larder; smoking is my drink. What need I then of wine?"

BELOW: still waters.

The grachtengordel

Each of Amsterdam's three main canals is approximately 3 km (2 miles) long, so it may not be an attractive proposition to walk the entire length of each one, although many enjoy the scenic stretch. As with the Jordaan, you can select small sections or, better still, simply follow your instinct. Since the waterways are not far apart, and are linked by side streets, it's easy to meander and switch between canals.

The **grachtengordel** canal network was created in the early 17th century to cater to a wealthier and expanding population. As these grand houses materialised, the merchant class gradually moved from the insalubrious Oude Zijds to the relative opulence of these new canals. The City Council imposed strict regulations to preserve the tone of the neighbourhoods: barrel-making was forbidden because of the noise; brewing was forbidden because of the bad smell; and sugar refining was out of the question as it posed a severe fire hazard. But trade was not excluded altogether: these steep-roofed houses were also intended to double as warehouses, with storage space in the attics and basements. Taxes were levied according to the size of the frontage, a system which often encouraged ostentation and vulgarity. The maximum permissable width was 10 metres (30 ft) but the depth could extend to 60 metres (190 ft).

Gable styles

If these canal houses remain special today it is largely for their decorative gables. The old-fashioned pointed or spout gable was gradually replaced by the simpler step gable, while in the 1630s the gracious neck gable became fashionable and remained so until the mid-17th century. From about 1660 onwards, the flowing bell gable was popular but, in grander houses, was superseded by the Italian style straight or triangular cornice. By the end of the Golden Age, the most ostentatious patrician houses had broad pedimented façades decorated in neoclassical style with garlands or extravagant sculptures.

The grandest of these 17th-century mansions were built with a warehouse in the basement, lavish reception rooms on the ground floor and, above, a dining room and banqueting room. Inventories from the time describe Persian silk furnishings, Turkish rugs, Japanese lacquerware, Venetian or ebony-framed mirrors as well as oil paintings or alabaster statues in most rooms. All in all, the

The façades of 17th-century gabled houses were decorated with heraldic motifs, or other religious or self-promotional devices. Typical designs feature coats of arms, trade signs, mythological animals, cherubs or Biblical scenes.

BELOW: Magna Plaza (shopping gallery) in the restored former post office.

greatest houses outshone even the *palazzi* of Venice – in a Republic which claimed to put virtue before gold! Although they might not have the best interiors, the **Museum Willet-Holthuysen** on Herengracht 605 and **Museum Van Loon** at Keizersgracht 672 are fine examples of 17th- and 18th-century stylish burghers' households.

Walks along the three concentric canals reveal significant differences in style. **Prinsengracht** (the Prince's Canal) is perhaps the humblest of the three, with a greater number of warehouses. **Keizersgracht** (the Emperor's Canal) is the most approachable and varied waterway, especially the stretch of renovated gables near No. 324. To Amsterdammers, however, **Herengracht** (the Gentlemen's Canal) is the undoubted star. The stretch between **Brouwersgracht** and **Raadhuisstraat** has a number of fine warehouses as well as the Bartolotti mansion (Nos. 170–172), a Renaissance cascade of decoration. The east bank, from Huidenstraat to Leidsestraat, provides the greatest variety of gables spanning Renaissance and classical styles.

But it's the elegant **Golden Bend** section, between Leidsestraat and Vijzelstraat, that Amsterdammers most admire. There is much to enjoy in the quirky sculptural details and gables decorated with dolphins or mermaids. Outsiders might find this stretch a vain exercise in grandeur. Great double-fronted mansions, once the residences of wealthy merchants, compete with each other in size, while a sumptuous copy of a classical Loire château (380 Herengracht), its gables and windows embellished with reclining figures, cherubs and various mythical characters, dwarfs the adjoining Renaissance gables. Most of these mansions are now austere hotels, offices and banks, and one of them is the residence of Amsterdam's *burgemeester*, or Mayor.

Map on pages 124–5

BELOW: 17th-century bell gables.

The Amsterdammers have kindly lined the route with benches from which to admire the view; so, if you question their choice of vantage points, do so quietly, in the privacy of a brown café.

Taking it easy at Amsterdam's new Museumplein.

The Museum District

For art lovers, the real centre of Amsterdam is **Museumplein** ◗, situated to the southwest of the canal circle's Golden Bend, in an area known as the Old South. With the recent redevelopment of the new Museumplein, Amsterdam has acquired a new public space which links its three major museums and the century-old Concertgebouw concert hall. Grassy areas will extend uninterrupted, offering a pleasant refuge for relaxation. A large pond is planned at the side of the Rijksmuseum for winter skating, and cultural events will continue to take place on site, including the Uitmarkt theatre festival every August. Although hundreds of trees were chopped down to accommodate a new underground car park for some 600 cars, the controversy over this project might just turn into contentment over the next few years.

For a different type of relaxation, there is the popular **Vondelpark**, a year-round refuge for joggers, cyclists, dog walkers and skaters where lively concerts and dance events are held in summer. Visit the Filmmuseum and the popular Café Vertigo with its happening summer terrace.

Avid shoppers may prefer a stroll along P. C. Hooftstraat, the choicest designer street in town, though it's nothing special compared with other European capitals. Your money is better spent on the **Spiegelgracht**, the city's antiques shopping centre, where each shop resembles a mini-museum. Asian antiquities, old Dutch tiles, Art Deco objects, Russian icons and pewter are just some of the spe-

BELOW: beauty at dusk: the Rijksmuseum.

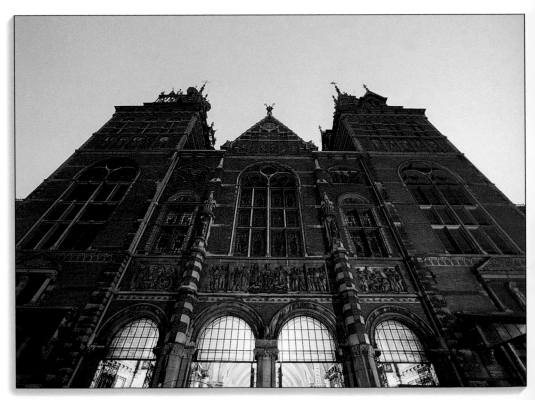

cialities here. Feel free to browse and don't be intimidated by the grandeur. The proprietors are friendly and helpful. If you fancy a break there are some good cafés and a pancake house.

Modern art

The **Stedelijk Museum** (13 Paulus Potterstraat, tel: 020-573 2911; open 11am–5pm daily, closed pub. hols; entrance fee) specialises in modern art, from the mid-19th century to contemporary. Foreign highlights include works by Chagall, Braque and the German Expressionists, as well as many new names from the USA and UK. For a Dutch flavour, however, Mondrian and Karel Appel are outstanding, as are contemporary artists like Jan Dibbets, Ren Daniels and Stanley Brouwn. Exhibits from the permanent collection are constantly changing, so if you come looking for your favourite Picasso, don't be surprised to find a Matisse in its place.

The Stedelijk is waiting for approval to proceed with extensive restoration of the old building and the addition of two new wings, one to house a permanent collection of 20th-century art. The project was designed by Portuguese architect Siza, and sometime around late 2001 or early 2002 the museum will be temporarily closed so that the building work can be completed.

Note that the Mondrian collection in The Hague is even more comprehensive, and the focus on Appel, Constant and Corneille, members of the celebrated COBRA movement, has been shifted to the new COBRA **Museum** in Amstelveen. Take tram 5 to the end of the line and visit the modern building filled with the work of these experimental painters who, by breaking away from constructions of traditional art, proved to be ahead of their time.

The **Van Gogh Museum** 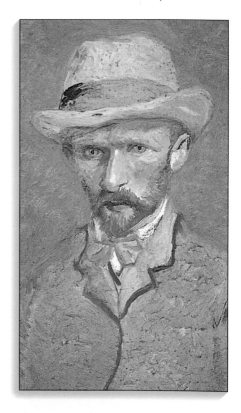 (7 Paulus Potterstraat, tel: 020-570 5200; open 10am–6pm daily; entrance fee), next door to the Stedelijk, completed an extensive renovation and saw the addition of a striking new wing in 1999. Almost double the size, and with major improvements to the facilities, including air-conditioning and better lighting, it is like a new museum.

The existing building, designed by the Dutch architect Gerrit Rietveld, remains devoted to the permanent collection of works by Van Gogh and other 19th-century artists. The new wing, designed by Japanese architect Kisho Kurokawa, is being used exclusively for changing exhibitions. With its austere style, inspired by geometric elements such as cones, ovals and squares, and its titanium roof and side wall, the building gives a very firm nod to the 21st century. The use of natural stone on the curved gable is also an original gesture. A tranquil pond makes a strong Zen statement and serves as a resting place between the two buildings, linking old with new.

The permanent collection, at once chronological and thematic, is, like Van Gogh's art, eminently approachable. The main focus is on Van Gogh's development, from his dark landscapes painted in the Dutch provinces of Noord-Brabant and Drenthe, to his light-strewn Parisian Impressionist phase, and finally to the climax of his life's work in the visionary Mediterranean atmosphere at Arles.

Map on pages 124–5

The Van Gogh Museum has almost doubled in size following an extensive renovation. Its new wing is a showpiece for changing exhibitions.

BELOW: Van Gogh self-portrait.

BELOW:
Zuiderkerk and the redeveloped Jewish quarter.

Packed with treasures

Compared with the simplicity of the previous museum, the **Rijksmuseum** ❶ (42 Stadhouderskade, tel: 020-674 7000; open 10am–5pm daily; entrance fee) needs more guidance. The Van Gogh Museum, representing the artistic development of a maverick genius, is self-explanatory and not specific to Amsterdam's cultural past (although the new wing is very much a fixture of the present and future). The Rijksmuseum, however, is a vast, unwieldy collection which draws much of its inspiration from the city itself.

Concentrate on the Dutch Masters – unless you wish to follow one of the Museum's thematic walks, such as "still life" or "paintings as narrative". Time permitting, there is also the renovated Dutch History collection, a vast sweep from the Middle Ages to 1945, and Painting: 18th-19th Century, a glance at Dutch Impressionism and the schools of Amsterdam and The Hague. The main course, however, has to be the 17th-century Golden Age.

The greatest paintings are on the top floor, and masterpieces are signalled by dutiful crowds of bored schoolchildren and attentive tour groups listening to guides. Luckily, if you avoid the scramble to see *The Nightwatch*, the great works of Frans Hals, Jan Steen, Pieter de Hooch, Jacob van Ruisdael and Vermeer can be enjoyed in relative peace, as can the works of 15th- and 16th-century painters such as the Master of Alkmaar (Room 202).

Jan Steen (Rooms 216–219) is a genre painter whose work humorously captures the lower orders at play. Steen's *The Morning Toilet* is full of sexual innuendo, while in *The Merry Family,* even the baby looks drunk. Adriaen van Ostade (Room 218) also has a nice line in revellers. Pieter de Hooch (Room 221) is the undoubted master of Dutch interiors, usually with a door left open to shed a homely light on the scene. But his paintings also offer moral comfort, even if, as in *Maternal Duties*, it is only a mother consoling her child after a punishment. There are also four masterpieces by Vermeer here.

As far as 17th-century painting is concerned, even the lesser Masters deserve to captivate. Van de Valkaert (Rooms 206 and 208), for instance, is one of many to see beyond the sobriety of the black-clad burghers, militia or City Regents; the sombre cloth or stance is used to direct one's eye to the expressiveness of the faces. Even so, with the exception of Rembrandt, Dutch painters tend to rehearse the same litany of facial expressions, from circumspect to careworn, complacent to vain, virtuous to lascivious. Morality is never far away in 17th-century Dutch painting.

A sense of place

Many painters, though, looked to place rather than people for spiritual and emotional values. Portraiture was, after all, the most conservative of genres: if it failed to please the sitter, the painter had no future. Pieter Saenredam's cool church interiors are deeply truthful, while Vermeer's street scenes (Rooms 207 and 210) are luminous, vibrant and absorbing. The brooding Dutch landscape is exposed by Jacob van Ruisdael (Rooms 217 and 218); his variants on lowering sky, boat, mill and man have rarely been bet-

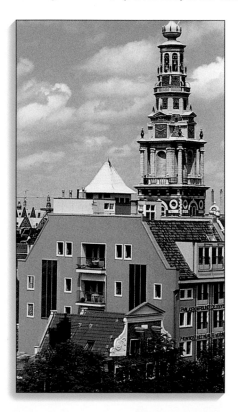

tered. The Dutch seascapes are almost as atmospheric but tend to be overladen with too much battle narrative for modern tastes.

Naturally, Rembrandt's *The Nightwatch* dominates the Gallery of Honour but, after admiring the scope and scale of the group composition, return to the more intimate portraits. His 1629 *chiaroscuro* self-portrait is deeply expressive, as are his portraits of Maria Trip, his son, his mother, and his wife, Saskia.

Jodenbuurt (old Jewish quarter)

Admirers of Rembrandt's work might like to visit the remains of Amsterdam's Jewish quarter, where the artist lived for much of his life. The Jodenbuurt (sometimes called Jodenhoek) stretches east of the Dam and waterfront area. Even though the quarter has been sadly neglected and, in recent years, partly demolished, the indomitable Jewish spirit seeps through the ruins.

From the Centraal Station, an intriguing walk leads southeast to Rembrandt's House and the Jewish Historical Museum on Jonas Daniel Meijerplein. The quickest route is via sleazy Zeedijk but far safer would be to take Tram 9 or the metro to Nieuwmarkt or Waterlooplein. If arriving by metro, look at the demolition ball on display inside the station. A reminder of the wanton destruction of this area, it's a typically Dutch indulgence in self-mortification.

Gem selecting at one of Amsterdam's diamond factories.

Jewish migrants

By the 17th century, up to 10 percent of Amsterdammers were Sephardic Jews from Spain and Portugal who, although relatively prosperous and well-integrated, were not allowed to join trade guilds. They worked in the cloth, tobacco, sugar or book industries. From 1620 waves of poorer Ashkenazic Jews from Poland and Germany settled in the east of town and, unable to speak Dutch, turned to menial ghetto jobs around St Antoniesbreestraat. Still, in polyglot Amsterdam, it was possible to be at once an insider and an outsider. Poet Andrew Marvell recorded this religious melting pot in the 17th century: "Hence Amsterdam, Turk-Christian-Pagan-Jew/Staple of sects and mint of schism, grew."

By 1900, 95 percent of the residents in this area were Jewish and played a visible role in Dutch society until World War II. However, between 1940 and 1945, the area became a sealed ghetto (the Joodse Wijk) and over 70,000 Jews, 90 percent of the Jewish population, met their deaths in Auschwitz, Sobibor or Bergen-Belsen. About 25,000 Jews now live in Amsterdam, once known as the "Jerusalem of the West".

St Antoniesbreestraat is now a shadow of its colourful self. Even so, amongst the shoddy modern buildings peer several original gables and even a Jewish bakery. Although it is still a working-class area, many new residents include an international "alternative" crowd, often congregating in the trendy Tisfris café, or the Café Dantzig at the nearby Opera house.

At No. 69 is the **De Pinto House**, once owned by a Portuguese merchant but now a public library. After admiring the decorative scrollwork around the windows, glance inside at the elaborate painted ceiling.

BELOW: Jewish Historical Museum.

The authentic 17th-
century interior of
the Portuguese
Synagogue, where
services are still held
by candlelight, is
worth a look. Do not
be deterred by a
locked door: persistent
knocking brings
results.

BELOW: stained
glass section of
Rijksmuseum by
Hendrick de Keyser.

Urban renewal

Just over the road is one of Hendrick de Keyser's famous gateways, surmounted by a skull and crossbones. It leads to another de Keyser masterpiece, the **Zuiderkerk** (South Church). Its elegant spire valiantly tries to rise above the ugliness of the surrounding "nieuwbouw" (new housing) but a sense of desolation hangs stubbornly in the air. Even though the church is currently a "centre for urban renewal", it will forever be associated with Jewish misery. In 1945 it was turned into a temporary morgue for Jews killed in Nazi raids.

St Antoniesbreestraat crosses the **Oude Schans** by means of a windswept bridge. On the near side is a quaint lock-keeper's house and a cluster of gabled houses; on the far side, the rambling BIMhuis, Amsterdam's premier jazz club, brings life to the canal during every season but summer. To the right of the bridge, the edges of Waterlooplein market spill over the quayside and it is worth taking a stroll through the surrounding neighbourhood and exploring the quaint Staalstraat, with its welcoming cafés and bookshops.

Jodenbreestraat takes over from St Antoniesbreestraat but the only vestige of its 17th-century self is the **Rembrandt House Museum** (4 Jodenbreestraat, tel: 020-520 0400; open Mon–Sat 10am–5pm, Sun 1-5pm; entrance fee). The painter lived here from 1639 to 1660, until bankruptcy forced him to move. The recently restored mansion which has doubled the museum space, contains over 250 of his drawings and etchings, including a portrait of Jan Six, one of Rembrandt's patrons. In painting his patron as a refined art lover, instead of the ostentatious merchant that he was, Rembrandt won a permanent place in the magnificent Six Collection (closed to the public). Van Gogh, Vermeer and Rembrandt continue to be the Netherland's most beloved, as well as most famous, painters. Among the best works in the Rembrandt House are the sensitive portraits of his wife Saskia and his homely portrayals of beggars, barrel-organ players and a rat-catcher. The trades have moved elsewhere, but Rembrandt's physiognomies are recognisable in the faces of present-day Amsterdammers. The museum's admission fee includes a visit to the Holland Experience, a 25-minute multimedia trip through the Netherlands.

Diamonds and dockers

From here, make a brief sortie into **Uilenburg**, formerly a maze of back alleys and sweat shops. The building on the right was the Boas diamond-polishing works, a major source of employment for Jews in the 19th century. Today, it is the site of the **Gassan Diamond Factory** (Nieuwe Uilenbergerstraat 173) and visitors are welcome, preferably by appointment.

Jodenbreestraat peters out in chaotic Mr Visserplein but it is worth negotiating the traffic hazards to see Mari Andriessen's posturing statue of a docker. De Dokwerker commemorates the round-up of 425 Jews in February 1941. The event provoked a general strike, led by the dockworkers, in which outraged Amsterdammers expressed solidarity with their fellow citizens using the slogan: "Keep your dirty hands off our rotten Jews". The short-lived strike was a unique protest against Nazi inhumanity in Occupied Europe. On the far side of the traffic island is the **Portuguese Synagogue** (open Sun–Fri 10am–4pm, except for Jewish holidays) which, in the 1670s, had the distinction of being the largest synagogue in the world. Originally a "clandestine" synagogue, it had the same status as the "secret" Catholic churches.

On Jonas Daniel Meijerplein, just opposite the synagogue, is the **Jewish Historical Museum ®**, (open daily 11am–5pm, except on Yom Kippur). housed in a complex of four former Ashkenazic synagogues. Beginning in the domed New Synagogue, the exhibition traces the spread of Judaism through the Netherlands from its humble beginnings to the years of prestige in the 18th century, and finally to the decimation of the community during the Holocaust. The displays are fascinating and extremely touching. Highlights include an 18th-century Ark, the ritual baths and wartime memorabilia. (Unfortunately, although there is a leaflet in English, exhibits are only labelled in Dutch.) The gift shop offers an interesting selection of books and Judaica. If it does not seem too irreverent amidst a record of so much suffering, call in at the Kosher Café for a sandwich or a slice of cheesecake before leaving.

By St Antoniesbreestraat is a statue of a turtle, representing Time and its loss for the Jewish community. Towards the newly extended Artis Zoological Gardens, Botanical Gardens and **Plantage Middenlaan**, is a prosperous 19th-century Jewish neighbourhood, where doorways are occasionally adorned with pelicans. According to Jewish legend, the pelican will, in adversity, feed its starving young with its own blood. More positively, let your eye run over the Portuguese names that still speak of Jewish blood in the quarter: the Coelho, Quendo and d'Oliveira families have all returned to the nest. ❏

Map on pages 124–5

BELOW: plenty of bargains can be had in the flea markets.

HET TWISKE RECREATIONAL PARK

To the north of Amsterdam, between Zaanstad and Purmerend, lie the recreational parklands known as Het Twiske, which takes its name from the river Twisck, a tributary of the River Wormer.

This vast park has something for everyone, be they fisherman, sailor, diver, swimmer, cyclist or ornithologist. If fishing or bird watching proves too strenuous, one can always set up a barbecue or picnic in one of many designated areas. The landscape came into being as a result of centuries of turf-cutting, and more recently sand quarrying, which left a lake with many islands. Eventually it was converted into a multiple-use recreational area. It is not uncommon to see Scottish Highland cattle and Shetland ponies grazing in the meadows amongst the splendid and sometimes rare flora and fauna. With so much water, it is a logical location for a sailing school where sailing craft, canoes and rowing boats can be hired.

In keeping with its natural charms motorised craft are banned. By far the most pleasant way to get there from Amsterdam is by bicycle from the back of Centraal Station, with a free ferry crossing to Amsterdam North, around 12 km (7½) round trip. The route is well-marked. For further information, tel: 075-684 4338. The parklands never seem crowded, so you are almost guaranteed a peaceful day.

BROWN CAFES, GRAND CAFES, AND YOUR CAFE

The Netherlands is big on cafés, and half the fun for visitors lies in wandering in and discovering for themselves the cafés' unique personalities

The Netherlands has a long café tradition. Some claim that the first bar, euphemistically called café, opened its doors in Amsterdam in the 13th century, when two men and a dog in a boat drifted ashore on the marshy banks of the (then) river IJ. By the 17th century, there were countless taverns in Amsterdam, which slowly and surely would extend to other cities. Dutch cafés have as much cultural value as museums and a visit to one is essential.

Traditional brown cafés (so-called because walls and ceilings have turned brown from age and smoke) are identified by dark, cosy, wooden interiors. The only audible sound is the buzz of lively conversation and the tinkle of glasses being rinsed. Coffee is generally brewed, not machine made, and if you fancy a snack to go with your beer or spirit, there is usually a plate of olives or cheese. These cafés define the Dutch word *gezelligiheid*, which means state of cosiness or conviviality. This is where locals come for a few beers after work, to play cards, engage in political debates and tell tall tales.

The more elegant and stylish grand cafés serve lunch and desserts and tend to have high ceilings, more light, reading tables and a variety of music. There are also cafés where you can play chess, throw darts, or play pool or billiards. There are men's cafés, women's cafés and even night cafés, which close around 5am. Remember that the Dutch take pride in speaking English, so there should be no loss for conversation, if desired.

▷ **CAFÉ LIFE BEGINS HERE**
Warm weather offers the perfect excuse to sit on a bar or café terrace and sip a beer in the sunshine with friends.

WHAT'S THE ALTERNATIVE?

◁ **GREENHOUSE EFFECT**
There are cafés to suit one's every mood, including those offering "space cake". But don't over-do it on an empty or jet-lagged stomach.

△ **LIVING ROOM**
Local, or brown cafés, remain a strong tradition. Serving as a type of living room, for some they offer a home away from home.

Hash cafés attract their own mellow public, and most tourists who fancy a walk on the wild side place a visit to a hash coffee shop at the top of their itinerary. Although the police have clamped down in recent years, due to a rise in "hard" drug selling, you won't have to look too far to find one. Alternative cafés attract their own clientele by hanging green and white placards in the window to distinguish themselves from regular ones. These placards have replaced many of the marijuana leaf logos and Bob Marley imagery.

Other cafés which have opened in recent years, include those known as "energy" or "smart drug" cafés, which sell psychedelic mushrooms and mood-enhancing drugs made of natural ingredients.

And for those hooked on the Internet, there are plenty of cyber cafés throughout the Netherlands where you can sip coffee while communicating via the Internet.

◁ **HANGING OUT**
The hectic but lively Leidseplein remains a popular haunt for locals as well as tourists, particularly during the the alfresco summer period.

△ **SOCIAL OR SOLITARY**
In a densely populated city like Amsterdam, the café is often regarded as a solitary retreat where one can read or sit in peace.

A NIGHT OUT

A night on the tiles should be the highlight of every Amsterdam itinerary. But where to go? There's something for everyone, and the only difficulty lies in choosing from a vast array of options

Map on pages 124–5

Amsterdam

There's a local saying decreeing: "The café is my church" – a tribute to the conviviality of café life. In this city, an intimate bar can take precedence over a sophisticated night at the opera or ballet. That said, what may start as an after-work drink in a *proeflokaal* (tasting house) can end hours later on the dance floor of a converted warehouse on the far side of town. An evening often begins with a *borreltje* (small glass) of spirits in somewhere cosy like De Drie Fleschjes (Gravenstraat 18) or Papaneiland (Prinsengracht 2). Customers must be prepared to follow custom by leaning over the bar, hands clasped behind their backs, to slurp down the first glass of spirits.

There are around 1,400 bars for alcoholic experimentation. The only difficulty is choosing between a *bruine kroeg* (brown café) or a designer bar. The most famous brown café is **Hoppe** (Spui 20), and not just because it sells more draught beer than any other bar. The smoke-stained interior is decorated with old paintings and threadbare Persian rugs, but the view is obscured by crowds of university students and businessmen in suits who have made Hoppe their home. Next door is its spiritual opposite, Luxembourg (Spui 22), a chic "white" café popular with yuppies. The absence of music, clutter and colour encourages the owners to call it "the brown café of the Nineties."

LEFT: the Herengracht canal meets the river Amstel at dusk. **BELOW:** dining out fashionably.

What to eat

Amsterdammers combat excessive drinking by eating, usually well before 9pm. Long-term residents complain that Amsterdam's cuisine is more limited than in most European capitals, but visitors are spoilt for choice. Amongst the 900 restaurants, exotic Indonesian fare, particularly the *rijsttafel*, offers a tasty variant on the sweet and sour theme. Many such restaurants are centred around the hectic Leidseplein, but are often over priced and mediocre. For a quieter, more authentic experience there is **Speciaal** (Nieuwe Leliestraat 142), with a diverse menu (including a vegetarian *rijsttafel*) served in a soothing setting of Indonesian raffia-work and prints. **Kantjil en De Tijger** on the Spuistraat 291 offers Indonesian fare in a trendy ambience.

As far as upmarket dining is concerned, Amsterdam is no longer under the spell of French cuisine and many of its best chefs have started looking East for inspiration, Elsewhere, the culinary high ground is captured by exquisite fish restaurants such as Lucius (Spuistraat 247) and D'Theeboom, a French-style bistro in a restored warehouse (10 Singel).

If in search of high culture, Amsterdammers often call in at the **Café Americain** (Leidseplein 28) to luxuriate in Art Nouveau splendour. From here, the next-door Stadsschouwburg (Leidseplein 26) is a convenient choice for a dance performance or English

play. This is alsoa venue for Dutch classical theatre and visiting theatre companies. Dine at the adjoining Café Cox, before or after the performance. Just a short walk or tram ride south of here, Amsterdam's major concert hall, the **Concertgebouw** (Van Baerlestraat 98), is home to one of the world's most respected orchestras. Free lunch-time rehearsal concerts can be booked the same morning.

Music and dance

Back towards the centre is the huge **Muziektheater** (Waterlooplein 22), the city's most controversial, and very costly, modern monument, and despite the presence of the reputable Netherlands National Ballet and Opera Company, many music lovers prefer a more subdued setting, including, perhaps, a concert by The Netherlands Philharmonic Orchestra in the Beurs van Berlage (former Stock Exchange on the Damrak) or a church organ recital in the mysterious Oude Kerk (Old Church) or tranquil Engelse Kerk (English Church, Begijnhof).

Amsterdam is equally proud of its reputation for cutting-edge pop and rock music. Although there is no major rock venue, the Melkweg entertainment complex (Lijnbaansgracht 234) remains a prime locationfor a blend of African bands, "alternative" discos and world music.

The **Melkweg** and its rival Paradiso (Weteringschans 6) are barely awake before 9pm, so there is time before the main gig to savour neighbourhood nightlife at its most exuberant. Paradiso offers more mainstream bands along with unknown up-and-coming acts. Drop in at Mulliner's Wijnlokaal (wine bar) at Lijnbaansgracht 266, to snack on tapas and perhaps catch some live music. The Maxim piano bar (Leidsekruisstraat 35) is a favourite with locals. Or if you're feeling lucky, visit the Holland Casino on the Max Euweplein, and take your passport.

BELOW:
Muziektheater.

If this is not your scene you can head east towards **Rembrandtplein** for gay clubs, burlesque and bondage shows, piano bars and disco madness. There's something for everyone, but the locals get restless the later it gets. Crowds in the streets around Rembrandtplein are game for anything, especially late at night when the disco crowd and piano bar clientele emerge. Beware of walking along deserted streets off the busy Leidseplein and Rembrandtplein late at night as tourists have been robbed of late. Take advantage of the taxi stands and stay street smart.

Stylish drinking

Style-conscious Amsterdammers turn their backs on such pedestrian neighbourhoods in favour of bohemian bars and *eetcafés*, often situated around the edge of red light districts or between canals. The hallmark of these designer bars is a slickness encapsulated by white marble interiors. Frascati (Nes 59, behind Rokin) and Blincker (Sint Barberenstraat 7) attract theatre-lovers, cabaret artistes and designers to nibble late-night snacks in spacious, mirrored interiors. A few streets further, La Strada (Nieuwezijds Voorburgwal), inspired by Fellini's film, proudly calls itself an Art Café. Apart from live music on Saturdays, there are regular art exhibitions, experimental plays and video shows. As the evening wears on, the jazz clubs warm up, not an easy feat considering their cold warehouse locations.

The newly restored BIMhuis (Oude Schans 73) is the city's major jazz and blues venue, but near Leidseplein there are also some small clubs including Café Alto (115 Korte Leidsedwaarsstraat), which has jam sessions during the week, and Bourbon St (6 Leidsedwaarsstraat). Currently most popular in the Amsterdam scene are Latin American, African and Middle Eastern music. Akhnaton (Nieuwezijdskolk 25) provides special evenings throught the month from "Les Nuits Africains" to salsa and tango extravaganzas.

Map on pages 124–5

After midnight

After midnight, Amsterdam's discos kick in. Escape (Rembrandtplein 10) attracts Amsterdammers of all ages and persuasions, while the Odeon (Singel 460) aspires to yuppified elegance in a gabled town house. The Arena youth hotel complex also has a popular disco (s' Gravesandsstraat 51). The Roxy burnt down in 1999 and the It club was closed down by the police for drug infractions. Sinners in Heaven (Wagenstraat 37) attracts a glamorous crowd and Dansen Bij Jansen (Handboogstraat 11) hosts a university crowd.

Jordaan's notorious "singing" brown cafés offer an equally frantic end to an evening, seeing the night out with hearty bonhomie and raucous sing-alongs. Not for those with a business appointment the following morning. For real night owls, there are late bars which stay open until 5am, including some that serve food into the night. Try Café de Koophandel (49 Bloemgracht) or P96, unsurprisingly at 96 Prinsengracht.

But, despite the best of intentions, a typical night on the town all too often ends in an alcoholic stupor. As the bartender claims in true Amsterdammer logic: "The second beer only has an effect after you've downed the fourth." ❑

BELOW: bars, clubs and cafés in Leidseplein.

Streetwise in the City

uriously, smaller Dutch cities tend to have relatively higher crime rates than Amsterdam. When asked about their notorious drugs problem, Amsterdammers shrug and say that it is no worse than in any other major city, only more public and sensationalised. Since the city's relatively successful battle against hard drugs, this half-hearted defence is almost true.

Contrary to popular belief *all* drugs are illegal, soft or hard, but in reality, police would never pursue anyone with less than 30g of soft drugs unless suspected of dealing. In the early 1990s the number of registered "coffee shops" was reduced from 750 to 250 to stem the tide of harder drug dealing, and to maintain the line between soft and hard drugs, thus making it easier for the authorities to observe and control. A registered coffee shop now displays a green

and white license plate in its window instead of the tell-tale cannabis-leaf logo. It cannot hold more than 500g of soft drugs in stock, or sell more than 5g per deal and the lower age limit is 18. In 1999 the ever popular 'It' disco was closed down because of drug-related evidence amassed by the HIT team; a combination of vice-squad, customs and tax officers.

Coffee shop names – and aromas – are a giveaway: Maloe-Meloe, Just a Puff and Extase continue to puff away peacefully. To avoid any misunderstanding, coffee shops often display "No dealing" or "No smoking" notices in English. Despite the efforts of the police, and assertions by the authorities to the contrary, Amsterdam remains a place where drugs are readily available. After midnight, the bridges off Warmoesstraat attract junkies and dealers, while Zwarte Handsteeg (Black Hand Alley) is as ominous as its name suggests. Beware of street dealers who invariably sell fake goods. Do not mistake a lack of sensationalism for an absence of danger: Thai Skunk and Ketama Gold are sold in the station area; the occasional desperate addict lurks along the dingier streets leading to the Amstel. For visitors, common sense should prevail: resist "space cake" in coffee shops; avoid eye contact in sinister alleys; and beware of admiring medieval gables on the central canals after midnight.

Yet there is no need to be alarmist about drug-related issues. The Dutch have long conducted a delicate balancing act between individual freedom and the collective well being, between permissiveness and orderliness. The majority of Dutch soft-drugs users are tolerated even by strict Calvinists, provided that they don't infringe on others' rights.

The same tolerance has always applied to sex in the city. Known as the *walletjes*, the red light district is a sex supermarket offering every variant on pornography and prostitution. Rembrandtsplein and Thorbeckeplein, just south of the red light district, provide a foretaste of things to come. Peep shows and pick-up clubs, boisterous gay bars and saucy striptease shows, give way to sex without the frills in brash Oudezijds Achterburgwal, just around the corner.

There are between 1,700 and 2,500 registered female prostitutes in Amsterdam, but most first-time visitors are drawn inexorably to the titillating prospect of the girls in the goldfish bowls. Energetic Thai women dance to music only they can hear behind their glass cages, others sit on padded red window seats and, between clients, paint their fingernails, smoke, or desultorily flip through a paperback. Apart from the girls' semi-nudity and a blankness about the eyes, there is little sense of their profession, let alone simulated eroticism. In padded chambers nearby, overweight Dutch housewives look uncomfortable in their bondage gear.

If business is slack, the women hiss or click their tongues at passing men. Female onlookers are given a glassy-eyed stare, though sometimes they get a lascivious wink. Although solitary women may be intimidated by the district at any hour, night is not necessarily the most dangerous time. Avoid the early morning desperation of passing junkies and an early afternoon edginess when pimps wait for the evening's business to begin. The *walletjes* is a safe area, but the northern end of Spui and Geldersekade are just far enough from the tourist crowds to exude a quiet sense of menace. Other areas to avoid – easily recognizable by their stillness – are the borders where social control is lacking and pickpockets, petty dealers and aggressive beggars are more apparent.

In between the *kamer te huur* (rooms to hire) signs are sex shops boasting "Marilyn Monroe special discount" and "100 percent hard porno." However, even some of the bars offering "orgasm" cocktails do so tongue in cheek. Many are friendly neighbourhood bars catering to shopkeepers and students as well as to working girls. In 1990 the government legalised brothels, restricting prostitution to non-residential areas, but in the past few years there has been a policy shift, with the focus very much on brothel owners, who are regularly checked. Key issues of concern are age, nationality, health and safety of the girls and or boys (gay clubs, brothels and escort agencies have grown in number). The brothel proprietors are compelled to ensure that their

employees are over 18, have regular health checks, are not press-ganged into prostitution and are not illegal immigrants. The latter being very important, since the opening of Eastern and other borders did for a while stimulate sex-slavery and the exacerbation of HIV and Aids related problems. Any breach of these conditions results in the proprietor losing his license.

Amsterdam is second only to San Francisco in its social acceptance of homosexuality. HIV has led to more efficient health programmes and increased solidarity within the gay community. Today, the city has a number of recognisable gay districts, all dotted with gay hotels, clubs and bars. The friendliest district is centred on Kerkstraat and Reguliersdwarsstraat, but elsewhere the city offers everything from sing-along bars to sinister cellars on the central canals. Women's Amsterdam is equally liberal, with women-only bars and disco nights and women-oriented sex boutiques such as Female and Partners on Spuistraat. Attempts to start male brothels, though, have not taken off. ❑

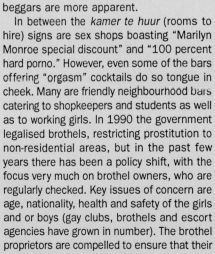

LEFT: coffee shops often have more than a little caffeine on the menu.
RIGHT: the red light district.

AMSTERDAM ENVIRONS

You don't have to travel far from Amsterdam to discover a wealth of worthwhile sights. Among these are historic Haarlem, and Edam, famous all over the world for its cheese

Map on page 169

This section covers the rest of the province of Noord-Holland, bounded to the east by the IJsselmeer, to the south by the provinces of Utrecht and Zuid-Holland, and to the west by the North Sea. Haarlem (population 152,500) is the provincial capital. It is an attractive old Dutch town on the edge of the Kennemer Dunes, with a famous collection of paintings by Frans Hals. Further north is **Alkmaar** (population 83,800), a pleasant market town. The towns along the River Zaan, known collectively as the Zaanstad, lie only a few miles northwest of Amsterdam.

The flat landscape of Noord-Holland is familiar from paintings by Dutch Masters such as Ruisdael. Large areas in this province consist of reclaimed polder lying below sea level.

Schiphol airport, 13 km (8 miles) southeast of Amsterdam, lies 4.5 metres (15 ft) below sea level on a former lake, the Haarlemmermeer, where a great sea battle took place against the Spanish during the Dutch Revolt. Three huge pumping houses were built in the 19th century to drain the lake. These distinctive neo-Gothic industrial buildings still stand; a museum which charts the Dutch struggle against the sea is housed in the former pumping house, **De Cruquius**, in Heemstede, a suburb of Haarlem.

Bookshops to bulbs

The most rewarding areas for walking or cycling in the Amsterdam environs are the dunes along the west coast and the woods of Het Gooi. Bulb fields extend along much of the eastern fringe of the dunes. The area's main flower and plant auction takes place in a vast complex at **Aalsmeer** ❶ 19 km (12 miles) southwest of Amsterdam. Another curious auction, the Broeker Veiling, is held in **Langedijk** ❷ village, near Alkmaar, where boats laden with vegetables are navigated through the auction sheds.

Haarlem ❸ is an interesting historic town on the winding river Spaarne, and it has clung to its ancient character more than any other town in the *Randstad* – the great conurbation, also known as the big village, that spreads south to Rotterdam and embraces Leiden and Utrecht, Delft, Gouda and Amsterdam as well as Haarlem itself.

Although only a 15-minute train journey from Amsterdam, Haarlem still seems very much under the sway of sober 17th-century virtues. It has an abundance of antiques dealers in the brick-paved lanes to the south of Grote Markt, and many curious old shop interiors, such as the violin seller's, found at Schagchelstraat 16, the comic strip store at Jacobijnestraat 8, and the cheese shop at Nieuwe Groenmarkt 39.

PRECEDING PAGES: plenty of flat space for cyclists to enjoy. **LEFT:** messing about on the river. **BELOW:** Keukenhof Gardens, Lisse.

H. de Vries' bookshop at Jacobijnestraat 3 has a Dutch Renaissance interior, reminiscent of paintings by Pieter de Hooch. Also on this street, at No. 22, is Galerie Année, which exhibits contemporary paintings, sculpture, ceramics and glass. But perhaps the most curious shop in Haarlem is the chemist A. J. van der Pigge at Gierstraat 3, where you can buy herbal teas or *drop* (liquorice), in a dark, wooden interior crowded with ancient apothecary jars.

Haarlem was the birthplace of many famous Dutch artists, including Geertgen tot Sint Jans (who lived in a monastery in the St Jansstraat) and the landscape painters Salomon van Ruysdael and his nephew Jacob van Ruisdael (so spelled). Jacob painted the dramatic View of Haarlem seen from the dunes at Overveen, now in the Mauritshuis in The Hague.

Renowned artist

The most famous artist of Haarlem was Frans Hals. Probably born in Antwerp, Hals spent most of his life in Haarlem, where he specialised in group portraits of military guilds and governors and governesses of charitable institutions. Eight of these extraordinary works, which inspired the French Impressionists and Van Gogh, are now hanging in the town's Frans Hals Museum.

The best place to begin a walking tour of Haarlem is the **railway station Ⓐ**, a handsome art nouveau building of polished wood and tile pictures dating from 1908. Now head down Jansweg and turn left into Korte Jansstraat to reach the **Bakenessergracht**, named after a Gothic church whose delicate 16th-century spire overlooks the canal. Groenebuurt (a lane to the right) brings you to the former Begijnhof quarter, of which all that survives is the church, a curious edifice with several houses built within the nave.

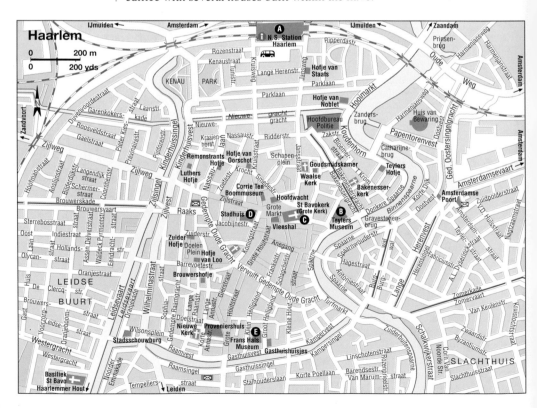

The Netherlands' oldest museum

Maps:
Area 169
City 166

Continuing along Bakenessergracht brings you to the broad River Spaarne. Standing on the waterfront nearby is the **Teylers Museum** Ⓑ (16 Spaarne, tel: 023-531 9010; open Tues–Sat 10am–5pm, Sun noon–5pm; entrance fee), the oldest museum in the Netherlands. This magnificent relic of the Dutch Enlightenment has been preserved in its original state.

The museum was founded in 1778 by Pieter Teyler van der Hulst, a prosperous silk merchant who amassed a large collection of fossils and scientific instruments. The round entrance hall of the museum, with its marble statues and bas reliefs depicting the sciences, has all the grandeur typical of a country house. More splendid still is the Oval Hall, a two-storey neoclassical hall built in 1779, with glass cabinets filled with antique scientific instruments, and bizarre pyramid-shaped display cabinets for minerals. The museum also houses an important collection of Dutch and Flemish prints, and 19th-century Romantic paintings.

Damstraat leads from the Spaarne to the **St Bavokerk** Ⓒ (Grote Kerk). This enormous Gothic Church was a favourite subject of 17th-century artists such as Pieter Saenredam and Gerrit Berckheyde. It dates from the 15th century, though the ornate bell-tower above the crossing is a 16th-century embellishment. The church is a marvellous jumble of roofs and gables, with several low buildings attached, such as the Vishal (once a fish market, now used for art exhibitions) on the north side, and several tiny 17th-century houses (rented out by the church authorities to raise revenue) along the south wall.

The Frans Hals Museum houses a collection of famous group portraits by the eponymous artist.

The entrance to the church is through one of these little shuttered houses, which adds to the dramatic impact of the vast nave. Though the church seems rather empty, it contains many fascinating features, including some curious medieval misericords, and several decorated graves of shoemakers in the ambulatory. St Bavokerk is renowned for its 18th-century Muller organ, which brought Mozart (aged 10), Händel and Liszt to this town.

BELOW: flowers are everywhere: fresh or dried.

The Grote Markt

Haarlem's imposing and atmospheric main square is worth more than a few minutes of your time. The **Grote Markt** (or main square), still looks very much as it did in the 17th-century townscapes of Gerrit Berckheyde in the Frans Hals Museum. The **Vleeshal** (meat hall) on the south side was designed in 1602 by Lieven de Key in a crowded Dutch Mannerist style, with a giant ox head to indicate the building's function. Opposite, exhibiting the more restrained classicism typical of the mid-17th century, is the **Hoofdwacht**, a guard house.

The **Stadhuis** Ⓓ (city hall) on the west side, standing on the site of a banqueting hall of the Counts of Holland, is an attractive mixture of buildings dating back to the medieval and Renaissance periods. The old town is dotted with some 18 *hofjes* (almshouse courts) founded by wealthy burghers, mostly situated in quiet streets to the west of Grote Markt, though there are three stately 18th-century almshouses on the east side (including one on the Spaarne founded by Pieter Teyler in 1787). The other main reason to visit Haarlem is the **Frans Hals Museum** Ⓔ (62

Groot Heiligland, tel: 023-511 5775; open Mon–Sat 11am–5pm, Sun noon–5pm; entrance fee), which is easily reached from the church down Warmoesstraat (notice the curious patterned pavements of brick), Schagchelstraat and Groot Heiligland.

The museum occupies a Dutch Renaissance building which was designed by Lieven de Key in 1608 as a hospice for old men, but two years later was converted to an orphanage. It contains several attractive period rooms and a detailed dolls' house, but its principal treasure is the collection of eight group portraits by Frans Hals.

Three paintings show members of the Guild of St George, and two depict the members of the Guild of St Adrian – whose guild house (the Kloveniersdoelen) is still standing in Gasthuisstraat. These military guilds seem to have been more interested in banqueting than in exercising, and Hals' portraits marvellously capture the slightly tipsy guild members, with their distinctive pointed beards and flowing orange and pale blue silk sashes. The other group portraits are extremely sombre by comparison. One shows the governors of St Elizabeth's Hospital and the other two are rather embittered portraits of the governors and governesses of the old men's home, painted when Hals, aged over 80, was an inmate.

Visiting the wood

BELOW: art in the Frans Hals Museum.

To the south of the old town is a large wood, the **Haarlemmer Hout**, all that remains of an ancient forest that once extended from Haarlem to The Hague, where the Counts of Holland were fond of hunting. Standing on the old waterway to Leiden, to the west of the town, is the **Basiliek St Bavo**, a bizarre

19th-century church of considerable architectural impact (best appreciated from Koorstraat). An extensive area of bulb fields extends along the eastern edge of the dunes from Haarlem to Leiden. These intensely cultivated fields are mainly situated on the polder that was created when the Haarlemmermeer was drained. This new land is extremely fertile, and provides enormous yields of tulips, daffodils and chrysanthemums. A visit to the busy Aalsmeer Flower Auction, near Schiphol airport, provides a marvellous glimpse into the workings of this efficient Dutch industry.

Map on page 169

Cheese capital

The town of **Edam** ❹, 22 km (14 miles) northeast of Amsterdam, is a cheerful, interesting little place with attractive canals crossed by narrow wooden bridges. Like many towns of the region known as Waterland, Edam was once an important whaling town, as the quay named Groenland (Greenland) recalls. In the 17th century it was an important port with large shipyards situated on the water-

Tulip bulbs find fertile ground around Haarlem and Leiden.

Amsterdam Environs

way to the east of the town. Edam is now world famous for its round cheeses, which are produced by farms on the fertile Beemster and Purmer polders. Edam cheeses, wrapped in a protective skin of red wax for export, can still be bought in the 16th-century Waag (weigh house) on Waagplein.

The main attraction

The main attraction in the town is the curious **Edams Museum** (1 & 8 Damplein, tel: 0299-372 644; open late Mar–Oct 1.30–4.30pm; entrance fee). This occupies a late Gothic house with a curious floating cellar that rocks to and fro as you walk across it. Opinions differ as to the purpose of the cellar; the romantic theory is that it was built by a retired captain to remind him of the sea, while a more prosaic explanation is that it was built this way to keep the cellar dry in times of flooding.

The museum proudly displays the portraits of three eccentric local characters: Jan Claeszoon Clees, who was extremely fat; Trijntje Cornelisdochter Kever, who was very tall; and Pieter Dirkszoon Langebaard, who (as his name suggests) had an extremely long beard. "Long Beard" toured the country displaying his beard to raise money for the local **Weeshuis** (orphanage), which is still standing on Kerkstraat.

The museum faces an unusual square; **Damplein** is built in the form of a long arched bridge to allow ships to pass beneath. South of here stands the solitary tower of a 15th-century church, with a beautiful 16th-century carillon of bells from Mechelen. Further south, you come to Edam's most attractive canal, the Schepenmakersdijk (shipbuilders' dyke), with curious tea houses on the water's edge on one side.

BELOW: Alkmaar cheese porter.

Exploring Alkmaar

Alkmaar ❺ is a modest inland town 40 km (25 miles) north of Amsterdam whose one moment of glory came in 1573 when it successfully withstood a Spanish siege, prompting the quip "from Alkmaar to victory." It is now a busy market town where a "traditional" cheese market is staged on Friday mornings during the tourist season. The yellow-skinned cheeses are piled on to wooden sledges by porters in traditional garb, before being taken to the Waaggebouw, a 14th-century chapel which was converted to a weigh house in the 16th century by the addition of a Renaissance gable and a jaunty bell tower. It now contains a small museum of cheese-making techniques. To explore Alkmaar on foot, take Stationstraat from the station, then follow the moat to the right, which brings you to a bridge leading to the **Grote Kerk**.

Map on page 169

An architectural mix

The Grote Kerk, an imposing 15th-century church, was built of mellow Brabant limestone by the Keldermans family of Mechelen. The 17th-century organ was designed by Jacob van Campen, the architect of the Amsterdam town hall. Heading into town along Langestraat, you come to the **Stadhuis** (Town Hall). The east wing and tower were built in late-Gothic style *circa* 1510; the west wing was added in 1694 in baroque style.

North of here is the **Stedelijk (Municipal) Museum Alkmaar**, which has a local collection of guild group portraits, antique toys, tiles and paintings. Situated in the attractive Renaissance guild house of the archers, it is worth a visit solely to see the panoramic view of the *Siege of Alkmaar*, painted by an unknown Master in the 16th century, and including nice touches of typical Netherland humour such as a drunken soldier and a couple making love as the battle rages on.

Heading east from here, you will eventually come to the **Waagplein**, scene of the Friday cheese market. Further east, the canal Verdronken Oord leads to the Noord-Hollands Kanaal, which has an animated maritime atmosphere. The curious **Accijnstoren** was built in 1622 to collect tolls on local shipping. In a delicate operation in 1924 the tower was moved by some 4 metres (13 ft), using a system of rollers, thereby (but only temporarily) improving traffic flow.

A more elegant quarter lies to the south of the Waagplein. The simple baroque-style **Wildemanshofje** on Oude Gracht was founded in 1714 for 24 elderly women. The statue of a wild man above the entrance is a curious play on the name of the founder, a certain Gerrit Wildeman. A thin ribbon of landscaped park runs along the town moat south of here, making this a pleasant route back to the station.

The industrial towns of Zaandam, Koog aan de Zaan and Zaandijk are strung out along both banks of the Zaan River, forming the conurbation of **Zaanstad ❻**. In 1592 a windmill-powered sawmill was invented in the Zaan region, leading to the development of a large timber industry which supplied nearby shipyards. Other windmills were built along the river banks to supply power for oil-mills, paintmills, flour-mills and mustard-mills (which produced

Architecture enthusiasts will find Alkmaar particularly interesting for its varied display of architectural styles including Renaissance, Gothic and Baroque.

BELOW:
cheese market
and public weights.

Bell-shaped gables typify gable styles of the Zaan district.

BELOW: Zaanse Schans windmill.

the celebrated Zaanse mustard). By the 18th century there were more than 1,000 windmills slowly turning in the breeze.

In 1697 Tzar Peter the Great travelled incognito to Zaandam to visit the famous shipyards on the river Zaan. A tiny wooden house is preserved in Zaandam, the **Czaar-Pieterhuisje**, where he stayed with Gerrit Kist, a local smith he knew from St Petersburg. The building developed an alarming tilt and is now propped up by a 19th-century frame. Occasionally large groups of Russian sailors descend upon Zaandam to see the small wooden bed into which the Czar used to squeeze his 2-metre (7-ft) frame.

Zaandijk a few miles north, has the sole surviving example of a complete street built in the old Zaan district style, with a small museum, the Zaanlandse Oudheidkamer, in an 18th-century merchant's home. The adjacent river was once the region's main thoroughfare. The abundance of timber in the Zaan region led to a distinctive local style of green wooden houses decorated with pointed or bell-shaped gables. In the 1950s many of the surviving houses and windmills in Zaan style were relocated to an open-air museum, the **Zaanse Schans**, situated on the river bank opposite Zaandijk. A working windmill here produces local mustard, and a clog-maker demonstrates his craft. The new **Zaans Museum** (7 Schansend, tel: 075-616 8218; open Tues–Sat 10am–5pm, Sun noon–5pm) uses the locally themed collections formerly at the Zaans Historisch Museum.

To the east of Amsterdam is the restored **Muiderslot** (1 Herengracht, tel: 0294-261 325, open (guided tours) Apr–Oct: Mon–Fri 10am–4pm; Nov–Mar:, Sat and Sun 1–3pm; Dec 18–27: noon–5pm; other pub. hols 1–4pm; entrance fee), situated where the River Vecht enters the IJsselmeer. This attractive brick

IJMUIDEN: FISH AND SHIPS

To the casual observer, Ijmuiden may appear to have little to offer, and may even seem a little grey. However, with a bit of effort, one soon begins to appreciate the importance of this fishing and shipping centre. Located to the northwest of Haarlem, it forms the entrance of the Noordzee Kanal, where ships from all over the world pass through some of the biggest sea locks and sluices in the world in order to reach Amsterdam.

The huge tankers and the graceful lines of the grand ocean liners gliding majestically along are an impressive sight. The Haarlem vvv organises round trips that start in the afternoon with a bus ride passing through country estates. Upon arrival in Ijmuiden, passengers transfer to a small cruise ship which sails around the fisherman's wharves, harbours, sea locks and the North Sea approach. Finally the bus returns to Haarlem, but it is worth catching a later bus so that you can take advantage of an excellent fish dinner in one of the many restaurants dotted around the fishing harbour. (Haarlem vvv, Stationsplein 1, tel: 0900-6161 600).

Keen anglers can even catch their own fish, by joining the crew of the fishing cutter *Tonijn*, for a day, and bringing home their catch. An optional extra is a three-course fish supper at the Meerplaats restaurant. Good luck! (Ijmuiden vvv, Plein 1945, 105, tel: 0255-515 611).

Map
on page
169

castle was built in 1285 by Count Floris V of Holland, the founder of many Dutch towns. Floris V was murdered here 11 years later by a group of nobles enraged by his policy of encouraging urban development. In the 17th century the poet and historian P.C. Hooft occupied the castle in his capacity as bailiff of Gooiland, and it became the meeting place for the illustrious Muiderkring (Muiden Circle) group of poets and writers; members included jurist Hugo Grotius, diplomat and poet Constantijn Huygens, and the prolific Amsterdam poet Joost van den Vondel.

From Amsterdam, you can take the bus 136 from Amstel train station. Alternatively, a boat leaves from behind the Centraal Station (Rederij Naco landing 7, tel: 626 2466; May–Sep) on excursions to Muiden as well as to the Fort Pampus Island fortification. In Muiden, the Rederij Toman ferryboat landing is next to the castle.

Also worth a visit is Oudekerk-on-the-Amstel, a picturesque village just 15 minutes southeast of Amsterdam that is too beautiful to miss. Located at the spot where the Bullewijjk, a picturesque tributary, joins the Amstel river, this pastoral landscape of windmills and farmhouses dates back to the 12th century, making it the oldest village in the Amstelland region. Its name is derived from the Catholic Church which was founded in the area in AD 1000, and which now houses a row of charming houses built around 1733.

Remembering a massacre

Further east along the IJsselmeer coast is the historic town of **Naarden** ❼. In 1572 the Spanish army under Don Frederick of Toledo murdered almost all the inhabitants. The massacre is commemorated by a 17th-century stone tablet on a building at Turfpoortstraat 7. The town fortifications were demolished by the Spanish and Naarden became a virtual ghost town.

More advanced defences were erected in the 17th century. These fortifications still completely encircle the town and are fascinating to explore. Their history is explained in the **Vestingmuseum** (6 Westwalstraat, tel: 035-694 5459; open mid-June–Aug: Mon–Fri 10.30am–5pm; Sept–mid-Dec: noon–5pm; entrance fee) which is located within a bastion connected to underground passages and casemates, themselves now home to a complex of up-market restaurants and interior design stores known as the Arsenaal.

Naarden is also associated with Comenius, a 17th-century philosopher and pedagogue who fled here from Moravia (now part of the Czech Republic) in 1621. The **Comenius Museum** (33 Kloosterstraat, tel: 035-694 3045; open Tues–Sat 10am–5pm, Sun noon–5pm; entrance fee) contains a small exhibition devoted to him.

The woods of Het Gooi, south of Naarden, attracted wealthy Amsterdam merchants in the 17th century. Dutch Impressionist, Anton Mauve, lived in Laren and painted the Gooiland countryside. **Hilversum** ❽ the main town of the area, is the home of Dutch national radio and TV. Its town hall was designed by W.M. Dudok in 1931. The town also has the Pinetum Blijdenstein and a botanic garden (Costerustuin). ❑

BELOW:
Hilversum café life.

THE HAGUE AND ENVIRONS

Maps:
City 176
Area 202

More than just the home of the Dutch government, The Hague and neighbouring Delft and Leiden offer visitors attractive architecture, historical buildings and museums packed to the rafters with art

The Hague and the neighbouring cities of Leiden and Delft lie in the prosperous northern part of Zuid-Holland province. Each of these venerable Dutch cities has played a crucial role in the Netherlands' history and the development of Dutch painting, and, not surprisingly, they have some of the best museums and art galleries in the country. Unlike most Dutch cities, The Hague does not owe its existence to trade or the sea; its principal activities are government and administration.

The seat of government

As the third largest city in The Netherlands, with some 445,000 inhabitants, **The Hague ❶** (Den Haag in Dutch) is referred to as "the political capital of the Netherlands". Its government buildings cluster around the Binnenhof, and it is also home to the majority of the Dutch ministries, the Royal residence of the Queen, various Royal palaces, the International Court of Justice, the world famous Peace Palace and the location of some 80 embassies and consulates. It is also known as the "widow of Indonesia", the former Dutch colony which gained independence in 1945. Between 1850 and 1900, the Archipel residential area was built to accommodate thousands of returning Dutch and also Indonesians who chose to adopt Dutch nationality and settle in the Netherlands. This accounts for the number of fine Indonesian restaurants throughout the city, such as Garoeda, Djawa and Poentjak Pas.

For a feel of Old World Indonesia, visit the Hotel des Indes for afternoon tea. Isadora Duncan spent her last night in this stylish hotel. A combination of culture and history, monumental and modern architecture, museums, stately hotels, antiques shops, gastronomy and natural beauty lend The Hague an air of sophistication and elegance. The city centre is manageable on foot, and public transport – both trams and buses – makes travelling from town to the sea quick and comfortable.

The Hague is also easily accessible from Leiden and Delft – under 15 minutes by train and just a few minutes more from Rotterdam and Amsterdam, making day trips a pleasant possibility. It is the only European capital bordering two seaside resorts, Scheveningen and Kijkduin, giving it a second reputation as a "seaside city" with miles of dunes and woods to explore.

The Hague was originally a hamlet close to the castle of the Counts of Holland, built in the 13th century. The hamlet grew up around a hunting lodge that belonged to the counts, and this gave rise to The Hague's curious Old Dutch name, 's Gravenhage (the Count's hedge). The village first became important in 1586 when the States General of the new Dutch

LEFT: ironwork at the Binnenhof (royal residence) courtyard.
BELOW: the royal residence.

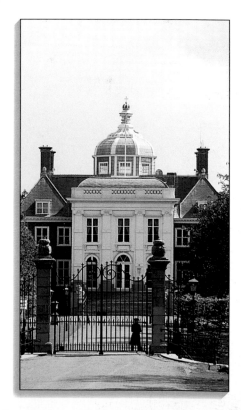

Republic met here, and The Hague gradually assumed the role of political capital, even though it was not officially a town, since it had no city walls or medieval privileges. Although The Hague was never granted a charter (it still doesn't have one), it does have its own Town Arms; officially laid down in 1861, it depicts a stork with an eel held tight in its beak. It is likely that this image pays tribute to the medieval storks which used to build their nests on the small island in the Hofvijver pond. Their presence was seen by The Hague residents as a sign of good fortune, as the storks would finish off all the remains from the fish market that would otherwise rot and possibly cause infectious diseases to spread amongst the town's inhabitants. Thus, in appreciation of the bird, the stork is now depicted on all municipal institutions.

Knight's Hall at The Hague's parliament buildings.

Village life

The main attraction of this "village", which is still referred to as "the largest village in Europe," was that it offered a neutral meeting ground for representatives of the seven northern provinces, who each jealously guarded their independence. Attractive streets and squares were laid out around the old castle in the 17th century, including the Plein and the Korte Vijverberg, which were designed by the diplomat and poet Constantijn Huygens. Further improvements were made in the 18th century along the Lange Vijverberg and Lange Voorhout.

The gracious style of the 18th century reached its highest expression in the former Royal Library at Lange Voorhout 34, begun by Daniel Marot in 1734 with wings added in 1761 by Pieter de Swart. By the 19th century The Hague had become a fashionable literary and artistic centre, while the nearby village of Scheveningen was one of the most elegant resorts on the North Sea.

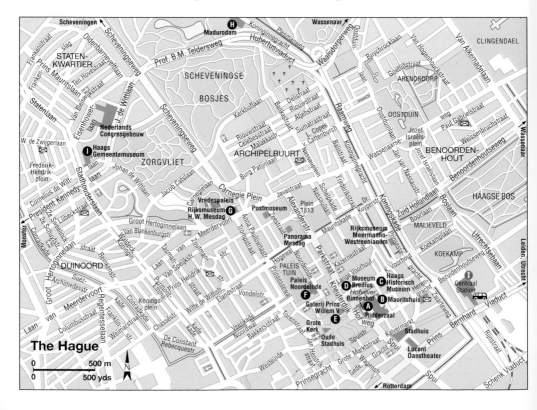

During the post-war years, The Hague lost much of its allure, due to the disappearance of many of its canals and the unchecked development of roads and office blocks. Fortunately, the extensive woods where the Counts of Holland hunted have been preserved, and the windswept dunes where the Impressionists of The Hague School painted remain as wild as ever.

Map on page 176

Modernisation

The Hague celebrated its 750th anniversary in 1998. In the 1980s, it began an extensive plan to create a modern city centre. It began with such projects as the Anton Philipszaal concert hall on the Spuiplein, which is home of The Hague Philharmonic Orchestra and host to many other cultural events. The AT&T Danstheater, designed by acclaimed architect Rem Koolhaas, is the home of the equally acclaimed Netherlands Dance Theatre.

The latest additions to the New Hague will offer considerable improvements, thanks to the contributions of such respected architects as Michael Graves, Cesar Pelli, Richard Koek and Rob Krier. This area between the Utrechtsebaan and the Prinsegracht will complement The Hague's historic centre, with new shops, modern housing developments and office buildings. Existing streets will be renovated, department stores given a face-lift and overall accessibility will be greatly improved.

The impressive new town hall, designed by the award-winning architect Richard Meier, also houses the public library and municipal records department, which employs a staff of more than 1,000 civil servants. With its two office wings forming a wall to the glass-covered atrium, the town hall has become a meeting place for locals and visitors alike.

The Hague is undergoing a serious face-lift with a number of exciting cultural and architectural projects bringing the city into the 21st century.

BELOW:
the Ridderzaal.

Seat of the Dutch government

The most attractive area of the city is situated around the old castle of the Counts of Holland. The gateway on Buitenhof leads into the Binnenhof, the former courtyard of the castle. The building that resembles a chapel in the middle of the courtyard is the **Ridderzaal Ⓐ**, a 13th-century hall built by Count Floris V and heavily restored in the 19th century. This small building has come to be a symbol of the Dutch Parliament, although it is now used only for ceremonial occasions. A new building has been designed for the Second Chamber on Hofsingel. Its glass façade is intended to give the public a glimpse of the government in action.

There is another gateway behind the Ridderzaal that leads to the **Mauritshuis Ⓑ** (8 Korte Vijverberg, tel: 070-302 3456; open Tues-Sat 10am–5pm; Sun 11am–5pm; entrance fee), which rises out of the water like a Venetian palace. This was the former home of Count Johan Maurits, an enlightened governor who ruled over Brazil on behalf of the Dutch West Indies Company. Built between 1633 and 1644 by Pieter Post, using plans drawn up by Jacob van Campen, the classical building perfectly embodies the Dutch principles of reason and balance. In a letter to Johan Maurits, Constantijn Huygens praised "the beautiful, very beautiful, and most beautiful building."

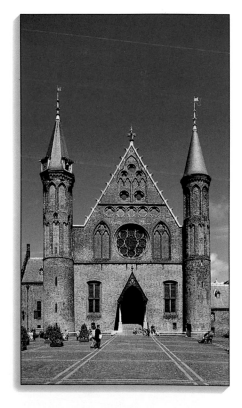

The Mauritshuis was once famed for its "cabinets of curiosities" – rooms filled with exotica brought back by Dutch trading ships. In the 19th century the Koninklijk Kabinet van Schilderijen (Royal Picture Cabinet) was moved here to create one of the most beautiful small picture galleries in the world. More like a private house than a museum, the Mauritshuis has a choice collection of Flemish, Dutch and German Old Masters. Works are hung in a series of handsome period rooms, ranging from grand gilded salons to intimate wood-panelled chambers.

Works by Rembrandt

The permanent collection on the ground floor is mainly devoted to Flemish paintings, including *Descent from the Cross* by Rogier van der Weyden and *Portrait of a Man* by Hans Memling. The rooms on the first floor contain some of the finest works of the Dutch Golden Age, including a number of Rembrandts. The most famous of these is *The Anatomy Lesson of Dr Tulp*, the artist's first major commission in Amsterdam, executed in 1632. The figure of Susanna painted in 1637 was probably modelled on his wife Saskia. There are also several self-portraits from different periods of Rembrandt's life. In the earliest, dated 1629, he looks almost arrogant, but by the time of the 1669 portrait (painted the year he died), the artist's face has weathered to an expression of infinite sorrow.

One of the more unusual paintings in the collection is *The Goldfinch*, by Carel Fabritius (a pupil of Rembrandt). It is one of the few works by Fabritius to have survived, and was painted in 1654, the year the artist was killed in a gunpowder explosion in Delft at the age of 22.

BELOW: Vermeer's *View of Delft.*

Map on page 176

Six years later, Vermeer painted *View of Delft*, which shows no evidence of the destruction. In 1994, this painting, as well as his *Girl with a Pearl,* were restored. The Mauritshuis also has a striking *View of Haarlem* by Jacob van Ruisdael, and several white church interiors by Pieter Saenredam.

Museums old and new

Wandering through the Mauritshuis, you are inevitably struck by the impressive views of the Hofvijver, all that remains of the castle moat. Several small museums overlook this lake, including the new **Haags Historisch Museum** ❻ (open Tues–Fri 11am–5pm; tel: 070-364 6940) on the east side. This museum of local history occupies the Sebastiaansdoelen, a Dutch Classical building commissioned by the archers' guild in 1636. In Room 1, which looks out on the Hofvijver, you can see several old paintings of the lake, almost invariably featuring the distinctive 15th-century octagonal tower still standing alongside the Mauritshuis. You also see the archers' doelen, or firing range, that once stood on the east side of the lake. The museum's other main attraction is a dolls' house beautifully furnished in 19th-century style.

After many years of closure, the **Museum Bredius** ❼ (open Tues–Sun 12am–5pm; tel: 070-362 0729; entrance fee) has reopened in a handsome 18th-century house on the north side of the Hofvijver. Its collection of paintings was formed by Dr Abraham Bredius, a director of the Mauritshuis at the turn of the 19th century, and contains works by both well-known names and unknown artists of the Dutch Golden Age.

A pleasant walk around the lake brings you to the **Schilderijengalerie**, also known as **Galerij Prins Willem V** ❽ (35 Buitenhof; open Tues–Sun 11am–4pm; entrance fee; tel: 070-362 4444), the oldest picture gallery in the Netherlands. Founded in 1774 by Prince William V, this small stately gallery has been restored to its original appearance, and paintings are crammed on the walls in several tiers (as they are in the painting in the Mauritshuis by Willem van Haecht of Alexander the Great Visiting the Studio of Apelles). The collection of Dutch Old Masters of the 17th and 18th centuries does not compare with the Mauritshuis, but this eccentric gallery is well worth a visit.

Royal shopping street

Buitenhof divides the government quarter from the old town, now an area of pedestrianised shopping streets. The Passage, off Buitenhof, is an elegant shopping arcade dating from 1885. Groenmarkt, not far from here, is the centre of the old town. Here stands the **Grote Kerk**, a 15th-century Gothic church with an early 16th-century choir. The Oude Stadhuis (Old Town Hall) opposite was built in 1564–65 in spirited Renaissance style, and a large wing was added in the 18th century.

Noordeinde is the most elegant shopping street in The Hague, and has a number of well-preserved art nouveau shop fronts. There are many fine restaurants in the neighbourhood, including It Rains Fishes and Les Ombrelles. This is where you will find the 16th-

The Hague runs the gamut of museums, with top works by Rembrandt and other well-known Golden Age artists, while smaller lake-front museums include The Netherlands' oldest picture gallery.

BELOW: Mauritshuis Museum.

century **Paleis Noordeinde G**, also known as the **Binnenhof**. The history of the palace goes back to 1559 when Emperor Charles V assigned Prince William of Nassau to the post of stadtholder of the provinces of Holland, Zeeland and Utrecht. It is now the royal residence of Queen Beatrix.

Trompe l'oeil seascape

Continuing down Noordeinde and across a canal, you reach the **Mesdag Panorama** (65 Zeestraat, tel: 070-310 6665; open Mon–Sat 10am–5pm; Sun noon–5pm; entrance fee). Inside, you enter a darkened tunnel and ascend a spiral staircase to a mock pavilion, from where it's possible to view a very lifelike panoramic scene of the coast and dunes at Scheveningen. The panorama was painted in 1881 by The Hague based Impressionist painter Hendrik Willem Mesdag on a canvas 120 metres (400 ft) long by 14 metres (46 ft) high. In executing this work, Mesdag was assisted by his wife (who painted the village of Scheveningen), Theo de Bock (who was delegated to paint the sky), and the Amsterdam based Impressionist G.H. Breitner (who added his favourite theme – a group of cavalry officers charging on the beach). The astonishingly realistic effect is obtained by the indirect daylight falling from above and the artificial foreground strewn with real objects.

Not far from here is the **Rijksmuseum H.W. Mesdag G** (71 Laan van Meerdervoort, tel: 070-362 1434; open Tues–Sun noon–5pm; entrance fee) occupying a house built in 1887 by the artist. This once neglected museum is now under the same management as the Van Gogh Museum in Amsterdam. It contains Impressionist paintings by Mesdag himself and other members of The Hague School, as well as a large collection of dark, melancholy works

BELOW: Indonesian mask in Leiden's Rijksmuseum voor Volkenkunde.
RIGHT:
Hooglandse Kerk.

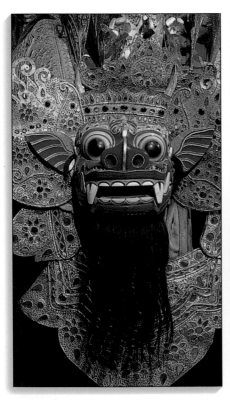

by members of the Barbizon School, including paintings by the likes of Corot and Millet, who greatly inspired Mesdag. **The Vredespaleis**, or Peace Palace, (2 Carnegieplein, tel: 070-302 4137; open June–Sept: Mon–Fri 10am–4pm; Oct–May: 10am–3pm; entrance fee) is just north of the museum. Built to house the Permanent Court of Arbitration set up after the 1899 Hague conference on the suppression of war, this stately pile was paid for by the Scottish millionaire and philanthropist Andrew Carnegie. Completed in 1913, its work failed to prevent the hostilities that led to World War I. The building is now used as the seat of the International Court of Justice, and contains a curious miscellany of objects donated by member states.

The Netherlands in miniature

The Scheveningseweg runs north of here towards the sea, cutting a path through the vast wooded area of the Scheveningse Bosjes. Situated on the edge of the woods to the east, **Madurodam** ❶ (1 George Maduroplein, tel: 070-355 3900; open daily Jan–Mar: 9am–6pm; Mar–June: 9am–9pm; July–Aug: 9am–11pm; entrance fee) is a miniature town, which has been renovated and extended. With its precise – albeit tiny – reproductions of historic buildings in the Netherlands, it provides a handy shortcut to a sightseeing itinerary. It also has a working port, an extensive railway network and some interesting details reflecting contemporary Dutch life.

The elegant quarter to the west of the woods contains a cluster of interesting museums. The **Haags Gemeentemuseum** ❶ (41 Stadhouderslaan, tel: 070-338 1111; open Tues–Sun 11am–5pm; entrance fee) houses an excellent collection of modern painting and decorative art in an attractive low brick building

Map on page 176

TIP

Don't miss the Haags Gemeentemuseum. A work of art in itself, it also houses a substantial collection by Mondrian and an impressive Delftware collection.

BELOW: Pilgrim Fathers Documents Centre, Leiden.

overlooking an ornamental pond. This was the last work designed by the founder of Dutch modern architecture, H.P. Berlage, who died a year before its completion in 1935.

Berlage's modern masterpiece provides an appropriate setting for an extensive collection of works by Piet Mondrian, ranging from early paintings in the style of The Hague School to abstract works composed of blocks of red, yellow, blue and white, with black lines delineating the pictorial space. Especially popular is Mondrian's *Victory Boogie Woogie* painting which was purchased from a collection in America in 1998 for US $40 million!

The museum also has a renowned Delftware collection, an exquisite Dutch dolls' house, a large collection of musical instruments and a section devoted to fashion. In recent years, the collection has been revitalised and is well worth a visit for the building itself, let alone its eclectic contents. The nearby **Museon**, which is built in a style that echoes Berlage's Gemeentemuseum, is a modern science museum with many working models. Also in this area is **Omniversum**, where films are projected onto the surface of a planetarium dome to achieve a striking visual effect.

There are several other specialised museums in The Hague, including the **Rijksmuseum Meermanno-Westreenianum** (30 Prinsessegracht, tel: 070-346 2700; open Tues–Fri 11am–5pm, Sat and Sun noon–5pm; entrance fee) which contains an important collection of illuminated manuscripts and classical antiquities, and the Postmuseum (opposite the Panorama Mesdag). If you are keen to follow in the footsteps of The Hague Impressionists, the coastal resort of **Scheveningen** is just a short tram ride from the city centre. The trams follow the Scheveningseweg, a broad straight road created to link The Hague to the coast

BELOW:
the Kurhaus,
Scheveningen.

in the 17th century by Constantijn Huygens. Every July the famous North Sea Jazz Festival weekend attracts visitors and top musicians from around the world.

Like most resorts on the sea, Scheveningen is a mixture of faded elegance and brash modernity, in recent years increasingly dominated by ugly high-rise buildings. The most striking buildings are the Kurhaus, a grand 19th-century hotel, and the modern Pier, which has an observation tower, a children's playground and a café. There is a Holland Casino opposite the Kurhaus hotel if you prefer more challenging entertainment.

The **Scheveningen Sea Life Centre** (open Mon–Sat 10am–5pm; Sun 1–5pm; entrance fee) exhibits underwater life of the North Sea by presenting it in its natural habitat. Walking through an underwater tunnel, visitors can experience life in the blue depths or on the seabed itself without ever getting wet. If you want to avoid the bustling resort atmosphere that thrives along the frantic promenade, head in the opposite direction to **Kijkduin**, a smaller, more peaceful seaside resort, with expansive dunes and miles of sandy beach. Whichever beach you go to, be sure to try some *poffertjes*, delicious miniature pancakes.

Syrian heads are on display at Leiden's Museum of Antiques.

University town

Leiden ❷, on a branch of the Rhine in the bulb-growing region between The Hague and Haarlem, is a likeable university town full of cafés and student bookshops. Leiden University is the oldest and most renowned in the Netherlands. It was founded in 1575 by William of Orange in recognition of the town's heroic resistance to the Spanish. Despite hunger and disease, the townspeople withstood a siege of 131 days. They were finally liberated by a drastic measure; the sea dykes were broken, allowing the sea to flood a large area to the south of

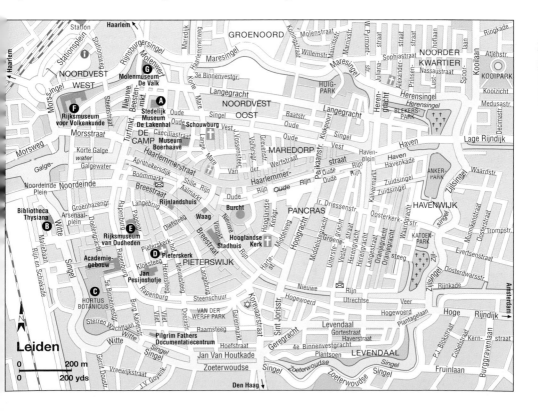

Rembrandt

Rembrandt Harmenszoon van Rijn was the greatest painter of the Dutch Golden Age. He was born in Leiden in 1606, the eighth child of a prosperous miller. Rembrandt was sent to the Latin School, a 1599 Renaissance building that still stands near the Pieterskerk. In 1620 he enrolled as a student at Leiden University, but soon abandoned his studies in favour of painting. His father sent him to study under Jacob van Swanenburgh, who owned a step-gabled house still to be seen at Langebrug 89. After three years, Rembrandt moved to Amsterdam and spent six months in the studio of Pieter Lastman, a famous painter of classical and historical subjects.

In 1625, by now an ambitious young artist, Rembrandt was advised by the diplomat Constantijn Huygens, an early admirer of his work, to study in Italy. He replied that he was too busy and said he could see all the Italian work he wanted in Holland. The self-portrait in

the Mauritshuis painted in 1629 shows the young Rembrandt as supremely confident and slightly haughty.

In 1632, and now settled in Amsterdam, he received his first major commission, *The Anatomy Lesson of Dr Tulp*, painted for the Amsterdam guild of surgeons and now displayed in the Mauritshuis Museum in The Hague. Two years later Rembrandt married Saskia van Uylenburg, the daughter of a prosperous burgomaster. He painted Saskia many times, including once as Flora in a marvellous painting in London's National Gallery.

In 1639 Rembrandt moved to a handsome Renaissance house in the Jewish quarter of Amsterdam (now the Rembrandthuis Museum). But Saskia fell ill and died in 1642, having borne four children. Only one, Titus, survived. A stone simply inscribed "Saskia" in Amsterdam's Oude Kerk marks her grave.

Ironically, this was the period of Rembrandt's greatest triumph, *The Night Watch*, now his most famous and valuable work. The work was completed in 1642 for the Amsterdam guild of arquebusiers, and now hangs in the gallery of honour in Amsterdam's Rijksmuseum. At about this time, Rembrandt appointed Geertghe Dircx,as a nurse for Titus. Living together as a couple, they never married, as this would have deprived Rembrandt of income from Saskia's will. They parted in 1649 after a quarrel.

In 1656 Rembrandt was declared bankrupt, and was forced to move to a more modest dwelling in the Jordaan. Though beset by personal and financial problems, Rembrandt painted one of his greatest works in 1656 – the now-damaged *Anatomy Lesson of Dr Deyman*, which hangs in the Amsterdam Rijksmuseum. His work continued to mature, and in 1661 he executed the famous *Syndics of the Drapers' Guild* – also to be found in the Rijksmuseum.

Titus died at the age of 27 in 1668, and eleven months later, in October 1669, Rembrandt also died. He was buried in an unmarked pauper's grave in Westerkerk in Amsterdam, and his exact burial place, which had been lost for three centuries, was only rediscovered early in 1990, during restoration of the interior of the church. ❑

LEFT: Rembrandt self-portrait 1629.

Leiden, so that Admiral Boisot could sail a fleet of ships up to the city walls. A magnificent tapestry in the Lakenhal Museum depicts this historical episode.

Map on page 183

Cradle of talent

Many distinguished academics have taught at Leiden University, including Herman Boerhaave, professor of medicine, and Carl Linnaeus, the Swedish botanist. Several notable Dutch artists were also born in the city, including Rembrandt, Lucas van Leyden, Jan van Goyen, Gerrit Dou and Jan Steen. The **Stedelijk Museum De Lakenhal** Ⓐ (32 Oude Singel, tel: 071-516-5360; open Tues–Fri 10am–5pm; Sat, Sun and pub. hols noon–5pm; entrance fee) provides an interesting introduction to the history of this important Dutch town. The museum occupies a distinguished canal-side building designed in Dutch Classical style in 1640 by Arent van 's Gravesande. The windmill flanked by cloth and wool above the entrance symbolises the building's original function as a cloth hall. Cloth making, which was introduced to Leiden by Flemish weavers fleeing the Black Death in the 14th century, was the town's main industry until the 18th century. Five stone tablets on the façade illustrate the stages in cloth making, beginning with spinning and ending with the inspection by the Staalmeesters (syndics, who applied a metal seal to certified Leiden cloth).

Lakenhal's art

A small art gallery in the Lakenhal contains works by 16th and 17th-century Leiden artists. Pride of place is given to Lucas van Leyden's *Triptych of the Last Judgement*, a faltering early Dutch Renaissance work painted in 1526 for the Pieterskerk. There is also an interesting scale model of the chapel of Marienpol Abbey, illustrating the locations of two altarpieces by Cornelis Engebrechtszoon now in the museum.

BELOW: gables in Leiden.

The Lakenhal has just one painting by Rembrandt, an unremarkable historical work dating from 1626, which is hung for comparison alongside a somewhat better work by Jan Lievens, with whom he probably shared a studio in Leiden. There is also a gloomy painting by Jacob van Swanenburg, Rembrandt's teacher in Leiden. But probably the most alluring work in the collection is the View of Leiden painted by Jan van Goyen in 1650 eschewing bright colours in favour of muddy brown tones.

The Lakenhal also has a number of period rooms rescued from old buildings in Leiden, including an 18th-century kitchen and a room in Biedermeier style. The most attractive rooms are in the wings on the first floor. The room in the east wing comes from the brewers' guild house, and is decorated with five murals depicting different steps in the brewing process. The Staalmeesterskamer in the west wing, which is hung with sumptuous gilt leather, was the chamber in which the syndics of the cloth guild used to meet.

The best view of Leiden is from the **Burcht**, a 12th-century castle surmounting an ancient artificial mound built at the convergence of two branches of the Rhine. From the battlements, you can see the two vast churches of Leiden which appear in Van Goyen's painting in the Lakenhal. The nearer of the two, the

Hooglandse Kerk, has a very curious appearance. Its 16th-century nave was never completed in length or height, and is dwarfed by the 15th-century Flamboyant Gothic choir.

To reach the university area, head down Hartesteg to the Nieuwe Rijn, then continue along Gangetje. The park you pass stands on the site of several houses destroyed in 1807 when a barge laden with gunpowder exploded. The park contains a statue of Burgomaster Pieter van der Werff, who refused to surrender the city to the Spanish army in the siege of 1574.

University quarter

On to Rapenburg, a handsome canal enlivened with many university buildings in Dutch Classical style – the finest undoubtedly being the **Bibliotheca Thysiana** Ⓑ at No. 25, which was built in 1655 by Arent van 's Gravesande. The University began in the former chapel facing the Nonnenbrug. A lane alongside leads to the **Hortus Botanicus** Ⓒ, one of the oldest botanical gardens in the world. Founded in 1587 it was originally stocked with numerous exotic species brought back from the Dutch East Indies and from the Americas.

Across the Nonnenbrug, an attractive lane leads to the **Pieterskerk** Ⓓ, a 15th-century Gothic church containing the tombs of Leiden academics, including Herman Boerhaave and the Remonstrant theologian Jacobus Arminius.

The university law faculty is situated opposite the church in the Gravensteen, a gloomy former prison of the Counts of Holland. The attractive cobbled lanes around the Pieterskerk contain antiquarian bookshops and pleasant cafés. This quarter also has associations with the Pilgrim Fathers, who spent 12 years in Leiden before setting sail from Delfshaven on the *Speedwell*. John Robinson, the

BELOW: modern architecture by Richard Meyer.

spiritual leader of the English religious community, lived on the south side of the Pieterskerk in the Jan Pesijnshofje. He had hoped eventually to join the Pilgrim Fathers in America, but died in 1625 in Leiden and was buried in the Pieterskerk. A plaque in the nearby Pieterskerk-Choorsteeg commemorates the Pilgrim Press run at No. 17 by William Brewster.

Map on page 183

This lane emerges on **Breestraat**, the principal street of Leiden. The long façade of the **Stadhuis** on the right was designed in Dutch Renaissance style by Lieven de Key in 1595. The **Rijnlandshuis** to the left was designed by the same architect one year later for the powerful local water authority. De Key also built the beautiful **Stadstimmerwerf** on Galgewaard, which when floodlit at night is particularly striking.

A relaxing walk alongside the leafy canal of Oude Delft takes in some interesting historical buildings.

Egyptian treasures

Several outstanding national museums are situated in Leiden, including one of Netherlands' oldest, the **Rijksmuseum van Oudheden** ❸ (28 Rapenburg, tel: 0715-163163; open Tues–Fri 10am–5pm; Sat, Sun and pub. hols noon–5pm; entrance fee) founded in 1818. This attractive museum has an extensive collection of archaeological finds from the Netherlands, ancient Greece, Rome and Egypt. The mysterious floodlit Temple of Taffel in the entrance hall was presented by the Egyptian government in gratitude for Dutch aid in rescuing buildings threatened by the Aswan High Dam project.

The national ethnographic collection in **Rijksmuseum voor Volkenkunde** ❻ (1 Steenstraat, tel: 0715-168800; open Tues–Fri 10am–5pm, Sat, Sun and pub. hols noon–5pm; entrance fee) was founded in 1837. The museum has particularly interesting displays on the Dutch East Indies Company and the countries

BELOW: the miniature town of Madurodam.

A WALK AMONG THE SCULPTURES

Admirers of royal statues can take a leisurely 90-minute walk starting from Plein 1813 and ending at the Lange Voorhout. Head out from Sophialaan at the Independence Monument of King William I. Proceed along the Bazarstraat to Anna Paulownastraat and the site of the city's newest statue of Queen Anna Paulowna, the former wife of King William II.

A short way along the road are the Royal Stables, where the Queen's golden coach is housed. The eclectic neo-Renaissance complex has a façade with horses heads in the pediments, an imposing carriage gateway and an octagonal tower crowned with a spire above the mansard roof. One of the wings is now a museum.

Along the Noordeinde by the Kneuterdijk Palace, a remarkable building which has served a number of functions since it was built in 1716 as the Palace of the Oranges, is an extraordinary statue of Queen Wilhelmina. Its robustness and lack of detail symbolise the queen's strong personality and steadfastness. The Noordeinde Palace has a history closely associated with the House of Orange and has been the Royal Residence since the 17th century. Today Queen Beatrix uses it as her workplace and for receptions. Look for the large statue of Prince William I of Orange, thought to be the oldest free-standing statue in The Hague.

Delftware

D elftware is the name given to a distinctive blue and white tin-glazed pottery produced in Delft and other Dutch cities. The earliest known tin-glazed pottery in the Netherlands was called majolica, after the Mediterranean island of Majorca where it was produced. The Italians were the main majolica producers in the 16th century, using techniques derived from Moorish and Spanish craftsmen. The term *faïence*, which is sometimes applied to Delftware, derives from the Italian town of Faenza, another important centre of majolica production.

In the early 16th century, the Italian potter Guido da Savino moved to Antwerp, where he established the first majolica workshop in the Low Countries. After the fall of Antwerp in 1585, skilled craftsmen fled from the Spanish terror to Holland or England. The Antwerp majolica workers mainly settled in Dutch towns such as Delft and Haarlem, where they began to produce wall tiles for kitchens and

fireplaces. These provided protection against damp and dirt, the two great enemies of the Dutch housewife. Gradually new motifs were introduced to suit Dutch taste.

In the early 17th century trading ships of the VOC (United Dutch East Indies Company) returned from the Far East laden with delicateChinese blue and white porcelain, leading to a drop in demand for the coarser Dutch majolica. Many pottery workshops went bankrupt, while others responded by producing blue and white pottery modelled on Chinese porcelain, often decorated with Biblical episodes or scenes from Dutch life. In 1645 civil war in China caused a sharp decline in imported supply and a temporary upswing in demand for local pottery.

In the mid-18th century the Dutch pottery industry suffered another major blow when cheap mass-produced English creamware began to flood the market. By the mid-19th century "De Porceleyne Fles" (founded in 1653) was the only pottery left in Delft. In 1876 Joost 't Hooft revived the art of hand-painted blue decoration. Traditional designs were reintroduced, and later Art Nouveau motifs began to appear. Today many museums in the Netherlands possess large Delftware collections. The Gemeentemuseum in The Hague has one of the finest in the world, mostly from the famous Van den Burgh legacy. The Rijksmuseum in Amsterdam also has a splendid collection, including curious tulip vases which were especially popular in Britain and the Netherlands during the reign of William and Mary. There is an interesting collection of Delftware tiles in Delft's own Rijksmuseum Huis Lambert van Meerten. In particular, the collection illustrates the wit of Dutch tile painters.

The Museum Het Prinsenhof in Leeuwarden contains the world's largest collection of tiles, with examples from Persia, Spain, France and Holland. The visitors' centre at "De Porceleyne Fles" exhibits numerous vases, plates and tiles and ceramic architectural details made in Delft. But the most remarkable decoration made at the pottery is the tiled interior of the bodega in the Hotel Port van Cleve, Amsterdam.   ❑

LEFT: modern Delftware ceramic ornaments at Singel flower market, Amsterdam.

with which it traded, such as China, Japan and the islands of Indonesia. Anyone for whom a trip to Holland is not complete without seeing a windmill should visit the **Molenmuseum De Valk** ⑥ (1, 2e Binnenvestgracht, tel: 071-516 5353; open Tues–Sat 10am–5pm, Sun 1–5pm; entrance fee). Like the mill owned by Rembrandt's father, this 18th-century working windmill was erected on the site of a bastion and contains several unusual rooms once occupied by the miller and his family.

Maps:
Area 202
City 191

Picturesque town

Delft ❸ is situated on the River Vliet, midway between The Hague and Rotterdam. This pleasant old town has changed very little since Vermeer painted the *View of Delft*, now in the Mauritshuis in The Hague. Standing on the Hooikade, where, one day in 1660, Vermeer painted his home town under a sky that threatened a summer storm, you can still recognise many features from the painting, such as the dusky red brick of the Armamentarium and the slender white spire of the Nieuwe Kerk.

In the Middle Ages, Delft was a typical Netherlandish town of weavers and brewers, with numerous monasteries and convents within its walls. But its tranquil mood was shattered during the Dutch Revolt when William of Orange chose the town as his military headquarters, taking up residence in the Prinsenhof, a former monastery. He was assassinated here in 1584 by Balthasar Gerards, a fanatical Catholic, and is buried in the town's Nieuwe Kerk.

In the 17th century Delft had the dubious distinction of being the main arsenal of the Dutch Republic. In October 1654, the town was devastated by an explosion in the Secreet van Hollandt (a gunpowder store hidden in the garden

BELOW:
old Delftware.

TIP

To capture something of the atmosphere of medieval Delft, veer away from the centre and follow the canal east along Oosteinde to Oostpoort. Built around 1400, this is the only one of Delft's eight medieval gates still standing.

BELOW: Nieuwe Kerk, Delft.

of a former convent), which destroyed one-third of the houses in the city and killed 200 people. One of the victims was Rembrandt's gifted pupil Carel Fabritius, the painter responsible for the beautiful study, *Goldfinch*, in the Mauritshuis in The Hague.

A canalside walk

A walk along **Oude Delft**, a narrow leafy canal, takes you past some of the most interesting buildings in the city. The letters VOC marked on a Renaissance house at Oude Delft 39 is a reminder that Delft was once one of the cities that bonded together to form the Verenigde Oostindische Compagnie – the United Dutch East Indies Company.

The massive brick building rising up from the water opposite is the **Armamentarium**, formerly the arsenal of the provinces of Holland and West Friesland. Its function is symbolised by the bearded figure of Mars, the god of war, perched awkwardly on a lion and a heap of weapons. Appropriately, it is the **Koninklijk Nederlands Legermuseum** (Royal Dutch Army Museum, 1 Korte Geer, tel: 015-215 0500; open Mon–Fri 10am–5pm, Sat and Sun noon–5pm; entrance fee) that now occupies the building. The bridge at the end of Oude Delft marks the site of a medieval city gate, the Rotterdamse Poort, which appears in the foreground of Vermeer's *View of Delft*.

A narrow canal, which begins as Lange Geer but changes its name four times, runs north from here. The curious **Museum Paul Tétar van Elven** (67 Koornmarkt, tel: 015-212 4206; open Tues–Sun 1–5pm; entrance fee) on the section of canal called Koornmarkt was the 19th-century home of an artist who attempted to recreate rooms reminiscent of Vermeer paintings.

Vermeer lived on **Markt** , Delft's broad market square lined with cafés and restaurants. The **Nieuwe Kerk** ❸ was begun on the east side of this square in the 14th century on the site of a medieval miracle. The slender spire of the church manages to appear harmonious though it was built in separate stages from the late 14th to the early 16th centuries, and subsequently damaged several times by fire.

Founder of the Dutch Republic

The lofty late-Gothic choir, which dates from the 15th century, contains the marble and bronze **Mausoleum of William the Silent**, founder of the Dutch Republic. Begun by Hendrick de Keyser in 1614 (long after William's assassination) and completed eight years later by his son Pieter, it is richly decorated with uplifting motifs for the young Dutch Republic; the dog at William's feet symbolises fidelity, and the four female figures represent liberty (holding a hat), justice, religion and courage. The epitaph was composed by the statesman and poet Constantijn Huygens. The tombs of subsequent stadholders and monarchs are in the crypt of the Nieuwe Kerk.

The jurist Hugo Grotius, who was born on the Nieuwe Langedijk in Delft in 1583, is commemorated by an 18th-century memorial. In 1618 Grotius was imprisoned in Slot Loevestein for his support of the Remonstrants, but two years later his resourceful wife helped him to escape in a book trunk (possibly the one that is now displayed in the Prinsenhof Museum in Delft, though the Rijksmuseum in Amsterdam also has a chest which is claimed by some historians to have been the jurist's historic hiding place). Grotius spent the rest of his life in exile, and died in Rostock in 1645. His most famous work, *De Jure Belli*

Jan Vermeer (1632–75) is thought to have spent his whole life in Delft. Though only 40 paintings have been ascribed to him, he is regarded as one of the greatest Dutch painters, alongside Hals and Rembrandt.

BELOW: picturesque canal walk, Delft.

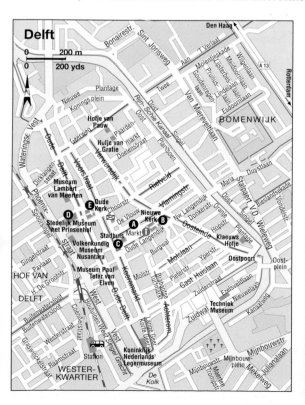

et Pacis, laid the foundations of modern international law. A plaque was attached to the monument by delegates to the International Peace Conference in The Hague in 1899. In recent years, the writings of Grotius on justifiable warfare have been cited to shed light on the nuclear weapons debate.

The Renaissance **Stadhuis** (city hall) opposite, was built in 1618 by Hendrick de Keyser. It is decorated with ferocious lions' heads, a characteristic feature of buildings of the early Dutch Republic. This square building incorporates the stone tower of a medieval town hall gutted by fire in 1618. Botermarkt, a covered canal, leads to the most fashionable quarter of Delft. The weathered stone house at Oude Delft 167, built in the Flamboyant Gothic style of Brabant in 1510, was one of the few houses to survive the great fire of 1536.

Scene of the crime

A lane north of here leads to the **Stedelijk Museum het Prinsenhof** (1 Sint Agathaplein, tel: 015–260 2358; open Tues–Sat 10am–5pm, Sun 1–5pm; entrance fee) which contains an excellent collection of topographical paintings of Delft (frequently commissioned to illustrate one calamity or another), medieval sculpture, portraits of prominent figures of the Dutch Revolt, Delftware and maps that give a clue to the history of the Netherlands and the development of its cities.

The museum occupies a beautiful 15th-century Burgundian Gothic convent with ancient tiled floors and leaded windows looking out on leafy gardens. This nunnery was the unlikely setting for the murder of William the Silent in 1584 by the Spanish sympathiser Balthasar Gerards. The bullet holes in the wall of the Moordzaal have been carefully preserved behind glass.

TIP

Thursday is market day on Delft's central square. It's a good day to visit if you enjoy the colour and bustle of a local market, but not ideal if you want to take in the sights.

BELOW: outdoor café at The Hague.

Opposite the convent stands one of Delft's finest buildings, the Gothic **Oude Kerk** ❸ (open Mar–Oct, Mon–Sat 9am–6pm; Nov–Feb Mon–Sat 11am–4pm; entrance fee). The tower, which dates from the 14th century, has a pronounced lean and its bell sounds a suitably melancholy note. The church was built over the course of the 14th and 15th centuries, and a magnificent Flamboyant Gothic north transept was added in the 16th century by Anthonis Keldermans of Mechelen (though the effect is rather weakened by the absence of a south transept).

Map on page 191

Pepys' approval

Within the whitewashed interior, the **tomb of Admiral Piet Hein** is given pride of place on the site of the main altar. Admiral Maarten Tromp, the hero of some 50 sea battles, is also buried in the Oude Kerk. His memorial is decorated with a marble relief depicting a sea battle. The Engligh writer Samuel Pepys, on visiting the church, was particularly impressed by the quality of the carving on this tomb, and noted that the smoke depicted was "the best expressed that ever I saw".

Another monument commemorates the Delft scientist Anthonie van Leeuwenhoek, who is credited with inventing the microscope, thus enabling him to observe such organisms as bacteria, red blood corpuscles and spermatozoa for the first time. A modern sculpture symbolising a yeast cell in the park at the end of Oude Delft commemorates Van Leeuwenhoek's discoveries. Perhaps fittingly, the air is now filled with a pungent yeasty smell from a neighbouring biochemical factory.

In a nearby clump of trees lies the derelict tomb of Karl Wilhelm Naundorff, who claimed he was the son of the executed King Louis XVI of France. ❏

BELOW: parliament buildings, The Hague.

ROTTERDAM AND ENVIRONS

From bombed out ruin to dynamic, modern city, Rotterdam has exceeded its ambition to become one of Holland's major urban centres – it is now the world's busiest port

Maps:
Area 202
City 196

Amsterdam

Rotterdam

The southern part of Zuid-Holland province is dominated by the port of Rotterdam, which extends for 37 km (23 miles) along both banks of the Nieuwe Maas river, from Rotterdam to Hoek van Holland (the Hook of Holland). The port activities, however, hardly impinge on the city of Rotterdam, which is unexpectedly quiet and attractive.

Dordrecht to the south retains much more the atmosphere of an old Dutch river port, with crumbling brick warehouses and canals lined with barges. The eastern part of this region is still largely rural, with several pleasant small towns, such as Gouda to the northeast of Rotterdam, and Schoonhoven and Nieuwpoort on opposite banks of the River Lek to the east.

In recent years, the face of **Rotterdam ❹** has changed almost beyond recognition. With its dynamic modern skyline, it is now the largest and busiest port in the world. Strolling along the Weena, the bustling downtown area, it is easy to see that this is a city on the move. One interesting landmark is the World Trade Center, a flattened green ellipse built on top of the Koopman Stock Exchange building. Another is the Nationale Nederlanden insurance building in the 150-metre (492-ft) high Delftse Poort, which is the highest office block in the Netherlands. There is now even life after dark in Rotterdam as opposed to 10 years ago when the city shut down as soon as the last office worker had gone home.

LEFT: cube houses designed by Piet Blom. **BELOW:** statue of Erasmus in front of Grote Kerk.

Re-emergence

This is not the first time in its history that Rotterdam has undergone major redevelopment. It emerged as an important shipping centre towards the end of the 17th century when the Dutch were prospering from trade in the East Indies. After a period of decline, its status as a European trade centre was elevated again in the 19th century by the construction of the Nieuwe Waterweg (New Waterway) canal to the sea (1866–72). In 1898, the 10-storey, 45-metre (148-ft) high Witte Huis was erected beside the old harbour.

After the port was bombed in 1940 (Witte Huis was one of the only buildings that didn't crumble), it was rebuilt, with massive investment, to meet modern requirements (*see page 210*). The spacious, pedestrianised streets of the Lijnbaan quarter, completed in 1953, inspired similar developments elsewhere.

No longer in the shadow of Amsterdam and The Hague, Rotterdam seems to have resolved its identity crisis and is realising its ambition to become one of Holland's major cities. It has a prestigious orchestra and hosts an internationally respected film festival. In summer, free dance, music and theatre festivals are staged in its parks and squares. The city centre reflects a fascinating cultural and culinary diversity.

TIP

In summer the Circle Bus Tour follows a route through the city, with stops at a number of museums, shopping areas and other points of interest – all for the price of a single day ticket.

Rotterdam is easily accessible. The city and its environs are served efficiently by trams, buses and the underground. It's worth paying a visit to the **VVV office** (Coolsingel 67; open Mon–Thurs 9.30am–6pm, Fri 9.30am-9pm, Sat 9.30am-5pm; tel: 0900 403 4065). As well as providing brochures, tourist information and a concert and theatre ticket service, it gives out free transport maps.

As in any city, be aware of, but don't be put off by the beggars and down-and-outs lingering around the station, many of them in their own drug-induced world. In typical Dutch style, the Rotterdam police have created a specific area near the station to keep a close eye on them in an attempt to reduce crime. The rest of the city feels comfortably safe and easy to explore, unless the local football team, Feijenoord, has played a championship game, in which case it's a good idea to avoid the centre of town altogether. It has been known for the peaceful city streets to be transformed within minutes into a riot of broken glass and plundered buildings by gangs of hooligans looking for trouble after a match.

Architectural highlights

The **Oude Haven**, Rotterdam's former harbour, has some exciting modern architecture. For many years after the bombardment of the city in 1940, the devastated area around the old harbour remained a wasteland. In the late 1980s it was rapidly transformed by the construction of a huge public library in glass and steel. The building offers fantastic views over the port and the modern city as well as its own hanging gardens. A collection of redundant Rhine barges owned by the Maritime Museum is also on permanent display here.

The only medieval building still standing is the **Grote Kerk Ⓐ** (open Tues–Sat 10am–4pm; Oct–May closed Thurs; entrance free). Also known as St

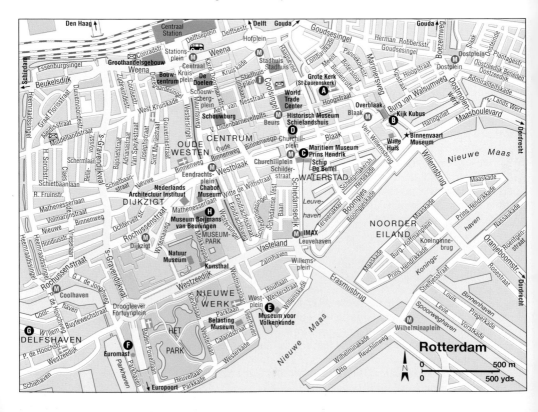

Rotterdam

Map
on page
196

Laurenskerk, the church was gutted during the war, but subsequently restored with great skill. On a bleak square in front of the church stands a statue of Erasmus, the philosopher and scholar, noted for his satire, who was born in Rotterdam in 1469. Although Erasmus left home at the tender age of six to study in Deventer and later Oxford, he spent most of his life in Rotterdam, and the city's university is named after him. The bronze statue by Hendrick de Keyser in front of the church dates from 1622.

The **Blaakse Bos** nearby is a bizarre cluster of tilted cube houses supported by tall concrete columns, designed by Piet Blom. A raised pedestrian street lined with shops (Promenade Overblaak) runs beneath the houses to create a modern version of the Ponte Vecchio in Florence. You can visit the exhibition house **Kijk Kubus ❸** (Cube House; open Mar–Oct: daily 11am–5pm; Nov–Feb: Fri–Sun 11am–5pm; entrance fee) for an impression of life in these strange futuristic dwellings, where all the furniture has to be adapted to the sloping walls.

The VVV has a brochure on architectural excursions, from pre-war Rotterdam and post-war reconstruction to the Museum Park and the newly developed Kop van Zuid city quarter.

On the waterfront

The waterfront promenade along Boompjes brings you out on **Leuvehaven**. A good place to stop and have a beer is the **Cambrinus Café**, which specialises in quality Belgian brews. There's an IMAX cinema facing the waterfront but the tourist-oriented restaurants on the waterside are pricy and mediocre, and best avoided.

The birth of Erasmus in 1469 caused a great scandal – his father was a Catholic priest and his mother, the housekeeper.

BELOW: old and new architecture.

*Clocktower detail
atop the lively
Hotel New York.*

At the end of Leuvehaven, behind a disused red lighthouse, is the **Maritiem Museum Prins Hendrik ❻** (1 Leuvehaven, tel: 010-413 2680; open Tues–Sat: 10am–5pm, Sun: 11am–5pm; July and Aug: 10am–5pm; entrance fee), a modern museum devoted to Rotterdam's maritime history. The interior is reminiscent of a ship, with long steel gangplanks leading to the upper floors. The café terrace offers one of the best views in Rotterdam, looking down the Leuvehaven to the river. The museum also displays a number of exhibits on the quayside, including a reconstructed rope walk. The fully restored 19th-century warship *De Buffel* is permanently moored here, and is worth visiting for the opulent officers' quarters, furnished in the style of a Victorian club.

In the middle of the windswept square beside this museum stands the sculpture *De Verwoeste Stad* (The Razed City). Designed by Ossip Zadkine in 1953, it symbolises the destruction of Rotterdam in 1940. A figure contorted with fear holds up his arms to the sky; the large hole in the sculpture represents the destruction of the city's heart.

Hemmed in by modern office blocks opposite, the **Historisch Museum Schielandshuis ❶** (31 Korte Hoogstraat, tel: 010-217 6767; open Tues–Fri 10am–5pm, Sat and Sun 11am–5pm; entrance fee) occupies a handsome 17th-century classical building once owned by the Schieland district water board. This small museum has a collection of paintings, period rooms and dolls' houses which provide a visual history of art and culture in Rotterdam. The famous Atlas van Stolk, an extensive collection of historic prints and maps, is housed here, and frequently forms the basis for interesting temporary exhibitions.

BELOW: Rotterdam's
metro station.

Occupying a pastel neoclassical building further along the waterfront, the **Museum voor Volkenkunde ❺** (open Tues–Fri 10am–5pm, Sat–Sun 11am–

Map on page 196

5pm; entrance fee) regularly organises stimulating temporary exhibitions on non-Western cultures and his its own reputed ethnic restaurant. Drop in at the **Grand Café-Restaurant Loos** on the Westplein for lunch or dinner in a chic ambience. Or else you can walk across the street to the small yacht harbour and take a speedboat ride across the river Maas to visit the **Hotel New York**. Although it keeps a very low profile, it is one of the liveliest places in town to have a drink or something to eat. Located in the former offices of the Holland America Line, most rooms have magnificent views of the river and all are uniquely furnished.

Old and new

Overlooking the small **Veerhaven** beyond are several 19th-century shipping offices decorated with telling maritime details. Westerkade leads from here along the waterfront to the attractive English-style **Het Park**, with a curious wooden church for Norwegian seamen. On the west side of the park, the **Euromast ⑦** (open Apr–Sept: daily 10am–7pm; Oct–Mar: daily 10am–5pm; entrance fee) rises above the trees to a height of 185 metres (600 ft). The observation platform at 100 metres (330 ft), offers a panoramic view of the city and port. Those with a head for heights can continue to the top of the mast by means of a slowly revolving cabin. The view from here is breathtaking.

The Euromast's observation platform affords fine views.

With the opening of the Erasmus Bridge in 1998, the city centre was extended further into the harbour area where an ambitious, well-conceived Docklands-style development of shops, cafés and housing has been created. The new tram and metro line provides easy access to the area.

Further downstream, beyond the park, lies **Delfshaven ⑥**, founded in the 14th century as the port of Delft, but now part of the municipality of Rotterdam. Delfshaven survived the bombardment in 1940, and most of its buildings are protected monuments. Admiral Piet Hein, who seized the Spanish silver fleet in a daring escapade in 1626, was born here. The port also has associations with the Pilgrim Fathers, who set sail for the New World (via Plymouth where they joined the *Mayflower*) in 1620 from the Middenkous quay.

A lofty double-gabled warehouse dating from the 19th century, **De Dubbelde Palmboom** (Voorhaven 12; open Tues–Sat 11am–5pm; entrance fee) has been attractively converted into a museum of Rotterdam history. As befits a city that prides itself on toil, the museum is devoted to work in the Maas river delta from prehistoric times to the present day. The nearby **Zakkendragershuisje** (Voorstraat 13; open Tues–Sat 10am–5pm, Sun 1–5pm; entrance free), built in 1653 as the guild house for the Grain Sack Carriers, now houses a small museum where pewter manufacture is demonstrated.

Museum Park

The best known of Rotterdam's 34 museums is the **Boymans van Beuningen Museum ⑧** (open Tues–Sat 10am–5pm, Sun 11am–5pm; entrance fee). Founded in 1847, it houses one of the best art collections in the Netherlands (though many of the paintings

BELOW: Delfshaven.

Rotterdam Port

Rotterdam is now the world's largest and busiest port, stretching for 37 km (23 miles) along the waterfront of the Nieuwe Maas. Each year Rotterdam handles around 250 million tons of goods, representing about 4 percent of the total world tonnage shipped by sea. About 85 percent of citrus fruits consumed in Europe are shipped through the port, and more than 50 percent of Europe's tobacco imports and 40 percent of all the tea drunk in Britain arrives via Rotterdam.

It was the completion in 1890 of the Nieuwe Waterweg between Rotterdam and Hoek van Holland that provided Rotterdam with a direct link to the North Sea; previously ships were compelled to navigate a series of notoriously difficult channels. The port has several natural advantages, the most important being its situation on the main branch of the Rhine (the Lek), the world's busiest river. Rotterdam is also connected to France and

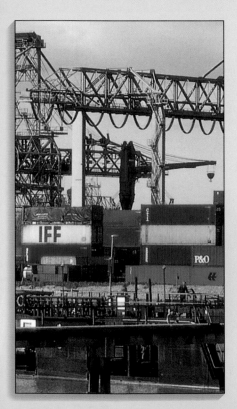

southern Belgium by the River Maas, and with northern Belgium by the River Schelde. The Waalhaven, a predecessor to the modern port, was completed in 1930, and was then the world's largest harbour. Much of the Waalhaven is now devoted to container ships, a form of mass transport pioneered by Rotterdam. In 1972 the first container ship between Europe and Japan docked in the Waalhaven. Container ships can transport 3,000 containers – which if placed end to end would stretch 18 km (11 miles).

The world's largest container port is the Europe Container Terminal in the Eemhaven, the next harbour downstream. This terminal, with its 14 giant cranes, can easily handle one million containers annually. Rotterdam is also the world's most important oil terminal. Today five major companies – Shell, BP, Esso, Q8 and Gulf – have storage tanks and refineries in the port.

The harbour now constitutes about 50 percent of the area of Rotterdam. The best way to see the wharfs, quays, docks and silos is to take a 75-minute Spido harbour tour from the Leuvenhoofd. Each kilometre of the Rhine is numbered, beginning at kilometre 0 on Lake Constance, and reaching 1001 at the Spido quay. At kilometre 1008 the boat turns across the busy shipping lanes and enters the Eemhaven, then heads back upstream to enter the Waalhaven.

Although covering only 7 km (5 miles) out of the 37 km (23 miles) of quays between the city and the North Sea, the trip provides a fascinating glimpse of port activities, as it darts beneath the bows of ships stacked with containers, or passes vessels in dry dock for repair.

There are dinner cruises year round, and in the summer months other tours explore the flood barrier, the Delta works and Dordrecht and Europoort. The *Flying Dutchman* offers a speedy trip in a hydrofoil along the harbour and surrounding areas. There is even a Dutch "pancake" cruise boat.

A route for cars signed "Rotterdamse Haven Route" covers almost 100 km (60 miles) from Rotterdam to the Europoort, and those interested in making "industrial" tours should contact the vvv Rotterdam. ❑

LEFT: Rotterdam port.

donated by Frans Boijmans were destroyed by fire in 1864). The original museum was rebuilt in 1935 and extended in 1972. An ambitious renovation has now created more space for its permanent and changing exhibitions. The museum owns a number of well-known early Flemish paintings, including *The Prodigal Son* by Hieronymus Bosch and one of the two versions of *The Tower of Babel* by Pieter Brueghel the Elder. The collection of Old Masters includes Rembrandt's tender portrait of his son Titus, painted in 1655. The modern collection features canvases by Monet, Van Gogh and Kandinsky, and several surrealist works by Magritte and Dali. The collections of industrial art and arts and crafts span an extensive period from the 14th century to the present day.

Boijmans stands on the edge of the Museum Park, an innovative project linking a green oasis known as the "people's park" with cultural institutions like the **Kunsthal**, the **Dutch Architectural Institute**, the **Nature Museum**, and the **Chabot Museum**.

The **Kunsthal** exhibition gallery (341 West Zeedijk, tel: 010-440 0301; open Tues–Sat 10am–5pm, Sun noon–5pm; entrance fee), focuses on contemporary art, occupying a building by renowned architect Rem Koolhaas. The logo on the tower is inspired by the "This Way Up" sign stencilled on to crates. The Kunsthal has no permanent collection of its own, but presents a wide choice of exhibitions ranging from art (Picasso), photography (Helmut Newton and Alice Springs) and architecture to jewellery, cars and football clubs.

The **Nederlands Architectuur Instituut** (**NAI**); (25 Museum Park, tel: 010-440 1200; open Tues–Sat 10am–5pm, Sun noon–5pm; entrance fee) is worth visiting just to admire the glass building itself, designed by Jo Coenen. A striking installation by Peter Struycken illuminates the gallery under the long archive section and is particularly impressive at night. The NAI hosts exhibitions and lectures on architecture and is divided into different building sections which are arranged to resemble an urban landscape. The stylish **Café Coenen** is open for lunch and dinner and has one of the most attractive terraces in the city.

BELOW: Museum Boymans van Beuningen.

Most of Rotterdam's private art galleries are concentrated either in the streets bordering the Boymans-Van Beuningen Museum or in Delfshaven. Attractive cafés and restaurants in the area are not so easy to find. But if you take a stroll along the Witte de With-straat or the Westersingel, there are one or two hidden treasures to be discovered, such as **De Harmonie** and **Van Popering**, which serve French and Belgian specialities. Conveniently close to the Boymans-Van Beuningen Museum, the **Café De Unie** at Mauritsweg 35 is a faithful reconstruction of a building designed in 1924 by the Rotterdam architect J. J. P. Oud. Like the Rietveld-Schröder House in Utrecht, it obeys the tenets of the De Stijl movement, using vertical and horizontal lines and blocks of primary colour for decoration. The quayside of the Oude Haven is another good spot for attractive cafés.

River Junction

The old river port of **Dordrecht** ❺ lies at the confluence of three busy waterways, about 15 km (10 miles) southeast of Rotterdam, and provides a pleasing contrast to the modernism of Rotterdam. A castle was built here by Count Dirk III in the early 11th century to control vital shipping routes into and out of Holland. The town that grew up around the castle is the oldest in Holland, and was granted a charter by Count Willem I in 1220.

Dordrecht played an important role in the emergence of the Dutch state; in 1572 this was one of the first towns to side with the Protestant rebels, and later the same year the United Provinces met in the Statenzaal (still standing in a courtyard known as Hof, which once belonged to an Augustinian friary).

Dordrecht was also the scene of the famous Synod of Dordt, held in 1618–19, at which the hardline Dutch Calvinists rejected the more moderate tenets of the Remonstrants. This led, in 1619, to the imprisonment in Slot Loevestein of Hugo Grotius, a leading Remonstrant, and the execution in The Hague of the statesman Johan van Oldenbarnevelt.

Dordrecht's waterfront

The waterfront at Dordrecht is the town's most interesting area, though many of the old warehouses are abandoned and decaying. A number of them are inscribed with the names of German towns or rivers, a reminder that Dordrecht was once a major port for the shipment of German wine.

The best approach to the harbour is down **Wijnstraat** (whose name recalls the wine trade). This is an old street lined with damp warehouses and curiosity shops. including an interesting antiquarian bookshop crammed with dusty novels in many languages, old records, faded prints, framed paintings and second-hand navigation maps. The overspill stock is stored in old St Emilion crates, suggesting that Dordrecht is still a wine port of some importance.

TIP

If you want to venture further afield, the area around Dordrecht has some pretty country-side, while the Kinderdijk windmills and the Biesbosch nature reserve are not too far away.

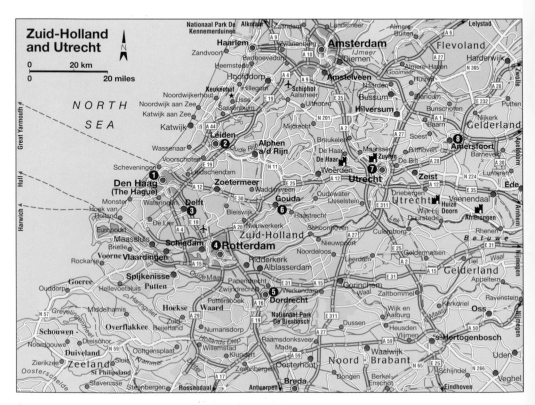

Zuid-Holland and Utrecht

Turning left at the end of this street, you come upon the **Groothoofds Poort**, a magnificent city gate built in the 17th century on the site of its medieval precursor. Once the principal entrance to Dordrecht, it is designed in grand Renaissance style, with a large cartouche depicting the Maid of Holland, symbolised by a plumpish woman behind a wicker fence. The gate occupies a spectacular site at the confluence of three major waterways. To the right, the Beneden Merwede carries river traffic east to Gorinchem and the River Maas. Straight ahead, the Noord is used by barges travelling north to the Lek and Rotterdam, and to the left, De Dordtse Kil carries shipping bound for Holland's Diep and Antwerp. An estimated 1,500 barges and ships pass by this spot every day, making it the busiest river junction in Europe. The quayside is now sadly deserted, except occasionally in the summer months when the *Pieter Boele*, a steam tug built in 1893, leaves from here on a round trip through the local waterways.

The Van Gijn collection

Turning left along the waterfront, then across the little drawbridge, will bring you to **Nieuwe Haven**, a picturesque harbour filled with creaking boats and surrounded by the cluttered premises of ships' chandlers. This harbour is overlooked by the **Museum Simon van Gijn** (29, Nieuwe Haven, tel: 078-613 3793; open Tues–Sun 11am–5pm; entrance fee), a richly furnished merchant's house built in 1729. In 1864 it was acquired by the banker and art collector Simon van Gijn, who lived here until his death in 1922. Although it is now a museum, the house still has a lived-in feeling, and its handsome period rooms convey a sense of quiet prosperity. The kitchen, with its tiled walls and gleaming brass pots, dates from the 18th century, while a room on the first floor contains a Renaissance fireplace dating from about 1550.

Decorated with curious figures of savages, it once heated the banqueting hall of the guild of arquebusiers (marksmen). Also of interest is the study on the first floor built by Van Gijn in neo-Renaissance style to evoke the 17th-century interiors of Vermeer.

The Van Gijn collection includes paintings, Flemish tapestries, glass and historical relics. On the first-floor landing is an attractive 17th-century shop sign, thought to have been painted by Albert Cuyp for a relative who sold wine. The most popular exhibition is the delightful collection of antique Dutch toys displayed in the attic and garden house, which includes dolls' houses, miniature shops, mechanical models (some still working) and magic lanterns. The museum also contains a model of Dordrecht as it was in 1544.

From the top of the tower of the nearby **Grote Kerk** (open Apr–Oct: Tues–Sat 10.30am–4.30pm, Sun noon–4pm; Nov–Dec: first and third Sat of the month 2–4pm; entrance free), you can see how the town has changed since then. The Grote Kerk itself was built in the 15th century by Evert Spoorwater of Antwerp in a subdued Brabant Gothic style. The distinctive squat tower dates back even further; it was begun in 1339, but never completed. The enormity of the first tier indicates that it was intended to support a very lofty edifice, but instead it is surmounted rather oddly by four 17th-century clocks.

Map on page 202

There's no shortage of windmills around Kinderdijk.

BELOW:
trawlerman in Dordrecht harbour.

Voorstraatshaven is the narrow canal running alongside the church that leads into the centre of town. The view of the **Stadhuis** (old city hall) from the Visbrug is particularly impressive. This 19th-century building spanning the canal rests on the foundations of a 14th-century exchange established by Flemish merchants. Just across the bridge at Visstraat 3–7 is an attractive café, **Crimpert Salm**, which occupies a Renaissance building, dating from 1608, where the guild of fishmongers used to meet.

Dordrechts Museum

The **Dordrechts Museum** (40 Museumstraat, tel: 078-648 2148; open Tues–Sun 11am–5pm; entrance fee), formerly a lunatic asylum, has a fine collection of paintings by 17th-century Dordrecht artists, including Albert Cuyp, Samuel van Hoogstraten, Nicholas Maes and Ferdinand Bol. The self-portrait by Ferdinand Bol clearly shows the influence of Rembrandt, under whom he studied. Jan van Goyen, though not a local, painted an alluring *View of Dordrecht* in 1651, seen from the north bank of the Oude Maas. The low horizon and threatening sky are characteristic of 17th-century Dutch landscape painting.

A panoramic view of Dordrecht by Adam Willaerts, hanging on the staircase shows the busy waterfront in 1629. A room of 19th-century works by the Dordrecht-born artist Ary Scheffer is furnished attractively in Victorian style. An interesting painting by a fellow artist portrays Scheffer in his Paris studio working on one of the paintings now in the Dordrecht collection. The museum has several 17th-century "vanity paintings", still lifes depicting symbols of mortality such as snuffed candles and pipes. This popular Dutch motif of human mortality is echoed on the portal of the nearby Arend Maartenshof, a

BELOW: kitchen at the Simon van Gijn museum.

17th-century almshouse at Museumstraat 56, where a Latin inscription above the entrance reminded its elderly residents that *Vita Vapor* – roughly translated it means "life is but a wisp."

Map on page 202

Gouda

Gouda ❻ is a pretty little town on the river Gouwe, at the point where it enters the Hollandse IJssel, about 25 km (16 miles) northeast of Rotterdam. Though its harbour activities have ceased, Gouda remains a lively market town, especially on Thursday morning from June to September when a traditional cheese market is staged at the Markt. Local farmers bring their home-produced cheeses here to be weighed and graded. The town's main activity revolves around the **Markt**, which is unusually spacious by Dutch standards. In the middle stands the Stadhuis, built in 1450 in a Gothic style reminiscent of Flemish town halls, with numerous statues of Burgundian dukes and duchesses, and lofty step gables sprouting pinnacles. The **Waag** (Weigh House) on the north side of the square is an imposing Dutch Classical building, built in 1668 by Pieter Post, which has been converted into a **cheese museum** (open Apr–Oct: Tues–Sat 10am–5pm, Sun noon–5pm; entrance free). An interesting relief in the tympanum depicts the weighing of Gouda cheeses.

Kerkstraat leads from the Markt to a beguiling medieval area of quiet cobbled lanes surrounding **St Janskerk** (open Mar–Oct: Mon–Sat 9am–5pm; Nov–Feb: Mon–Sat 10am–4pm; entrance fee). This elongated Gothic church, rebuilt after a fire in 1552, is renowned for its exceptional stained-glass windows. Most of these were given to the church during its reconstruction by a wide range of donors, including municipalities, abbeys, guilds, princes and burgomasters. The

The Dutch consume Gouda in large quantities, whether as jong *(a young creamy cheese),* belegen *(matured),* oud *(10 months old), or* extra belegen *(a crumbly old cheese).*

BELOW:
St Janskerk, Gouda.

FOUR ARCHITECTURAL WALKS

A combination of rich docklands history and modern architecture that combines living, working and recreation with alfresco cafés and shops, makes for an interesting Rotterdam walk. Kop van Zuid is the newest development in the dockland area, on the left bank of the Maas, connected to the city centre by the striking Erasmus Bridge. Take the Metro to Wilhelminaplein or a train to Rotterdam Zuid.

The Museum Park walk begins and concludes at the Netherlands Architecture Institute (NAI), a modern urban park ringed by the NAI, the Chabot Museum, Museum Boijmans van Beuningen, the Kunsthal and the Natural History Museum. The walk also leads into the Scheepvaart (maritime quarter). The Waterstad walk begins at the Leuvehaven at the Maritime Museum Prins Hendrik. The focus is on the Oude Haven (old harbour) where the celebrated cube-shaped Paalwoningen (pile dwellings) stand in stark contrast to 18th-century mansions on the southern side of the Haringvliet.

The City Centre walk focusses on the post-war reconstruction of Rotterdam's city centre from 1945 to the present. You will see a broad range of architecture beginning at the VVV Tourist Office building at 67 Coolsingel. A brochure about these walks can be obtained from the VVV office in Rotterdam.

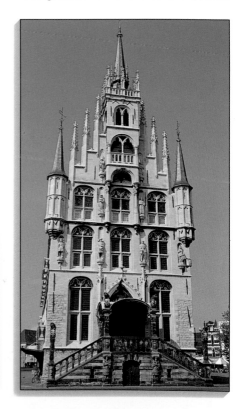

Map on page 202

14 finest windows were designed by the brothers Wouter and Dirck Crabeth in 1555–77, in a transitional style between Gothic and Renaissance art. The guilds usually commissioned representations of Biblical episodes that were connected in some way with their trade. The window depicting *Jonah and the Whale* (window 30) was presented in 1565 by the guild of fishermen, while the butchers' guild donated *Baalam and his Ass* (window 31). The *Last Supper* (window 7) was donated by Philip II in 1577, when Gouda was still a Catholic city, while in 1561 William of Orange presented the church with *Christ Driving the Money-lenders out of the Temple* (window 22).

A number of other interesting windows were executed after Gouda fell to the Protestants. Window 25, illustrating the relief of Leiden in 1574, was given by the city of Delft in 1603. In 1596, the city of Haarlem donated window 2, showing the capture of Damietta by Dutch Crusaders, while Dordrecht proudly presented window 3, illustrating its own attractions, the following year. In the 19th century, Jan Schouten of Delft added three very curious windows (numbers 1A, 1B and 1C) made up from old fragments of glass.

Stedelijk museum

BELOW:
market day, Gouda.
RIGHT: 16th-century
stained-glass
window in St
Janskerk.

Opposite the church is the **Lazarus Gate**, a handsome sandstone portal, dated 1609, that leads into the leafy garden of the **Catharina Gasthuis**. Founded in the 14th century as a hospice, it was later used as a hospital. Today the complex is used to display objects from the varied collection of the municipal **Stedelijk Museum** (open Mon–Sat 10am–5pm, Sun noon–5pm; entrance fee). Several of its rooms are furnished in period style, including a Dutch kitchen. The collection of paintings is remarkably good for a town of this size, and includes several works by the Gouda-born artist Pieter Pourbus the Old, a moving portrait of a dead child by Bartholomeus van der Helst, a series of civic guard group portraits, and some Impressionist paintings by members of the Barbizon and Hague Schools.

Achter de Kerk street leads to a curious brick chapel modelled on the Church of the Holy Sepulchre in Jerusalem. Turning right here down Spieringstraat takes you past the ornate 17th-century portals of the orphanage (on the left) and an almshouse (opposite). Turning right along Minderbroederssteeg, a narrow street with some old warehouses, you reach Oost Haven, a former harbour now bereft of shipping.

On the opposite quay stands a 17th-century building with a Renaissance façade, originally a shop selling tobacco, coffee, tea and snuff. It is now the **De Moriaan Museum** (Westhaven 29; open Mon–Sat 10am–5pm, Sun noon–5pm; entrance fee, but free with Stedelick Museum ticket). The name De Moriaan, which means "The Moor", arose from an 18th-century belief that the Moors were avid pipe smokers. The beautiful 17th-century interior houses a large collection of clay pipes, the manufacture of which was introduced to Gouda in about 1620 by some English pipe-makers. The long thin-stemmed pipes, familiar from paintings of crowded inn scenes by Jan Steen and Adriaen Brouwer, had particularly small bowls because of the high price of tobacco at this time. ❑

UTRECHT

Founded as a Roman garrison, the "Ford on the Rhine" blossomed into a Christian stronghold defended by fairytale castles, its power symbolised by the cathedral that still dominates the historic centre

Maps:
Area 202
City 212

The small province of Utrecht owes its existence to the Christian Church. In the late 7th century, Pepin II, King of the Franks (a recent convert to Christianity) consolidated his power here by defeating the Frisian King Radboud at Wijk bij Duurstede. He then set out to convert his lands to Christianity and appointed a Bishop of Utrecht. Het Sticht, as the see was called, gradually extended its power, and by the 11th century its boundaries reached as far north as Groningen.

The most striking symbol of the power of the Church in Utrecht province today is the 14th-century tower of the Utrecht Dom (cathedral), which can be seen from as far away as Culemborg. The numerous other churches, monasteries and convents that have survived in Utrecht and Amersfoort are further evidence of the extent of Het Sticht's influence.

City of churches

Utrecht **❼** itself is one of the oldest cities in the Netherlands. It stands on a tributary of the Rhine, and was founded in AD 47 as a Roman garrison. A posting to *Trajectum ad Rhenum* (the Ford on the Rhine) must have seemed a bleak prospect to any soldier used to sunnier climes. This frontier was constantly being attacked from the east and the Roman settlement at Utrecht was destroyed five times before it was totally eradicated by Germanic tribes in the 3rd century. All that now remains to show for two centuries of Roman occupation are a few pottery fragments in the Centraal Museum.

King Pepin II took control in 689. He appointed Willibrord, a missionary from Northumberland, his first bishop (commemorated by a statue opposite the Janskerk). Willibrord built two churches on this strategic site and set about converting the people of his bishopric to Christianity.

In the 11th century Utrecht flourished under the protection of the German emperors. Bishop Bernold embarked on an ambitious project to make Utrecht a great spiritual centre of northern Europe and drew up a plan to create a cross of four churches, with the Domkerk at the centre. Only two of these remain standing – Janskerk to the north and Pieterskerk to the east – but the position of the other two is easily identified. The cloister on Mariaplaats belonged to Mariakerk, the church at the west end of the cross, while a portal on Nieuwegracht leads to the ruined transept of the Paulusabdij, built at the southern point.

Numerous other churches and monasteries were built within the city walls, and the skyline of Utrecht was once a mass of spires. But many of these were toppled by a hurricane that struck the city in 1674.

PRECEDING PAGES:
Kasteel de Haar.
LEFT: happy pigs
in Oudewater.
BELOW:
Bunschoten local.

The Old Canal

Oudegracht, the oldest canal in the city, is a good starting point for a tour of the old city. It was dug in the 11th century below street level to allow for sudden changes in the level of the Rhine. The canal is lined with brick quays and cavernous cellars that extend back to connect with the houses on the street above. Once used to store goods shipped from the Rhine and Flanders, the vaulted cellars are now occupied by student restaurants and bars. In summer, café terraces are crammed into the short stretch of sunlit quayside between the Bakkerbrug (Baker's Bridge) and the Stadhuis (Town Hall). Out of season these quays remain silent and derelict.

Several medieval town houses still stand on Oudegracht. **Oudaen** (No. 99) is a stern, fortified house built in 1320, when the Netherlands was gripped by an obscure dispute between two rival gangs called the Hoeken (Hooks) and Kabeljauwen (Cods), rather like the 14th-century quarrel in Verona that ensnared Romeo and Juliet. Now restored, it has a magnificent café on the ground floor and a restaurant above. Opposite there is an even older building called **Drakenborch** (No. 114), dating from 1280 and restored in 1968.

Soaring tower

From the Bakkerbrug there's a good view of the **Domtoren ❹** (cathedral tower), one of the architectural marvels of the Gothic age. Built between 1321 and 1383, it rises to an ethereal octagonal lantern 112 metres (376 ft) high. It was for several centuries the tallest spire in the Low Countries, and even today it is impossible to remain unmoved by the elegance and sheer daring of the structure. Imitations of the Domtoren were built in Amersfoort, Delft, Groningen, Maas-

Utrecht's Domtoren was not without its critics. Geert Groote, a disapproving monk, published a diatribe against it warning that it would encourage "vanity, boasting and pride" and predicted its collapse. As it turned out, this was one of the few spires to survive the 1674 hurricane.

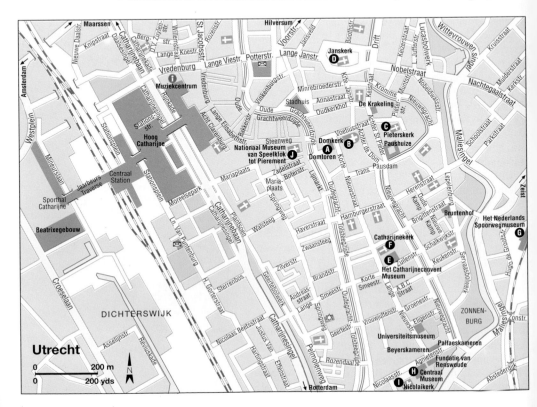

tricht and Breda. Its unmistakable silhouette also appeared in several medieval paintings, such as the Van Eyck altarpiece in Ghent (a reproduction can be seen in the Janskerk).The 465-step climb up the tower is worthwhile if only for the panoramic view. Tickets, which include a guided tour, are available from the **Rond Dom visitor's centre** in the square (open Mon–Sat 10am-5pm; Sun noon–5pm; the last guided tour of the day is at 4pm). "Rond Dom" also provides information about the museum quarter and a film of the history of Utrecht.

Map
on page
212

Cathedral remains

By following Oudegracht as it bends southwards, then turning left into Servet-straat, you come to the foot of the tower. A Renaissance gate on the right leads into the secret Bishop's Garden, where you get a superb view of the soaring tower. The archway beneath the Domtoren once led into the cathedral of Utrecht. A road now runs under the tower, and any traveller examining the Gothic vault-ing runs the risk of being hit by a bus.

All that remains of the **Domkerk ❸**, which was begun in 1254, are the choir and transepts on the far side of the road (open May–Sept: Mon–Fri 10am–5pm; Sat 10am–3.30pm, Sun 2–4pm; Oct–Apr: Mon–Fri; 11am–4pm, Sat & Sun same as May-Sept). The nave, which had been built with inadequate buttress-ing, came crashing down during the freak hurricane in 1674.

French-Gothic overtones define Utrecht's cathedral.

Bishop Bernold's cross

The **Pieterskerk ❹** (open Tues–Fri 11am–4.30pm, Sat 11am–3pm; free), the first church of Bishop Bernold's cross, was the bishop's favourite, and he elected to be buried here rather than in the Dom. Completed in 1048, it stands on the Pieterskerkhof, a tranquil square near the Domkerk. It is a rare example of the German Romanesque style. Utrecht was then part of the Holy Roman Empire and the building materials were shipped here from the Eif-fel: grey tuffa walls and red sandstone columns form a striking contrast to the ubiquitous Dutch brick.

BELOW:
Huize Doorn castle.

Sadly, the storm of 1674 brought down both of the Pieterkerk's spires and caused considerable structural damage. The necessary repairs to the church were funded rather drastically by demolishing the west-work (an important architectural element of Roman-esque church design) and selling the stone.

Turning right along Achter St Pieter brings you to an unusual house called De Krakeling (the pretzel) at No. 8. It was built in 1663 by Everard Meyster, an eccentric local aristocrat who once laid a bet that he could persuade the people of Amersfoort to haul a nine-ton boulder, the kei, into the town (*see page 220*). He won his bet and spent the money on a lavish feast of beer and pretzels for the 400 people who dragged the stone into Utrecht. The pretzel-shaped bell pull on the front door recalls this curious event.

Keistraat (renamed to commemorate Meyster's tri-umph) leads to the second of Bishop Bernold's churches, the **Janskerk ❺** (open Mon–Fri 1–5pm, phone ahead to ensure there is a curator available; free). Completed about 1050 in a similar German Romanesque style to the Pieterskerk, it originally had

Those who enjoy local markets should visit Utrecht on a Saturday. The best and busiest markets include the plant, general and second-hand markets, along with the colourful Saturday flower market. Its enormous bunches of blooms sell at bargain prices.

red sandstone columns but these had to be encased in brick when the church showed signs of collapsing. One of the original columns has since been laid bare in the nave. As with the Pieterskerk, this church lost its Romanesque westwork: one tower fell in the 14th century, the other followed on that bleak day in 1674.

After the Reformation, the choir – which had been rebuilt in the 16th century in Flamboyant Gothic style – was used to house the university library. In 1660 one of the chapels in the north aisle was converted into a guard house and adorned with a brightly painted coat of arms bearing the motto of the Dutch Republic: *Concordia res parvae crescunt* (Unity makes small things great).

New canal

Back on Drift, you can turn off down the elegant Kromme Nieuwegracht, the canal which bends along the former course of the Rhine, to reach Pausdam. This attractive bridge is overlooked by the **Paushuize** (Pope's house), a Flamboyant Gothic building dating from the early 16th century. It was built for Adriaen Floriszoon of Utrecht, who was appointed Pope by Charles V in 1522. Pope Adrian VI, the first and only Dutch pope, immediately made himself highly unpopular in Rome by embarking on a vigorous programme of reform; none of his proposals was implemented before he died in the following year.

Nieuwegracht (new canal), a deep narrow canal, runs south of here. Not exactly new, it was built in 1393, in the same century as the old canal. Like Oudegracht, it has a lower quay lined with cellars, but these have all been abandoned. Nieuwegracht has some attractive examples of Dutch domestic architecture, such as the tiny classical house at No. 37.

BELOW: Bunschoten town harbour.

Several religious orders built monasteries and convents on this canal. A former Carmelite convent now houses the **Het Catharijneconvent Museum** Ⓔ (Nieuwegracht 63; open Tues–Fri 10am–5pm, Sat & Sun 11am–5pm; entrance fee). It has the finest collection of art from the Middle Ages in The Netherlands, with displays of illuminated manuscripts, statues, altar pieces and paintings by Jan van Scorel, Rembrandt, Frans Hals and Pieter Saenredam among others. Liturgical and other religious objects demonstrate the cultural and social differences between the Dutch Protestants and Catholics.

The adjacent **Catharijnekerk** Ⓕ occupies a curious place in Dutch ecclesiastical history. Formerly the chapel of the Carmelites, it became the national cathedral of Dutch Catholics in the 19th century, when the ban on Catholic worship was officially lifted. The jubilant Catholics attempted to improve the chapel by adding a spire modelled on that of Kampen Stadhuis, and decorating the interior in rich neo-Gothic style. This offended the Dutch Protestants, who insisted that it be restored to its pristine whiteness.

Relics of the railway age

Across the bridge from the Catharijneconvent museum, Brigittenstraat leads to a park bordering the city moat. Across the park, over an ornate iron bridge is the **Het Nederlands Spoorwegmuseum** Ⓖ (National Railway Museum; open Tues–Fri 10am–5pm; Sat & Sun 11.30am–5pm; entrance fee) housed in a disused

19th-century railway station. It has more than 50 historical locomotives, trains, wagons and coaches. You can take a short ride on an old steam train, or try your hand at driving a diesel locomotive, switching points, or driving an inter-city train on a simulator.

Map on page 212

Almshouses

Outside the museum, turn right along the cobbled lane to reach the **Bruntenhof**, a row of whitewashed almshouses founded in 1521 by Frederik Brunt. A Renaissance portal leading to the Governors' Chamber (No. 5) bears a reminder of mortality in the form of an hourglass and skull. Three more almshouses at the southern end of the old town are worth a glance. Twelve homes known collectively as the **Pallaeskameren**, after their founder Maria van Pallaes, stand on Agnietenstraat. The date of foundation, 1651, and the Pallaes family coat of arms appear on every door lintel. In Lange Nieuwstraat, the **Beyerskameren** consists of 16 terraced houses founded by Adriaen Beyer. The foundation date, 1597, is cut in the keyhole casing of the Governors' Chamber (No. 120).

When Maria Duist van Voorhout, Baroness of Renswoude, decided in 1757 that she was going to found an institution to educate poor boys, she spared no expense. The **Fundatie van Renswoude** on Agnietenstraat is a magnificent sandstone rococo building, decorated with the coats of arms of the founder and of the 13 members of the original board of trustees.

The former convent next door houses the **Centraal Museum** ❻ (Agnietenstraat 1; Tues–Sat 11am–5pm, Sun noon–5pm; entrance fee) which has an excellent collection of local history, furniture, costumes, sculpture and paintings. Highlights include paintings and art works by Saenredam, Van Scorel (the most

When the city walls were demolished in the 19th century, the municipal authorities created a series of landscaped parks around the circumference of Utrecht.

BELOW: medieval painting, Rijksmuseum Het Catharijneconvent.

TIP

If your time in the Centraal Museum is limited, highlights to single out include the *Jerusalem Brotherhood* portraits by Van Scorel, Terbrugghen's *The Calling of St Matthew* and the furniture collection of the De Stijl designer, Gerrit Rietveld.

notable of Utrecht artists), Bloemaert, Moesman, Koch, Toorop and Droog Design, and the largest Rietveld collection in the world. Recent refurbishment incorporated a new multimedia information centre as well as a children's museum. A re-created medieval garden contains various moss-covered fragments rescued from demolished buildings. A path leads through the museum garden to the **Nicolaikerk ❶**, built in 1150, which once boasted two spires, but one was replaced by an octagonal bell tower in 1586 and the other was felled by the storm in 1674.

Along the ramparts

The most pleasant route back to the centre is along the landscaped ramparts. You will pass an abandoned Gothic Revival church, the **St Martinuskerk**, which overlooks a series of 19th-century workers' terraced houses known as **De 7 Steegjes** (the seven lanes), where patterned brick pavements create the impression of an outdoor carpet. The fact that the huge church is now neglected, while the humble dwellings alongside have been saved from demolition by a vigorous campaign, shows how the Dutch aspire not to grandeur but to *gezelligheid* (snugness).

Heading down Springweg, past a row of 11 almshouses founded in 1583 (Nos. 110–30), you come to the **Mariaplaats**, where a cloister is all that remains of the fourth of Bishop Bernold's churches. Turning right down Zadelstraat, then left into the Buurkerkhof brings you to the **Buurkerk**, the oldest parish church in Utrecht, where one Sister Bertken was walled up for 57 years at her own request, in order to escape the evils of the world.

Begun in the 13th century, it was converted into a hall church with five aisles

BELOW: Centraal Museum, Utrecht.

in the 16th century. The church now houses the delightful **Nationaal Museum van Speelklok tot Pierement** ❶ (10 Buurkerkhof, tel: 030-231 7789; open Tues–Sat 10am–5pm, Sun 12–5pm; entrance fee), a collection of mechanical musical instruments, ranging from a glass case of twittering birds to several ear-splitting dance hall organs.

Map on page 212

Guided tours are given by enthusiastic music students from the university, whose job includes playing the piano and singing a lusty Berlin *lied* to the accompaniment of a street organ. English-speaking guides are available and music is played on the hour every hour with a repertoire ranging from classical and torch songs to waltzes and house music. Those who want to compose their own little ditties can have lots of fun in the 'pling plong' room. The presentation is unforgettable, though one wonders what Sister Bertken would make of it all.

Castles and Kings

The Bishops of Utrecht erected a number of castles to defend the region from the Dukes of Gelderland to the east and the Counts of Holland to the north. Many are still standing along the Rivers Kromme Rijn and Vecht. **Huize Doorn** (Doorn, off the A12 between Utrecht and Arnhem; open mid-Mar–Oct Tues–Sat 10am–4pm and Sun 1–5pm; guided tours only; entrance fee), built in the 14th century, and rebuilt in the 18th century, was the residence of the deposed Kaiser Wilhelm II of Germany (1859–1941), who lived here from 1921 until his death.

Before moving to Huize Doorn, the Kaiser lived (from 1918 to 1920) in **Kasteel Amerongen** (Amerongen, 8 km/5 miles east of Doorn; open Apr–Oct Tues–Fri 10am–5pm, Sat & Sun 1–5pm; entrance fee). This medieval castle,

Statue of a mermaid at the 14th-century castle, Huize Doorn.

BELOW: Utrecht is a province of castles.

BY HORSE OR BOAT?

Probably the most romantic way to see the city of Utrecht is by horse-drawn carriage. Traditional coaches drawn by beautiful Gelderland horses take you around the outer canals, parks, narrow alleyways, the inner canals and buildings of special interest. Most impressive is the Maliebaan, along a wide tree-lined boulevard where centuries ago a form of polo was played, just as it was at the Mall in London. Carriages extend their seating to a maximum of five people, and thus are not just for romantics. (Information from Mr Groen, tel: 030-271 0235. Departures from Domplein Apr–Oct: 11am–6pm; Nov–Apr weekends only).

Opposite the Oudegracht 85 is a small kiosk where tickets are available for a *rondvaart* (canal boat) excursion. Included in the price is a leaflet in English which describes the route. The trip takes about an hour and is by far the best way to become acquainted with the unique wharves of Utrecht. Of particular interest are the lampposts that line the canals. At the base of each one is a carved stone representing the activities or trades practised at that particular place. For example at the fish market (*Vismarkt*), there are fish carvings. To a lesser extent, the bridges are embellished in the same manner. (Rondvaartbedrijf Schuttervaer, Bemuurde Weerde O.Z. 17, tel: 030-272 0111.)

Map
on page
202

TIP

Friday is an ideal day
to visit Amersfoort,
when the weekly
flower market is set
up on the Havik
quayside.

BELOW: Oudegracht
and the Domtoren.

rebuilt in the 17th century, is one of the most interesting in Utrecht province, rich with furnishings and curiosities.

The aristocratic Van Zuylen family occupy a prominent place in Utrecht's history. Of their many castles in the province, the most interesting is **Kasteel De Haar** 20 km (12 miles) west of Utrecht (open Tues-Sun 1pm-5pm; entrance fee). In the 19th century the ruined medieval castle was transformed into an ornate Gothic Revival edifice by Cuypers, architect of Amsterdam's Rijksmuseum. An entire village was demolished to create the extensive castle gardens. Just north of Utrecht on the river Vecht lies Slot Zuylen, another family pile. The castle is a curious mixture of medieval turrets and 18th-century baroque.

Medieval attractions

Amersfoort ❽ is a sober provincial town on the river Eem, 23km (14 miles) northeast of Utrecht, with small neat houses and simple Gothic chapels. Its traditional industries were brewing, cloth-making and tobacco, and in the Middle Ages it was an important place of pilgrimage. An old town by Dutch standards, its first wall dates from about the 12th century. It was presumably aprosperous place, as a new wall was begun in the 14th century enclosing a much larger area. The **Muurhuizen** (wall houses) which stand on the foundations of the inner city wall, are an unusual feature. They form an almost complete circle of lanes, which makes a very attractive walk through the old town (beginning from the Museum Flehite). The outline of the old wall can still be seen quite clearly in the façade of Groot Tinnenburg at Muurhuizen 25.

At the northern end of Muuirhuizen is the **Museum Flehite** (Westsingel 50; open Tues–Fri 10am–5pm, Sat & Sun 2–5pm; entrance fee). It contains a local history collection, including painful reminders of a camp for deportees built during World War II in the suburbs of Amersfoort. When the second wall was demolished in the 19th century, some parks were laid out on the site, as in Utrecht. Several medieval gates are still standing from the second ring, including the unusual **Koppelpoort** near the Museum Flehite, a 15th-century watergate on the river Eem defended by two towers. An unusual museum, housed in a former convent is the **Culinair Museum Mariënhof** which covers the history of Dutch eating habits from prehistoric times. Amersfoort's main church, the **Onze Lieve Vrouwekerk**, was destroyed in the 18th century by an accidental explosion. All that is left is the **tower**, a replica of the Domtoren in Utrecht.

South of here, on the edge of the old town, is the famous Amersfoortse *kei* (the Amersfoort boulder), a large glacial rock which Everard Meyster persuaded the locals to drag into Utrecht in 1622. The gullible folk of Amersfoort immediately became the butt of jokes, and resolved to bury the boulder. In 1903 they plucked up the courage to unearth it.

Bunschoten-Spakenburg were two separate fishing towns which were subject to flooding and thus became rather isolated. As a result old traditions continue to be observed. Monday, when locals are dressed in costume and going about their work, is the best day to pay a visit. ❑

Rebels with a Cause

Utrecht may seem strait-laced compared with Amsterdam, yet it counts many radical women among its citizens. In 1529 a certain Zuster (Sister) Bertken made the bold resolution, at the age of only 30, to retreat from the world in a bricked-up cell in the choir of the Buurkerk. At that time, this part of the church was older and considerably lower than the nave, and the church authorities decided they should replace it. They had to wait until 1586, however, when Sister Bertken finally died at the age of 87.

Catharina van Leemputte was a spirited local woman who, in 1577, headed a band of women in an attack on Vredenburg citadel which had become a symbol of Spanish tyranny during the Dutch Revolt. As a result of this women's revolt, little remains of Vredenburg except for some fragments of masonry near the tourist office.

Isabella Agneta van Tuyll van Serooskerken was born in Utrecht in 1740. She came from a powerful local aristocratic family, which owned numerous castles and houses in Utrecht province. Adopting the pen name of Belle van Zuylen, she published Le Noble, a satirical novella involving a foolish aristocrat who inhabited a crumbling castle clearly modelled on one owned by her father, who promptly forbade Belle to write any other novels, so she reverted to letter writing.

Truus Schröder was a 20th-century rebel. Her burning ambition was to be an architect, but there were no openings for women when she was young. When her husband died in 1923, she decided to build herself a new house, and enlisted the help of the Utrecht architect Gerrit Rietveld. Together they designed a small family house that permanently changed the direction of Dutch architecture. The Rietveld-Schröder house was tacked on to the end of a row of dull 19th-century houses in a calculated attempt to shock the bourgeoisie of Utrecht. The exterior is reminiscent of an abstract painting by Mondrian, with flat surfaces rendered in red, blue, yellow and various shades of grey. To give the house a truly modern appearance,

the external brick walls were concealed under a layer of plaster.

The interior design is equally radical, and its most striking feature is the ingenious method by which all the dividing walls can be folded away to create a single room. Rietveld was particularly adept at inventing space-saving solutions, such as a bathroom door that doubles as a slide projector screen and a cupboard in the hall that holds a child's wooden beach cart (designed by Rietveld and now in the Centraal Museum in Utrecht).

This unconventional partnership took a more personal turn when Gerrit Rietveld moved into the house, working in a studio on the ground floor originally intended as a garage. Up until 1963, the house enjoyed an enviable situation on the southern edge of the city. In 1963 this situation was shattered by the construction of an elevated section of the N222 ring road a few yards from the house. This proved too much for Rietveld, who died the following year – a victim of the modern age which he and Truus Schröder had done so much to create. ❑

RIGHT: authoress Belle van Zuylen.

ZEELAND

Map
on page
222

*This cluster of islands, linked to the mainland by dykes and dams,
is Holland's sunniest spot, with beaches for relaxing, nature
reserves for walking and gentle terrain that is perfect for cycling*

Zeeland ("Sealand") is well named. The southwestern province seems more part of the North Sea than of the Netherlands, to which it is so tenuously attached. Even in a country where a close, stormy relationship with the sea is the stuff of legend and everyday life, Zeeland seems a place apart, isolated from the mainstream of Dutch life, slashed by great jagged stretches of water.

In the past, this detachment was even more pronounced, as illustrated by old maps of Zeeland. The further back in time you go, the more the landscape breaks up into a pattern of little islands, all below sea level, uncertainly protected by dykes and dunes. As the centuries rolled past, the Dutch patiently stitched these islands together with typical ingenuity and hard work.

That process is as complete as it is ever likely to be. The former islands now form long peninsulas connected to the mainland and Zeeland has emerged from isolation. Two factors more than any others have accounted for this: disaster and tourism. Disaster struck – not for the first time – during the night of 1 February 1953, when a deadly combination of tide and storm sent the North Sea crashing through the protective dykes and across the spirit-level flat landscape beyond. More than 1,800 people lost their lives and there was immeasurable destruction.

LEFT: Middelburg
woman in
traditional
constume.
BELOW: elegant
Zierikzee.

Protection plan

The Delta Plan, a decades-long project subsequently launched to shut out the North Sea forever, has, as a by-product, given Zeeland superb road links along which visitors pour from the rest of The Netherlands and neighbouring countries. They discover a land of vast horizons infiltrated on every side by lakes and sea channels, a water wonderland of beaches and harbour towns. There are few urban centres, though now sleepy villages once sent their adventurous spirits as explorers and merchants to the farthest reaches of the globe. New Zealand is just one legacy of Zeeland's seafaring traditions. Tourism, fishing and farming are Zeeland's main sources of wealth. The first two depend on the ever-present sea which, though it has threatened much, has given much in return. The third comes from superb farmland created by centuries of land reclamation. Fields that stretch endlessly under broad skies, market garden centres and orchards ensure that Zeeland will never go hungry.

Two-wheel benefits

There is no better way to explore Zeeland than on a bicycle. At the busiest times in summer, traffic is often bumper-to-bumper on the main roads. This gives a misleading impression of a congested province – Zeeland is too big to get congested and its back

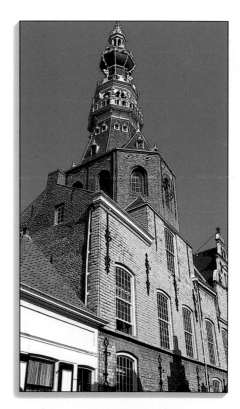

roads are a largely unused resource. On a bike you can escape from sweltering traffic jams in minutes, and pedal into another world of pretty villages and quiet cafés, little islands of civilisation in a sea of green fields. Zeeland has no hills so it is perfect for cycling, but watch out for unobstructed winds that make the going harder.

You can hire bicycles in most towns and at main railway stations. There are signposted cycling routes all over Zeeland; you can get information on these from most local tourist (VVV) offices. If touring by car, the signposted **Delta Route** combines all aspects of the Zeeland experience – town, country, coast, history and the Delta Works. The province-wide route breaks down into easily managed segments covering each of the islands and Zeeuws Vlaanderen. Information is available from VVV offices.

The Delta works

The Delta stretches across the mouths of the Rhine, Maas, Waal and Schelde rivers that all drain into the North Sea. What were once islands are now linked to each other and the mainland by the giant causeways of dams, barriers and raised dykes. Begun soon after the 1953 disaster, these huge dams and movable barriers that form the Delta Works have become tourist attractions in their own right. Over a period of 30 years, at immense cost, sea inlets that pierced Zeeland's coast, leaving it at the mercy of the North Sea, were closed off, shortening the coastline by 700 km (440 miles) and forming sheltered lakes that are a paradise for watersports and nature lovers. Coastal and river dykes were also raised and strengthened. The scale of these engineering works staggers the imagination.

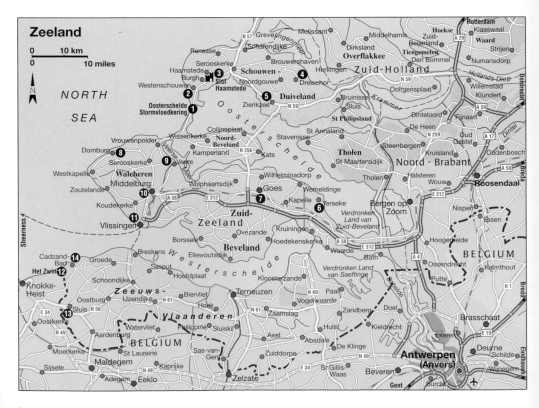

Zeeland

On the highways that sit on top of them, travellers flow effortlessly from one former island to another. Pride of place goes to the **Oosterschelde Stormvloedkering ❶** (Oosterschelde Storm Surge Barrier), which opened in 1986 after a 10-year construction programme. In bad weather, the Barrier's 65 enormous gates can be slammed shut on the North Sea, while at other times they remain open to preserve the inlet's valuable saltwater shellfish beds and mud flats.

The **Delta Expo** (open Apr–Oct: daily 10am–5.30pm; Nov–Mar: Wed–Sun 10am–5pm; entrance fee, includes boat trip in summer) on **Neeltje Jans**, an artificial island in the middle of the Eastern Scheldt, tells the story of Zeeland's 2,000-year struggle with the sea. Models demonstrate the 1953 flood and the operation of the Storm Surge Barrier, and you can go on a boat trip to see the real thing. Other works protect threatened areas in Zeeland, and yet more lie to the north in the delta area of neighbouring Zuid-Holland province. The sea still presents a threat – albeit a much diminished one – and it's said that no one sleeps soundly in Zeeland when the North Sea rages beyond the defensive walls.

Schouwen and Duiveland islands

It's as well that the sea offers compensations – and Zeeland takes advantage of every one of them. Coming into the province by the coast road from Rotterdam, over the broad back of the Brouwersdam, you arrive at the one-time islands of **Schouwen** and **Duiveland**. On the seafront, 17 km (11 miles) of magnificent sands form the main attraction, with beach cafés at strategic points. Behind the beach are 1,100 hectares (2,750 acres) of dunes – hilly, sandy terrain crisscrossed by a network of paths that are great for walking, cycling and horseriding. Campsites have been tucked out of sight behind the dunes, yet between holidaymakers and day-trippers even this amount of beach fills up on sunny summer days.

From **Westenschouwen ❷** beach you have a fine view of the Storm Surge Barrier, and its serried ranks of giant towers stretching into the distance. You can get an even better view by taking a flight on a glider from nearby Nieuw-Haamstede airfield and asking the pilot to swing out over the water. The small towns of Schouwen are mostly residential. **Slot Haamstede ❸**, (tours mid June–mid Sept Wed 10.30am and 11.30am; entrance fee), is a castle with elements from the 13th century and a well-appointed Ridderzaal (Hall of Knights). Near **Burgh-Haamstede** it is worth a visit. Further east, the north coast of Duiveland is a windsurfer's paradise. The now freshwater **Grevelingenmeer** (Grevelingen Lake) provides a huge expanse, ideal for practising. There is fishing too, with boat trips leaving from the harbour villages of **Scharendijke** and **Brouwershaven**.

The farmland interior of Duiveland offers motorists – and cyclists even more so – one of Zeeland's delights: exploring side roads that lead either nowhere in particular, or to tiny villages, identifiable only by their church towers, that appear from the haze on the horizon. **Dreischor ❹**, neat and peaceful, its 14th-century church ringed by a canal and a circle of enchanting houses, is foremost among these must-see Zeeland gems.

Map on page 222

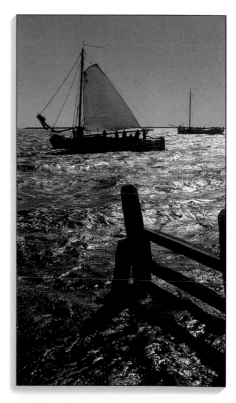

BELOW: oyster boats working the Oosterschelde.

TIP

From a small airfield near Arnemuiden, you can hire a light aircraft for a *rondvlucht* (round trip) over Zeeland – an ideal way to view the flat, watery landscapes that characterise the province.

BELOW: statue of a mussel man.

In **Zierikzee** ❺, founded around 800, Duiveland has one of Holland's most elegant towns, so nearly perfect that you could easily believe beauty to have been its creators' prime requirement. Though the approach to Zierkzee is through unappealing modern suburbs, the road soon brings you to the old town's attractive cobbled streets, rows of stately merchants' houses and snug sailors' cottages dating from the 16th to the 18th centuries, and a medieval harbour, fronted by two towers.

Zierikzee looks like an open-air museum but is a living town, with *gezellig* (cosy and friendly) bars and some fine restaurants. A long inlet, lined with yachts in summer, leads to the Oosterschelde; **boat trips** (tel: 0111-414995) leave from here to tour the Storm Surge Barrier. The town's maritime history is presented at the **Maritiem Museum** (Mol; open Apr–Oct: Mon–Sat 10am–5pm, Sun noon–5pm; Nov–Mar: during school holidays only, same times; entrance fee). This building, 's-Gravensteen, dates from the 13th century and was originally the town jail.

Zeeland's least developed "island", **Tholen**, and neighbouring **St Philipsland**, bordering the adjacent province of Noord-Brabant, are mainly agricultural. Their long coastlines provide plenty of watersports opportunities, and they are quieter and closer to the mainland than Zeeland's main tourist centres. Sport fishing is the main draw on Tholen. Boats leave from **Stavenisse** harbour and anglers take up position along the shore. A nature reserve near **St Maartensdijk** attracts birdwatchers and ramblers.

An island once connected to its neighbours only by ferry, **Noord-Beveland** is now linked by one road to Schouwen-Duiveland via the Oosterschelde Storm Surge Barrier and the 5-km (3-mile) long Zeeland toll bridge, and by two other

ZEELAND FLEXES ITS MUSSELS

Before starting their journey to consumers' plates, Zeeland mussels rest in beds off Yerseke in the Oosterschelde (Eastern Scheldt) estuary. Whip-like branches sticking out of the shallow water mark the location of each merchant's "parcel". During April and May, fishing boats "plant" mussel-seed: young mussels that will form next year's crop. By the time they have grown to 4 or 5 cm (1½ inches), they have joined together in dense carpets for mutual support against tidal pull. The boats scoop them up and move them to other parcels, called "wet warehouses", which are freer of sand, for the final two-week growth to maturity. At between 6 and 7 cm (2½ inches), they are ready for harvesting.

At this stage, the mud-encrusted mussels would scarcely be appealing to devotees. The salt tang of the sea merges with danker smells dredged up from the bottom. They spend between 4 and 16 hours in the merchant's treatment works being sluiced by constantly running seawater to remove sand and other impurities. Each mussel filters more than 50 litres (11 gallons) of water a day. A falconer employed by the Mussel Bureau at Bergen op Zoom helps keep seagulls, and their cargoes of seagull poop, away from the mussel beds.

dam-top roads to its southern companions, Walcheren and Zuid-Beveland. Agriculture, fishing and tourism are the main activities here. The freshwater Veerse Meer (Lake Veere) is an exceptional yachting and windsurfing area and the Schotsman holiday centre just behind the Veersegat dam recalls nearby Veere's former maritime trading links with Scotland. Like the rest of Zeeland, Noord-Beveland's coastline is dotted with picturesque fishing villages such as Colijnsplaat, and yachting harbours like Kortgene on the Veerse Meer.

Fruits of the sea

Off **Yerseke** ❻, on the eastern landward coast of **Zuid-Beveland**, lies one of the reasons why a movable barrier rather than a solid dam was built to protect the Eastern Scheldt. Zeeland mussels and oysters are renowned for their quality, and special deliveries rush the pick of the crop from Yerseke's auction house to fancy shops and restaurant tables across Europe. Eating a steaming potful of mussels is an essential Zeeland experience.

You can buy Zeeland mussels by the truck-load – quite literally.

During the mussel season, between July and April, a shuttle service of fishing boats from Yerseke lift ton after ton of "black gold" from offshore beds (see box). Restaurants throughout Zeeland brandish *Zeeuwse Mosselen* signs and a feeding frenzy for this fresh, inexpensive delicacy develops. (The finest are exported to Belgium, where demand is even greater.). A visit to Yerseke's mussel auction is a must.

One of the province's few large towns, **Goes** ❼, on Zuid-Beveland, has added a modern shopping centre to its Zeeland Renaissance-style town and harbour front, but the Tuesday market in the Grote Markt makes for a more colourful shopping experience, as local women dress in traditional Zeeland costume.

BELOW: Domburg is known as the "Zeeland Riviera".

Windsurfing is popular on the "Zeeland Riviera."

BELOW:
Zierikzee's
medieval
fortifications.

Old-world charm also lives on in the **Zuid-Beveland Stoom Trein** (South Beveland Steam Train), that puffs its leisurely way southwards from Goes through a beautiful landscape of dykes, lakes and woods.

Zeeland's two most important transport arteries, the A58 motorway and the only regular railway line, run through Zuid-Beveland. They connect Goes, Middelburg and the busy port of Vlissingen with the "mainland"; both are crowded during summer peak times.

Walcheren

Zeeland is a holiday area *par excellence* and **Walcheren** is its star performer. Ringed by beaches and dunes, the historic island is a magnet for beach lovers, but even at the busiest times of year there always seem to be wide stretches of sand that no one has occupied.

The North Sea and Westerschelde coasts together form the most obvious attraction, with a constellation of small resort towns that shelter behind the dunes, rather fancifully dubbed the "Zeeland Riviera". The principal resort is **Domburg ❽** where people have come for centuries to take the curative waters, and where, in the early 1900s, an artists' colony developed that counted Mondrian among its number. A 7-km (4½-mile) bike ride away is the quieter resort of **Westkapelle**, with its giant lighthouse, and not much further, the small resort of **Zoutelande**. Hotels, campsites and bed and breakfast lodgings are plentiful.

From the Westerschelde shore, you can watch an endless parade of cargo ships of all sizes streaming through the narrow (and unfortunately polluted) estuary, heading into or out of Antwerp.

On the banks of the Veerse Meer stands picturesque **Veere ❾**, a well preserved medieval town with a Gothic town hall built in the 1470s that has a 48-bell carillon in its Renaissance belfry, and a 15th-century fortified harbour tower, the **Campveerse Toren**, now a hotel and restaurant. Veere once held a monopoly on the Scottish wool trade and beside the harbour, at 25 and 27 Kade, are the two 16th-century **Schotse Huizen**, which were once the offices and warehouses of prosperous Scottish wool merchants. Nearby **Vrouwenpolder** has a tranquil beach on the Veerse Meer, with the adjacent North Sea shut out by the Veerse Gatdam.

Middelburg

Middelburg ❿, the provincial capital, is a busy yet elegant canalside town of 40,000 inhabitants, whose beautifully ornamented **Stadhuis** (guided tours Mar–Oct Mon–Sat 11am–5pm; entrance fee) on the Markt (Market Square) is one of The Netherlands' finest town halls. The Gothic façade dates from the 15th century and the belfry is 55 metres (180 ft) tall.

Zeeland's provincial government is housed in the old **Abdij** (Abbey) founded in the 12th century, part of the abbey complex that dominates the town centre. Its famous spire, known as **Lange Jan** (Long John) (open Easter–Oct Mon–Sat 10am–5pm; entrance fee), looms 91 metres (300 ft) above the town. The view of Middelburg and Walcheren from the upper reaches of the tower makes the climb worthwhile.

Map on page 222

The ancient Romans had a fleet base in this area, and at the **Zeeuws Museum** (Zeeland Museum) (open Mon–Sat 11am–5pm, Sun noon–5pm; entrance fee) in the Abbey, you can see Roman finds that include an altar and votive offerings to a local sea goddess, Nehallenia. Other rooms display 16th- and 17th-century tapestries depicting naval actions during Holland's war of independence against Spain, Chinese porcelain, furniture, silverware, traditional Zeeland costumes, and more besides.

Visitors from the United States may be interested in the **Roosevelt Study Centre** (tel: 0118-631590; open Apr–Oct: Mon–Fri 10am–12.30pm and 1.30–4.30pm; other times by appointment; free). It covers local history aspects of US presidents Theodore and Franklin D Roosevelt, whose ancestors emigrated from Zeeland to America in the 1640s.

The abbey itself is the star of the **Abdij Historama** (open Mon–Sat 11am–5pm, Sun noon–5pm; entrance fee) which takes you on a tour of the cloisters, cellars and crypt, and introduces you to its former occupants, the Norbertine monks, as well as such historical characters as William of Orange, who had some influence on the abbey's history.

Frequently choked beyond its capacity with peak-time summer traffic, Middelburg is the hub of Zeeland. Many of the town's cafés and restaurants merit the prized description *gezellig*, and its cobbled streets reward the casual stroller.

Island in miniature

Miniature Walcheren (open Apr–Oct daily 10am–5pm; entrance fee) in Molenwater Park is a walk-through depiction of the island, showing scaled-down models of its main buildings and centres seen from a bird's-eye view. Its miniature

In 1944, during operations to clear the approaches to Antwerp harbour, Allied planes bombed Walcheren's dykes, flooding the island and forcing its heavily entrenched German defenders to withdraw.

BELOW: Zeeuws Vlaanderen.

Map on page 222

houses, churches and public buildings are brilliantly executed. Radio-controlled trains and boats, and Lilliputian carillons add to the sense of realism.

Vlissingen ⓫ (Flushing) is the industrial heart of Zeeland and an important port with a ferry service across the Westerschelde to Zeeuws Vlaanderen (see below) and across the North Sea twice a day to Sheerness. There is not much to do or see here and most visitors go straight from the ferry port to the station, where there are hourly connections to Amsterdam that stop at various other places en route.

The sea-wall walkway offers a pleasant stroll beside the harbour and another view of Antwerp-bound cargo ships. A statue of the famous 17th-century admiral Michiel de Ruyter gazes out across the water.

Zeeuws Vlaanderen

Just as Zeeland seems a place apart from the Netherlands, its southernmost section, **Zeeuws Vlaanderen** (Zeeland Flanders), bordering Belgium, is different from the rest of the province. The area is connected to the rest of Zeeland by car ferry only, which operates between Breskens and Vlissingen in the west, and Perkpolder and Kruiningen in the east. Road links run through Belgium's Flemish region, specifically via Antwerp.

At both its western and eastern extremities are nature reserves associated with that inexhaustible Zeeland resource: water. In the east is the **Verdronken Land van Saeftinge** (Drowned Land of Saeftinge), a birdwatcher's paradise comprising mudflats once reclaimed from the Schelde and now mostly reclaimed by the river. On the North Sea coast is another birdlife sanctuary, **Het Zwin** ⓬, which continues across the border into Belgium.

BELOW:
adapting quickly to provincial life.
RIGHT:
a mussel boat.

Sluis ⓭, on the border, is possibly better known in Belgium than in Holland, because many Belgians hide their "black" money from the taxman in its banks and patronise the town's numerous porn shops and sex clubs – some cultured souls might even pause to glance at the Stadhuis (Town Hall), which has the only surviving 14th-century belfry in the Netherlands, although it had to be rebuilt after being knocked down in 1944.

Beaches and mussels

There are popular beaches around **Cadzand-Bad** ⓮, from where it is possible to walk through Het Zwin to the nearby Belgian resort **Knokke-Heist**. Other handsome Belgian cities – among them Brugge, Gent and Antwerpen – lie within a short distance of the border.

Along the canal from Terneuzen to Gent, the terrain is mostly industrial, although there is another nature zone nearby at **De Braakman**, a former inlet on the Westerschelde, which is now dammed off to form a lake.

Philippine, a neighbouring village, is the place to go for mussels. It has some of the best mussel restaurants in this part of Zeeland and has become a place of pilgrimage for mussel fanciers.

As in most of Zeeland, fishing in Zeeuws Vlaanderen is a primary recreation; you can make sea-fishing trips from **Breskens** and **Terneuzen**. ❏

Map on pages 232–3

NOORD BRABANT

From the flamboyant architecture and riotous carnivals of Den Bosch and Bergen to the peaceful reed forests of the Biesbosch and lonely fenlands beyond, the Catholic south caters for many moods

N oord-Brabant (North Brabant) is one of the country's largest provinces. A variety of landscapes are contained within its boundaries including forests, moorland (*Kempenland*) and fens (*Peelland*). Its northern limits are bounded by the River Maas (Meuse), to the south it borders Belgium and the east adjoins hilly Limburg. Apart from the polderland west of Breda, most of the province lies above sea level.

During the 15th century, the southern provinces were ruled by the Dukes of Burgundy, whose legacy is reflected in the culture and religion of Northern Brabant. The Catholic influence is still strongly felt. Religious festivals are important events on the calendar, and carnival (*see page 247*), so much a part of Dutch life today, is celebrated with as much enthusiasm and colour as it was during the southern Golden Age.

Town of a thousand perils

Founded in the 9th century in the eastern reaches of the River Schelde estuary, **Bergen op Zoom** ❶ developed as an independent, fortified harbour town. Thanks to its powerful defences, it fended off five Spanish sieges between 1581 and 1622, before yielding to the French in 1747. Though its fortifications were demolished in 1868 and the shabby Butter Market is no longer full of sailors' wives, Bergen's centre still has pockets of architectural splendour, grand red-brick warehouses and glinting weathervanes in the shapes of mermaids and dolphins.

LEFT AND BELOW: colourful contrasts in the country's largest province.

The Oosterschelde coastline around Bergen op Zoom is a classic Dutch setting: polderland so flat it looks as if it's been ironed, windmills and sea. In the great flood of 1953, this part of Noord-Brabant went under the waves and rowing boats bobbed in Bergen's streets. Now, guarded by the distant ramparts of Zeeland's Oosterschelde Storm Surge Barrier (*see page 225*), shoppers flood the Dutch Renaissance town centre and soak up the atmosphere in the Markiezenhof's illuminated courtyard.

In the **Grote Markt**, the main square, reminders of Bergen's stormy past include an inscription from 1611 on the Stadhuis (Town Hall) that says *Mille periculus supersum* (I overcome a thousand perils), referring to fears of flood, fire and lack of faith in the declared Spanish truce. The first town hall was destroyed by fire in 1397, and the builders of this one seemingly lacked confidence in their handiwork's survival. As Bergen op Zoom expanded, so did the Stadhuis, swallowing up the adjoining English Merchant Centre and a burgher's house.

Also in the Grote Markt is a Gothic belltower topped by an 18th-century pepper-pot lantern turret,

the *Peperbus*, added after much of the church was destroyed by fire in 1747. This is all that remains of the 14th-century **Sint-Gertruidiskerk** (St Gertrude's church), whose motto could just as easily have been "I fail to overcome a thousand perils". The church was looted in 1580 and destroyed in 1747 by the French. A replacement burned down in 1972.

At night, the pepper-pot tower, gold weathervane and herringbone brick are illuminated. Around the square, restaurants and open-air cafés serve traditional local delicacies, such as asparagus and oysters.

Northwest of the Grote Markt, in Steenbergsestraat, is the town's finest building, the **Markiezenhof**, former palace of the marquises of Bergen op Zoom. Although comparable to The Hague's Ridderzaal, the 15th to 16th-century Markiezenhof is closer in spirit to the architecture of Brugges in Belgium than to any other building in the Netherlands. An imposing gateway (see below) leads to an illuminated inner courtyard adorned by a delicate gallery and well. Inside this part of the palace, now restored, is the **City History Museum** (open Apr–Sept: Tues–Sun 11am–5pm; Oct–Mar: Tues–Sun 2–5pm; entrance fee) that displays a mixture of Flemish tapestries and Louis XV furniture.

In the rear courtyard you may catch a whiff of tempting aromas wafting over from the city's best restaurant, *La Pucelle*, housed in late Gothic splendour. Before sitting down to eat, visit the **Gevangenpoort** (also known as Lieve Vrouwepoort), Bergen's only remaining medieval gateway. Gothic in style and Flemish in spirit, this turreted stone and red-brick gateway leans against sturdy walls, the remains of the early fortifications. Formerly used as the city prison, the Gevangenpoort is now a focus of the town's pre-Lenten carnival procession *(see page 245)*.

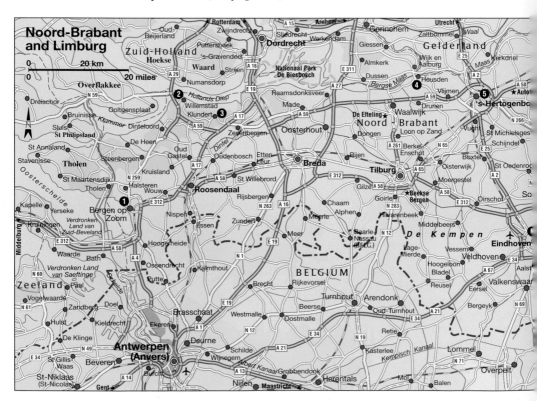

Northwards to Willemstad

From Bergen op Zoom, the N259 leads north across the polders to **Willemstad ❷**, a handsome village on the Hollands Diep and formerly a fortress town with a strategic importance far beyond its size. Approaching Willemstad, the wide estuary of the **Hollands Diep** comes into view. Cars on the raised road into the town are dwarfed by the slow-moving barges on the Diep. If you are willing to face the wind that blasts the observation tower at the southern end of the **Haringvlietbrug** (Herring River Bridge), overlooking the nearby Volkerak sluice, you'll be rewarded with a view of marine traffic jams, as barges queue to pass through locks connecting the Maas and Waal rivers with ports in southwest Holland. An information board modestly points out that Dutch barges handle 70 percent of western Europe's canal and river traffic.

A narrow bridge leads into Willemstad's star-shaped bastions, a stronghold bounded by canals, moats and the Hollands Diep. In 1583, William the Silent completed the transformation of a fishing village, celebrated for its herring catches, into a fortress town that he named after himself. Built to guard the entrance to the Hollands Diep, Willemstad is one of the best-maintained fortress towns in the country, its perfect geometry shown in 17th-century prints, topographical maps and aerial photographs.

The compact town is centred on the inner harbour, now a marina full of Dutch, Belgian and German boats. Looking down on them is the **Mauritshuis**, also known as the **Prinsenhof**, a severe, red-brick Dutch Renaissance building from 1587. Originally a hunting lodge for Prince Maurits, it was later the provincial governor's residence, then the town hall. A mermaid weathervane on the roof once graced the Markiezenhof in Bergen op Zoom and now enjoys a fine

Map
on pages
232–3

Willemstad is the country's best-kept fortress town.

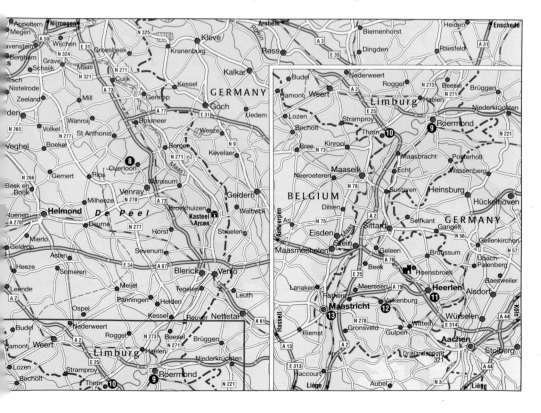

view of Willemstad's inner harbour, with its watchtower, warehouses, the old Arsenal converted to a hotel, windsurfing school and seafood restaurant. Beside the tower, a wooden bridge leads across the bastions.

A walk past outdoor cafés, clog shops and half-hidden disco suggests that Willemstad is only a thin shell concealing a modern bazaar, yet tourism never swamps local life. Neat white houses, duck-filled canals and tiny wooden bridges may make Willemstad look unreal, but this is an illusion. Doorsteps here really are washed on Monday and the church is filled on Sunday.

The octagonal **Reformed Church**, from 1607, surrounded by a shady cemetery, was one of the Netherlands's first Protestant churches. Enclosed by a small moat, it lies at the end of a leafy arbour. A short walk brings you to the **Oranjemolen**, a cosy 18th-century windmill beside the ramparts and the old outer harbour, beyond which is a wide estuary dotted with barges.

From the ramparts, a long walk leads along the old fortifications and main canals while a shorter walk traces smaller waterways back to the inner harbour. Behind the inner harbour, perched like ant-hills on top of the star-shaped bastions, are concrete bunkers from World War II. Nearby is a cemetery for 134 Belgian prisoners-of-war who died in 1940 when their ship struck a mine.

If you are tired and hungry at this point, stop at the **Arsenal**, rebuilt in 1793 by the French and now a fish restaurant, which is as good a place as any to recall the time when Willemstad was the main fishing port on the Haringvliet.

The Reed Forest

From Willemstad, an inland route leads past Oudemolen, Klundert, Zevenbergen and Made to Drimmelen, a village that makes a good base for exploring the nearby wetlands in De Biesbosch National Park. The most appealing village on the route is **Klundert ❸**, which has a free-standing, Flemish Renaissance **Stadhuis**, with a well, double staircase and lion statues reflected in its blue-green windows. Facing the town hall, the renovated **Prinsenhof** bears the town's blue and yellow insignia.

Drimmelen, an unremarkable port on the River Maas, is the gateway to the watery wilderness known as De Biesbosch ("reed forest"). The flat, dreary landscape around the village gives no hint of the ecologically rich wetlands beyond.

The **Biesbosch** owes its unique character to a great flood on St Elizabeth's Day, 1421. A storm broke the dykes along the rivers Waal and Maas, flooding the polderland. The waters reached Geertruidenberg, Drimmelen and Heusden, turned Dordrecht into an urban island and created an inland sea. The *St Elizabeth's Day Panel* in Amsterdam's Rijksmuseum shows houses submerged to their gables, floating churches and marooned sheep. More than 10,000 people drowned and 70 villages were lost underwater.

Gradually, sludge and sand deposited by the Maas and Waal accreted and the area became overgrown with rushes, reeds and willows. In 1685 and again in 1904 parts of the Biesbosch were reclaimed for farming and for gathering materials for thatching and basket-weaving. The opening of the Haringvlietdam in

1971 changed the ecological balance of the area. Today, the Biesbosch is an ever-changing pattern of water and land, but still home to rare plants and animals – among the latter are beavers, which are being reintroduced. As exhibits at **De Biesbosch Visitor's Centre** (open Tues–Sun 10am–5pm; entrance fee) suggest, you have plenty of opportunity to see what makes the Biesbosch the Netherlands' richest nature reserve. As you explore on foot, by boat or by bike (most tourist facilities are concentrated in a small area on the northern perimeter of the reserve, a few kilometres east of Dordrecht), look out for hawks and heron, swans and spoonbills, cormorants and kingfishers, as well as wild duck and geese. Squirrels and bats inhabit the willows, and beavers and polecats may be lurking among the marsh marigold and yellow irises.

Heusden

After the wild and scenic Biesbosch, civilisation beckons at **Heusden ❹**, an ancient fortified town similar to Willemstad, on the Maas east of Drimmelen. After the Union of Utrecht was formed in 1579, Heusden declared allegiance to the Protestant cause and star-shaped bastions were built around its castle and harbour. Within the safety of the walls, an elegant canal-lined town thrived on boat-building, arms dealing and herring fishing. Heusden remained a Protestant stronghold and garrison town until the French invasion of 1795. Although shelled in 1940, the town has been restored to its 16th-century glory and, four centuries later, even the local trades remain little changed.

The liveliest spot in town is the former fish market, sandwiched between the butter market and the harbour. Both the **Vismarkt** and **Botermarkt** are framed by assymetrical gabled houses, many of them converted to fish restaurants. At

TIP

A relaxing way to explore the Biesbosch nature reserve is by bike. Dordrecht station is a good place to rent bicycles and the vvv supplies brochures with suggested cycle routes. It's about a half-hour ride from town to the reserve's northern perimeter.

BELOW: collecting rushes for furniture weaving.

one end of the Vismarkt is an incongruous-looking stone portico, built in 1591, that looks more like a Roman arch than the Custom House (Commiezenhuis) it is. But once you pass through the arch onto a wooden landing stage, the Vismarkt's hustle and bustle is forgotten. It's as if you've gone behind the looking-glass to be presented on the other side with an altogether calmer scene: a circular sheet of water, its surface unbroken but for reflections of a feathery tree, a miniature bridge, a raised windmill and a neat lock-keeper's house. The Dutchness of this scene lies in its scaled-down perfection and simulated naturalness.

Heusden, like an emblematic Dutch town, appears to grow organically out of the landscape. Yet the landscape is itself landscaped: the pool is a basin; the river a canal; the river banks ramparts and sea walls. Here, nature is unnatural, down to the over-domesticated ducks.

Nor does the rest of the town disappoint in its Dutchness, from Gothic **St Catherinakerk** (Saint Catherine's church) to the functional Stadhuis, gabled houses and 17th-century market halls. As if for confirmation, there is yet another windmill, a tumbledown castle and the provincial governor's house, enclosed by courtyards and gardens. The Woonhuis also represents a very Dutch welcome: built on the site of a medieval arms factory, this ornate 18th-century building remained a family-run armaments business until quite recently.

For a traditional Dutch farewell, return to one of the fish restaurants around the Vismarkt and be comforted that the herring and hospitality are real.

The Duke's Woods

The Dutch call **'s-Hertogenbosch** ❺ Den Bosch, pronounced "Den Boss". The full title means "the Duke's Woods", a reference to the fact that the town

BELOW:
Heusden.

grew up on the site of a 12th-century hunting lodge owned by Henry I, Duke of Brabant, who in 1185 gave the town its charter. Den Bosch flourished as a wool town and, after absorption by Burgundy in 1430, became a noted centre of the arts. It was governed by Spain until 1629 when William the Silent's son took the town after a long siege.

When the Kingdom of the Netherlands was proclaimed in 1814, Den Bosch and the rest of Noord-Brabant soon joined it, while southern Brabant declared allegiance to Belgium. This division of allegiances has left its mark on Den Bosch which is moored to the Netherlands politically and economically, though the stronger cultural pull is towards Catholic Flanders and the hearty tastes that characterised the old Burgundian empire.

In today's Den Bosch, rustic cuisine, locally brewed beer, a noisy carnival and lively cultural scene ensure that Burgundian instincts survive. There are classical concerts and modern dance, and the North Brabant Orchestra in residence at the Schouwburg, near the cathedral. The shape of the old city, a triangle centred on the cathedral and bounded by the Binnendieze, the inner canals, has changed little.

A visit to Den Bosch opens with a view of soaring **Sint-Janskathedraal** Ⓐ (Saint John's Cathedral; open daily, Easter–Oct: 8am–5pm; Nov–pre-Easter: 9.30am–4pm; free), the greatest Gothic church in the Netherlands and the most Flemish of cathedrals. **Parade**, the town's central square, accords Sint-Janskathedraal the space it demands. Enough of its plain, Romanesque belltower remains to provide a severe counterpoint to this flight of Gothic fantasy. But unadorned red brick loses out to Flamboyant Gothic at its most exuberant. As the house of Hieronymus Bosch overlooks the cathedral, you can imagine that

Maps:
Area 232
City 237

Interior detail at the superbly Gothic Sint-Janskathedraal.

BELOW: street facades in Tilburg.

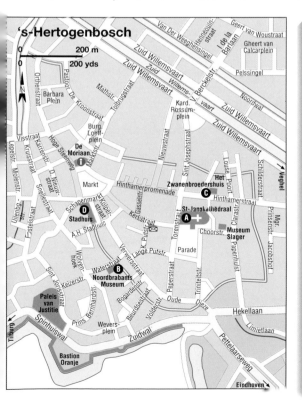

The Catholic South

T he Dutch are half-baked, without fire, melancholy and stale" was the damning judgement of Lepeintre, the 19th-century French traveller to the Calvinistic northern provinces. By contrast, the southern provinces have always revelled in their Burgundian heritage. As the Dutch specialist, William Shetter, puts it: "Residents of the southern provinces may well feel themselves to be religious, bourgeois and dominant, but they do not easily fit the Dutch stereotype of unemotional, reserved or earnest."

Instead, these latter-day Burgundians pride themselves on their warmth and generosity and accuse their northern neighbours of meanness. In fact, niggling miserliness (*krenterigheid*) is the defect that southerners find synonymous with the Dutchness of Holland, along with the smugness known as "Calvinistic fascism".

The northerners are not slow to respond: southerner jokes feature in the standard cabaret routines of Den Haag and Amsterdam. Southerners are mocked for their soft Flemish accents, liberal Catholicism and suspect morals. The term "southern Lowlands" is something of a misnomer since Noord-Brabant and Limburg form the High Netherlands, a mainly sandy region lying above sea level.

At the heart of differences are the great rivers forming the most prominent cultural boundary in the Netherlands. The term *beneden de Moerdijk* refers to people "below the rivers", the Moerdijk being the the wide river delta south of Rotterdam. The term can also embrace Belgian Flanders, thereby implying a Flemish solidarity which transcends or ignores modern boundaries.

The Flemish are often called the only Romance people to speak a Germanic language and certainly many southern Dutch feel a greater cultural affinity with the Belgian Flemish rather than with "Hollanders", the northern Dutch. The origins of the southern provinces predate Dutch statehood. In the Middle Ages, Flemish culture was the predominant one in the region and, as a result, Noord-Brabant's medieval towns, such as Den Bosch, have more in common with Bruges and Leuven than with Amsterdam or Den Haag.

From the 16th century the southern provinces were conquered by the Princes Maurits and Frederik Hendrik and, with the 1648 Treaty of Münster, became part of the United Provinces. Dutch Brabant and Limburg were allowed to remain Catholic but were otherwise alienated and excluded from power by the rising Dutch Republic. In the 17th century the Protestant Dutch Republic was a forward-looking maritime nation. By contrast, the southern provinces, populated by Flemish-speaking Catholics, looked to the rural hinterland and, alienated from the Dutch state, dwelled on past glories.

There was no equality of wealth until the late-19th century. The reversal of the cultural brain-drain from south to north only began with the electronics-led economic boom, and more recently the region has been termed the "silicon flatlands" thanks to its ability to attract high-tech industries. ❑

LEFT: roadside crucifix.

the view of richly carved sculptures and surreal symbols must have wormed its way into the painter's work.

The cathedral was built between 1330 and 1550 and, in keeping with the religious politics of the Netherlands, switched its allegiance frequently. In 1629, it was seized by the Protestants but returned to the Catholics by Napoleon in 1810, a change more in tune with its spirit. You enter the cathedral through its great west door, your first impression being one of space followed by disappointment that a 1980 restoration has left it too neat and sparse, Dutch rather than Flemish.

The grandeur of conception is clear in the vaulted ceiling, yet the eye is drawn to artistic details. After looking at the magnificent organ, choir stalls and carved baptismal fonts, your gaze falls upon aisles decorated with statues of calm women staring at stony-faced men. One small chapel off the left aisle contains dramatic Byzantine icons, including a dark-faced Christ against a rich orange background.

In the north transept there are *grisaille* figures of the Virgin and St John, reputedly by Bosch, which originally decorated the cathedral's doors. Even in this minor work, there is a sense of the charge levelled against Bosch in his lifetime: "He had the audacity to paint mankind as he is on the inside." Ultimately declared a heretic, Bosch is not much celebrated in his home town. Most of his works are in Rotterdam's Boymans-Van Beuningen Museum and in the Prado in Madrid, to which Philip II spirited away his favourite Flemish treasures.

Splendid vaulting overshadows the nave in Sint-Janskathedraal.

Nearby is the flowery, over-restored **Chapel of Our Lady**, which houses a 13th-century statue of the Virgin, traditionally associated with miracles. In adjoining **St Anthony's Chapel**, the cathedral's finest work, the *Altar of the Passion*, is an early 16th-century panel-painting that depicts the life of Christ through a combination of vivid Flemish paintings and carved figures.

BELOW: Sint-Janskathedraal.

Outside, in the bustling Parade cafés, a crowd drinks under the stern gaze of a statue of Bosch. The painter also supervises the Markt, site of the town hall and De Moriaan, the Duke of Brabant's fabled hunting lodge. Turning your back on Bosch, walk down **Verwersstraat**, to see among its attractive gables a 14th-century bakery, still in use, and, at No. 78, a façade decorated with Delft tiles.

A small alley, **Oud Bogardenstraatje**, leads over a canal to an enclosed gateway, a restored mews and a rear view of the **Noordbrabants Museum** ❸ (open Tues–Fri 10am–5pm, Sat noon–5pm; entrance fee), its gardens dotted with modern sculpture.

This 18th-century patrician building houses a collection reflecting the province's medieval origins and Burgundian traditions. In addition, works by Brueghel and Rubens pay tribute to the population's Flemish Catholic character. Van Gogh's paintings of Brabant peasants stress the region's rural roots and the painter's attachment to the wooded Meierij area outside town. The popularity of brooding works by Flemish-Belgian Expressionist Constant Permeke underlines the local affinity with Flemish culture, an affection that continues to transcend modern political boundaries.

Frogs are treated like princes in the Strabrechtse heathland near the Belgian border. Roadside trenches ensure that their annual mating migration from the River Dommel doesn't become a dice with death. In the early hours, youthful volunteers free them from the trenches so that nature can take its course unhampered by speeding cars.

BELOW:
cattle market, Den Bosch.

From the museum, narrow Beurdsestraat leads you back to Verwersstraat, and a left turn along Peperstraat returns you to the cathedral. En route, the mayor's gilded residence is indicated by a miniature **statue of Atlas**, his back burdened by the (minor) cares of office.

At the cathedral, turn right into **Hinthamerstraat**, once home to Bosch. Sadly, the painter's undistinguished gabled house has no architectural flights of fancy and is devoid of winged demons and gluttonous monks. The house grounds the imagination with the reminder that Bosch led a comfortable burgher's existence here, even though his works were collected fanatically by Burgundian and Spanish rulers, including Charles V and Philip II. Bosch is still seen as a solitary genius, belonging to no artistic school. The painter's spirit, if it lives at all in his home town, hovers above the cathedral gargoyles or floats into the city's Burgundian restaurants.

Almost next door to the house of Bosch, **Het Zwanenbroedershuis** ⓒ (open Fri 11am–3pm, free) houses one of the country's oldest religious societies. Founded in 1318, the Swan Brotherhood is signalled by statues of the medieval stations in life, from lawyer to priest. Bosch belonged to this medieval society which, then as now, promoted and popularised church music, religious art and encouraged Christian good works.

In 1629 the Brotherhood opened its doors to Protestants as well as Catholics and has attracted active support from the Dutch royal family ever since. Although the Swan Brotherhood's small collection of antiques, books and statuary is rarely visited by foreigners, Dutch people find comfort in its musty, unchanging displays. The characteristic reverence shown by Dutch visitors partly explains – even if retrospectively – Bosch's need to rebel.

The rest of Hinthamerstraat's devotion to earthly pleasures is exemplified by the number of gabled shops and restaurants in adjoining streets. But older trade is suggested in Korte Waterstraat, a blind alley leading to the original town ramparts, and in the **Binnenhaven**, the Inner Harbour. To reach the Markt from the main train station turn right and walk along the Visstraat in the direction of Centrum. Turn right at the end when you reach the Hoogsteenweg. It's worth stopping at the **Stadhuis ❿** (Mon–Fri 9am5pm) for a closer look at the classical façade and carillon. If you happen to stop by on a Wednesday between 10 and 11am you will see the mechanical horsemen trot out to its half-hourly chimes. The brasserie in the 16th-century cellar is also worth a visit.

Some 11 km (7 miles) northwest of Den Bosch, medieval **Kasteel Ammersoyen** (Ammersoyen Castle) (open for guided tours mid Apr–Oct Tues–Sat 10am–5pm, Sun 1–5pm, last tour 4pm; entrance fee) has been restored as closely as possible to its 14th-century condition, which means not much in the way of life's comforts and conveniences. You can tour the castle's interior apartments as well as the defensive works of the powerfully fortified, square keep with its four round towers and moat.

South to Eindhoven

From Den Bosch, the motorway south to Eindhoven passes through **De Kempen**, an unspoilt region of woodland, heaths and sand dunes. Unlike coastal dunes that protect the inland plains, the sole function of these sands is to be the green lungs of the Den Bosch, Tilburg, Eindhoven industrial triangle. The landscape runs through deeply wooded river valleys until the trees peter out among dunes and broom-covered heath.

Until the 19th century De Kempen was neglected by inhabitants and visitors. The poet Potgieter poured scorn on the bleak landscape: "Grey is your sky and stormy your beach. Naked are your dunes and flat your fields… Nature created you with a stepmother's hand." Yet today's visitors appreciate these sandy expanses and horizons seemingly placed so low that the heath merges with the cloudy sky. The views towards Eindhoven are reminiscent of Van Ruysdael's spacious, forlorn landscapes.

Eindhoven ❻ needs to be placed in this rural perspective if it is not to be dismissed as a soulless metropolis. Often referred to as "Philips Town", home of the multinational electrical company, the city can afford to be materialistic and monolithic because it has the countryside to keep it sane. De Kempen stretches south and west while the marshy Peel overlaps the Brabant-Limburg border. Now the high-tech centre of the Netherlands, Eindhoven was a mere village until the arrival of the Philips dynasty around 1900. Although no architectural beauty (it was heavily damaged during World War II, and rebuilt in modern style), Eindhoven has a reputation for its strikingly modern sculpture, inspired or funded by the family firm. Just outside the station is an imposing statue of Dr Anton Philips while, on Emmasingel, the original **Philips building** has been preserved, complete with low-tech chimney and sculpted bust of G. L. Philips.

Maps:
Area 232
City 237

BELOW:
Heineken brewery,
Den Bosch.

Symbols of the "old Netherlands" are still visible today.

Outside another Philips building, on Mathildelaan, is *Natuursteen*, Fred Carasso's tribute to nature in the form of a dancing, globe-shaped bronze.

By contrast, Mario Negri's statue of an automaton on the central **Piazza** represents the dehumanising nature of city life. As if confirming this idea, it shields a sharply metallic library and clinical shopping centre; the only humour lies in the steel tubing, designed to look like a cross-section of a Philip's component.

Eindhoven's artistic focus is the **Van Abbemuseum** at Bilderdijklaan 10 (under renovation until 2001; temporary exhibition space at Vonderweg 1; open Tues–Sun 11am–5pm; entrance fee), housing a unique modern art collection and with many innovative exhibitions through the year. Set beside landscaped gardens on the River Dommel, the museum was established by industrialist H.J. van Abbe. Cubist works by Picasso and Braque complement Surrealist paintings by Chagall and Delvaux, and Expressionist works by Kokoschka, Kandinsky and Permeke. The Dutch De Stijl movement, with Mondrian at the forefront, is well represented, as is the COBRA school. Pop Art, Conceptual art and modern German art feature prominently.

Van Gogh's Peel

As if to compensate for modern Eindhoven, the surrounding countryside contains much of historical interest, with Kempen farmhouses and, at **Heeze**, a 17th-century castle with period furniture and Gobelin tapestries. A quiet route from Eindhoven leads northeast to **Nuenen** ❼, Van Gogh's home village. In 1883 Van Gogh came to stay in the family rectory at Nuenen. Returning home was an admission of his defeat as a preacher in Belgium and followed a troubled relationship with Gien Hoornik, a prostitute and artist's model in The Hague. In

BELOW:
Den Bosch.

Nuenen Van Gogh made his first studies of peasant life, spending more time in the fields than in his small studio. His sketches of faces and hands were awkward and rough, echoing the timbre of his life.

The culmination of the artist's explorations in Nuenen was the first of his early masterpieces, *De Aardappeleters* (*The Potato Eaters*). Vincent's brother, Theo, was at first shocked by the coarseness of the work but Van Gogh, equating manual labour with honesty, replied that: "These people, eating potatoes in the lamplight, have dug the earth with those very hands they put in the dish."

Nuenen today is a shrine to Van Gogh; the rectory, with its green shutters and neat hedgerows, remains frozen in time. A monument honours the painter's memory, as does a permanent exhibition in the **Van Gogh Documentatiecentrum** (Van Gogh Documentation Centre; open Mon–Fri 9am–noon 2–4pm; entrance fee), near the town hall. **St Clemenskerk**, the solitary, pointed church, is a reminder that the painter's friendship with the verger resulted in the loan of a studio. In 1885 Van Gogh's father died and the painter abandoned the Netherlands for Antwerp, Paris and the radiant Mediterranean light near Arles.

Just east of Nuenen, Helmond is a characterless town bordering the mysterious **Peel** marshland that stretches between Helmond and the Limburg border. Its most characteristic sections, De Grote Peel and Helena Peel, are peatland nature reserves. For background information on the area, you can visit the **Natuurstudiecentrum** (Nature Research Centre; open Sat–Mon 1–5pm, Tues–Fri 9.30am–5pm; entrance fee) in Asten, south of Helmond.

For centuries this part of Noord-Brabant was deserted or, in the popular imagination, haunted by spirits, outlaws and vagabonds. In the 1850s, impoverished peat-cutters moved in to the area, using the old defensive canals for transport-

Map on page 232–3

De Peel National Park is one of the few wild and inhospitable places left in the densely populated Netherlands. It aims to protect and ensure the survival of this landscape, but allows access to walkers via lonely trails through the boggy terrain.

BELOW: Van Gogh's *The Potato Eaters.*

Map
on page
232–3

ing peat. As the peat was removed, bogs and lakes gradually formed and, in the process, attracted black-headed gulls and marsh birds. The lakes were not drained and transformed into polders because the soil underlying the peat, unlike the rich clay of North and South Holland provinces, is sandy and infertile.

Large-scale reafforestation has turned parts of De Peel into heath and woodland, with an occasional village built using traditional pile dwellings. The authentic Peel landscape has contracted but not disappeared. East of Eindhoven, **Helena Peel** and **Peel de Veluwe** still lie among bird-filled swamps, open waters hooded by hump-back *knuppel* bridges.

Access to the nature reserve is via Moostdijk near Meijelsedijk. Black-headed gulls are visible between March and July and are most vocal in early spring, when they nest among the reeds. To many hikers, rare insects and views over bleak fens encrusted with World War II pillboxes are reason enough to visit the area at any time of year.

The poet De Genestet aptly described De Peel on an overcast November day:

O land of manure and mist, of dirty clammy rain
Soggy patch of ground, full of chilly dews and damp.
Full of bottomless mire and unwadeable roads,
Full of gout and umbrellas, of toothache and cramps.

Despite this jaundiced, albeit realistic, view, there is much to enjoy in De Peel, especially if you like to be alone with nature.

Theme parks

If you're travelling with children, they'll be glad to hear that there's more to Noord-Brabant than scenic variations and historic towns. The **De Efteling** theme park (open daily, Apr–Jun and Sep–Oct: 10am–6pm; Jul–Aug: 10am–9pm; entrance fee; tel: 0416 288111) at Kaatsheuvel north of Tilburg, is one of the Netherlands' best. From the Fairy Tale Forest, through mystical Arabia of The Thousand and One Nights, and the Flying Pagoda, De Efteling recreates the world of goblins, fakirs, wizards and sprites.

Beekse Bergen Safari Park (open daily, Jan and Dec: 10am–4pm; Feb and Nov: 10am–4.30pm; Mar–Jun and Sep–Oct: 10am–5pm; Jul–Aug: 10am–6pm; entrance fee) at Hilvarenbeek near Tilburg takes you on a trip through the real world, but the experience is equally exciting. Herds of elephants and giraffes, prides of lions, flocks of brightly coloured birds and many other exotic animals patrol the Noord Brabant "savannahs". All in all there are around 800 animals from 125 species. You view most of the animals on drive-through excursions, but there is also a walk-through area where you can see penguins, flamingos and monkeys, among others.

Autotron (open daily, Apr–Jun and Sep–Oct: 10am–5pm; Jul–Aug: 10am–6pm; entrance fee) at Rosmalen east of Den Bosch sees classic car enthusiasts driving up in droves. Said to feature the world's second finest collection, with 250 cars, the exhibition is a vision of gleaming paint and chrome, an image of the age of automobiles when "the open road" really was open. ❏

Riotous Fun

Carnivals In Amsterdam pale in comparison to the celebrations held in Bergen op Zoom and Den Bosch during *Kermissen*, a concept embracing most folkloric festivities. Carnival is a heart-felt tradition in the southern Lowlands, and harks back to the 15th century when the southern provinces were ruled by the Dukes of Burgundy. Burgundian rule coincided with the southern Golden Age, a time of opulent town halls, noble mansions and artistic excellence. The region acquired a taste for open-air theatricals, feasting and banqueting and, above all, riotous carnivals, which remain an integral part of southern Dutch life today.

Seven weeks before Easter the carnival is at its pre-Lent peak, but preparations begin months before. Bergen op Zoom's 700 brass bands practise in neighbouring towns; the witches' costumes are created; the totemic giants are repainted; the carnival cabaret is rehearsed; a new carnival song is composed in local dialect. A Carnival Prince is also elected as master of ceremonies. In the weeks leading up to the carnival, shops are decorated with folkloric characters and bands perform in local bars and children's clubs. Masked children torment passers-by with off-key renditions of the carnival song, *Wa d'n Kemedie* (What a comedy).

The traditional Old Wives Ball, held a few days before the grand carnival weekend, is a colourful pub crawl attended by young women (and occasionally men) dressed as old hags, harridans and witches. At midnight, the women and "transvestites" are unmasked and, if female, are kissed by male revellers hovering in the wings.

During the carnival weekend, restaurants are full of brass bands and cooking plays second fiddle to performing. The weekend is for adult revellers but Monday is Children's Day, a private occasion when local youngsters wear fancy dress and meet the Carnival Prince in the Grote Markt. The Prince, or an imposter with a head for heights, greets the children from his eyrie in the Peperbus,

the church tower. Dressed as a giant, the Prince dangles huge arms and legs over the side of the tower and challenges children to hunt him through the town. A mad chase ensues, while truanting parents can be found ensconced in cosy bars.

The carnival procession itself, led by giants, floats and the long-suffering Prince, is a stage-managed occasion designed to appeal to the thousands of visitors. The Bergen op Zoom carnival is a peacock's public display. Community spirit can verge on exhibitionism. At midnight, the celebrations stop and Lenten austerity begins.

Jan Steen's *The Fat Kitchen* depicts the Dutch love of carnival, but it's left to a southern painter, Bruegel the Elder, in *Battle of Carnival and Lent*, to suggest the yin and yang of "fat" carnival and "skinny" Lent. In this symbolic confrontation between Church and inn, a merry band of guzzlers is pitted against crippled beggars and Calvinist moralists. The victory appears to be with the beer barrels, pancakes and giant-tailed fish: a southern vision of the world. ❏

RIGHT: carnival costume.

Lakes and water gardens

After this harrowing pilgrimage, you can escape to the Maas. Following the river south through Limburg provides plenty of opportunities for leaving the motorway to visit riverside castles, and enjoy watersports or water gazing. Just off the N271, graceful **Kasteel Arcen** (open Apr–Oct daily 10am–6pm; entrance fee) is an 18th-century moated château and estate set amidst a series of islands interspersed with water gardens. A walk past the château leads you to an orangerie, ornamental lake and a vivid rosarium. Oriental gardens, tropical gardens, terraces, waterfalls and pergolas delight garden-loving visitors.

Roermond 9 is a modern industrial city, though its Prinsenhof (governor's palace), Gothic cathedral and Munsterkerk have been restored since 1945. The city's greatest attraction lies just outside it: the **Maasplassen** are artificial lakes in former sand and gravel pits, whose landscaped shores are popular with sailors and windsurfers. At Maasbracht is what looks like a giant parking lot for barges with names like *Fatima*, *Tulipe* and *Marjan*. Some of the massed boats sport the last word in high-tech appliances while others are more like river tramps, but a fine smell of shipboard cooking emanates from all.

Between borders

Below Roermond, Limburg narrows to a finger of land squeezed between the Belgian and German borders. Almost on the Belgian border, **Thorn 10** is a picturesque, but self-conscious village that barely escapes being twee. Cobbled streets lead past former almshouses, converted abbey buildings and white-washed brick cottages. Its saving grace is a quiet spirituality, in keeping with its earlier incarnation as a religious centre.

BELOW: between acts, Maastricht carnival.
RIGHT: Roermond.

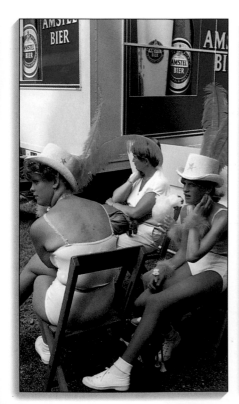

The original religious community was centred around the 10th-century **Abdijkerk** (open Mar–Oct: daily 10am–5pm; Nov–Feb: Sat & Sun noon–5pm; entrance fee) run by an abbess and a chapter of noblewomen. The church's Romanesque crypt remains but the rest of the church is Gothic with a baroque face-lift. An overblown Rubens painting competes for attention with the mummified remains of past canons and canonesses.

South of Thorn, the Maas runs along the Belgian border and South Limburg's rolling landscape ushers in wilder, less classically Dutch views. A romantic flavour is added by border castles and fortified farms. South of the Susteren lakes, two feudal castles, Wittem and Limbricht, survey a wooded scene. North of Heerlen, **Kasteel Hoensbroek** (open daily 10am–5.30pm; entrance fee), with its 14th-century red-brick towers squatting in a murky green lake, is the finest castle between the Maas and Rhine. Inside, 16th and 17th-century furnishings reflect the period of Hoensbroek's first major restoration. Views towards distant narrow river valleys and hills beyond shatter another Dutch stereotype of iron-flat landscapes.

Imaginative museum

Skirt industrial Sittard and Geleen in favour of **Heerlen ⓫**, a diffuse yet rewarding town, which at first glance is an overgrown shopping centre. Heerlen, though, has a rich past.

A Roman trading post on the Cologne–Calais road, Heerlen supplied glassware, earthenware and provisions to the legionnaries. The remains of Roman *Coriovallum* were excavated during the 1960s and a small museum built to house the circular Roman baths, furnace room, shops and sports field. The result

Map on page 232–3

From the late 19th century until 1975, Heerlen was the centre of the Dutch coal-mining industry. The discovery in 1960 of natural gas in Groningen spelled the end of Heerlen's "black fairytale".

BELOW: south Limburg, hilly enough to be called the "Dutch Alps."

is the imaginative **Thermenmuseum** (open Tues–Sun 10am–5pm; entrance fee), a metal hangar painted red, yellow and blue. Inside, a raised steel walkway provides views over the complex below, in which Roman bathers went from the sauna to warm, lukewarm, cold, and full immersion baths. In one room are the remains of a stone temple, a reconstruction of a potter's workshop and a collection of excavated jewellery, coins and statuettes.

Southern Limburg

Visually, southern Limburg is not classic Dutch and, for that reason, attracts many Dutch tourists. Its novelty is an undesigned natural landscape, an irregular patchwork of woods, meadows and hills with forbidding castles and half-timbered farms set at jaunty angles. For many foreigners, the novelty lies more in historic caves and castles rather than in landscape. The "Dutch Alps" could easily pass for Belgium's Ardennes, Germany's Eifel or England's rolling Dorset countryside. Yet there is enough Dutchness to enjoy in its shallow valleys and freshly whitewashed farms.

Valkenburg ⑫, in the wooded Geul valley, is the most popular non-coastal destination among Dutch visitors. The spa-town atmosphere and casino provide stimulation when country walks pall. For a more history-oriented stay in the region, you can spend a weekend at **Kasteel Erenstein** (tel: 045 541 1333; fax: 045 546 0748) or the farmhouse hotel **Winselerhof** (tel: 045 546 4343; fax: 045 535 2711), each with a gourmet restaurant.

At **Thermae 2000** (open daily 9am–11pm; entrance fee), an invigorating spa centre in the hills, treatments include Roman, Turkish and Swedish baths, as well as *Medizinisches Heilwasser*, German health cures. Housed under a glass pyramid, mineral-rich springs are channelled to allow swimmers to glide between exotic water experiences. (Reservations: 043 601 9419; fax: 601 4815.

Following Grotestraat from the Spaans Leenhof (the tourist office) to the castle provides a snapshot of Valkenburg. At the lower end of the street is the **Streekmuseum** (open Tues–Sun 10am–5pm; entrance fee), a cluttered collection redeemed by an elegant marlstone building, decorated with stained-glass windows and a stone falcon. Glimpses of the tumbledown castle overshadow unpromising lines of gift shops and tawdry bars. As the Netherlands' only elevated fortress, its jagged ruins, towering over modern excrescences, have a dramatic appeal.

At the foot of the castle, turn left into Berkelstraat and walk through the medieval **Berkelpoort** gateway before visiting the castle. From the De la Ruine hotel, steep steps lead past a curious sandstone grotto hewn into the rock; during carnival, a dummy of a witch is suspended over the entrance.

Still higher is the **castle** itself (open Apr–Oct daily 10am–5pm; entrance fee) which offers fine views over the River Geul valley. The 11th-century fortress was built by the feudal lords of Valkenburg ("Falcon Castle"). It attracted Flemish, Spanish and French hunters and finally succumbed to Louis XIV after a siege. On retrieving control from the French in 1672, William III ordered that the castle be demolished. The

TIP

For a fine view of the gently rolling countryside around Valkenburg, take a ride on the open cable car that takes you up to the Wilhemina Toren, a bar-restaurant on top of the hill above the castle.

BELOW:
Valkenburg caves.

remains (restored in 1921) include a tower, chapel and arsenal, and a network of secret tunnels leading to the **Fluwelengrot** caves (guided tours Apr–Nov: daily 10am–5pm; Dec–Mar: Sat & Sun 11am–4pm) and former quarries.

Map on page 232–3

Caves and grottoes

Return to Berkelstraat and turn left into Munstraat. After passing under Grendelpoort, the second medieval gate, glance back at the statue of a Virgin in a niche, a foretaste of the Lourdes grotto to come. The **Lourdesgrot** on Cauberg was built as a replica of the French shrine and attracts sick pilgrims, particularly on the Feast of the Assumption. Valkenburg's hills are pitted with such caves, among them reconstructions of modern coal mines and Roman catacombs. The most incongruous are the **Gemeentegrot** (open for hourly guided tours daily 10.30am–4pm), the municipal caves between Grendelpoort and the Lourdes grotto. As with all Dutch caves, they are man-made but exceptional in that they have been quarried since Roman times. Marlstone, a type of limestone, was worked here until recently. Now prohibitively expensive, marlstone's use is restricted to restoration work and statuary.

The ruined castle of the lords of Valkenburg, the country's only hilltop castle.

The caves are vast, covering 110 hectares (275 acres) and 75 km (47 miles) of tunnels, of which about 5 km (3 miles) are open to the public. Given the constant temperature of 11°C (52°F), it is best to see the caves in cold weather when it feels warmer inside. Earlier visitors followed this logic, and amused themselves during winter by carving and painting the caves' porous marlstone, which is soft underground. Once exposed to the outside air, it hardens rapidly. The oldest known cave sculptures and paintings date from the 15th century, but some of the modern ones are no less intriguing.

BELOW:
Thermae 2000 spa.

While you're waiting for a guided tour by "train" or on foot, expect to be accosted by an enterprising sculptor who, working on the captive-audience principle, is willing to carve anything on the spot, from family crests for Belgian aristocrats to statuettes of beloved pets for homesick, globe-trotting Canadians.

The cave's first section is covered with abstract art carved by students of Breda University. Many of these 1960s designs are primitive, even by prehistoric caveman standards. The 15th- and 16th-century works include a sculpture of St George, an impressive lion rampant and a painting of Knight Willem, a local hero. The best modern picture is of the Dutch royal family: different generations of royals attended sittings in this damp site between 1885 and 1950.

The strangest sculptures are by a 19th-century blacksmith who, inspired by the prehistoric world, spent all his time underground, carving dinosaurs. One looks like the Loch Ness monster while another, a life-size megalosaurus, resembles a demented crocodile.

The caves have played an important role in local history as well as local art. During World War II, 3,000 citizens hid inside, leaving behind their names, messages and, occasionally, paintings. The Germans gained control of the caves and built a secret factory to produce flying bombs. Now mostly ruined, the factory was dismantled by liberating American forces in September 1944.

To Maastricht

From Valkenburg, a short route leads across the plains to **Maastricht** , the provincial capital and most Burgundian city in the Netherlands, a sophisticated, open-minded border town, far removed in spirit from the regimented northern provinces. Aficionados of the south consider Maastricht the country's most

TIP

If you have exhausted Maastricht, why not take a summer cruise down the River Maas to Liège in neighbouring Belgium. Ask at the vv for information.

BELOW: tomb of Count Gueldre Gerare IV and wife, Notre-Dame church.

user-friendly city, combining quality of life with standard of living in a way northerners haven't quite got the hang of yet. In his satirical novel, *In Nederland*, Cees Nooteboom decries the north as "an orderly human garden" and praises the south as a land of untamed cave-dwellers leading freer lives.

Maps
Area 233
City 255

Of all the southern towns, Maastricht has the least trammelled spirit, and as the Netherlands' oldest city, it has been open to foreign influence from Roman traders, Charlemagne's soldiers and Burgundian merchants.The result of such a cosmopolitan history is no bland internationalism, but a relaxed society confident of its traditions and its dialect, which, unlike many parts of the Netherlands, Maastricht has retained. So distinctive is it that locals half-jokingly claim not to speak Dutch. Before the euro the city accepted three currencies, reflecting its position in the important economic triangle delineated by Maastricht, Aachen and Liège. Germans cross the border for art exhibitions; Belgian students for the nightlife and northern Dutch for the hilly countryside and a chance to release their Calvinistic inhibitions.

Maastricht started out as a Roman garrison and trading post commanding an important river crossing. From there, all roads led to Cologne, London and Rome. The establishment of a 4th-century bishopric under St Servaas brought the town great prestige and wealth. However, its role as a frontier town resumed in 1204 when the Duke of Brabant shared power with the Prince-Bishop of Liège. For over 200 years, this dual authority was reflected in the city's geography: upstream from St Servaasbrug, the Bishop of Liège held sway while Brabant governed the area downstream from the bridge.

In the 15th century the city was absorbed by the Burgundian empire and became a great trading centre, matched by a flourishing reputation for *Maasland (Mosan)* art. At its apogee in the early 16th century, Maastricht rivalled Flemish Ghent and Antwerp. Thereafter, its fortunes fluctuated according to the effects of repeated Spanish and French invasions. From the successful 1579 Spanish siege to the last French invasion, in 1794, Maastrichters became used to adapting to foreign tastes.

BELOW:
Bonnefanten
Museum,
Maastricht.

Rich heritage

Architecturally, foreign influence brought greater diversity than you see in most Dutch cities. The city's Roman remains and rings of medieval fortifications are still in evidence. It has Romanesque arches and murals, French Gothic churches, indigenous *Maasland* Renaissance architecture, onion towers imported from the East, and, from the 17th century, the classical style favoured by northern Dutch Calvinists.

Under Louis XIV, an aristocratic French community encouraged the creation of Baroque residences. Later in the 18th century, symmetry gave way to frenzied rococo lines. As for German influence, Maastricht's helm roofs are a copy of the Rhineland's. The city's architecture continues to be inspired by the past, particularly in its saddle-back roofs. More imaginatively, bold modern statues delight in holding a distorting mirror to the past. At best, as in Mari Andriessen's *Mestreechter Geis* (Spirit of Maastricht), there is both a past memory

and the essence of the city today. Maastricht may be a result of dynastic bargaining but its spirit remains intact.

Maastricht's centre is on the west bank of the Maas and stretches towards the Belgian border. Most visitors arrive in the Wijk district on the east bank and so need to cross the river. Once in the historic heart, you can explore the city's three most appealing districts. The centre, including two major squares, churches and the town hall, is the civic and spiritual core. The Stok quarter, the Roman and medieval district, is bounded by Sint-Servaasbrug to the north, the Maas to the east, Onze Lieve Vrouwebasiliek (Basilica of Our Lady) to the south, and Wolvenstraat to the west. The Jeker quarter, south of the Stok quarter, embraces the city's medieval fortifications, mills and almshouses, and follows the course of the river Jeker to the south and Tongersestraat to the northwest.

The heart of town

The *Stad aonde Maos* ("the town on the Maas") has two main central squares, the largest of which is the spacious **Vrijthof** . Approached via inward-looking alleys that typify the old centre, this light-filled square seems out of keeping with Maastricht's nature. Its origins are disputed: built over marshes along the River Jeker, the area was originally unsuitable for building and, by medieval times, was used as a military parade ground, execution site and pilgrims' meeting place. Every seven years, the "Fair of the Holy Relics" attracted pilgrims, craftsmen and traders to the lively square. Something of this chaotic spirit is recaptured in the Vrijthof at carnival time.

One side of the square is lined with cafés and in summer, the wide pavements are filled with tables which draw a constant stream of human traffic. On the other side of the square the two magnificent churches of **Sint-Servaasbasiliek** and **Sint-Janskerk** survey the scene, almost reproachfully. They provide a sombre counterbalance to the carnival spirit and café culture.

Sint-Servaasbasiliek (open Sept–June: Mon–Sat 10am–5pm, Sun 1–5pm; Jul–Aug: Mon–Sat 10am–6pm, Sun 1–5pm; entrance fee) is one of the oldest churches in the Netherlands and is a fitting tribute to its Armenian founder, Saint Servaas, who became Maastricht's first bishop and brought the town fame and fortune. The church is said to stand on his burial site and contains his relics. Begun in the 11th century, the Romanesque basilica was enlarged and embellished over the next four centuries. Its front façade has the grim impregnibility of a fortified town, but this forbidding impression is a feature of Romanesque *Maasland*, a style prevalent along the Maas. The heavy apse is flanked by square, twin towers beyond which soars the Gothic spire of Sint-Janskerk.

Sint-Servaasbasiliek hides its lyrical side around the corner, in the **Bergportaal** on the south side of the church (entrance during services). The 13th-century, French High Gothic doorway is a *trompe-l'oeil* of inner arches. Each section is adorned with sculpted vegetation, mythological animals, Biblical scenes and hidden symbolism. Viewed from the sloping steps

TIP

If you're visiting Holland at carnival time (third week of February) be sure to head for the southern towns: Maastricht, Breda and Den Bosch are all renowned for their energetic carnivals.

BELOW: structural detail on an old tavern.

Map below

beside this doorway, Sint-Janskerk appears to offer a severe Protestant rebuke to the fanciful aspirations of St Servaas. The interior of St Servaas has been somewhat over-restored. Its 10th-century crypt, Gothic porch, chapels and cloisters are more authentic than the clinical-looking choir. Catholic Maastrichters ruefully say that the restorers must have been Protestants.

Bright, zig-zag patterns on the capitals are a preparation for the jewellery-shop appearance of the **Schatkamer** (Treasury) in the former sacristy. This Aladdin's Cave glitters with silver, gold, copper and precious stones. In addition to a 12th-century cross encrusted with amethysts, treasures include a lovely statue of St Anne, a platter depicting St John's head on a plate, ivory reliquaries and illuminated manuscripts. The undisputed masterpieces, however, are a 16th-century silver bust of St Servaas, ornamented with reliefs telling his story (it is carried through the town in Easter processions) and a bejewelled 12th-century chest reliquary that is a high point of *Maasland* art. Craftsmanship shines through the rich decoration so that it is not the profusion of emeralds and sapphires that you admire but the workmanship itself.

Outside, the faded 15th-century exterior of **Sint-Janskerk** (open Apr–Oct Mon–Sat 11am–4pm), Maastricht's main Protestant church since 1632, awaits you. Surrounded by gabled houses and flower beds, the structure is more remarkable for its location and exterior than for its stark interior. Apart from the impressive red Gothic tower (which you can climb for a fee), the Louis XVI pulpit, a smattering of marble tombs and testaments to local notables, the church is a disappointment.Before leaving the Vrijthof in the direction of Dominikanerplein, have a look at the **Spanish Government House ❶**, 16th-century seat of the provincial government. Its exterior is adorned with Habsburg symbols,

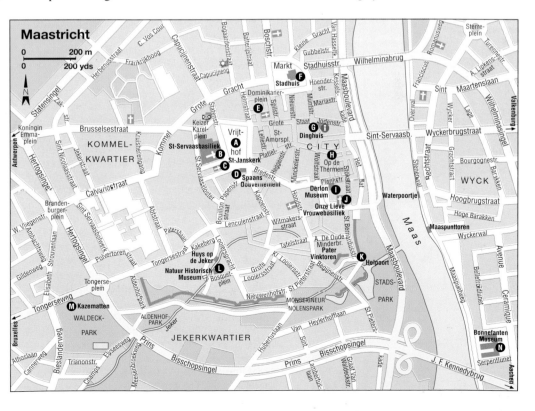

including the motto: *"Plus oultre"* (Still further). The Renaissance arcade is attractive, but there is nothing remarkable about the collection of French 18th-century furniture, paintings and other assorted exhibits inside.

Dominikanerplein , the adjoining square, is a small, intimate affair, crowded with café tables. A sober Gothic church, the Dominikanerkerk, dominates the scene. The austerity and rigor of its exterior is in keeping with the Dominican ethos. The friars were renowned for their scholarship and intellect, and played an unbending role in the Inquisition. The dark interior contains faded murals and the overall impression is sombre. Only at carnival does the church come alive with children's displays of monsters and figures of fun – the Dominicans would not have approved.

The bars in and around Markt are a popular meeting place. The statue of a plump stallholder, 't Mooswief, on the square is usually surrounded by chattering students.

The market square

From Dominikanerplein, attractive alleys and shopping streets lead to the Markt, another busy square which vies with the Vrijthof as a city centre. On Wednesday and Friday mornings the Markt wins out because these two market days attract crowds of locals as well as day-trippers from Aachen and Liège. The ever-popular herring stall is rarely without a queue and is as good a place as any to sample the Dutch speciality. Even on other days, the bars in and around the square are crowded.

Centrepiece of the square is the **Stadhuis** (open Mon–Fri 8.30am–12.30pm and 2–5.30pm; free) a severe, 17th-century classical town hall by Pieter Post, a pupil of Jacob van Campen. You approach its interior by two flights of stairs, designed so that the two competing city authorities of Brabant and Liège could literally go their own way. The entrance chamber radiates cool gravity but its exuberant rococo ceiling adds a touch of frivolity. It is here that the Mayor hands over the keys of the city to the Carnival Prince. You may be lucky enough to hear the 43-bell carillon – in typical Maastricht style, the 17th-century council abandoned solemn dirges in favour of spirited folk tunes; happily the practice continues.

BELOW: the Vrijthof, heart of Maastricht.

The medieval quarter

Grote Staat, the main shopping street, leads from the northern end of Vrijthof to the Stok quarter, the heart of the medieval and Roman city. Grote Staat, like most other streets in this area, is well provided with bars, *pâtisseries* and cheese shops. There are frequent opportunities to sample local specialities, including a *Limburgse vlaai* (fruit flan) and *rommedou* cheese. If you can resist the aroma of asparagus omelette and trout, you may succumb to tempting displays of *pralines* and gingerbread delicacies, washed down with a glass or two of local beer, or a bottle of rare Maastricht wine. (Napoleon closed most of the region's vineyards, but three small ones still produce 25,000 bottles a year).

At the end of Grote Staat stands the **Dinghuis** , a narrow Gothic building with a steep saddle-back roof. Now the city's friendly and efficient vvv tourist office (open Mon–Fri 9am–6pm, Sat 9am–5pm), it has barred ground-floor windows, left over from its Napoleonic days as a prison.

The compact Stok quarter is the oldest part of the city, dating back to Roman times. Its northern boundary is the Gothic **Sint-Servaasbrug**. Built of grey Namur stone, it is the oldest bridge in the Netherlands. Alongside it, Mari Andriessen's *Mestreechter Geis* statue represents the spirit of Maastricht and guards the entrance to the old quarter.

Stok quarter buildings date from medieval times, when it was the central market area. Street names testify to the presence of grain, fish, meat and timber markets, though **Stokstraat** got its name from the nearby stocks and city prison. In the 17th and 18th centuries the area became fashionable and a number of intricate façades and gable stones remain from the period. Number 26 is one of the finest, a *Maasland* Renaissance masterpiece that owes more to freely interpreted Gothic than to Renaissance symmetry. Number 17 has an ornate rococo façade decorated with scallop shells which was peeled off a town house on Grote Staat: proof that wandering is not restricted to gable stones.

Off Stokstraat is a handful of medieval squares, including **Op de Thermen** ⓗ, a chic square with boutiques, a half-timbered medieval tower and a statue of a decapitated *Amazon*. The square lies on top of the Roman baths, whose outline is traced on the pavement.

Around the corner, in Plankstraat, the **Derlon Museum** ⓘ (open Sun noon–4pm; free) houses a small Roman collection unearthed when the Derlon hotel was built. Remains dating from the 2nd century include a wall, gate, well, part of a temple to Jupiter and a section of cobbled Roman road. Tired visitors can view the display from the comfort of the hotel's tea rooms.

In the 19th century, the fashionable centre moved to the Markt and Vrijthof, leaving Stokstraat to degenerate into a cholera-infested slum with open drains

Map on page 255

Sign of a Wijnkelder, or wine seller.

BELOW: in Den Ouden Vogelstruys café, Vrijthof.

and brothels. Sensitive 1960s restoration, however, has made the Stok quarter a perfect place for strolling and window shopping. Designer boutiques rub shoulders with friendly working-class bars, modern statues and old gable stones. Swans, lions, cherubs, grapes, trees, even a sphynx, are clues to their previous owners' trades and professions.

Romanesque treasure

The **Onze Lieve Vrouwebasiliek** ❶ (Basilica of Our Lady; open Sept–June: daily 10am–4pm; Jul–Aug: daily 10am–5pm; entrance free to church, fee for treasury), surrounded by cafés and restaurants on shady Onze Lieve Vrouwe-plein, grandly delimits the district's southwestern end. On the site of a vanished Roman temple, the fortified Romanesque church is the city's oldest. Built in the year 1000, it is flanked by two circular turrets, pierced by arrow slits, and topped by a squat helm roof. Its forbidding west front owes more to German Rhineland architecture than to Flemish or Dutch styles.Inside, the atmosphere is slightly eerie, heightened by the delicate sculpted capitals decorated with scenes from the Old Testament and an apse decorated with gauzy Romanesque frescoes. Christ is depicted against an azure backdrop, with stars and angels beyond. Onze Lieve Vrouwe's struggle for supremacy over St Servaas ended in failure: by the 15th century it was banned from displaying relics and selling indulgences. As a result, the basilica has a much smaller collection of treasure.

BELOW:
St Servaaskerk
and St Janskerk.

Student quarter

From the Onze Liewe Vrouwe square, St Bernardusstraat leads south to the **Jeker quarter,** a gently tumbledown district of narrow winding streets, mill

streams and ruined fortifications. This area is popular with Maastricht's big student population so bars and "alternative" shops are tucked into the side streets. Compared with the Stok quarter, this relatively large area has fewer grand old churches. It is characterised by its mills and almshouses and the quiet pathways running through parks and gardens, or along the three tiers of ramparts (a popular jogging route).

Helpoort **🅚** (Hell's Gate), at the end of St Bernardusstraat, built in 1229, is a sinister steep-roofed gateway marking the city's medieval boundaries. Beside it a lone tower, the **Jekertoren**, marks the former territorial demarcation between Liège and Brabant. Beyond Helpoort, a tranquil walk along the city walls leads to Heksenstraat and the University quarter, passing the main park, a mini zoo and various derelict towers.

The fast-flowing **River Jeker**, on the far side of Helpoort, is flanked by an old tower and a row of neat 17th-century cottages that once formed part of the city's Begijnhof (Beguine's Convent). On the river's opposite bank is the **Anker**, a water-driven paper mill on the site of the former Pesthuis (Plague House), built to keep plague victims safely out of harm's way – which meant outside the city walls.

Instead of tracing the city walls, you can follow atmospheric alleys from Helpoort to Lang Grachtje, a filled-in river enclosed by the city walls. This leads to **Grote Looiersstraat**, one of the city's loveliest spots. Until the 16th century, it was filled with tanneries but later became a sought-after residential area. Although the canal is now filled in, gracious 17th and 18th-century houses remain. Several bear witness to virtuous 17th-century Dutch society: No. 27 was once a Catholic almshouse, and No. 17 a Poor House – an admonitory motto

Map on page 255

TIP

A good place to catch an English or American movie in its original version (i.e. not dubbed but with Dutch subtitles) is the Lumière Filmhuis at 40 Bogaardenstraat.

BELOW: Mondrian leaves his mark on a 2CV.

over the door says: "He who gives to the poor shall suffer no harm." En route, look out for an informal group of bronze figures sitting on a stone bench. The sculpture is dedicated to Fons Olterdissen, a local storyteller.

Musical city

It is thought that Comte d'Artagnan, the fourth Musketeer, was killed in Maastricht during an attack on King Louis XIV's forces in 1673.

Grote Looiersstraat leads to **De Bosquetplein** and the University quarter, between the arms of the Jeker. The **Natural History Museum** (De Bosquetplein 6; open Mon–Fri 10am–12.30 pm and 1.30–5pm, Sat–Sun 2–5pm; entrance fee) houses a small exhibition on the flora and fauna of the area and has a well-kept garden.

As you walk along the steep Heksenstraat (Witches' Street) and admire the clear views over the river, you will pass a mill and a stone carving of a witch on the wall – hence the name. Heksenstraat adjoins the Academy of Music so the air here is often filled with conflicting snatches of classical music and jazz. Also on this stretch of the Jeker is the **Huis op de Jeker**, a perfectly preserved *Maasland* Renaissance house spanning the river. Nearby, the former Grey Sisters Convent is a poetic if dilapidated haunt favoured by romantic couples in search of privacy.

From here, most streets lead back to the centre via Platielstraat and **Sint-Amorsplein**, a fashionable square overlooked by a reproving statue of the saint. On the square, the Troubadour Chantant is a lively student café which lives up to its name with regular performances of singing, dancing, cabaret and even poetic monologues.

Maastricht is a musical city, offering everything from classical music to cabaret, opera to musical puppet shows and, in October, hosts a well-known jazz festival. Churches, including St Servaas, hold regular organ recitals and on Sunday mornings, the voices of the Mestreechter Staar male choir can be heard rehearsing in the Staargebouw concert hall.

Visitors with any energy left can visit the **Kazematten** , the city's old fortifications, or explore the galleried St Pietersberg and Sonneberg caves just outside town. These are similar to the Valkenburg caves, but had a more pronounced military function, used both in 17th-century sieges and during World War II.

Below: one of Maastricht's venerable bars.

Italian and Flemish Masters

The stylish, modern **Bonnefanten Museum of Art and Archaeology** across the rivier (Avenue Ceramique; open Tues–Sun 11am–5pm; entrance fee) has works by Italian and Flemish Masters, and holds the country's finest collection of *Maasland* art. The Italian collection, covering work between 1300 and 1550, includes some of the greatest Sienese, Florentine and Venetian artists, from Sano di Pietro to Filippo Lippi and Bellini. Domenico di Michelino's *Expulsion from Paradise* approaches the power of Masaccio's Florentine frescoes, while Sano di Pietro's luminous *St Catherine* is the envy of Sienese museum curators.

It is no accident that the Netherlands' ever-growing Italian collection is housed here: national museum policy confirms the view that, as the nation's most

Latin city, in spirit and in reality, Maastricht is the rightful home for such southern European works.

The same logic applies to the museum's collection of Flemish Masters, tactfully known as "South Netherlandish" painters. Covering the period from 1480 to 1650, these paintings embrace the region of old Flanders, stretching from Bruges and Antwerp to Den Bosch and Maastricht. The collection includes Pieter Brueghel's *Wedding in front of a Farm* and the *Census at Bethlehem*, as well as local landscapes, still lifes and portraits. Although Amsterdam's Rijksmuseum collection is far bigger, Maastricht's pre-17th-century works are comparable with those on display in the capital.

Museum highlights

Pride of the museum is its *Maasland* art collection, paintings from the River Maas area dating between 1270 and 1550. Often known by the French term, *Mosan*, this important school is best represented in Maastricht and over the border in Liège. *Maasland* art is rooted in craftsmanship and expressive detail, and is at its best in silver work and sculpture, especially wood carvings. Sadly, the frequent incorporation of jewels and precious metals meant that many works were stolen, dismantled or melted down in former times.

Enough precious works of art remain to confirm the theory that "Maastricht doesn't feel part of the Dutch Golden Age – all that belongs to northerners. Here, the Golden Age came much earlier and had different influences." Highlights include a 15th-century wooden *Pietà*, a life-size 16th-century *Mary in Sorrow* and a serene Liège School angel that looks graceful enough to fly away at any moment. ❏

Map on page 255

The Bonnefanten Museum, Maastricht, highlights the works of Dutch and Italian masters.

BELOW: restoration of Onze Lieve Vrouwe church.

HOW THE DUTCH LIVE ON WATER

God made the world but the Dutch made Holland. The Dutch have always had an inextricable link with water – whether reclaiming it or enjoying it

Any visitor to the Netherlands could be forgiven for thinking they had arrived on a carpet of islands. There are boats everywhere, ranging from rowing boats to supertankers (Rotterdam is the largest harbour in the world). Because waterways are quite shallow, many boats are flat-bottomed and of narrow build. In appearance they are similar to Britain's Norfolk wherries or Thames barges, but offer a wider variety of sizes and functions. Many of the old tugboats, known as *sleepboten*, that were once used to tow boats around narrow canals are now used for pleasure purposes instead.

The Netherlands' wealth of vintage vessels, however, are by far the most charming. Where deeper navigation is possible, you are almost certain to see tall ships and multi-masted vessels from days gone by with names reflecting their place of origin. Given the universal love of all that is maritime, the Netherlands provides probably the best retirement home for these ageing ladies of the sea.

Numerous boat festivals underline the local passion, the most famous of all being Sail Amsterdam, which extends its welcome to the world (*see page 88*). Launched in 1975 to celebrate Amsterdam's 700th birthday, it is now repeated every five years and has become a truly international maritime event attracting thousands of boats, whole fleets, and millions of visitors. The impressive opening parade includes around 800 traditional Dutch sailing vessels.

△ **WATER MARGIN**
Though of little commercial use, "retired" waterways such as this one in the environs of Overijssel, still function as peaceful recreational routes for locals and holidaymakers.

▷ **ALL ABOARD**
The bus-like *rondvaart* is one of the few remaining means of commercial transport on Amsterdam's inner canal ring, and is well worth the ride.

△ **GENERATION GAP**
Pleasure boats cater for seven passengers or several hundred. Many old ferries and steamers have found a new lease of life as "party ships".

◁ **DAY TRIPPERS**
Excursions along picturesque rivers, such as the Vecht, are popular in summer, although some stretches of natural river are closed to powered craft and give nature the upper hand.

HOME IS WHERE THE BOAT IS

The Dutch have a passion bordering on the religious for all forms of water transport, be it a modern hydrofoil or a graceful old sailing ship of the former Dutch East Indies Company. Boats rival bicycles as a favoured means of transport, and when people are not cruising the waters in whatever craft they have chosen from the vast range available, many retire to their homes on the water.

Houseboats come in three basic varieties. First is the purpose-built modern and palatial *woonarken*, or residential "ark", built on a pontoon or flotation chamber. Prices for these often rival those for freehold property. Second is the old barge that has had its cargo hold converted into living quarters. It remains mobile by using either a sail or motor. Last is the converted smaller vessel that remains moored in one place. Its unique construction and domestic compromise makes this houseboat the most interesting and amusing for onlookers to observe.

◁ **MARKET PRICES**
There's more to the country's tranquil harbours than boats. In many former fishing villages the quaint fishermen's homes are listed properties.

△ **WE COME IN PEACE**
Once a major trading port, as testified by its sea-facing cannons, Hoorn harbour remains a busy spot for locals and visitors alike.

*In the grounds of the
Kröller-Müller
Museum.*

(*see page 243*). The extensive collection also includes works by other modern European masters such as Mondrian, Van der Leck, Seurat, Redon, Braque, Picasso and Gris.

In the grounds of the museum is Europe's largest **Sculpture Park** (open Apr–Oct: Tues–Sun 10am–4.30pm; free). Try to pick a fine day and wander at will through beautifully kept gardens where you will come across the work of Rodin, Moore, Lupchitz, Tajiri, Volten, Visser, Paolozzi and Marini. Nature and Art are in peaceful harmony here. Within the Rietveld-designed pantheon you can enjoy the work of Barbara Hepworth under the open sky; and admire Marta Pan's beautiful white sculpture, *Otterloo,* that floats in a pond. This just perceptively moving piece looks like a strange and silent mating of two swans frozen in time – or, to be more mundane, like a meringue in an *île flottante.*

A ticket to the Kröller Muller Museum also entitles you to visit the gardens of the **Jachtslot St Hubertus** at the northern end of the park, about 3 km (2 miles) from the visitor's centre (open May–Oct: Mon–Fri 10–11.30am

2–4.30pm; guided tours only, every half hour; free). The Art Deco hunting lodge was built in 1920 by Dutch architect, Berlage, and dedicated to St Hubert, the patron saint of hunters.

Map on page 268

Achterhoek

The second area of Gelderland lies between the River IJssel to the west and the German border to the east. Once covered with marshes, land reclamation over the last few centuries has turned the **Achterhoek** into a fertile expanse of fields and meadows hemmed on all sides by woods. Stately castles, farmhouses, pristine gardens and tiny, unexpected museums all lie along the hundreds of bicycle routes, waiting to be discovered.

In the eastern section of the Achterhoek, around the town of **Winterswijk ❸**, you can still find marshland areas where rare plants and flowers flourish, including certain varieties of orchid. To the north of Winterswijk is another beautiful rural area with woodland streams and masses of wild flowers, perfect for long walks. Here you'll come across the famous "mosaic floor of the Netherlands", an area where ancient stones have risen to the surface, and where palaeontologists claim to have found dinosaur traces.

The IJssel, which is a tributary of the River Rhine, forms the western border of the Achterhoek. This is a lovely meandering river with green banks and bays which are used for watersports such as windsurfing and swimming.

One of Achterhoek's most historic centres is **Zutphen ❹**, a fortified town founded in the 11th century, bounded by magnificent old walls complete with look-out towers. The huge Gothic **Grote Kerk** (open May–Sept open Mon 2–4pm Tues–Sat 11am–4pm; entrance fee) houses the medieval **Librije**. This was one of the first public libraries in Europe and has some wonderful illuminated manuscripts and 16th-century tomes on display. Not far from the church is one of the old city gates **Drogenapstoren**, an impressive 15th-century brick tower in the ramparts.

About 19 km (12 miles) south of Zutphen is the old town of **Doesburg ❺**, another beautifully restored centre worth a visit if you're passing by.

The River Area

The third area of Gelderland lies between the Rhine and the Maas. The River Waal, a wide tributary of the Rhine, cuts through it, linking the German Ruhr area and the North Sea to form the busiest shipping route in Western Europe.

This region is also watered by the delightful River Linge, which flows through the fruit and vineyard district of the Betuwe (literally "Good Land"). The Rhine and the Maas are excellent for watersports. Some of the river meanders, now cut off from the main stream, have been turned into watersports resorts with marinas, beaches and campsites.

A particularly attractive trip can be taken either by bike or car from **Zaltbommel**. It runs along the top of the gently stepped dykes and offers wonderful views, with the River Linge on one side and orchards and picturesque houses actually built into the dykes on the other.

The collection of paintings and sketches by Vincent van Gogh in the Kröller-Müller Museum is one of the most complete collections of his works in the world.

BELOW: kids enjoying the Kröller Muller Museum.

The Battle of Arnhem

As September 1944 began, the population of the Nazi-occupied Netherlands waited in expectation. The Allied armies of liberation were poised on the Dutch–German border and the German army was on the run. It seemed that the four-year nightmare of occupation was about to end. But the Allied offensive from Normandy was beginning to run out of steam. Soldiers were exhausted by three months of continuous fighting, German resistance on the Dutch border stiffened and the advance ground to a halt. Something was needed to break open the front and the strategy called Operation Market Garden was born.

British Field Marshal Montgomery's plan was simple in essence, but breathtakingly daring. Some 35,000 parachute and glider-borne troops of the 1st Allied Airborne Army would drop from the sky to capture each of the river, stream and canal bridges along a 100-km (60-mile) road running from the border through the cities of Eindhoven, Nijmegen and Arnhem. Meanwhile, an armoured column would punch a hole in the German front then race along this road, over the captured bridges, and cross the Rhine at Arnhem, gateway to Hitler's Reich.

It was a high-stakes roll of the dice that could end the war by Christmas. The Airborne Commander, General Browning, thought the operation feasible, but told Montgomery: "We might be going a bridge too far." Battle commenced on 17 September. Dutch civilians watched in amazement as thousands of parachutes blossomed in the daylight sky. Troops of the US 101st and 82nd Airborne Divisions quickly secured most of their objectives, but an important canal bridge near Eindhoven was blown up and the vital bridge over the River Waal at Nijmegen was strongly defended by the Germans. The ground assault was held up.

The British had played down Dutch Resistance reports that German armoured formations were in the area, and many troops were shot even before hitting the ground. Of those that landed safely, only some 600 fought their way to the Rhine bridge along what became known as Hell's Highway, before running into SS tanks and artillery. This handful of "Red Devils" held the bridge at Arnhem for four days against overwhelming odds, but eventually they were overcome.

The Battle of Arnhem ended in defeat for the Allies. Much of Eindhoven, Nijmegen and Arnhem was destroyed. Today, the only evidence of former conflict is in the peaceful military cemeteries that dot Hell's Highway. The Liberation Museum outside Nijmegen and the renovated Airborne Museum at Oosterbeek contain mementoes of the fighting, and record the struggle of the soldiers who came from the sky.

Though their numbers lessen with every year that passes, veterans still return to the now rebuilt "bridge too far" in Arnhem, where an occasional solitary figure wearing his red beret with pride can be seen looking down into the muddy water, pondering the past, and remembering. ❑

LEFT: scene from the 1977 film *A Bridge Too Far*.

Arnhem

Gelderland has three main cities. **Arnhem ❻** will always be associated with the Allied paratroopers who landed here in September 1944 in a brave attempt to invade Germany and end the war. The Battle of Arnhem actually took place around **Oosterbeek ❼**, about 8 km (5 miles) west of Arnhem. Here, on the north bank of the Rhine, in the beautifully kept **Oosterbeek War Cemetery**, lie the remains of the 1,748 Allied troops who tried to take the Arnhem Bridge.

The cemetery lies in a peaceful green clearing surrounded by trees, and is maintained by the staff of the War Graves Commission. Each year in September a touching memorial service is held, usually attended by about 3,000 people, including ex-servicemen and the widows, children and grandchildren of the dead. A touch of poignancy is added by children from the local schools who place bunches of flowers on each grave during the ceremony.

War museum

The devastating story of the Battle of Arnhem can be traced at the **Airborne Museum** (open Mon–Sat 11am–5pm, Sun noon–5pm; entrance fee) in Oosterbeek, located in the former Hotel Hartenstein, which served as the headquarters of General Urquhart who kept vigil here during the harrowing days of the battle (see opposite). Visitors can follow the various stages of the bloody confrontation with the aid of large-scale dioramas, a spoken commentary and photographic display.

If you are visiting the original Arnhem Bridge, a detour to the **Nederlands Openlucht Museum** (Schelmseweg 89, Arnhem; open Apr–Oct; entrance fee), on the outskirts of the city, is also worthwhile. The open-air museum spans 300

Map on page 268

BELOW: Het Loo Palace, Apeldoorn.

years of Dutch rural history reflected in over 100 different period buildings ranging from a wealthy merchant's house to a primitive paper mill. It also has one of the more interesting exhibitions on traditional costume. A vintage tram ferries visitors around the complex (wheelchairs are also available).

Nijmegen

Nijmegen ❽ is the oldest city in the Netherlands. Formerly called Noviomagus, after the Roman fortress that was built here, it was granted city rights 1,900 years ago under the Roman emperor Trajan. During the early Middle Ages it was controlled by the Franks. Under Charlemagne's rule, it was an important administrative centre and the Emperor built an imposing **palace** on the Valkhof. It was later destroyed by the Normans and only scant remains can be seen (in the park east of the main square). Nevertheless, the city centre is rich in grand medieval buildings, relics of the city's former wealth and power. Despite extensive shelling during the war the **Grote Markt** is well preserved.

Built on seven hills overlooking the River Waal, Nijmegen is the most important city of the Catholic south and many religious institutions are situated here, including the main Catholic University, with a student faculty of 15,000.

The **Museum Het Valkhof** (Kefkensbos 59, open Tues–Fri 10am–5pm; Sat–Sun noon–5pm; entrance fee) is largely a celebration of the city's Roman past. An extensive range of coins, glassware, jewellery and ceramics unearthed by local archaeologists, are on display here. But the museum, which opened in 1999, is not confined to the Roman collection. There are also art galleries dedicated to pop art and modern expressionism, and exhibitions of less contemporary art including etchings, sculptures and silverware.

TIP

The Apenheul monkey reserve in Appeldoorn is open from April to October. Roam among the many different monkey species and watch – from a distance – the gorillas at play in their wooded enclosure.

BELOW: café at Nijmegen's waag (public weights).

A Royal family home

Apeldoorn ❾ is known as the "Penpushers Paradise" because of its large population of civil servants; they arrived in the 1960s when many government offices were relocated from Amsterdam and The Hague to Apeldoorn.

Map on page 268

The town itself is nothing to write home about, but just outside is one of the loveliest Dutch palaces, **Paleis Het Loo** (open Tues–Sun 10am–5pm; entrance fee). This beautiful 17th-century palace was first occupied by William III, Stadholder of the Netherlands and King of England and Scotland, who built Het Loo between 1685 and 1692 as a country seat. In the 18th century William III's successors, the Stadholders William IV and V, used it frequently. In the 19th century Kings William I, II and III all lived here. For the Dutch, Het Loo is especially associated with Queen Wilhelmina, who retired to this country residence after her abdication in 1948 and lived here until her death in 1962.

Now the palace is a museum which traces the history of the House of Orange-Nassau and its ties with the Netherlands, which have existed since 1403. The palace itself is the result of magnificent restoration work which entailed peeling off the white plaster façade to reveal the original brickwork, hidden since the 19th century when Louis Napoleon, installed by his brother Napoleon I as King of Holland in 1806, took over Het Loo and "renovated" it. Mercifully his idea of what constituted good taste proved reversible.

Detail at the country-side Het Loo Palace near Apeldoorn.

The **gardens**, too, have been restored to their former 17th-century glory, making them the best surviving example of the horticultural trends of William and Mary's reign. The **Royal Stables**, built between 1906 and 1910, now house a collection of carriages, coaches, sledges and vintage cars which were used by members of the royal household. ❑

BELOW: Queen Wilhelmina's study at Het Loo Palace.

GREEN FINGERS, HEALING HERBS

The Dutch, fond as always of gardening, go to the **Informatietuinen** in Appeltern to get inspiration. It is by far the largest model garden complex in the Netherlands, with more than 100 different types of garden represented. Ranging from simple patios and plant boxes to intricately manicured lawns, tea gardens and gazebos, all conceivable plants and materials available to amateur and professional gardeners alike are on display here.

The visitors' centre has an extensive library and a display of rare species. After you've feasted your eyes on all this, you can relax in the beautiful winter gardens or enjoy some refreshments in the garden café (Waalstraat 2a; open Mar–Dec; tel: 0487-541732).

The **Vogeltuinen** gardens contain the largest collection of medicinal and healing plants and herbs in The Netherlands. Visitors are greeted with a cup of coffee before being taken on an informative tour around the gardens which ends at the visitors' centre, where the plant-based healing techniques of Alfred Vogel are explained in gushing detail.

Guided tours are available from May to September. (A. Vogelbezoekerscentrum, Industriestraat 15, Elburg, tel: 0525-687373).

Smoke-free zone

Genemuiden **⑫**, awarded town status in 1245, is one of the few towns in the world with a street where smoking is illegal, but with good reason. The small street is called the **Achterweg** and smoking is forbidden because of the fire risk to the old wooden buildings with their hay storage areas. The prohibition, and one of the "No Smoking" signs, dates from 1899.

Fire is not the only elemental threat to Genemuiden. Like so many places in the Netherlands, the village is fighting a ceaseless battle against water levels. To appreciate the way they tackle the challenge here, visit the steam powered pumping station **Stoomgemaal Mastenbroek** (Kamperzeedijk 5; open first Sat in June, first and third Sat in Jul and Aug and first Sat in Oct 10am–4pm; visits outside these times can be arranged by appointment, tel: 038-4774229).

Calvinist tradition

Travelling south towards Zwolle, just off the motorway, is the village of **Staphorst ⑬** notable for its Reformed church and staunchly religious culture which, to the modern observer, may seem oppressive.

Many of the inhabitants wear traditional village costume, which is relentlessly black for men, but with a little intricately coloured relief for women and children. On Sundays, they sit silently behind their lace curtains reading the Bible or glaring at passing tourists, venturing out of doors only to visit the church. The bright green and blue painted farmhouses add a touch of colour to the place, but don't take a camera. Photography is frowned upon because the conservative Staphorsters see the camera as a dreaded symbol of modernity.

The people of Kampen are the butt of many a Dutch joke, but they don't take themselves too seriously either. In August, the ritual raising of a stuffed cow to the top of the Nieuwe Toren is a tongue-in-cheek symbol of their supposed stupidity – and a big tourist attraction.

BELOW: enjoying the scenery at Weerribben.

Towers and spires

Lying on the flood plain of the IJssel, the small town of **Kampen**  has the Netherlands' finest series of gables and façades and a plethora of towers and gateways, making it a lovely place for a leisurely stroll. It reached its peak as an important trading town in the 16th century, when the most beautiful of the buildings were constructed.

The **Kroonmarkt** is dominated by the graceful 15th-century Gothic **Church of St Nicholas**, and a 14th-century **town hall** (open Mon–Thurs 11am–noon 2–4pm; May–Sept: also Sat 2–5pm; entrance fee). This building was partly devastated in 1543 but was rebuilt in the same decade. The most interesting part of the old wing is the medieval "Magistrate's Hall", notable for its barrel-vaulted roof and splendid carved stone chimneypiece.

Not far from the town hall, is the **Stedelijk Museum** (Oudestraat 158; open Tues–Sat 11am–12.30pm and 1.30–5pm; free); a 15th-century town house with a collection of local curiosities.

Provincial capital

Zwolle , the economic and cultural centre of West-Overijssel, and capital of Overijssel, is an ancient town of great architectural beauty. Throughout the 15th century it prospered as one of the most important members of the Hanseatic League, an association of medieval towns formed to protect and advance their commercial interests. Most of the inner city's old buildings have been well restored and there are many beautiful old gateways, some dating from the 15th century. Its bastions and star-shaped moat date from the 17th-century. The city also has its supply of pretty canals, and a pleasant way of seeing it is by water-pedal boat.

Map on page 268

BELOW: Kampen's town hall.

The **Grote Markt** is dominated by the austere Church of St Michael. Next to it stands the **Hoofdwacht**, a beautiful 17th-century gabled building which once overlooked the site of public executions.

To appreciate the history, and understand the finer points of the town's evolution a visit to the **Stedelijk Museum Zwolle** (Melkmarkt 41; open Tues–Sat 10am–5pm, Sun 1pm–5pm) is a must. There are permanent and temporary exhibitions dedicated to the cultural and social history not only of Zwolle, but the entire province. The museum is situated in an 18th-century mansion, and its permanent exhibition includes several period rooms, a unique 18th-century kitchen, collections of archaeological finds, paintings, silverware, porcelain and textiles. There are also displays encompassing the economic, religious and municipal history and life of Zwolle. The entrance is located in the new wing, which focuses on cultural history and contemporary art.

One of Zwolle's greatest architectural gems is the **Sassenpoort** (Sassenstraat 53; open Wed–Fri 2pm–5pm, Sat, Sun and public holidays noon–5pm), an impressive medieval gatehouse dating back to 1409. It is now used as a visitors, information centre, dedicated to the history of the town with architectural models and various old photographs on display.

Gothic splendour

About 30 km (19 miles) south of Zwolle, in the Salland area of Overijssel, is the delightful old town of **Deventer** ⑯, another riverside town that prospered from the booming Zuiderzee trade. The 15th-century **Lebuinuskerk** (Groote Poot; open Mon–Sat 11am–5pm; free), a grand Gothic building, is the embodiment of Deventer's former wealth and importance and one of the finest

BELOW: crypt at St Lebuinuskerk.
RIGHT: windmill at dawn, Weerribben.

ecclesiastical buildings in the eastern Netherlands. Another rather impressive church is the 12th-century two-towered **Bergkerk** on Kerksteeg, again dedicated to St Nicholas.

A change from the usual display of local artefacts is Deventer's **National Toy and Tin Museum** (Nationaal Speelgoed en Blik Museum; Brink 47; open Tues–Sat 10am–5pm, Sun 1pm–5pm; entrance fee) whose collection of antique toys and games includes an incredible array of tin toys, moving or static (cars, trains, moving figures, tin soldiers). The museum also organises various seasonal exhibitions, and in August it hosts a popular antiquarian book market.

A walk in the woods

In the eastern Overijssel area of Twente, near the German border, you will come across the town of **Delden** ⑰ whose main attraction is **Twickel Castle** – which sounds just like a place in a children's storybook. The castle itself is not open to the public, but the gardens are (on Wednesdays and Saturdays). The castle is surrounded by a magnificent oak forest, the largest in Western Europe, which is great for walking.

Another very attractive town in the area is **Ootmarsum** ⑱. Most of its 18th-century houses have now been restored and there is a magnificent 12th-century church. But prettiest of all is the surrounding countryside, with walks through quiet fields past wonderful 16th-century windmills. Watermills are plentiful here too, and four of these are open to the public. **Watermolen Frans** (Oosteriksweg 26, Mander; open Sun 10am–5pm; June–Aug: Sun & Wed 10am–5pm) houses a permanent exhibition on the history of the mill, which dates from 1725, alongside informative displays about the local flora and fauna. ❏

Map on page 268

House of the Three Herrings in the old town of Deventer.

BELOW: the "boys room", Deventer toy museum.

HILL COUNTRY

If you get the yearning to see some hills, head for the Salland area. At Holten railway station you can pick up a map describing a bicycle route of about 26 km (16 miles). Known as the *heuvelrug* route (hill range route), it takes cyclists over the hill range formed in the last ice-age that now delineates the Salland/Twente border. The scenery, consisting largely of ancient forests and heathlands, is beautiful.

The best place to rent bicycles is from **Jan Stam Fietsverhuur** (Waagweg 7, Holten; tel: 0548-366802/ 361779) where you can also buy the aforementioned map. You'll need to present some form of identification and pay a returnable deposit for each bicycle.

Walkers can take the Holterberg route (maps are available from the Nijverdal railway station). The leisurely 14-km (9-mile) walk begins at the visitors centre (Sallandse Heuvelrug), which is run by forest rangers. Here you can buy a special ticket which allows you to continue your walk through a protected nature reserve. This is one of the few areas in The Netherlands where you can spot the black grouse in its natural habitat. There are a few steep hills, but none are too strenuous and all footpaths are in excellent condition. The walk ends at Holten railway station.

Map on page 284

Amsterdam

FLEVOLAND

*The Netherlands' newest province has few historic centres,
but it does offer excellent watersports facilities,
miles of sandy beaches and fresh green countryside*

Much of this, the flattest province in the Netherlands, is made up of recently reclaimed land ringed by a channel of water, and its modern towns are built on what was formerly the bottom of the Zuiderzee (*see page 291*). Reclamation of Flevoland began after World War II, but the work wasn't finally completed until 1986 when the newly created polders – Oostelijk Flevoland and Zuidelijk Flevoland – were officially declared the 12th province of the Netherlands.

Ships and planes

Lelystad ❶ is the capital of the new province, named after the engineer who pioneered the Zuiderzee reclamation scheme. The first inhabitants arrived, mainly from Amsterdam, in 1967, and since then the town has grown into an attractive place with many parks and nearby nature areas. Apart from some interesting housing developments, the main points of interest in the town itself are its museums. The **Nieuw Land Poldermuseum** (Oostvaardersdijk 1–13; open Mon–Fri 10am–5pm, Sat & Sun, 11.30am–5pm; entrance fee), occupying an eye-catching building, has a permanent exhibition centred on land reclamation which transports you through 15 different themes, ranging from the old Zuiderzee culture to current coastal defences. One of its most prized exhibits is the oldest skeleton found in the Netherlands. The museum is very child-friendly and also supplies audio guides in English.

BELOW: lighthouse at Marken.

The nearby **Batavia-Werf** (Batavia Wharf; Oostvaardersdijk 1-9; open July–Sept: 10am–9pm; Oct–June: 10am–5pm) is a popular attraction, and for good reason. The traditional shipbuilding yard initially gained its fame for its authentic working replica of the Dutch East Indies Company merchant ship, the *Batavia* which visitors are allowed to explore freely (due to return to her berth on 15 April 2001). The wharf is currently concentrating its efforts on building a replica of Admiral de Ruyter's legendary ship, *De Zeven Provincien* (*The Seven Provinces*), a 17th-century man-o-war constructed with traditional materials and crafts of the period, which is due for completion in 2005. De Batavia-Werf is a working museum, not only in shipbuilding but also in conservation. In a new wing, they are busy preserving the wreck of a 16th-century ship, under the supervision of the Dutch Institute of Shipping and Underwater Archaeology.

The Dutch have an aviation history of which they are justly proud and for aircraft enthusiasts, a visit to the **Vliegend Museum Lelystad** (Flying Museum in Lelystad; Maraboeweg 12; open Sat & Sun 11am–5pm), an extensive collection of modern and vintage aircraft, is a real treat.

Modern architecture

Almere was the province's fastest-growing new town, but although the ambitious town planners created a pleasing design, with modern sculpture an integral part of the town's layout, it is not the success people had hoped for. Unless you are interested in "progressive and radical" architecture – **De Fantasie**, completed in 1983, is a complex of unusually shaped family houses; **Bouw Rai** is another modern housing area with 225 homes designed by 15 different architects (for information tel: 036-538 6842) – there's nothing much to recommend it.

The reclamation of land threw up some interesting finds. As the sea was drained away sections of British RAF war planes, some with human remains still inside, and wrecks of 17th-century Dutch ships were revealed.

Nature trails

Near Almere, the Oostvaardersplassen region, with its 6,000 hectares (15,000 acres) of wetlands – small lakes, reed marshland and woods – is one of Europe's more important nature reserves. Half-wild horses and cattle have been imported to this area and there is an excellent protected natural bird sanctuary. There are even colonies of cormorants.

The town of **Dronten ❷**, 7 km (4 miles) east of Lelystad, is an excellent base for bicycle trips and walks in the surrounding nature areas and is ideal for camping holidays, too. Maps of walking and cycling routes are available from the local VVV (De Rede 149, tel: 0321-31 86 87). The *stadsbosbeheer gidsen* (state forest ranger guides) are particularly informative.

Protestant tradition

Urk ❸, formerly a small island, is an especially interesting place to visit. The 1,000-year-old fishing village is a very pretty, traditional place. The local dialect is still spoken and many of the older inhabitants still wear the local costume, examples of which are on display in the **Museum Het Oude Raadhuis** (Wijk 2; open Apr–Oct Mon–Sat 11am–5pm; entrance fee). The community is intensely Protestant, which means that everything stops on Sundays. Nowadays, attitudes are much more relaxed, but once upon a time anyone who dared sail into Urk harbour on a Sunday would have had their boat pelted with stones. Urk remains a hard-working fishing village, but has also become a yachting centre and is an ideal centre for a waterways holiday.

BELOW:
Monnickendam.

Fishing lakes

The chain of lakes which separate the "old land" from the newly created polders are shallow and bordered by wide, reeded areas – excellent conditions for fish. The province has nine lakes, and Flevoland fish are famous for their strength, making them a challenge to land for serious anglers, who take along special equipment according to the type of fish they hope to catch.

The Dutch take their fishing very seriously, and the fish are well looked after (until they reach the oven), the waters are clean and the lakes well stocked. Town lakes, in particular, are excellent for their sport: the **Gooimeer** is reached by crossing the Hollandse Brug and driving along the Gooimeerdijk towards Almere. The **Eemmeer** is popular with eel fishermen who catch large specimens near the sluices that control the water level in the lake. ❑

whom Lelystad new town is named), but it was a long time before work actually got underway. After endless debate, and the devastating floods of 1916 which spurred some action, the 32-km (20-mile) long *Afsluitdijk* ❹ was finally completed in 1932 and the Zuiderzee became the IJsselmeer. The roadway built on top of the dam to connect North Holland to Friesland is now a major artery in the country's road network.

Work then began on creating three new polders in the southern part of the lake. The Noordoostpolder was won back from the sea between 1937 and 1942, Oostelijk Flevoland between 1950 and 1957, and Zuidelijk Flevoland between 1959 and 1968.

While many towns prospered from land reclamation, the creation of the Afsluitdijk and the surrounding polders had enormous repercussions for the many fishing towns around the IJsselmeer. Access to the sea was now blocked and the traditional fishing communities that once thrived on the shores of the Zuiderzee eventually disappeared. A proposed fourth polder, the Markerwaard, was abandoned after strong objections from Hoorn and other affected towns, which did not want to end up, like Purmerend, landlocked. The dyke that would have enclosed the Markerwaard now carries a road linking Enkhuizen and Lelystad.

History on the waterfront

The Zuiderzee's fascinating history is vividly presented at the **Zuiderzee Museum** in Enkhuizen (Wierdijk 18; open Apr–Oct daily 10am–5pm; entrance fee). Though enthusiasts mooted the idea of a Zuiderzee museum back in the 1930s, the **Binnenmuseum** (indoor museum) didn't open until 1950; another 33 years were to elapse before the **Buitenmuseum** (open-air museum) joined it.

BELOW: yacht masts bob gently in the picturesque Hoorn harbour.

The Binnenmuseum is housed in a Dutch Renaissance, waterfront complex from 1625, a local merchant's combined home and warehouse. When the Enkhuizen Chamber of the United Dutch East Indies Company later acquired it, it became known as the **Peperhuis** because of the company's lucrative trade in Indonesian pepper.

Map on page 284

A large hall houses an extensive collection of traditional Zuiderzee fishing boats and pleasure craft. It is interesting to see how different styles of boat building developed in fishing towns only a short distance apart. Local furniture also varied in style from one town to the next. But the greatest diversity seems to be in the costume, as illustrated in the series of furnished rooms depicting different local styles. Terschelling Island, industrial Zaanstad, West-Friesland, Hindeloopen (famous for hand-painted furniture), Marken, Urk, Spakenburg and Volendam, are all represented.

Enkhuizen open-air museum

The only way to reach the nearby open air museum, is by boat (the return trip is included in the entrance ticket), either from the pier near the railway station or from a car park at the beginning of the dyke road to Lelystad. The inconvenience of this arrangement is outweighed by the thrill of arriving by boat, though the landing-craft boats built for the museum look out of place alongside traditional, brown-sailed boats in Enkhuizen harbour.

Old Dutch traditions are revived at the Enkhuizen museum.

The museum, a reconstruction of old fishing communities, is made up of around 130 buildings rescued from towns around the Zuiderzee. Some of the houses were shipped intact across the IJsselmeer, and one three-storey wooden cheese warehouse was transported from Landsmeer along Noord-Holland's inland waterways on two barges. The layout of the museum is based on *buurtjes* (quarters) modelled on different towns. The harbour, modelled on Marken's, has several old fishing boats moored at the quayside. There is even a small, reconstructed corner of Amsterdam hidden behind the museum shop.

BELOW: time out for a relaxing pipe.

Labels attached to houses provide interesting snippets of information about their former occupants. Large families, such as the couple with nine children who lived in the house from Venhuizen (VH1), often inhabited the tiniest houses. Many of the houses are neatly furnished in period style, with tea trays set out in front rooms as if the occupants might return at any moment. A grocery shop in the Harderwijk quarter sells delicious smoked sausage and boiled sweets, there's a post office from Den Oever and a baker's shop on the main canal sells traditional cakes. Demonstrations of local trades are given in some buildings, such as the painter's shop and the steam laundry.

The museum has three restaurants: one occupies the Landsmeer cheese warehouse, another is decorated with the tiled interior from a restaurant in Zandvoort, but the most attractive is the dyke house restaurant, with a gleaming tiled interior from Hindeloopen, that overlooks the harbour.

Ideally, you need a whole day to visit both parts of the museum, and another day to visit the town of Enkhuizen itself.

TIP

A great little trip,
especially if you're
travelling with kids, is
the hour-long steam
train journey from
Hoorn to Medemblik.
The service runs from
May to October. For
up-to-date information
tel: 0229-214 862.

A modest, well-preserved town (population 16,000) **Enkhuizen ❺** was Holland's foremost herring port during the 17th century, hence the three herring motif on its coat of arms. The most attractive spots are around the harbours, in particular at a secluded promontory overlooking the backs of the houses on Bocht. The fishing industry is not quite dead here, and a small fish auction is still held on **Buitenhaven**.

Many of Enkhuizen's most striking buildings, such as the **Munt** (Mint) of 1611 at Westerstraat 22, and the **Weeshuis** (Orphanage), at Westerstraat 111, built five years later, are designed in jaunty Dutch Mannerist style. North of Westerstraat is a peaceful, almost rural area, often overlooked, known as the **Boerenhoek** (Farmers' Quarter), where you still come across large farmhouses built alongside urban canals.

Steam train destination

A quiet old port 21 km (13 miles) northwest of Enkhuizen, **Medemblik ❻** is one of the oldest towns in the Netherlands. Its harbour is a popular mooring spot for visiting yachts, but its main attraction for tourists is **Kasteel Radboud**, (Oudevaartsgat 8; open May–Sept: Mon–Sat 10am–5pm, Sun 2–5pm; Oct–Apr: Sun only 2–5pm; entrance fee) a heavily restored 13th-century castle overlooking the harbour, named after a Frisian king defeated by the Franks in AD 689.

The summer steam train pulls in at the old railway station (where you'll also find the vvv). The **Stoommachine Museum** (Oosterdijk 4; open Apr–June and Sept–Nov: Wed–Sat 10am–5pm, Sun noon–5pm; July–Sept: Mon–Sat 10am–5pm, Sun noon–5pm; entrance fee) has an interesting collection of well-preserved old steam engines.

BELOW:
Marken harbour.

Hoorn ❼, 19 km (12 miles) to the south, was one of the Dutch Republic's great seafaring towns. Among many famous mariners born here were Abel Tasman, the first European to reach Tasmania, and Jan Pietersz Coen, founder of the Dutch Indonesian trading post Batavia (now Jakarta). Another Hoorn native, Willem Schouten, named Cape Horn after his home town. Today, the town is effectively a suburb of Amsterdam, but many mementoes of its maritime history have survived. The harbour quarter to the south of **Grote Oost** is particularly interesting to explore, with the best view from south of Binnenhaven towards a row of step-gabled merchants' houses on Veermanskade. Three curious, 17th-century houses on Slapershaven, named the **Bossuhuizen** after a Spanish admiral, are decorated with colourful friezes depicting a sea battle off Hoorn in 1573.

A magnificent Dutch Mannerist building overlooks the **Rode Steen** (main square, literally "red stone"). Built in 1632 for the College of the States of West-Friesland (Alkmaar, Edam, Enkhuizen, Hoorn, Medemblik, Monnickendam and Purmerend), it houses the **Westfries Museum** (open Apr–Sept: Mon–Fri 11am–5pm, Sat 2–5pm, Sun noon–5pm; Oct–Mar: Mon–Fri 11am–5pm, Sat–Sun 2–5pm; entrance fee) of local history, filled with the confidence of the Dutch Golden Age, and containing furniture, guild group portraits, ship models and period rooms. Opposite, the **Waag** is a handsome, Dutch Classical weigh house from 1609. Streets north of Rode Steen contain other relics of Hoorn's glorious past. These include the Dutch Renaissance **Statenpoort** from 1613 at Nieuwstraat 23, former government representatives' lodgings. In Muntstraat opposite, is the Hoorn Chamber of the Dutch East Indies Company, completed in 1682.

Map on page 284

Yachting and windsurfing

Monnickendam ❽, 16 km (10 miles) northeast of Amsterdam, is an attractive little port with picturesque canals. The harbour's vast collection of pleasure boats of every size and type, from dinghies to ocean-going luxury cruisers, as well as fishing boats and windsurfing facilities, is surprising for such a small place. An enticing smell of smoked eel wafts through narrow lanes by the harbour, where there are several old smokehouses.

The best place for fish is café-restaurant **Nieuw Stuttenburgh**, on the harbour. Its interior is filled with curiosities, including old mechanical musical instruments that are sometimes played to amuse customers. From the harbour, boats ply in the summer months across the Gouwzee to **Marken ❾**. Once an isolated and somewhat eccentric fishing community, Marken was "discovered" by 19th-century French tourists. Now linked to the mainland by a causeway, the island has lost something of its romantic appeal. But the community has held on staunchly to its identity, and Marken's traditional black and green wooden houses on stilts still form an attractive scene.

Havenbuurt (harbour quarter), a village, whose painted houses cluster around the tiny harbour, and **Kerkbuurt** (church quarter) get pretty crowded, but there are quiet corners to explore in the eastern part. The remainder of the island is farmland and you can reach the white lighthouse at its end by taking a brisk walk along the old sea dyke where it's possible to watch old-style IJsselmeer sailing ships, *boters* and *skûtsjes*, ply the waters offshore. The **De Taanderij** café overlooking the harbour is a convivial place for lunch or coffee.

BELOW: life moves at a gentle pace in North Holland.

Artists' haven

A boat service links Marken with the former fishing town of **Volendam ❿**, a few kilometres north of Monnickendam, and unusual in these parts because of its predominantly Catholic population. The populist face of Dutch tourism is on display here. Local people wear traditional costume and you can have your picture taken wearing clogs and short jackets, or long flowery aprons and milkmaid hats. Harbourside fish stalls do brisk business, especially with smoked IJsselmeer *paling* (eel).

The harbour front has unfortunately been ruined by tourist shops, though a few narrow canals behind the dyke are still worth exploring. During the 19th century, Romantic painters flocked here to paint the fisherfolk in traditional costume. The Spaander Hotel where they stayed, still stands; on its café walls are paintings that the owner accepted as payment.

In a pastoral setting a few kilometres from Volendam, **Broek-in-Waterland** is a cute-looking hamlet with distinctively painted farmhouses. ❑

WILDLIFE AND NATURE RESERVES

The Dutch have acted with characteristic resolve and attention to detail to preserve wild places in their small and densely populated country

With 16 million inhabitants living in 42,000 sq km, the Netherlands has one of the world's highest population densities. Though the entire country could fit inside America's Yellowstone National Park it has its share of protected places: national parks and nature reserves managed by the *Staatsbosbeheer* (State Forestry Service) and the *Vereniging tot Behoud van Natuurmonumenten* (Federation for Nature Conservancy). These bodies protect forests, heathland, dunes, marshes, lakes, rivers, an island, and the habitats of rare and endangered wildlife and plants. Despite their modest size, the parks and reserves are eclectic and varied. As with many Dutch landscapes the Biesbosch National Park, near Rotterdam, bears the imprint of flooding. This "forest of reeds" was once isolated and almost inaccessible, but now its flotilla of marshy islands have been partially stitched together and the flooded area reduced.

Equally memorable are the inland sand dunes of the Loonse en Drunense Duinen near 's-Hertogenbosch (Den Bosch). It seems as if desertification has struck the watery polders (reclaimed land), but only sand-grasses and scrubby trees maintained by the Nature Conservancy prevents this granular landscape from blowing away on the wind. In Noord Brabant and Limburg, the peat moors of Groote Peel National Park is another of those places, formerly wild and inhospitable, that must now be protected if its original character is to survive. Lonely trails through Groote Peel's boggy terrain are now being opened to the public.

▷ **WILD THINGS**
Deer, foxes and wild boar are among the few large mammals to survive in the Netherlands. Beaver are also being re-introduced.

▷ **TREE LINES**
Pine and silver birch trees pack the Veluwezoom National Park, northeast of Arnhem, which you can tour on an extensive network of walking and cycling paths.

△ **OUT AND ABOUT**
Strolling through the Groote Peel National Park, a zone of peat bogs, swampy moorland and lakes near Eindhoven, on the border of Limburg and Noord Brabant provinces.

△ **ON YOUR BIKE**
Free bicycles provide perfect motivation for exploring the heathland, forests and fens of Hoge Veluwe National Park north of Arnhem.

▷ **SHORE THING**
Tiny Schiermonikoog island in the Wadden Sea earned national park status for its tranquility and sea dunes lined with woods.

ON A WING AND A PRAYER

The absence of any large mammals in the Netherlands makes birdwatching, for species like the wood owl pictured above, a major draw. Taking a boat trip into the Biesbosch National Park is to drift into a far different world from the open polder land that surrounds it. The ecologically rich wetlands environment south of Rotterdam is a paradise for birds. Kingfishers dart along narrow channels and coots and hawks flutter overhead. Heron, storks, geese, ducks and cormorants are just some of the other avian species that make their homes in the park.

Although there is plenty of woodland habitat, however, the country's vast amounts of freshwater resources – rivers, lakes, canals – long coastline and wetlands, are especially attractive to water birds. Heron are a frequent sight as are oyster catchers, spoonbills and ducks. The white stork is rare and protected. One of the best areas for observing seabirds is the Wadden Islands.

▷ **HEATH COATED**
Heathland and peat bogs cover a large extent of protected landscapes in the Netherlands, as here at the Dwingelderveld National Park south of Assen in Drenthe.

▽ **DROWNED LAND**
Going by boat is the best way to get to grips with the Biesbosch National Park, a swampy area that mostly went underwater during the St Elizabeth Day flood in 1421.

▷ **BIRD OF PASSAGE**
Nature reserves and national parks provide badly needed protection for many bird species, such as this kingfisher. Its habitats are endangered by urban sprawl and the intensive agriculture now practised on the polder lands.

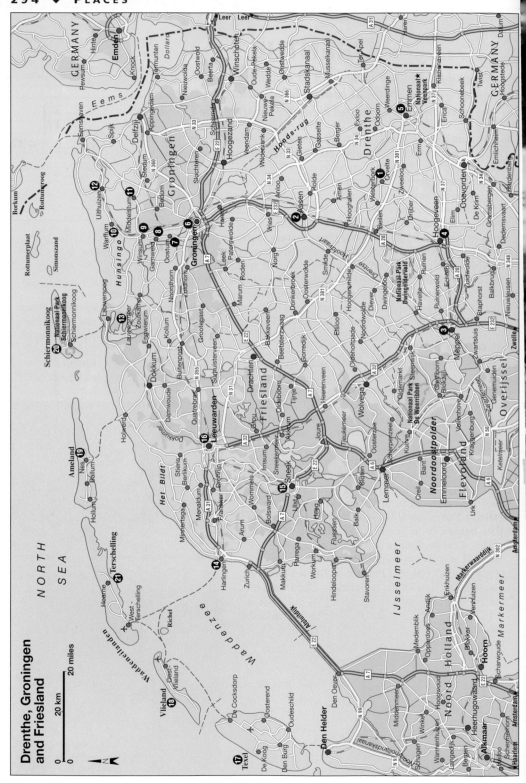

Drenthe, Groningen
and Friesland

between various European conquerors. The Romans came first, and the province still has traces of their roadways; then came the Frankish kings and German emperors. Later, when all the southern and northern provinces were confederated in the Republic of Holland, Drenthe had no separate representation; it was seen as being a backwater not worth bothering about.

Local people did not mind much and continued to enjoy the serenity of their cosy rural life. When the area was officially declared a province in 1815 life continued exactly as before. Even today Drenthe has that peaceful forgotten-world quality that is increasingly difficult to find in more developed northern European countries. Drenthe is the plce the Dutch now visit to relax and escape the crowds.

Village life

Many of the rural villages of the province still have their *brinken*, or village green, surrounded by beautiful traditional Dutch cottages, old-fashioned gardens and pristine cobbled streets echoing to the clatter of clogs. Though clearly not Scandinavian, there is something about the villages of Drenthe which conjures up images from Hans Christian Andersen. It's as if there could be inch worms measuring the marigolds, gingerbread houses in the woods and fairies at the bottom of every garden.

Not content with its collection of naturally preserved villages, Drenthe also has a "show" village called **Orvelte** ❶ (open Apr–Oct; Mon–Fri 10am–6pm; Sat and Sun 1pm–5pm; tel: 0591-38242), dubbed a "living monument of historically interesting rural architecture." Though this sounds pretty gruesome, it is quite unlike those so-called "native" villages in different parts of the world where the "natives" arrive in the morning, park their cars, and pretend to be honest-to-goodness villagers during the day while the cameras click. People born in Orvelte go to school, marry and die there. Maybe if Van Gogh had stayed there, the Netherlands would have had to wait a little bit longer than 1990 to commemorate the 100th anniversary of his death.

First stop in Orvelte should be the VVV (Dorpstraat 1a; tel: 0593-322335), where staff will help you plan a route around the vast array of cottage industries. Not all buildings have free entrance. Workshops specialise in flint-knapping, clog and candle making, a tin foundry and, of course, a village pub.

Similar in concept are two other museums close by. The **Nationaal Veenpark** (open Good Friday–Oct; 10am–5pm; Jul–Aug 10am–6pm; entrance fee; tel: 0591-324444), near the town of Barger Compascuum to the east of Emmen, is a museum-village illustrating life in a mid-19th-century peat colony. Exhibitions explain the process of extracting peat, primarily for use as fuel, but also for the construction of turf-walled cottages. Recent additions include a theme park for children, based upon the characters in the books by Herman Veen. You can then take a trip on a peat barge to the nearby village.

The **Open Air Museum** (De Zeven Marken; open Apr–Oct; Mon–Sun 10am–6pm; tel: 0591-382421) at nearby Schoonoord brings the story of life in Drenthe

TIP

If you're driving to Orvelte, Drenthe's "show village", bear in mind that traffic access is only for residents, but there are car parks at the edge of the village.

BELOW: Emmen zoological garden.

Assen's museum houses a collection of fine artefacts.

BELOW: at home: provincial style.

forward by some 50 years, recalling, through its buildings and exhibitions, life at the turn of the 19th century. It also has a children's farm.

Exploring the towns

Drenthe has four main towns. The best known among speed fans would be Drenthe's capital city, **Assen ❷**, where the famous TT Grand Prix Motorbike Race is held annually on the last Saturday in June. But the town also has its antiquities; the most beautiful and historically interesting is the 13th-century convent of the Cistercian order of Maria in Campis. The convent was originally built on bogland in 1245 in an area called Coevorden near Assen. However, the nuns found the area too damp and the building was moved lock, stock, barrel and bricks to the town. After the Reformation, in 1598, the convent was secularised and taken over by the district council.

Today, in the grounds of the beautiful 13th-century abbey church, you will find the **Drents Museum**, which has a fine collection of Germanic, Roman and medieval artefacts, as well as several bodies of prehistoric bog people discovered well-preserved in their peat graves.

Meppel ❸ is one of the oldest towns in Drenthe with a 15th-century church and some fine 15th-century houses. Also worth a visit is the circa-1840 Theekoepel (tea dome) in Wilhelmina Park. In neighbouring Nijeven is the *Boerkerk* or farmer's church, built in the style of a 15th-century farmhouse. This attractive town of 23,000 inhabitants is an important hub for land and water transport and has some of the area's best watersports facilities.

Hoogeveen ❹ used to be a busy inland harbour in the days when South Drenthe was a land of peat colonies. Today it is an attractive place to shop. On

Sunday mornings a drummer parades through the streets calling people to church, a custom dating back 300 years to the time when the inland waterway was the most important source of income for the town. The population wanted things to stay that way and so they followed the drummer to church every Sunday to enlist heavenly aid. Visit the water gardens, accessible by train (open Mon–Sat; tel: 0528-264636).

Emmen ❺ is the largest town in Drenthe. It has a lively market place where you can buy comfortable wooden clogs for walking around the nearby Noorder Dierenpark, a small zoo where animals roam freely in an open natural landscape. In nearby Erica, Industrieel Smalspoor Museum (open mid-May–mid-September; entrance fee; tel: 0599-235816), is an industrial narrow-gauge railway museum housing a collection of working and static 1930s diesel locomotives. Admission includes a round trip in one of these curious vehicles, taking in a peat moor and the only remaining turf-shredding factory of its kind in The Netherlands.

Kamp Westerbork

In the middle of Drenthe lies the infamous and haunting Kamp Westerbork (open Mon–Fri 10am-5pm; weekends 1am–5pm; closed Jan), a former World War II transit camp for unfortunate victims who were headed for concentration camps. The story of their every-day life in Kamp Westerbork is told in the remembrance centre. A partially furnished barrack room, a last-minute scribbled greeting thrown out of the train, a large model of the camp and a drawing of children playing combine to form a mental image of Westerbork's past. Personal stories in the exhibition and 1944 film footage help to make this period accessible to children. ❑

Map on page 294

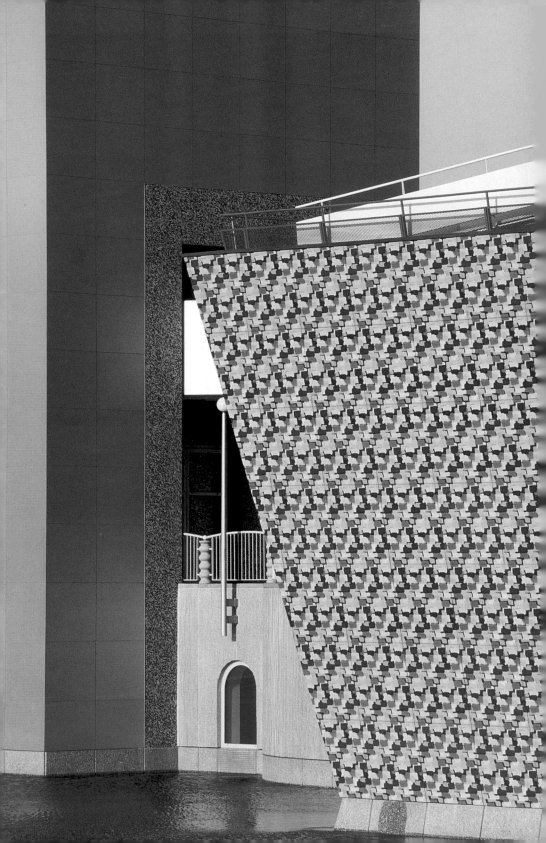

GRONINGEN

This is where many find the image of The Netherlands they've been looking for – a flat, green landscape dotted with small villages, windmills and friendly locals in wooden shoes

Map on page 294

Amsterdam

G roningen, like its neighbour Friesland, is terp country. These mounds – usually built on top of what was once a kind of communal rubbish heap – were used by the earliest inhabitants, the so-called "marsh Dutch", to raise their buildings above the floodplain.

Boating, biking or driving through the northern countryside, typically as flat as a billiard table and just as green, there are still many remaining terps that serve to elevate medieval churches and sometimes even whole villages. Eventually the northerners turned to dykes, in preference to mounds, building row after row of some of the biggest in the world as they painstakingly reclaimed the land from the sea – a process that is still going on and which can be witnessed today, especially in northern Groningen.

Amsterdam of the North

Groningen ❻ is the name of the capital as well as of the province. The city (population 170,000) is a busy commercial centre that regards itself as the Amsterdam of the North. Not much remains of the old city, which was pretty well destroyed during the Allied liberation in 1945. Groningen's attraction lies more in its atmosephere than in its appearance. One of the dominant aspects of Groningen is its youthful population and vibrant intellectual scene. The university is prestigious and an estimated 20,000 students live in the city, along with an equal number of other young people below the age of 30. It also attracts many artists.

Aside from the university, the main industry is producing sugar from beet. The locals, with the typical northern Dutch wryness of humour, like to say Groningen's sugar production makes it "the sweetest town in Europe" – unless the wind from the factory is blowing the wrong way.

Groningen gets few foreign tourists, other than passing Scandinavians and Germans. Locals ruefully admit that many of those tourists are en route to Amsterdam, often to buy drugs, and the drugs trade has now come to Groningen itself – another reason the city is called the Amsterdam of the North. But even for those not interested in drugs, Groningen's history and its lively pub scene are worth a visit.

The city centre, nearly 2km (1 mile) across, is encircled by a canal with further bisecting canals. One of the main landmarks is the **Martinikerk** (open June–Sept Tues–Sat noon–4pm; entrance fee), the imposing Gothic church that dominates the **Grote Markt**, one of the city's two main squares. The 95-metre (315-ft) spire, familiarly known as "The Old Grey Man", was destroyed and rebuilt several times. The interior is decorated with some beautiful 16th-

LEFT: the Groninger museum.
BELOW: local and imported cigars.

Rural scenes abound in the North Holland provinces.

BELOW: Groningen Maritime Museum.

century wall paintings. There are two series of frescoes: one portrays the story of Christmas, the other depicts the Easter story.

Like most Dutch towns, Groningen was made for strolling, and there are plenty of interesting sights in almost every corner of the city. This was an important trade centre and a rich town in the Golden Age, hence the various museums dedicated to shipping and the history of tobacco. The **Groninger Museum** (Museumeiland l; open Tues–Sat 10am–5pm, Sun 1–5pm; entrance fee), housed in splendid contemporary pavilions opposite the train station, boasts one of Europe's finest collections of oriental ceramics, as well as a fine display of local paintings, including several works by Jan Wiegers and other members of the well-developed Groningen School of Expressionism. Interesting temporary exhibitions are mounted in the east pavilion throughout the year.

More contemporary art is on show at the **Visual Arts Centre** (Oosterpoort, Trompsingel 27; open Tues–Fri 10am–5pm, Sat & Sun 1–5pm; entrance fee).

Near the Groninger Museum, on the northwestern edge of the circle, a couple of small streets make up Groningen's red light district with the same type of carnal window displays as in the much larger red light district of Amsterdam. Also keep an eye out for the many surviving *gasthuizen* and *hofjes*, almshouses built around pretty little courtyards providing accommodation for travellers, the elderly and the poor. You can peer in through the gates, but visitors should get permission before entering the courtyards to look around. Good examples can be found on Munnekeholm, Kerkstraat, Nieuwe Kerkhof and Visserstraat. One of the locals' favourites is the **Pepergasthuis**, on Peperstraat, dating from the 15th century. It has been renovated but still provides low-rent homes for the poor and elderly. Look out for Oude Kijk in 't Jatstraat ("I'm Just Looking into

the Street" Street), named after the evil-eyed statue that has been staring down for centuries from high up on a building wall.

Alongside the "official" events and curricula of the university, Groningen's cultural scene centres on the bars, pubs and "brown" cafés. They are ubiquitous, especially around the central squares and on Peperstraat and Poelestraat. Pubs are generally open most of the day, and seem to serve as much coffee as alcohol. People set themselves up at the big wooden tables with newspapers, books, note pads and sketch books, sip their coffee at leisure and wait for friends to arrive so that the conversation can begin.

A good example is **Café Mulder** (Grote Kromme Elleboog 22). Like many other pubs in this artistic outpost, Café Mulder is decorated with local paintings, and it is not unusual to find the artist relaxing beneath one. In fact, one of the best ways to get into conversation with the locals – and Groningers love to talk – is to ask them about the paintings. Likely as not, they'll have an anecdote about the painter, the subject (some, like the fat blonde lady with the huge breasts, are as well known in Groningen as the artists) and how the painting came to hang where it does.

The whole town has a comfortable, vaguely beatnik feel to it and, while it may not have a great deal to recommend it architecturally, it's certainly a lively place and ideal for those on a budget.

Hiking, biking and boating

The villages north of Groningen can be explored easily by car, but the quiet, flat roads and picturesque canals are a magnet for many Dutch, especially southerners, with the time and energy to spend a few days cycling, hiking or boating.

Map on page 294

Many Dutch village names rival those in rural England for originality: Doodstil means "Dead Quiet." Locals maintain the place is still as quiet – some say as boring – as when it was first named.

BELOW: water and wheels.

Map on page 294

TIP

Campsites around Groningen are plentiful, but many people prefer to knock on a farmer's door and ask for permission to pitch a tent. Sometimes they'll get breakfast into the bargain.

BELOW: traffic jam in Groningen.
RIGHT: pastures green.

Indeed, most of the week-long or fortnight holidays taken by the Dutch involve some combination of all three – whether making their way by bike or canoe between campsites, or travelling on a houseboat or covered pontoon and making daily jaunts out away from the canal into the countryside.

Several attractive villages, including **Oostum** ❼, lie barely 3 km (2 miles) from central Groningen and are easily reached by bicycle, boat (which can be rented in Groningen) or on foot by lunchtime. Nearly every village has a little café that serves passable food in what looks like, and often is, someone's sitting room. An especially popular stop for tea, coffee or a meal is **Café Hummingh**, a quaint little red-brick house in the even quainter village of **Garnwerd** ❽, just 11 km (7 miles) from central Groningen.

If canoeing appeals, **Winsum** ❾, the "canoe village", is an ideal starting point. Canoes can be rented and the locals are eager to give their recommendations on where to go and what to see. **Warffum** ❿, is a mecca for folk dancers, especially around the annual folk dancing festival in June.

In **Middelstum** ⓫, the village elders drink *jenever* (gin) in the local café at 10 am and pick up their daily conversations without even saying hello to each other. Middelstum is also recommended for its restored bakery, where you can taste lovely warm bread straight from the oven.

Feudal grandeur

Groningen has a number of grand old manor houses. The most interesting of these is **Menkamaborg** (open Apr–Sept: daily 10am–noon & 1–5pm, Oct–Mar: Tues–Sun 10am–noon & 1–4pm; closed Jan; entrance fee), in the village of **Uithuizen** ⓬, about 25 km (16 miles) north of the city. This fortified manor house dates back to the 15th century, was rebuilt in the late 17th century and has since been restored and refurbished to the casual, functional elegance of the 18th century.

Six rooms are open to the public, including the ladies' drawing room (walls covered in damask silk), the state apartment (a pipe organ in a fake cabinet), the library (several good paintings and an ornate desk) and – always the most interesting in any restored landmark home – the kitchen, with its big black pots and huge open fireplace, flanked by all manner of antique cooking tools and utensils.

Lakeland

The mud flats on Groningen's northern coast lack the attraction of Friesland's natural sand beaches and cosy coves, but the **Lauwersmeer** ⓭ is worth a visit. This huge freshwater lake about 35 km (22 miles) northwest of Groningen, cut off from the sea by the Lauwersoog dam, is another popular area for boating, fishing, windsurfing, cycling, and bathing from its man-made beaches.

Lauwersoog, the port on the lake, is the place to catch the ferry for the 50-minute journey to Schiermonnikoog (*see page 315*), the wildest and most isolated of the Frisian Islands. Naturalists should not miss the famous environmental centre at **Pieterburen** not far away. ❑

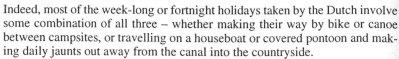

TIP

Although northerners are used to being the butt of many a joke among fellow countrymen, visitors should pay a little respect when it comes to the sensitive issue of Frisian independence.

It is easy to see why the jokes paint the northerners as country bumpkins, as hillbillies without hills. They don't speak as quickly or use the same city slang as southerners. The north has more than its share of windmills that still work, including at least one that is actually used as a mill, to make flour. And while two million pairs of wooden shoes manufactured in the Netherlands each year are sold to tourists, most of the remaining million are sold to people in Friesland (and Groningen) who wear them as everyday shoes, particularly in the wet. These aren't, of course, the big, sharp-pointed clodhoppers sold at the souvenir shops; instead, they are light and strong, made out of poplar, usually painted black, with some leather trim – and they last for years. Visitors seldom notice that the man riding by on a bike or the woman shopping with her children is wearing wooden shoes unless it's pointed out.

Frisian independence

One thing visitors, even other Dutch, are careful not to joke about is the issue of Frisian independence. There is a strong, long-time movement in the province to declare independence and secede from the rest of the Netherlands, and it would be unwise to mock the movement in the presence of its most ardent supporters, most of whom refuse to speak anything except Frisian but nonetheless understand both Dutch and English perfectly.

Most Frisians, of course, realise that secession is a political and economic unreality and have no interest in its actual realisation, but that, perhaps, helps them lend their casual support to the notion of Frisian independence. The VVV has entered into the spirit to the extent of issuing visitors a "Friesland Passport" which serves as a primer on provincial culture in several languages and

BELOW: taking time out in Hindeloopen.

offers discounts for a number of tourist attractions ranging from museums to restaurants to bowling alleys. Perhaps even more than other Dutch, the northerners love sports. Cycling, camping, canoeing, sailing and hiking are all typical weekend pursuits. In winter even the smallest villages have a field especially flooded so that the locals can skate with each other after work. In summer, many communities enjoy that strange form of pole vaulting peculiar to the Dutch – the vaulters plant their pole in the middle of a canal and leap to the other side, with the possibility of a hilarious mid-canal landing.

In the coldest winters, when the canals all freeze solid (it happens, on average, once every five or six years), Friesland has its Elfstedentocht, or "11-cities race", so named because skaters must traverse a 200-km (125-mile) loop of frozen canals between the 11 cities of the province. Twenty thousand people or more, some wearing the traditional wooden skates still popular in the north, may be gathered at the early-morning starting line for this punishing race. But only a fraction of them will finish it hours later, in darkness, sore and tired and sometimes frostbitten. When Crown Prince Willem-Alexander skated under an assumed name in 1985 and managed to finish the race (though well behind the winner), his public popularity soared.

First port of call

The ancient fishing village of **Harlingen** ⑭, on the Waddenzee (variously translated as "mud sea" or "salt flat sea"), is the first stop for many who enter Friesland after driving up from Amsterdam across the *Afsluitdijk*, the 32 km (20-mile) long, 90-metre (100-yard) wide dyke built to enclose the Zuiderzee, now the IJsselmeer. With a population of 16,000, nearly all of central Harlingen

Map on page 294

BELOW: the Elfstedentocht (11-cities race).

TIP

Get dressed in your oldest clothes and wallow in the mud of the Waddenzee, where the Fries have invented the rare sport of mud-flat walking. It is advisable to use a guide as variable mud depths and tides can be dangerous. Contact the vv offices in Friesland.

BELOW: knee-deep in mud sport.

– the part along the docks – is a national conservation area because of the exquisitely gabled 16th-, 17th- and 18th-century homes and buildings, including a number of old East Indies Company warehouses. In the dock area is the obligatory statute of the little Dutch boy who allegedly stuck his finger in the dyke to save the sea wall from collapsing. In the interests of civic pride and tourism, many Dutch seafront communities today claim the legendary boy as their own little hero.

Leading away from the harbour, the main street, **Voorstraat**, has many pleasant shops. It is especially attractive on Saturday market days, when colourful stalls and booths are run by people in local costume. **Harlingen** is still a working seaport, and in strolling along the harbour you can watch a variety of boats coming and going or look over the dockside to the fishing trawlers and small shipping steamers that carry cargoes to Germany and other Dutch ports. Harlingen harbour is also the place to catch ferries that run up to four times a day in season to two of the most popular Wadden Islands, Vlieland and Terschelling.

Stavoren

Having mentioned Harlingen, it would be unfair to leave out Stavoren. This legendary harbour, famous for its story dates back to 500 BC. Stavoren was once the seat of ancient kings, and thanks to its location became a major trading port with shipping and cargoes from France, England and Scandinavia. This easily explains the wealth which the city obviously enjoyed centuries ago, still visible in some of the rich buildings. Alas, Stavoren's merchant days are all but gone, but the harbour, like that in Harlingen, plays host to many clippers and cutters of a bygone era.

The ships that always draw the most attention, however, are the antique sailboats, many of them a century or more old. Many of them were designed specifically for sailing the peculiar waters of the Waddenzee, the shallow, and often wild corner of the North Sea that stretches from Friesland to Germany and Denmark. The Waddenzee is no more than 1 metre (3 ft) deep in many places, and rarely more than 3 metres (10 ft) deep in any one place, even at high tide. Consequently, when the tides go out, the salt flats and mud that gave the sea its name are revealed. The Fries, who seem to be able to make a sport out of almost any activity, subsequently invented *wadlopen*, or "mudwalking".

Map on page 294

Walking on mud

The first organised walk on the seabed was held in 1963. Since then, hundreds of thousands of people – always led by registered guides – have joined walks from the mainland to one of the outlying inhabited Wadden Islands a few miles away, or to one of the larger uninhabited salt flats. Some mudwalkers compare it to mountain climbing, given the amount of exertion required to make your way through the mud.

The walks are particularly popular among birdwatchers because of the many species, some quite rare outside Friesland, that feed on the exposed seabed. Besides the bird life, the Waddenzee serves as something of a nursery for many different types of fish that are spawned in the North Sea and then seek out the slightly warmer waters of the shallow Waddenzee until they mature and head back out to the bigger sea.

Wadlopen trips, usually undertaken only in the summer months, became very popular in the late 1960s and early 1970s, but Friesland officials have since severely restricted the number of walks for two reasons: to reduce the number of drownings among mudwalkers who set off on their own, without guides, and in order to avoid damaging the delicate Waddenzee environment. Because of these restrictions, and the limited number of groups licensed to sponsor *wadlopen* outings, interested visitors should make arrangements in advance. Various groups offer walks according to variable schedules from different seaside towns, so it is best to find the contacts through local vvv offices in Friesland.

The depth of the Waddenzee, or rather the lack of depth, makes navigation tricky, even for the antique sailboats with their remarkably shallow draft. The boats are all but flat-bottomed and, instead of keels, they have large wooden "swords" amidships to both port and starboard; the swords are lowered and raised by means of back-breaking cranks on the deck.

Sailboating

Antique sailboats are especially popular among Dutch and German school organisations or groups of families that hire them, along with a captain and mate, for a week or a weekend. With full galley facilities on board and berths for up to three dozen, the ships ply the Waddenzee, hopping from island to island, beach to beach, all the way to Germany, mooring in tiny island villages, or simply dropping anchor on an invit-

BELOW: it's a bird's life in the Waddenzee.

Friesland's quirky planetarium is well worth a visit.

ing sandbar. One of the attractions of such a trip is that, while the captain and mate can sail their boats themselves in any weather, the passengers are encouraged to learn and to take up as much of the running of the boat as they want. Various operators offer sailing packages on antique vessels, but one of the largest and best (open year-round) is a 32-boat co-operative supervised by Adrian Bakker. (For information write to: Rederij Vooruit Holland, Geeuwkade 9, 8651 AA IJlst, or tel: 0515-53 14 85.)

Watersports capital

There are many small villages in Friesland, and visitors who wander by car, bicycle, canal boat or on foot are rarely disappointed. For those interested in watersports, **Sneek** ⓑ, (pronounced snake) is a must; this town is the watersports capital of Friesland, a province whose numerous seaports and lakes make it the watersports playground of the Netherlands. Some non-boating places are appealing, too. **Franeker**, 10 km (6 miles) inland from Harlingen, was an influential university and market centre in the Middle Ages. It is little more than a pleasant small town today, though its elaborately decorated 1594 Dutch Renaissance town hall and several museums still draw many tourists.

Friesland's planetarium

Across from the town hall, one of the most popular museums – a home-made planetarium – is truly unique. **Eisinga Planetarium** (3 Eise Eisingastraat, tel: 0517-393 070; open mid-Apr–mid-Sept 15, Tues–Sat 10am–5pm, Sun and Mon 1–5pm; entrance fee) was built by Eise Eisenga, a wool-comber and amateur scientist, in the sitting room of his family home between 1774 and 1781, in an

BELOW: on the water in Hoorn.

attempt to quell local fears that a collision among the planets would lead to the Earth's destruction. To help convince the local burghers that devastation was not imminent, Eisenga made sure to put Franeker at the centre of the universe. Now the oldest planetarium in the world, Eisenga invited local people into his house to show them how the solar system worked – even though Uranus, Neptune and Pluto are missing because they hadn't yet been discovered.

In over 200 years, the timing of the planetarium's movements – hours, days, weeks, months, seasons and years – has been readjusted only once, and was off by just two degrees. Visitors can explore the whole house, not just the sitting room but also the attic, which houses the mechanism made of oak hoops and 10,000 hand-forged nails that Eisenga used to create his model on a scale of one millimetre to one million kilometres.

It is an inspiration to anyone who has ever tinkered in a workshop, and fascinating to everyone else. The house features other globes, telescopes, sundials, maps, models and timepieces, and is refurbished to show how a tradesman in 18th-century Friesland might have lived. There are also changing exhibitions related to the stars and the planets.

Leeuwarden, despite its relative isolation, has a lively after-hours scene with something for everyone, from billiards to jazz. What's good enough for Mata Hari...

Last resort

A few more miles inland is **Leeuwarden** ⓰, (population 85,000), the capital of Friesland. The city is pleasant enough and the people are charmingly self-deprecating, despite their pride in their province and its independent history. People will say, for example, that yes, of course, Leeuwarden gets tourists – when it's raining and all the people sailing from Harlingen or biking or camping elsewhere in Friesland head for the town to dry out.

In truth, there are several museums, a number of decent restaurants and an active pub scene. For example, on the Oude Doelesteeg, a small alley off the main shopping street, Nieuwestad, are several different inviting bars and brown cafés, ranging from one that draws a billiards crowd to another that pulses with heavy-metal rock music. Then there's the intimate Bar de Wipsluip, with table-top candles, red roses on the bar and mellow jazz.

BELOW: maritime influences in Texel.

The VVV office adjacent to Leeuwarden station offers a free brochure recommending a walk through town depicting buildings and provides interesting background on Leeuwarden. Of particular interest is the childhood home of Mata Hari (Margaretha Geertruida Zelle), the renowned dancer, supposed temptress and purported World War I spy who was born in Leeuwarden. She has been adopted as a heroine of modern tourism despite a shadowy career that ended when she was shot by the French. Her former home now houses the **Frisian Literary Museum**.

On a historical note

Also noteworthy in Leeuwarden are numerous small statues scattered on various corners, and two other museums: the **Frisian Museum** (11 Turfmarkt, tel: 058-212 3001, open Mon–Sat 11am–5pm, Sun 1–5pm; entrance fee), which displays antiquities and costumes and provides a comprehensive history of

TIP

The Wadden Islands, with their motor-vehicle restrictions, offer outdoors fans a fantastic opportunity to travel about on two-wheels. Plan accordingly so that you can get the most out of the islands' abundant natural beauty.

Friesland; and the **Resistance Museum** (11 Turfmarkt, tel: 058-212 3001; open Mon–Sat 11am–5pm, Sun 1–5pm; entrance fee), comprising a series of walk-through exhibits dedicated to the Dutch role in World War II. At the Resistance Museum, for a small fee, visitors get a headset and a 25-minute cassette that relates the hardships of Friesland under German occupation, when there were 30,000 deaths and a famine in the final winter of the war that forced people to eat anything they could find, including tulip bulbs, to survive.

Leeuwarden has a bare handful of cheap hotels. For those who can afford it, the VVV usually recommends the 80-room, modern Oranje Hotel across from the station. There are many more family-style restaurants, however, and a few places for the Leeuwarden trendy set, many of whom make a living as artists and designers. One of the most popular eating places in the town is **Het Leven** (The Life) situated on Druifstreek. This is a large restaurant, by Frisian standards, with plain wooden tables that easily accommodate the noisy group meals so loved by the Dutch in general and Frisians in particular. People who enter alone usually end up dining in company. Main courses are typically Dutch: hearty meat or vegetarian main courses with herring or baked cheese to start, and plenty of cold beer or French table wine, all at reasonable prices. Another place in Leeuwarden serving similar food and which draws the same sort of lively crowd, is **Café Silberman**, next door to Het Leven.

The Wadden Islands

BELOW: Texel treasure hunt.

The Wadden Islands, dividing the Waddenzee from the North Sea, are a natural wonder treasured by people looking for a certain kind of holiday: somewhere definitely out-of-the-way, a bit harder to get to, with plenty of outdoor activities.

Map on page 294

The islands represent the remains of an arching natural dyke that lay between the North Sea and a huge ancient marshland. That marshland is now the Waddenzee, flooded by a gradual raising of the sea level that took place when the Ice-Age glaciers melted. Because of their unique physical history, and the shallowness of the Waddenzee, all the islands are renowned as havens for feeding and migratory birds – and consequently for birdwatchers.

The largest and southernmost island, **Texel** ⓱, is the most accessible because it is reached by a short ferry ride, not from Friesland but from Den Helder, on the other side of the IJsselmeer. Texel is the most developed island, and is consequently quite crowded in summer, especially with cars, which are either rare or legally banned from the Wadden islands of Vlieland and Schiermonnikoog.

Apart from the seven villages, five museums and more than 300 species of birds, Texel's most famous inhabitants would have to be the sheep, which outnumber the human population. Wool products are almost as diverse as the many shops on the island, and for the confirmed carnivore, Texel lamb is famous for its slightly sweet yet delicately briny flavour.

Meat eaters should not miss out on Texel's tasty, sweet lamb.

On your bike

The next island, **Vlieland** ⓲, is accessible by ferry (90 minutes, depending on the weather), and limited high-speed catamaran service (45 minutes) from Harlingen, the busy little port where chartered antique sailboats and commercial ships nestle up to the foot of the historic town centre. Vlieland (population 1,200) offers the visitor an acquaintance with nature that Texel has difficulty in matching. Motorised transport is limited to inhabitants only, so one is compelled to hire a bicycle from Oost Vlieland, the island's only village, with shops, restaurants and two small "supermarkets". (West Vlieland was consumed by the sea centuries ago).

Cycle rentals are cheap and plenty of friendly shops cater to all needs, especially families with young children and the physically challenged. The island is crisscrossed with a labyrinth of excellent cycle paths traversing dunes, fragrant woods alongside cranberry fields, and moorlands where wild fowl, birds of prey, migratory birds and rabbits are plentiful. Vlieland's two claims to fame are 96 species of birds and the longest nudist beach in Europe. Amateur botanists may enjoy a broad spectrum of flora and fauna, including rare orchids.

The western side of the island is one expansive stretch of sand, some 8 km (5 miles) long, with a few vegetative dunes known as the Vliehors. It is used for part of the year as a firing range. Fortunately, the Dutch militia are very committed to conservation; just don't walk across their terrain when red flags are hoisted, as you might run the risk of being preserved in situ. Like all the islands, Vlieland has had its share of shipwrecks, and has arguably the most famous of all: the *Lutine*. In 1999, newly-minted coins commemorated the bicentennial of this sad incident and a Lutine walk was created with gold-coloured slabs commemorating other wrecks. The *Lutine*'s bell now hangs in Lloyd's of London, but in return Lloyd's donated a memorial plaque.

BELOW: sea shells, Terschelling.

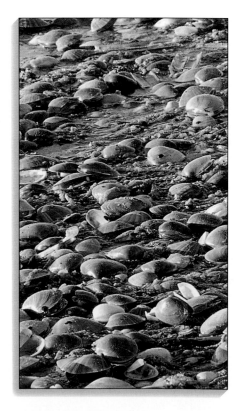

For a complete insight to the treasures of this island, natural or otherwise, a visit to the **Centrum for Informatie and Educatie De Noordwester** (150 Dorpstraat 150, tel: 0562-451 700; open Nov–Mar: Wed, Sat and Sun 2–5pm; Apr: Mon–Sat 1–5pm; May–mid-Sept: Mon–Fri 10am–noon, 2–5pm, Sat 2–5pm; mid-Sept–Oct: Mon–Sat 2–5pm; Dutch school hols: Mon–Fri 10am–5pm, Sat 2–5pm) is a must. Apart from its impressive collection of beach-combed finds the ground floor exhibits anything and everything pertaining to Vlieland. Seasonal exhibitions feature local painters.

Other attractions include **Trompshuys**, or the Admiral Tromp's house, (99 Dorpstraat, tel: 0562-451 600; closed for renovation and due to open in spring 2000; open Apr: Tues–Sun 2–5pm; May–Aug: 11am–5pm; entrance fee). The less energetic can board the **Vliehors Express**, a sort of luxurious army truck that makes a trip around the beaches to the Post House and Vliehors. Further information is available from the VVV office opposite the ferry terminal.

Ameland and Schiermonnikoog

The two northernmost islands, Ameland (population 3,000) and Schiermonnikoog (population 925), are too quiet for all but the most world-weary, privacy-seeking Dutch. **Ameland ⑲**, is undoubtedly the busiest of the two, boasting three villages, Hollum, Ballum and Nes, where a number of distinctive skippers' houses from the 17th and 18th centuries can be seen.

Hollum's **Cultuur-Historischmuseum Sorgdrager** (1 Herenweg, tel: 0519-554 477; open Mon–Fri 1.30–5pm, Sat and Sun 1.30–5pm; entrance fee) focuses on cultural history, and, in common with the other islands, exhibits memorabilia concerning the now politically incorrect whaling industry of a bygone era. On

BELOW: all paths lead to the sand in Terschelling.

a happier note, at Oranjeweg 18, is the **Reddingsmuseum Abraham Fok** (tel: 0519-554 243), dedicated to the history of lifeboats and sea rescue and presented via photographs and numerous artefacts.

The **Natuurcentrum**, or Nature Centre, is to be found in Nes, (Strandweg 38; open daily 10am–12am and 1pm–5pm; tel: 0519-542 737). It aims to make the visitor aware of the region's natural history and includes an impressive sea aquarium.

Active entertainment

If you are in the mood for a bird's eye view, a small fee of about 60 Dfl will buy you a 15-minute flight around the island (open year-round; tel: 0519-554 644). For those seeking more worldly entertainments, there is golf, an amusement arcade, tennis, a sports hall and horse riding. Relevant information is available from the VVV office in Nes (R. van Doniaweg 2; tel: 0519-546 546). Ameland's ferry is from Holwerd, a village about 40 km (25 miles) up the coast from Harlingen.

Schiermonnikoog ㉘, the most isolated island, is accessible only from the tiny port of Lauwersoog in northern Groningen. Lauwersoog harbour gives the traveller a foretaste of the isolation: the only things to be seen are its small fishing fleet and a row of sluices, while a simple restaurant takes 90 percent of its clientele from those leaving or arriving on the island. Travellers who find no contradiction in the words "bleak" and "beauty" should find it worth the effort.

Upon arrival a bus takes passengers to the only village, Schiermonnikoog. If you have arranged to stay at the island's oldest hotel, you will be picked up in

Map on page 294

Friesland's two northernmost islands are not for those who crave man-made entertainment. If there is beauty to be found in isolation, this is certainly it.

BELOW: sea mail, Friesland style.

a vintage charabanc, or bus. **Hotel van der Werf** is worth a visit if only to view numerous photographs depicting the social history of the island. Stepping into its lounge and dining room, with its rich wood-panelled walls and traditionally attired staff, is like stepping back in time. Not surprisingly it's a favourite haunt of authors and literary figures.

Nature reserve

By the statue of Schiere Monnik in the village are two upstanding whale jaws brought in by the famous ship, the *Willem Barentsz*. Green Peace would have adored these islands in their heyday. Predictably, the entire island (like Vlieland) is designated as a nature reserve, hence the no car policy. And again, one may get around on horseback, by bicycle or on foot.

Whatever mode of transport is employed, it would be sinful not to climb up the observation point known as the **Wasserman**, which offers a phenomenal panoramic view; the stirring North Sea on one side contrasted by the almost mill-pond quality of the Waddenzee.

The Visitor's Centre, the Oude Centrale (Torensteek 20; tel: 0519-531 641) is compulsory. All the information about the island's flora and fauna – which includes 50 percent of Europe's native species – can be found here. Rare plants include some varieties of orchid otherwise extinct in the wild.

An exceptionally entertaining alternative way of seeing the island is to book a seat on the **Balgexpress**; a sort of portable cabin on wheels, which is tractor-drawn and takes its passengers around the beaches and on occasion, in and out of the sea. Don't worry, it's perfectly safe – and, like the island itself, unforgettable.

BELOW: catching the breeze in Texel.

ELEVEN CITIES TOUR

Since not everyone can skate, or put up with freezing temperatures, no matter how much hot chocolate is on offer, the Fries Bureau voor Tourisme (tel: 0512-585 000) has put together numerous packages enabling visitors to see the 11 cities by alternative means of transport, be it bicycle, in-line roller skates, walking, horse or car. Cycle tours take from four to seven days, horseback tours at least five days, walking eight days and roller skating seven days.

The 11 cities tour starts in Leeuwarden and is then followed by Sneek, Ijlst, Sloten, Stavoren, Hindeloopen, Workum, Bolsward, Harlingen, Franeker, Dokkum, with the last leg returning to Leeuwarden. Other packages, varying from one to three days, are available for those who are of a shopping persuasion, and there are trips for culture vultures and restaurant lovers too.

Depending on the length of your stay in The Netherlands, these comprehensive arrangements make for a pleasant holiday in their own right, and are reasonably priced. There's plenty of scope to tailor tours to individual requirements. And don't forget the *Paspoort foar Fryslan*. Costing only 5 Dfl, it contains 45 Dfl worth of vouchers valid for reductions in museums and other attractions in the 11 cities. So, grab a hot chocolate, and happy non-ice skating.

Terschelling island

The second-largest of the five main Wadden islands, **Terschelling** ㉑ (population 3,000), offers a good compromise between crowds and desolation. Terschelling was important as a port in the 16th to 18th centuries and was a centre for the Dutch whaling industry. The harbour of the main town, **West-Terschelling**, is guarded by a 16th-century Brandaris lighthouse, the largest in the Netherlands. The town itself is known for its little 17th-century gabled houses. There is a small cultural museum on Commandeurstraat and there are a number of unpretentious family restaurants both in West-Terschelling and in nearby villages. Cranberries and the fruit's by-products, from wine to tarts, are a local speciality.

Terschelling offers exhilarating cycling on paved or dirt-packed paths through spectacular scenery, ranging from grassy dunes to mature forests whose tall trees block out the sun, emit a sweet scent and obligingly scatter pine cones for children to collect (bikes with child seats can be hired on the harbour front).

The vast North Sea beaches of Terschelling are backed by dunes that are constantly being formed and re-formed by the wind and currents. Considerable areas have been planted with grass, and breakwaters have been constructed to hold the dunes in place, keeping them from shifting eastward under the constant battering of wind and waves from the west.

Terschelling, like the other Wadden islands, is in effect a vast laboratory of wind, sea and land. And for anyone who travels as far north as Friesland, it would surely be a crime against the ethics of good travelling not to take a ferry out to one of these beautifully wild and, for the most part, undiscovered Netherland islands. ❑

Map on page 294

TIP

If the days of whaling fleets and maritime trade fascinate you, Terschelling's Museum 't Behouden Huys by the ferry terminus is full of interesting exhibits.

BELOW: North Sea beach dunes in Terschelling.

INSIGHT GUIDES

Travel Tips

✕ INSIGHT GUIDES

The world's largest collection of visual travel guides

Insight Guides – the Classic Series that puts you in the picture

Alaska	China	Hong Kong	Morocco	Singapore
Alsace	Cologne	Hungary	Moscow	South Africa
Amazon Wildlife	Continental Europe		Munich	South America
American Southwest	Corsica	Iceland		South Tyrol
Amsterdam	Costa Rica	India	Namibia	Southeast Asia
Argentina	Crete	India's Western	Native America	Wildlife
Asia, East	Crossing America	Himalayas	Nepal	Spain
Asia, South	Cuba	India, South	Netherlands	Spain, Northern
Asia, Southeast	Cyprus	Indian Wildlife	New England	Spain, Southern
Athens	Czech & Slovak	Indonesia	New Orleans	Sri Lanka
Atlanta	Republic	Ireland	New York City	Sweden
Australia		Israel	New York State	Switzerland
Austria	Delhi, Jaipur & Agra	Istanbul	New Zealand	Sydney
	Denmark	Italy	Nile	Syria & Lebanon
Bahamas	Dominican Republic	Italy, Northern	Normandy	
Bali	Dresden		Norway	Taiwan
Baltic States	Dublin	Jamaica		Tenerife
Bangkok	Düsseldorf	Japan	Old South	Texas
Barbados		Java	Oman & The UAE	Thailand
Barcelona	East African Wildlife	Jerusalem	Oxford	Tokyo
Bay of Naples	Eastern Europe	Jordan		Trinidad & Tobago
Beijing	Ecuador		Pacific Northwest	Tunisia
Belgium	Edinburgh	Kathmandu	Pakistan	Turkey
Belize	Egypt	Kenya	Paris	Turkish Coast
Berlin	England	Korea	Peru	Tuscany
Bermuda			Philadelphia	
Boston	Finland	Laos & Cambodia	Philippines	Umbria
Brazil	Florence	Lisbon	Poland	USA: Eastern States
Brittany	Florida	Loire Valley	Portugal	USA: Western States
Brussels	France	London	Prague	US National Parks:
Budapest	Frankfurt	Los Angeles	Provence	East
Buenos Aires	French Riviera		Puerto Rico	US National Parks:
Burgundy		Madeira		West
Burma (Myanmar)	Gambia & Senegal	Madrid	Rajasthan	
	Germany	Malaysia	Rhine	Vancouver
Cairo	Glasgow	Mallorca & Ibiza	Rio de Janeiro	Venezuela
Calcutta	Gran Canaria	Malta	Rockies	Venice
California	Great Barrier Reef	Marine Life of the	Rome	Vienna
California, Northern	Great Britain	South China Sea	Russia	Vietnam
California, Southern	Greece	Mauritius &		
Canada	Greek Islands	Seychelles	St. Petersburg	Wales
Caribbean	Guatemala, Belize &	Melbourne	San Francisco	Washington DC
Catalonia	Yucatán	Mexico City	Sardinia	Waterways of Europe
Channel Islands		Mexico	Scotland	Wild West
Chicago	Hamburg	Miami	Seattle	
Chile	Hawaii	Montreal	Sicily	Yemen

Complementing the above titles are 120 easy-to-carry Insight Compact Guides, 120 Insight Pocket Guides with full-size pull-out maps and more than 60 laminated easy-fold Insight Maps

CONTENTS

Getting Acquainted

The Place

Area: 33,950 sq km (13,000 sq miles)
Area Below Sea Level: one-fifth
Population: 16,000,000
Capital: Amsterdam
Seat of Government: The Hague
Time Zone: GMT + 1 hour in winter, + 2 hours in summer (last weekend in March to last weekend in September)
Language: Dutch
Religion: Roman Catholic (40 percent), Protestant (30 percent)
Weights and Measures: Metric
Electricity: 220 volts AC, round two-pin plugs
National Airline: KLM Royal Dutch Airlines
International Dialling Code: 31 + 20 (Amsterdam), 70 (The Hague), 10 (Rotterdam)

Government & Economy

The provinces of the Netherlands were united as an independent state in 1648, and the constitution was approved in 1848. The Head of State, Queen Beatrix, lives with her husband, Prince Claus outside The Hague. They have three sons.

From its position on the North Sea at the estuaries of three major rivers – the Rhine, the Maas and the Schelde – the Netherlands is, and has been for centuries, a maritime trading nation. Although a small country, it has increased its size by reclaiming land from the sea. The windmills, dykes, dams and locks are all witnesses to the success achieved by a hard-working people.

The country rose to greatness in the 17th century when explorers and merchants roamed the world. From the enterprising spirit of the Dutch, prosperity and spiritual wealth manifested themselves in treasures of crafted silver and gold, the unique architecture of canal houses and artistic masterpieces.

The Dutch have a highly organised economy and although the country suffered from unemployment when new technology replaced labour-intensive industry, it remains cushioned against the worst effects of recession. The European Union imports more than 75 percent of Dutch goods and 30 percent of all trade to European countries passes through the world's largest port, Rotterdam.

The Netherlands is the world's largest exporter of plants, flowers and bulbs and the second largest exporter of farm produce. Electronics, publishing and the processing of oil to produce petroleum products are major industrial sectors. The Netherlands has produced several multinationals, including Heineken, Shell, Philips and Unilever.

Climate

Amsterdam has a mild, maritime climate with much the same temperatures as the UK but is wetter and marginally cooler in winter. Summers are generally warm but you can expect rain at any time of year. Spring is the driest time of the year and a favourite time for tulip enthusiasts. The advantages of a visit in winter are the cut-price package deals and the fact that museums and galleries are pleasantly uncrowded.

The Provinces

The Netherlands is made up of 12 provinces, each administered by an elected Provincial Council and each with its own characteristics. There are also many beautiful towns in the provinces, of which 150 have a total of over 42,000 "protected" buildings, such as historic farmhouses, windmills and castles.

Friesland:
in the north, has a historic capital, Leeuwarden. There are daily ferry connections to four of the Frisian Islands. Frieslanders have an independent spirit and continue to speak their own language.

Drenthe:
has ancient Saxon villages scattered among woods and heathland. Perfect for cyclists to explore, there is no shortage of museums, castles and churches.

Groningen:
in the northeast, with its eponymous capital, has 33 museums, 80 windmills and 100 medieval churches.

Overijssel:
to the southeast, embraces the picturesque town of Giethoorn where you can travel by boat through canal "streets". The two Hanseatic towns of Zwolle and Kampen delight with their historic buildings and the villages of Urk and Staphorst still follow ancient customs and traditions.

Gelderland:
is the largest province, stretching from the great southern rivers to the northern sand dunes. It contains the country's largest open-air museum: the Hoge Veluwe National Park has deer, wild boar and sheep plus the treasures of the Kröller-Müller art gallery.

Flevoland:
the Netherlands' newest province, reclaimed from the IJsselmeer. The principal towns are Lelystad and Almere.

Utrecht:
in the centre, is like the Netherlands in miniature. There are historic towns, countryside, woods, lakes and polders; castles and country houses.

Noord Brabant:
in the lively south has 's-Hertogenbosch as its capital with the largest cathedral in the country: St Jan, built in the 14th century. Social occasions have undisguised zest – from the Carnival in February to jazz festivals held in Breda.

Limburg:
too enjoys life. The capital, Maastricht, is one of the Netherlands' oldest towns and a centre for haute cuisine, tradition and natural beauty.

Noord-Holland:
in the influential west – not in the north, as its name suggests – is particularly rich in folklore. Traditional dress is common in old towns such as Volendam, Marken, Edam and Monnickendam. Haarlem has influenced many painters and the Frans Hals Museum is one of the Netherlands' principal attractions. Alkmaar is famous for its weekly cheese market.

Zuid-Holland:
contains the seat of government, in The Hague, and other well-preserved cities such as Leiden, Delft and Gouda. It holds the nickname of the "vegetable garden of Europe" because tomatoes, cucumbers and peppers are grown here. Bulbfields also cover the north of the province in a riot of colour in spring.

Zeeland:
is the delta of the Netherlands – a little kingdom of peninsulas, inland seas and lakes. The most ambitious engineering project in the world, the Delta Works uses high technology to keep the sea in check. Seafood is its lifeblood. The old capital, Middelburg, has a wealth of Flemish-Renaissance architecture.

Business Hours

Normal shopping hours are 9am–6pm. Late-night shopping is usually Thursday, depending on which major city you are in. In recent years, food stores have extended their hours on Saturday to 7pm or 10pm, with some grocery chains such as Albert Heijn remaining open on Sundays from 1pm–7pm. Most shops close at 5pm on Saturdays, though some have extended to 6pm, and, in larger cities, many department stores and speciality shops are now open on Sundays.

All shops close for one half-day on Monday morning. Banks are open Monday–Friday 9am–4pm, with some larger branches open to 5pm.

Public Holidays

Banks and most shops close on the following days:

- 1 January (New Year's Day)
- Good Friday, Easter Sunday and Monday
- 30 April (Queen's Day)
- 5 May (Liberation Day)
- 1 June (Ascension Day)
- 12 June (Whit Monday)
- 25 December (Christmas Day)
- 26 December (Boxing Day)

Planning the Trip

Entry Regulations

Visitors from the European Union, the US, Canada, Australia, New Zealand and most other European and Commonwealth countries require a passport only. Citizens of most other countries must obtain a visa in advance from a Dutch embassy or consulate.

Customs

Personal possessions are not liable to duty and tax provided you are staying for less than six months and you intend to take them out again. There is no restriction on the amount of currency that you can bring into the Netherlands. Among prohibited or restricted goods are plants, flowers, weapons and narcotic drugs.

Duty-free
Duty-free allowances vary according to where you bought the goods.

As of 1 July 1999, the regulations for duty-free shopping have changed. Duty-free shopping is no longer available to travellers within the European Union. Despite the change in regulations, travellers departing from Schiphol Airport to destinations in and out of the EU may still take advantage of reduced prices on all goods except alcoholic

Animal Quarantine

An official certificate of vaccination is required for cats and dogs brought into The Netherlands from any country other than Belgium and Luxemburg.

beverages and tobacco. Travellers to the Canary Islands (Spain) and the Channel Islands (UK) are not affected by the ruling.

Health

No health certificates or vaccinations are required for European Union citizens.

EU citizens who have obtained an E111 form from their local social security office before departure are entitled to free treatment by a doctor and free prescribed medicines. This insurance is not comprehensive and won't cover you, for example, for holiday cancellation or the cost of repatriation. If you want full cover, you should take out separate medical insurance.

Money Matters

The Dutch monetary unit is the guilder (gulden), sometimes called a florin (for NLG). One guilder is equivalent to 100 cents. The euro will come into circulation in 2002, when it will replace the guilder.

Coins in current circulation are the stuiver (5 cents), dubbeltje (10 cents), kwartje (25 cents), guilder (100 cents), rijksdaalder (250 cents), and five guilder coin (500 cents).

Existing bank notes are 10, 25, 50, 100, 250 and 1,000 guilders.

CHANGING MONEY

GWK (Grenswis-selkantoren NV) is a national financial institution where you can exchange any currency and also use credit cards, travellers' cheques and Eurocheques. There are GWK offices located at 35 main railway stations in the Netherlands and at the country's borders. They open Monday–Saturday 8am–8pm, Sunday 10am–4pm and sometimes in the evening at main stations and airports. Although the Amsterdam Centraal Station GWK exchange office is open 24 hours a day, the station itself is closed for security reasons from 1am–5am.

Embassies

Australia
4 Carnegielaan Koninginnegracht, The Hague
Tel: 070-310 8200
Canada
7 Sophialaan, The Hague
Tel: 070-311 1600
Great Britain
44 Koningslaan, Amsterdam
Tel: 020-676 4343
United States
19 Museumplein, Amsterdam
Tel: 020-575 5309

Change is also available at post offices (at a good rate of exchange) and banks. There can be a considerable difference in commission charged between the various institutions and at the different times of night or day. Many banks with outside dispensers accept recognised bank cards for money exchange. GWK and other currency exchange outlets also accept major credit cards.

CREDIT CARDS

Credit cards are accepted at hotels, restaurants, shops, car rental companies and airlines. American Express, Diners Club, Eurocard, Visa, Mastercard and JCB card are all recognised, plus many more.

Package Tours

Numerous companies offer two to seven-day packages, principally to Amsterdam. These often (but not always) work out cheaper than fixing your own travel and accommodation. To qualify for the air packages, you have to spend a Saturday night away.

The packages range from all-inclusive (meals, excursions, welcome parties included) to basic travel and accommodation.

What to Bring

The unpredictability of the weather calls for a raincoat and/or umbrella at all times of the year. Light clothing should be sufficient in summer, but take a jacket or light coat for the evenings. Very warm clothing is advisable for winter. Comfortable footwear is essential for sightseeing and walking on the cobbled streets. Casual dress is the norm, though a very few of the smarter hotels and restaurants require men to wear jacket and tie.

Getting There

BY AIR

Most visitors, whether from America or other parts of Europe, fly into Schiphol Airport, 9 miles (14km) southwest of Amsterdam. The airport has connections to 248 cities in 97 countries. With its expanded terminals, casino, business centre, two hotels and a children's play area – along with its reputation for efficiency and easy access to all parts of the Netherlands – Schiphol remains one of Europe's most popular international airports. Together, British Airways (tel: 0870-544 4000), KLM Royal Dutch Airlines (tel: 0870-507 4074) and British Midland (tel: 0870-607 0555) operate an almost hourly service during the day from London Heathrow and from East Midlands airport (tel: 01332-852 852). (All telephone numbers are in the UK).

Best value of the lot for British visitors is the Amsterdam Air Express from Gatwick, departing on Friday afternoons only and returning on Monday evenings. Services from major regional airports are covered by various British and Dutch airlines.

Several airlines offer cut-price fares which work out to little more than the cost of a standard rail ticket. These cheaper flights usually mean that you have to spend a Saturday night in the Netherlands. Very regular flights link Schiphol with all major European airports, and there are several flights a week from North America, Canada and Australia. The Amsterdam Travel Service, which has offices in the UK and in Amsterdam, offers specially priced excursion packages to Amsterdam and other cities in the Netherlands. For further information contact:

UK office
Bridge House, 55–59 High Road, Broxbourne, Herts; EN10 7DT
Tel: 01992 456 056.
Amsterdam office
Dam 10
Tel: (020) 627 6236.

BY TRAIN

There are good rail connections to all parts of the Netherlands from Brussels, Paris, Antwerp, Cologne, Hanover and London, and the North Sea ports.

The Eurostar Channel Tunnel train goes direct from London (Waterloo) to Amsterdam via Brussels in neighbouring Belgium and takes about six hours (tel: 0990-186 186). Day and night services operate from London (Liverpool Street) to the Netherlands via the Hook of Holland – journey time is around 12 hours by ferry, 10 hours by jetfoil.

A further option is London (Victoria or Charing Cross) to Ostend via Dover, but there are several transfers involved. Or go via the Sheerness–Vlissingen rail ferry. British Rail European Enquiries, tel: 0990-848 848.

BY SEA

From the UK, P&O Stena (tel: 0870-570 70 70) operates two sailings a day from Harwich to the Hook of Holland: High Speed Service: 3 hours 40 minutes. North Sea Ferries (tel: 01482-377 177) has a daily sailing from Hull to Rotterdam, taking 14 hours. Sheerness Travel Agency (tel: 01795-666 666) is one of the main east coast agents dealing with this route. The fastest

sea route from the UK is from Dover to Ostend via Hoverspeed's seacat (tel: 0870-524 0241), which takes about 2 hours.

BY CAR

To drive in Holland, you must carry a current driving licence (an international licence is not necessary), vehicle registration document, Green Card insurance policy and a warning triangle for use in the event of an accident or breakdown. Holland has an excellent network of roads and signposting is good. But once you're in the cities, a car is often more of a hindrance than a help. In most large cities, you are required to buy parking tickets at specially posted vending machines along the

Tourist Offices

The Netherlands Board of Tourism (NBT) provides a number of useful publications, including *Holland's Seaside, Cycling in Holland, Watersports in Holland* and *Rail Holidays in Holland*, plus addresses of hotels and restaurants. For copies and information, visit or write to your nearest office:

● **Canada**
25 Adelaide Street East,
Suite 710,
Toronto,
Ontario M5C 1Y2.
● **Great Britain**
18 Buckingham Gate,
London SW1E 6LB.
● **Switzerland**
12 Rautistrasse 8047,
Zurich.
● **United States**
355 Lexington Avenue
(21st Floor), New York,
NY 10017; also
225 North Michigan Avenue,
Suite 1854,
Chicago, Ill 60601; and
9841 Airport Blvd,
Suite 710, Los Angeles,
California 90045.

streets, marked with a "P". Amsterdam is notorious for high fines, parking clamps and a very enthusiastic parking enforcement team.

From the UK, the Channel Tunnel's Le Shuttle provides a 35-minute drive-on service between Folkestone and Calais, France, from where there is a straightforward motorway connection through Belgium.

All the companies mentioned in the By Sea section above offer a car ferry service. Advance bookings are advisable in summer. From the Hook of Holland to Amsterdam, travel time is roughly 2 hours 30 minutes. If you don't mind a longer drive on the Continent you can, of course, take the shorter cross-Channel ferry route from Dover to Calais (P&O Stena, 1 hour 15 minutes to 1 hour 30 minutes; (tel: 01394-604 363). Hoverspeed's seacat takes 50 minutes and their hovercraft 30 minutes).

Practical Tips

21; (tel: 020-621 1211 for reservations to events). There are also special brochures available from the **VVV**, *Amsterdam Winter and Summer Arts Adventures*, costing around f.4. These are part of the extensive effort to present "language is no problem" performances and exhibitions.

Media

Newspapers and Magazines

The main national newspapers are *NRC Handelsblad*, the most respected paper, the more left-wing *De Volkskrant* and *De Telegraaf*, on the political right. English newspapers arrive on the same day they are published and are widely available.

The weekly English-language *What's on in Amsterdam* gives listings and reviews of what's on in the city (f.4 from the **VVV** offices). Brown café notice-boards are another good source of information on local events. The *Uitkrant*, available at the Uitburo on the Leidseplein is a free monthly publication, which, although published in Dutch, is easily readable for concert venues and dates of performances. Pick up their English brochure, *Culture in Amsterdam 1998–2001*, at their offices at Kleine Gartmanplantsoen

Emergency Numbers

● **Amsterdam (code 020)**
Police/ambulance: 112
SOS doctor/
dentist/chemist: 592 3434
Lost property
(noon–3.30pm daily): 559 3005

● **The Hague (code 070)**
Police/ambulance: 112
SOS doctor/dentist: 345 5300
            (night): 346 9669
Lost property: 310 4911

● **Rotterdam (code 010)**
Police/ambulance: 112
Doctor: 420 1100
Dentist: 455 2155

Television and Radio

On cable TV you can watch Britain's BBC1 and BBC2, plus Sky, CNN Fox and various other international networks. English-language films are frequently shown on Dutch TV channels, undubbed. On the radio, you can tune into the BBC World Service, BBC Radio 4 and Sky Radio.

Postal Services

Main post offices are usually open Mon–Fri; 8.30am–6pm; 8pm on Thur–Sat; 9am–1pm. Stamps are available from post offices, tobacconists, and some news stands and stationery shops.

Poste Restante facilities are available at main post offices – you need a passport to collect mail.

Telephones

Telephone boxes are mainly green, but are also recognisable in more compact and contemporary styles. Most take phonecards and/or 25c, f.1 and f.2.50 coins. You find them in post offices, large stores, cafés and in some streets. Larger post offices have international call facilities which work out cheaper than using a hotel phone. Beware of hole-in-the-wall shops offering so-called cheap long-distance telephone services, as many are actually overpriced.

Tourist Information

Tourist information offices (Vereniging voor Vreemdelingen-verkeer – or VVV for short) are clearly marked and usually located just outside the railway station in every main town and city. Here the multilingual staff will answer all

your questions, provide maps and brochures, handle your accommodation bookings and reserve tickets for the theatre. But there is a charge for most of them. It is useful to carry passport-sized photographs for various identity cards you may purchase.

The registered address of the head office is:
VVV Amsterdam Tourist Office
P.O. Box 3901
1001 AS Amsterdam
Tel: 06-3403 4066 or
0900-400 4040 (f.1 per minute)
Fax: 020-625 2869
To vist in person, go to: 10 Stationsplein (white building across the road to the left outside the Centraal Station). Open: daily 9am–5pm. There are also **VVV** offices inside the Centraal Station, (open 8am–8pm Mon–Sat, 8am–5pm Sun), and at 1 Leidseplein, Amsterdam, (open daily 9am–5pm). If you wish to write to a town tourist office, address the letter with **VVV** and the name of the town.

Doing Business

The Netherlands has always been a trading nation; lacking its own raw materials, it has survived by means of *entrepôt* trade and distribution, one reason why Schiphol Airport and the Port of Rotterdam are so important to the country's economy. Most of this trade is with EU countries, principally Germany, the UK and Belgium.

Doing business with the Dutch is usually a pleasure: they are informal, honest and excellent linguists. They are also efficient and expect their trading counterparts to be the same.

Travelling with Children

Children are treated with respect and affection. The notion that they should be seen and not heard is alien, and children are involved in adult life from an early age – one reason why Dutch children can seem unusually well-behaved and mature.

Children are welcome in restaurants and cafés, many of which serve a *kindermenu* (children's menu). It is easy to hire bicycles fitted with children's seats for getting about town or for excursions into the country.

Ask at the **VVV** for details of special activities for children. Several cities now have *kinderboerderijen*, or children's farms; in Amsterdam for example, there are city farms within the zoo complex and another at the Amstelpark (located near the Rai Exhibition Centre in the southern suburbs). Top children's attractions include Artis Zoo, Planetarium, Geographic and Zoological Museums, the New Metropolitan Museum of Science and Technology, Madame Tussaud's and the Tropenmuseum in Amsterdam; the Zuiderzee Museum in Enkhuisen; Burger's Zoo in Arnhem, the Omniversum Space Museum and the Madurodam miniature town in The Hague; the zoo and Maritiem Museum in Rotterdam, Utrecht's railway museum (Nederlands Spoorwegmuseum), and De Efteling amusement park in Tilburg.

This is, of course, far from being an exhaustive list; in fact the towns of the Netherlands, with their harbours, bridges, canals, parks and windmills, seem almost deliberately designed to appeal to children.

Disabled Travellers

Many train stations have lifts, which should be marked clearly at arrival points. Many older city-centre hotels have very steep staircases and no lifts; check before booking whether your hotel has wheelchair access and a lift. Most of the 4- and 5-star hotel chains have wheelchair access and lifts.

Students

University campus restaurants (called mensas) are open to anyone, and a good source of cheap, filling food, though they are only open for lunch Monday–Friday during termtime.

Service & Tips

Service charges and VAT are included in restaurant and bar bills. At cafés, the extra change can be left as an extra tip and at finer restaurants a tip of 10 percent is acceptable for extra attention or service, but this is by no means compulsory. Taxi meters also include the service charge, though it is customary to give an extra tip of a guilder or so. A lavatory attendant is usually given 50 cents.

Medical Services

The standard of medical and dental services in the Netherlands is very high, and most major cities have an emergency doctor and dental service; enquire at your hotel or consult the introductory pages to local telephone directories.

Security & Crime

Amsterdam and Rotterdam are major European centres for drugs, and much crime here is drug-related. As a visitor, you are unlikely to be affected directly by the drugs trade, but you should take sensible precautions against becoming a victim of petty crime. Keep a careful watch on wallets, bags and other valuables, especially on public transport. Leave large amounts of cash and jewellery at your hotel. Deserted areas should be avoided after dark.

Lost Property

You should report loss or theft of valuables to the local police immediately, as most insurance policies insist on a police report. Loss of passport should be reported immediately to the police and your embassy or consulate.

Most large cities have a police lost property office and there is usually a separate office for items lost on public transport.

Etiquette

The Netherlands has a reputation for tolerance. Foreigners, including minorities, are always welcome and, as a visitor, you are likely to find local people pleasant, polite and civilised. They may not be very demonstrative or vivacious, but they are rarely inhospitable or unfriendly. You may be surprised at the leniency towards drugs and prostitution, especially in cities like Amsterdam. There has been a crackdown on hard drugs, but you can still buy soft drugs in many city cafés. Many locals argue that the drugs problem is no worse than in other major cities – just more open.

Getting Around

Public Transport

Exploring the Netherlands is made easy by the excellent and inexpensive public transport system. All towns of any size have a railway station, which usually also acts as the main terminus for the bus, coach, tram and metro services. Bicycles can also be hired at most stations.

Tickets

Tickets are sold in the form of Nationale Strippenkaart to be used on buses, trams, metro and the train between certain stations anywhere in Holland. The easiest place to buy the cards is at a **vvv** office (or tel: 0900-4004040 (f.1.05 per minute); fax: 020-625 2869), though they are also sold at railway stations and many newsagents and tobacconists. You can buy tickets from the bus or tram driver, but they cost more than tickets purchased in advance. Transport routes are divided into zones; you must cancel one strip for your journey and one strip for each zone you travel through (i.e. cancel two strips for one zone, three for two zones, and so on). The stamp on your stripenkaart is valid for one hour. Within that time you can change from one route to another, or from one form of transport to another without cancelling more strips. Two strips cost f.4 and 15 strips cost f.12. An alternative is an unlimited travel ticket (called a *dagkaart*), valid for one, two or three days.

Tram 20 is a circle tram with two different routes which take you across the city to most of the museums and tourist attractions.

The trams run daily from 9am–7pm every 10 minutes. One ticket entitles you to unlimited use of the tram for one day.

BY AIR

Schiphol, near **Amsterdam** is the Netherlands' principal airport. Amsterdam Schiphol railway station is located below the arrivals hall. Trains leave for the principal Dutch cities every 15 minutes or so between 5.25am and 0.15am, and every 60 minutes or so during the remaining period.

Rotterdam has a small airport served by flights from Amsterdam, London and Paris, located 15 minutes from the city centre. A regular local bus service runs between the airport and the city.

Eindhoven and **Maastricht** both have airports, principally for domestic flights.

Domestic flights within the Netherlands are operated by KLM City Hopper.

For further information: tel: 020-474 7747.

Sightseeing by Air

Flights over south Limburg, neighbouring Germany and Belgium from Maastricht airport are organised by Air Service Limburg, tel: 043-364 5030. One-hour flights cost f.150 per person, with a minimum of two passengers and a maximum of three.

Maps

The **vvv** issues a useful road map of the Netherlands, updated each year, for f.2. For anyone who requires more detailed maps for walking or cycling, the ANWB 1:100,000 series is sold in many **vvv** offices and bookshops.

Most **vvv** offices sell street plans of towns and cities in their locality; when using them it helps if you remember that *straat* means street, *plein* means square and *gracht* means canal.

BY TRAIN

Netherlands Railways (Nederlandse Spoorwegen) has a national inter-city network of express trains linking major cities. There is a fast direct train link every 15 minutes between the airport Schiphol and Amsterdam. There is also an hourly night service between Utrecht, Amsterdam, Schiphol, The Hague, Rotterdam and vice versa. "Stop" trains provide connections to smaller places. Most stations are located centrally. There are at least half-hourly services on most lines with anything from four to eight an hour on busier routes. It is not possible to reserve seats on national train services.

Tickets & Passes

Train tickets and travel passes can be purchased at any railway station in the Netherlands, at the domestic (*Binnenland*) office or from the yellow ticket machines in the stations. Although instructions are in Dutch, the machines are not difficult to use. A return ticket is cheaper than two singles and valid for one day. First and second class one-day travel passes are also available, at f.114 and f.73.50 respectively, providing one day's unlimited train travel anywhere in the Netherlands.

A Weekend Return ticket provides economical travel from 7pm Friday to 4am Monday. The Holland Rail Pass was launched in 1999 and entitles travellers to 3–5 days train travel all over the Netherlands within one month. A companion receives a 50 percent discount; young persons under the age of 25 and senior citizens receive a 50 percent discount.

A Group Travel pass (*Meermanskaart*) offers substantial savings for two to six people. For children between the ages of four and eleven accompanied by an adult, there is a Railrunner option for f.2.50 per child, which is valid for one day's unlimited travel throughout the Netherlands. Any fare-paying adult above the age of

19 can take up to three children on Railrunners. Children under four travel free.

Eurodomino: This card entitles you to three, five or eight-day unlimited rail travel (within a certain period), with prices varying according to which countries are included in your itinerary. Prices start at about f.90 for three days. Brochures are available at larger train stations from the International windows.

Rail Idea: This offers supplementary transport and admission to 33 different attractions throughout the Netherlands, mostly between May and September. There is a booklet, *Er Op Uit*, available at a nominal price which provides further information; although written in Dutch, it is fairly easy to comprehend. You can purchase a Rail Idea together with your train ticket or it can be purchased separately if you already have a valid ticket or travel pass.

Information
For further information about public transport information and tickets:
Amsterdam GVB
1 Stationsplein,
Centraal Station
Tel: 0900-9292 (f.1.05 per minute);
(Monday–Friday 8am–10pm,
Saturday and Sunday 9am–10pm).
Nationwide
Tel: 0900-9292 (f.1.05 per minute).
For information on international trains: tel: 0900-9296 (f.50 a minute). More information on train travel in Holland may be found in the free booklet, *Exploring Holland by Train*, published in English.

TRAIN TAXIS

The *Trein Taxi* is a typical Dutch form of transport where you share a taxi with others at a reduced rate. Train taxis take you to and from over 100 stations in the Netherlands. The fixed price is around f.7.50 per person, regardless of distance. Train taxi

tickets are sold at train station offices, ticket machines or can be purchased at a slightly higher price from the driver. Train taxis travel within a certain area, which is displayed at the Train taxi rank.

Taxis

Taxis will not stop if hailed in the street. It is customary in Holland to book a taxi by phone, although they can always be found at taxi ranks near hotels, stations and busy road junctions. The taxi meter price includes service charge. A fare starts at f.6 then increases about f.5 per kilometre. A 3-mile (5-km) journey in town would cost approximately f.16; prices are slightly higher at night.

Driving

Highway Code
Stay on the right and overtake on the left. All road users should allow

free passage to approaching police cars, fire engines and ambulances that are using their sound and light signals. A tram may not be held up on its course. Seatbelts must be worn in the front seats of vehicles.

Speed Limits
Within a built-up zone the maximum speed is 50 kph (30 mph). In residential areas, indicated by signs of a white house on a blue background, vehicles may only be driven at walking pace. Outside the built-up area the speed limit is 80 kph (50 mph). A speed limit of 120 kph (75 mph) applies on motorways and a speed limit of 100 kph (62 mph) on most major roads in the Netherlands.

Fuel
Petrol stations situated on national highways are open 24 hours. Most major petrol stations sell LPG (car gas). Unleaded petrol is readily available.

Vehicle Rental

Here are the Amsterdam addresses of some rental firms:

● **Car Rental**
The main car rental firms have offices at Schiphol airport. These are their Amsterdam addresses:
Avis
380 Nassaukade, 1054 AD
Tel: 020-683 6061
Ansa International
6–7 Hobbe-makade, 1017 XK
Tel: 020-664 8252
Budget Rent a Car
121 Overtoom, 1054 HE
Tel: 020-612 6066
Diks Autohuur
278–280 van Ostadestraat,
1073 TW
Tel: 020-662 3366
Europcar
51–53 Overtoom, 1054 HB
Tel: 020-683 2123
Hertz
333 Overtoom, 1054 JM
Tel: 020-612 2441;
Schiphol Airport
Tel: 020-601 5416

Kuperus
Van der Madeweg 1/5, 1098 AM
Tel: 020-668 3311

● **Camper Van Rental**
Vans must be booked in advance. Deposit is often 50 percent of the rental. Hire charges from f.950 per week. The following rental offices are located in Amsterdam:
ACC
4 Akersluisweg, 1069 MD
Tel: 020-610 1819
A-Point
11 Kollenbergweg, 1101 AR
Tel: 020-430 1647
Braitman & Woudenberg
4/A Droogbak, 1013 GE
Tel: 020-622 1168

● **Bicycle Rental**
Damstraat Rent-a-bike
Damstraat 20
Tel: 020-625 5029
MacBike
Mr. Visserplein 2
Tel: 020-620 0985
See also under *Cycling*.

National Highways

A.1: Amsterdam-Hoevelaken-Apeldoorn-Holten-Borne
A.2: Amsterdam-'s-Hertogenbosch/Eindhoven-Maastricht-Eijsden
A.4: Amsterdam-Burgerveen-Leiderdorp-Den Haag
A.5: Amsterdam-Haarlem
A.6: Muiderberg-Flevopolder-N.E. Polder-Emmeloord
A.7: Amsterdam-Hoorn/Lambertsschaag-Den Oever-Zurich-Joure-Drachten-Groningen-Hoogezand
A.8: Amsterdam-Westzaan
A.9: Alkmaar-Haarlem-Schiphol-Ouderkerk
A.12: Den Haag-Utrecht-Arnhem-Bergh (German border)
A.13: Den Haag-Rotterdam
A.16: Rotterdam-Breda-Hazeldonk (Belgian border)

Cycling

Bicycles are ubiquitous. The 12 million bicycles in the Netherlands are used extensively by people of all ages for commuting, shopping, walking the dog, transporting young children, towing windsurf boards and sometimes even to move house (using an old-fashioned *bakfiets* – baker's bicycle).

Even on the coldest winter days, you will see hardy cyclists. The Dutch favour old-fashioned heavy-framed bicycles for town use, without gears or hand-brakes (you stop by back pedalling).

By hiring a bicycle, you join in the life of the nation. Though bicycles are discouraged on crowded Dutch trains, they can be rented cheaply for a day or longer at most railway stations (with a small reduction on production of a train ticket). Parents with young children can also hire a small seat which is fixed on the back of the bicycle. Most railway stations provide secure lock-ups especially for bicycles.

Principal railway stations with bikes for hire are:

The Hague: tel: 070-385 3235
Delft: tel: 015-2143 033
Leiden: tel: 071-5120 068
Rotterdam: tel: 010-412 6220
Gouda: tel: 0182-519 751

Dordrecht: tel: 078-6146 642
Utrecht: tel: 030-2311 159

Otherwise, **VVV** offices can supply a list of hire companies. There is usually a deposit of between f.50 and f.200, depending on the sophistication of the bike, and rental costs are about f.10 a day or f.40 a week.

Safety

Be warned: the Netherlands may be Europe's cycling heartland, but it is also a nation where theft is all too common, especially in the larger cities. Always lock your bike and, wherever possible, secure it to an unmovable object. When cycling in Amsterdam, keep in mind that anarchy reigns. Taxis are allowed to drive on tram tracks, daring cyclists go through red lights and every rider must be on the defensive at all times.

Cycle Routes

A network of almost 6,250 miles (10,000km) of cycle lanes has been created in the Netherlands, complete with separate traffic lights for bikes at road intersections. Though cycling is safer than in many other countries, it is worth familiarising yourself with the bicycle and the rules of the road before setting off into the traffic. Bear in mind that cars entering a road from your right usually have priority.

The best maps to use are the ANWB 1:100,000 series, on which cycle lanes (*fietspaden*) are indicated by a dotted black line. Cycle routes are well signposted and signs at important junctions are often numbered so you can pinpoint your location on the map. In planning a route through the country try to avoid large cities and busy intersections. Cycling across the flat Dutch polders or along long straight canals or roads can be bleak, especially in bad weather. Though the Netherlands is dotted with attractive camp sites, hotels are often difficult to find, particularly in rural areas. It is also worth bearing in mind that restaurants outside Amsterdam tend to close early in the evening.

River Routes

By far the most attractive routes in the north of the country are those that follow the rivers. The Lek (which changes its name to the Neder Rijn east of Wijk bij Duurstede) provides an attractive route between Rotterdam and Arnhem, passing through pleasant river towns such as Schoonhoven, Culemborg, Wijk bij Duurstede and Rhenen. There are hardly any bridges across the Lek; numerous small ferries link the two banks.

National Park

From Arnhem, the most interesting cycling country is to the north through the rolling hills and moors of the Nationaal Park De Hoge Veluwe. A unique feature of this park is the free white bicycles which can be used anywhere within the park boundaries (a similar scheme foundered in Amsterdam when all the white bicycles were immediately stolen and repainted). Beyond the park, you can continue through moorland to Zwolle, north of which is an extensive area of lakes stretching to the attractive Frisian town of Sneek.

The IJsselmeer

It may seem tempting to head west across the IJsselmeer by the 20-mile (32-km) Afsluitdijk, but this tends to be an ordeal, particularly in high winds. A far better way to cross the IJsselmeer is by the small ferries that ply between Stavoren and Enkhuizen in the summer.

Between the Towns

In the densely populated Randstad, safe cycle routes are often difficult to find. To cycle from Rotterdam to The Hague, the best route is to follow the River Schie to Delft, then the Vliet to the outskirts of The Hague. The meandering Oude Rijn is a good route to take from Leiden to Utrecht, keeping always to the quiet side of the river. Cycling from Leiden to Amsterdam, you can follow a string of lakes north to Uithoorn, then enter the city by the beautiful Amstel route.

To cycle from Amsterdam to

Utrecht, follow the Amstel to Ouderkerk, turn down the Holendrecht to reach Abcoude, then take the Angstel to Loenersloot. Here, you cross the Amsterdam-Rijnkanaal to reach the River Vecht, which then flows into the heart of Utrecht.

Among the Dunes

The dunes offer an alternative route along the west coast, linking Hoek van Holland, The Hague and Haarlem. Once across the Noordzee Kanaal at Ijmuiden, you can continue along the coast north to Den Helder, where the ferry departs for the quiet island of Texel.

Water Transport

A popular way to get to know Amsterdam is by taking a canal tour; numerous companies operate from the canal basin opposite Centraal Station and tickets can be booked in advance from the nearby **VVV** office. Tours take an hour or more; candle-lit dinner cruises are also available. Fuller information is given in the Excursions section.

While canal tours are geared essentially to visitors, you can also use Amsterdam's canal bus system. Modern glass-topped launches (equivalent to the Parisian *bâteaux mouches)* will pick you up at various points of the city and take you through some of the loveliest parts of Amsterdam. Day tickets with unlimited use are available. Be prepared to queue in summer.

The Museum Boat service stops at nine major museums at 75-minute intervals – well worth considering if you intend doing a lot of sightseeing. You can buy a day ticket from the VVV office opposite Centraal Station, where the boats leave. There is now also a canal bus offering a regular service through the canals between the Rijksmuseum and Centraal Station.

Where to Stay

Reservations

Wherever you plan to stay, it is wise to book in advance during the summer and holiday seasons and (in the case of North Holland) during the bulb season (April–May). This is especially true of Amsterdam, where the central hotels are usually booked up during June, July and August. Having said that, it is worth telephoning hotels if you visit Amsterdam at short notice, to check for cancellations.

You can book directly with the hotel; invariably the person who answers the phone will speak English. Alternatively, book in advance through: The Netherlands Reservation Centre, P.O. Box 404, 2260 AK Leidschendam, tel: 070-419 5500, fax: 070-419 5519. The services of The Netherlands Reservation Centre are free and cover the whole country. Tell them where you want to stay, the dates, the price you are prepared to pay, and the number of rooms, with or without private bathrooms. Booking forms are stocked by branches of The Netherlands Board of Tourism.

Alternatively, you can book in person by going to VVV offices in major towns (those that offer the service display the i-Nederland sign). You will be expected to pay for accommodation on the spot, plus a small booking charge, and you will be issued with a voucher confirming your booking. These offices will make reservations for any hotel in the Netherlands.

Choosing a Hotel

All hotels are graded according to their facilities. The Netherlands Board of Tourism issues a free annual hotels brochure listing around 200 of the 2000 hotels in the Netherlands along with their star rating and facilities, which include information for handicapped guests. This is available at many of the VVV offices or directly from the NBT office in The Hague/Leidschendam. The ANWB offers a complete listing of hotels in the Netherlands, with ratings and facilities; it costs around f.25 and is available from ANWB offices. As a general rule, the quality of accommodation in the Netherlands is high – but you do get what you pay for. Prices vary according to the season; winter prices are commonly 30–50 percent lower than the published rates. But you need to ask for a discount – it will not be offered automatically.

Hotel Price Guide

Approximate prices for a double room with bathroom, usually including breakfast, are:

££££	Over f.280
£££	f.200–275
££	f.85–195
£	Under f.85

Hotel Listings

The following is a selective list of hotels in the major cities and towns covered by this guide, listed alphabetically by region. Hotels in Amsterdam are divided into three price categories.

AMSTERDAM

Expensive

American
97 Leidsekade, 1017 PN
Tel: 020-556 3000
Fax: 020-556 3001
Outstanding Art Nouveau building on the lively Leidseplein. Comfortable well-equipped bedrooms, popular café famous for Tiffany-style decor and colourful clientele, Night Watch cocktail bar with converted terrace. **££££**

Amstel Inter-Continental
1 Professor Tulpplein,
1018 GX
Tel: 020-622 6060
Fax: 020-6225808
Lavishly furnished 19th-century
hotel, on the banks of the River
Amstel (20 minutes' walk from the
centre). Popular among visiting
celebrities and royalty. High-class
cuisine in 2-star Michelin La Rive
restaurant and lavish Sunday
brunch. Terrace bar. **££££**

Blakes
384 Keizersgracht, 1016 GB
Tel: 020-530 2010
Fax: 020-530 2030
Opened in 1999, this exclusive
hotel in a monumental canalside
building has 26 luxuriously
furnished rooms and is managed by
Blakes, a London boutique hotel.
The restaurant and bar attract an
interesting mix of locals and hotel
guests. **££££**

Golden Tulip Barbizon Palace
59–72 Prins Hendrikkade, 1012 AD
Tel: 020-556 4564
Fax: 020-624 3353
Nineteen old houses converted into
this luxury hotel overlooking
Centraal Station. Interior is a
combination of the old Dutch,
French and post-modern styles.
Facilities include sauna and fitness
room, one-star Michelin Restaurant
Vermeer and extensive congress
facilities. **££££**

Grand Hotel Krasnapolsky
9 Dam, 1012 JS
Tel: 020-554 8080
Fax: 020-626 1570
Spacious comfortable rooms on
main Dam square facing the Royal
Palace. Breakfast served in a glass-
roofed winter garden. **££££**

Grand Westin Demeure
Oudezijds Voorburgwal 197,
1012 EX
Tel: 020-555 3111
Fax: 020-626 6286
This elegant hotel in the heart of
the city was once the city hall and a
royal residence. Café Roux is a
popular dining spot for locals as
well as guests. **££££**

Hotel de l'Europe
Nieuwe Doelenstraat 2–8,
1012 CP

Tel: 020-531 1777
Fax: 020-531 1778
Grand late 19th-century hotel
overlooking the River Amstel and
the Mint Tower. Facilities include
swimming pool, open-air terrace,
meeting rooms, fitness centre and
two restaurants. **££££**

Jan Luyken Residence
Jan Luykenstraat 58,
1071 CS
Tel: 020-573 0730
Fax: 020-676 3841
Late 19th-century building close to
major art museums and the
Concertgebouw. Quiet rooms and
bar/lounge with adjacent patio.
££££

Apollo
1077 BA
Tel: 020-673 5922
Fax: 020-570 5744
Modern luxury hotel on the
waterside, 2 miles (3km) south of
the centre; two restaurants with
waterside terraces and rooms with
a view. **££££**

Okura Amsterdam
Ferdinand Bolstraat 333,
1072 LH
Tel: 020-678 7111
Fax: 020-671 2344
Essentially a hotel for business
travellers, not far from the RAI and
with car parking space. Twenty-three
floors and a top-floor bar with a
spectacular view, several excellent
restaurants, shops and luxurious,
well-equipped fitness centre. A good
choice for gourmets – see *Where to
Eat* for the Yamazato Japanese
restaurant. **££££**

Pulitzer
Prinsengracht 315-331,
1016 GZ
Tel: 020-523 5235
Fax: 020-627 6753
Terrace of 17th- and 18th-century
canal-side residences and
warehouses, converted into a
charming luxury hotel. Exposed
brick, old beams, antiques and
beautiful furnishings. Popular
restaurant and bar. **££££**

Moderate
Ambassade
341 Herengracht, 1016 AZ
Tel: 020-626 2333

Ijmuiden

Fast flying ferries have begun
service from behind
Amsterdam's Centraal Station at
Steiger (landing) 7 which make a
pleasant half hour excursion to
Ijmuiden. Weekdays every half
hour from 7am–7:30pm;
weekends every hour. For further
information, tel: 020-639 2247

Fax: 020-624 5321
Highly popular, very friendly B&B
converted from a series of 17th-
and 18th-century canal-side
houses. Lots of antiques, paintings,
steep steps and spiral staircases.
Book well in advance. **£££**

Canal House
148 Keizersgracht,
1015 CX
Tel: 020-622 5182
Fax: 020-624 1317
American-owned hotel, expertly
converted from merchant houses
on a quiet canal. Lots of antiques
and a charming breakfast room.
£££

Die Port van Cleve
176 Nieuwe Zijdsvoorburgwal,
1012 SJ
Tel: 020-622 6429
Fax: 020-622 0240
Well located behind the Royal
Palace and Dam Square, this older,
comfortable hotel has a popular bar
and restaurant featuring Dutch
cuisine. **£££**

Estherea
305 Singel, 1012 WJ
Tel: 020-624 5146
Fax: 020-623 9001
17th-century canal house, just
minutes from Dam Square. Steep
stairs but there is a lift. **£££**

Toren
164 Keizersgracht,
1015 CZ
Tel: 020-622 6352
Fax: 020-626 9705
This friendly, well-located hotel is
situated in two canal houses and
recently underwent an extensive
renovation. The rooms are
comfortably furnished and the
buffet breakfast is extensive. There
is also a bar. **£££**

Budget

Acro
40 Jan Luykenstraat,
1071 CR
Tel: 020-662 0526
Fax: 020-675 0811
One of the better value budget
hotels close to the art museums
and the Vondelpark. Pleasant
modern furnishings in good
condition. **££**

Concert Inn Hotel
11 De Lairessestraat,
1071 NR
Tel: 020-305 7272
Fax: 020-305 7271
A family-operated B&B near the
Concertgebouw and museum
quarter. **£–££**

Hotel Fita
37 Jan Luykensstraat,
1071 CL
Tel: 020-679 0976
Fax: 020-664 3969
In the museum quarter between the
chic PC Hoofstraat shops and the
Van Gogh and Stedelijk museums.
Small, cosy and eccentric. **££**

Keizershof
618 Keizersgracht,
1017 ER
Tel: 020-622 2855
Fax: 020-624 8412
This is a cosy family-run B&B
offering rooms with canal or garden
views. **£–££**

Prinsen
Vondelstraat 38,
1054 GE
Tel: 020-616 2323
Fax: 020-616 6112
Converted 19th-century houses
situated in quiet street, two
minutes from Leidseplein and
Vondelpark. **££**

Wijnnobel
Vossiusstraat 9,
1071 AB
Tel: 020-662 2298
Cheap, clean and cheerful, with
views of the Vondelpark, just five
minutes from the Leidseplein and
museum quarter. No private
bathrooms. **£**

Winston
Warmoestraat 129,
1012 JA
Tel: 020-623 1380
Fax: 020-639 2308

Like an Amsterdam counterpart to
New York City's infamous Chelsea
Hotel, this hip little hotel caters to
artists, and each room, though
small, has its own unique
ambience. On a street leading to
the Red Light District and various
leather bars – and just a stone's
throw from Dam Square – it has a
lively bar, with poetry readings and
music at the adjacent Winston
Kingdom. **££**

Hotel Price Guide

Approximate prices for a double
room with bathroom, usually
including breakfast, are:

££££	Over f.280
£££	f.200–275
££	f.85–195
£	Under f.85

NOORD-HOLLAND

Bergen
Appartementen Eikenhof
1 Guurtjeslaan, 1861 EV Bergen
Tel: 072-589 5926
Fax: 072-581 2597
Feel at home in a comfortably
furnished studio apartment just
minutes from the dunes, woods or
centre of town. All rooms have a
terrace or balcony. **£££**

Schoorl
Hotel Jan van Scorel
89 Heereweg, 1871 ED Schoorl
Tel: 072-509 4444
Fax: 072-509 2941
This large family hotel is in a
tranquil setting among the dunes
and woods, offering comfort and
luxury in a natural setting. Facilities
include a pool, a sauna and fitness
room. **££££**

Enkhuizen
Die Port van Cleve,
74–78 Dyk,
1601 GK Enkhuizen
Tel: 0228-312510.
Fax: 0228-318765.
Located at the old harbour in the
city centre, this cosy hotel has 26
rooms and a popular restaurant
that offers terrace dining in summer

months, with a view of the
Drommedaris tower. Lift. **££££**

Het Wapen van Enkhuizen
59 Breedstraat,
1601 KB Enkhuizen
Tel: 0228-313 434
Fax: 0228-320 020.
A comfortable family-run hotel next
to the Stadhuis (city hall), which
has similar architecture to
Amsterdam's stately Palace on the
Dam. **££**

Haarlem
Golden Tulip Lion d'Or
34–36 Kruisweg,
2011 LC Haarlem
Tel: 023-532 1750
Fax: 023-532 9543
Just across from the train station,
this hotel has a history dating back
to 1820. Today it is operated by a
reputable Dutch chain, and the 34
rooms are modern and well-
equipped. There is also a 24-hour
reception, a lift, a bar/lounge and
an à la carte restaurant. **££££**

Carillon
27 Grote Markt,
2011 RC Haarlem
Tel: 023-531 0591
Fax: 023-531 4909
Simple, well-located lodgings across
from the Grote Markt in the heart of
the old city. **££**

Ijmuiden
Augusta Hotel-Restaurant
98 Oranjestraat,
1975 DD Ijmuiden
Tel: 0255-514 217
Fax: 0255-534 703
This intimate hotel between the
North sea locks and the fish
auction houses is over 90 years old
and remains stylish, with well-
furnished rooms and a charming
ambience. The elegant Art Deco
restaurant specialises in the catch
of the day and is worth a visit even
if you are only passing through. **£££**

ZUID-HOLLAND

Delft
Best Western Museum Hotel
189 Oude Delft,
2611 HD Delft

Tel: 015-2140 930
Fax: 015-2140 935
Located in the picturesque old
quarter along the canal. **£££**

Juliana
33 Maerten Trompstraat,
2628 RC Delft
Tel: 015-256 7612
Fax: 015-256 5707
A cosy, family-run hotel with a
garden, located just outside the city
centre. **£££**

De Plataan
10 Doelenplein,
2611 BP Delft
Tel: 015-212 6046
Fax: 015-215 7327
A family-run hotel in the heart of the
old historic centre within walking
distance of the museums and
marketplace. Comfortable rooms,
friendly staff, excellent breakfast
and a pantry for making tea and
coffee. **£££**

Hotel Price Guide

Approximate prices for a double
room with bathroom, usually
including breakfast, are:

££££	Over f.280
£££	f.200–275
££	f.85–195
£	Under f.85

The Hague

Carlton Ambassador
2 Sophialaan,
2514 JP Den Haag
Tel: 070-363 0363
Fax: 070-360 0535
Located in the quiet, historic
Mesdag quarter, near the
embassies, museums, Peace
Palace and main shopping streets.
The service is friendly, and each of
the 80 rooms is decorated in Old
Dutch or English style. **£££**

Corona
39–42 Buitenhof,
2513 AH Den Haag
Tel: 070-363 7930
Fax: 070-361 5785
Luxurious hotel on a central square
across from the Binnenhof and
shopping quarter, with a highly
regarded restaurant. **££££**

Esquire
65 van Aerssenstraat,
2582 JG Den Haag
Tel: 070-352 2341
Fax: 070-306 3366
This comfortable, friendly hotel is in
the charming Statenkwartier, with
many shops and restaurants
nearby. The hotel is easily
accessible via trams 7 and 10 from
The Hague's Centraal Station. It is
also close to Scheveningen if you
want to take in the sea air. **£££**

Inter-Continental Des Indes
54–56 Lange Voorhout,
2514 EG Den Haag
Tel: 070-363 2932
Fax: 070-345 1721
Former palace built in the 1850s,
once the haunt of Mata Hari and
Pavlova, now used by diplomats and
well-heeled travellers who rely on
the attentive service and luxurious
rooms. Even if you are not a hotel
guest, it is a great spot for
afternoon tea. **££££**

Steigenberger Kurhaus
30 Gev. Deynootplein,
2586 CK Scheveningen
Tel: 070-352 0052
Fax: 070-416 2646
Architecturally splendid with
marvellous views and elegant
rooms, located in Scheveningen,
the seaside resort town on the
outskirts of The Hague. The
Kandinsky Restaurant is the hotel's
pride. **££££**

**Restaurant-Hotel Savelberg (in
park Vreugd & Rust)**
14 Oosteinde, 2271 EH Voorburg
Tel: 070-387 2081
Fax: 070-387 7715
Situated in a small village, 15
minutes from The Hague city centre
by car. Early 18th-century manor
house with 14 rooms in a park
environment and a top culinary
restaurant frequented by
government heads and other
movers and shakers, where
owner/chef Henk Savelberg proudly
presides. Even if you don't stay
here, it is worth a summertime visit
to dine on the terrace. **££££**

Leiden

Golden Tulip Leiden
3 Schipholweg, 2316 XB Leiden

Tel: 071-522 1121
Fax: 071-522 6675
Just opposite the train station, this
dependable hotel has all the usual
amenities. **££**

Nieuw Minerva
23 Boommarkt, 2311 EA Leiden
Tel: 071-5126 358
Fax: 071-514 2674
Homely hotel furnished with
antiques, located in a group of
historic buildings on a quiet
tributary of the River Rhine. **££**

Rotterdam

Best Western Pax Hotel
658 Schiekade,
3032 AK Rotterdam
Tel: 010-466 3344
Fax: 010-467 5278
This small hotel is known for its
friendly atmosphere and
personalised service. Centrally
located, just 10 minutes' walk from
downtown shopping, the Doelen
concert hall and the World Trade
Centre. The 53 rooms are
comfortably furnished and there are
also studio apartments – each with
its own kitchen. **£££**

Bilderberg Park Hotel
70 Westersingel,
3015 LB Rotterdam
Tel: 010-436 3611
Fax: 010-436 4212
Well-located hotel along a canal in
the heart of the city, bordering
Museum Park and near the
shopping and entertainment centre.
The Empress Restaurant is
recommended and the fitness
centre offers facilities for working
out and relaxing. Within walking
distance of the train station,
accessible by tram and also has
parking facilities. **££££**

Golden Tulip Rotterdam
Coolsingel/4 Aert von Nesstraat,
3012 CA Rotterdam
Tel: 010-411 0420
Fax:010-413 5320
Housed in a historic building in the
heart of the city, this large hotel is
geared to the business traveller.
Rooms are fully-equipped and you
can enjoy breakfast with a view on
the roof terrace. **££££**

Hilton Rotterdam
10 Weena, 3012 CM Rotterdam

Tel: 010-414 4044
Fax: 010-411 8884
The focus of Rotterdam's business
life by day and its social life by
night. Located close to the train
station in the heart of the concert
and congress centre in "downtown"
Rotterdam. There are 254 air-
conditioned rooms and eight suites,
fully equipped with all the
amenities. A Holland Casino is in
the same complex. **££££**

Hotel New York
1 Koninginnenhoofd,
3072 AD Rotterdam
Tel: 010-439 0500
Fax: 010-484 2701
Located across the Maas river in
the former headquarters of the
Holland America Line, this is a
splendid and very popular hotel,
with uniquely furnished rooms and
waterfront views. Try to book the
room in the Clock Tower, which has
a waiting list of many months. The
bar and restaurant are both lively.
££££

NOORD-BRABANT

Den Bosch
Eurohotel Best Western
63–65 Hinthamerstraat,
5211 MG Den Bosch
Tel: 073-613 7777
Fax: 073-612 8795
Just opposite the majestic St Jan
Cathedral and near the quaint,
narrow roads and walkways of the
old city, this family hotel offers
typical Brabant hospitality. Rooms
are comfortable and fully equipped.
£££

Golden Tulip Central
98 Burg. Loefplein,
5211 RX Den Bosch
Tel: 073-692 6926
Fax: 073-614 5699
Centrally located near the
marketplace in the heart of the old
city. All the rooms are well-equipped
and comfortable, especially the
bathrooms. There are two
restaurants and a bar. An extensive
buffet breakfast is served in a
14th-century Gothic cellar. Limited
facilities for handicapped guests.
££££

LIMBURG

Kerkrade
Kasteel Erenstein
6 Oud Erensteinerweg,
6468 PC Kerkrade
Tel: 045-546 1333
Fax: 045-546 0748
A romantic 13th-century moated
castle that is part of the Camille
Oostwegel group (see page 246),
where you can dine lavishly in an
elegant setting and then stay
overnight in the adjacent Hotel
Brughof, an 18th-century former
farmhouse, run by the same
management. **££££**

Hotel Winselerhof
99 Tunnelweg,
6372 XH Landgraaf
Tel: 045-546 4343
Fax: 045-535 2711
Majestic 16th-century farmhouse
with lodging around a historic
courtyard. Authentic Italian cuisine
in the Restaurant Pirandello with
terrace dining in warm weather.
££££

Maastricht
De La Bourse
37 Markt, 6211 CK Maastricht
Tel: 043-321 8112
Fax: 043-321 7706
A friendly, family-run hotel in the city
centre, close to the train station.
Ask for a quiet room. **££**

Golden Tulip Derlon
6 Onze Lieve Vrouweplein,
6211 HD Maastricht
Tel: 043-321 6770
Fax: 043-352 1933
Charming hotel in old quarter built
on Roman foundations (with a
permanent exhibition of
archaeological finds in the lower
level of the hotel). **££££**

Holiday Inn Crown Plaza
1 Ruiterij, 6221 EW Maastricht
Tel: 043-350 9191
Fax: 043-350 9192
On the Maas river near the
Bonnefanten Museum. Ask for a
room with a view. **£££–££££**

Hotel Bergère
40 Stationsstraat,
6221 BR Maastricht
Tel: 043-325 1651

Fax: 043-325 5498
An elegant hotel with friendly staff
and comfortable rooms opposite
the train station. Has special
arrangements with Thermae 2000
(see page 247). **££££**

Valkenburg
Hotel Château St Gerlach
1 Joseph Corneli Allée,
6301 KK Bad Valkenburg
Tel: 043-604 2444
Fax: 043-604 2883
Restored to its former glory, this
spectacular complex dates from the
18th century. Gourmet restaurant
and modern facilities, including an
indoor swimming pool and spa.
Situated on the banks of the
romantic river Geul in the heart of a
400-hectare nature reserve. **££££**

Thermaetel
25 Cauberg,
6301 BT Bad Valkenburg
Tel: 043-601 6050
Fax: 043-601 4777
This modern hotel, with 60 rooms
and suites and an excellent
restaurant, is attached to the
Thermae 2000 health resort (see
page 247). **£££–££££**

UTRECHT

Grand Hotel Karel V
1 Geertebolwerk,
3511 XA Utrecht
Tel: 030-233 7555
Fax: 030-233 7500
This luxury hotel in the historic city
centre opened partially in Autumn
1999, and is due to be fully
completed in Winter 2000. On the
site of a former military hospital
with an illustrious history dating
back to the 14th century, this is
Utrecht's first 5-star hotel. Worth a
visit, if only for lunch or afternoon
tea. **££££**

Holiday Inn
24 Jaarbeursplein,
3521 AR Utrecht
Tel: 030-297 7977
Fax: 030-297 7999
Caters for business visitors to the
next-door Exhibition Centre, with a
panoramic restaurant and a bar on
the 20th floor. **££££**

Tulip Inn
10 Janskerkhof
3512 BL Utrecht
Tel: 030-231 3169
Fax: 030-231 0148
Charming hotel and restaurant in
the heart of the old quarter
opposite St Janskerk and local
shops. **££–£££**

OVERIJSSEL

Zwolle
Bilderberg Grand Hotel Wientjes
Stationsweg,
8011 CZ Zwolle
Tel: 038-425 4254
Fax: 038-425 4260
This monumental hotel in the city
centre dates to 1876 when it was
built as the residence for the mayor.
It has been a hotel since 1929 and
in recent years has been restored
to incorporate modern amenities.
The restaurant Bonaparte attracts
non-hotel guests for its inspired
cuisine and seasonal menu. **££££**

Blokzijl
Kaatje bij de Sluis
4 Domineeswal,
8356 DS Blokzijl,
Tel: 0527-291 833
Fax: 0527-291 836
This gourmet hideaway opened its
doors in 1974 and in 1985
expanded into an exclusive hotel-
restaurant with the addition of eight
luxury rooms in an adjacent
restored luxury mansion. **££££**

Bed & Breakfast

VVV tourist offices in major towns
keep lists of *pensions* (rooms in
private houses) where you can
stay the night inexpensively.
Prices are usually quoted per
person, rather than per room,
and breakfast is usually extra.
  The standard of
accommodation in *pensions*
does depend on the attitude of
the owner – varying from
spotless to appalling. It is best
to check the room on offer first,
before parting with your money.

Harlingen
Anna Caspari
67–71 Noorderhaven,
8861 AL Harlingen
Tel: 0517-412 065
Fax: 0517-414 540.
This family-run hotel is just minutes
from the harbour and the ferry
landing, and is situated on a busy
canal lined with yachts and old
sailing ships. If you don't mind
sacrificing the view, choose a quiet
room in the back. The restaurant
has an impressive wine list. **££**
Zeezicht
1 Zuiderhaven,
8861 CJ Harlingen
Tel: 0517-412 536
Fax: 0517-419 001
Close to the ferry landing on the
South harbour, this hotel has a
popular restaurant with a terrace
thronging with customers in
summer months. **££**

Leeuwarden
Leeuwarder Eurohotel
20 Europaplein,
8915 CL Leeuwarden
Tel: 058-213 1113
Fax: 058-212 5927.
A modern hotel with many
amenities in the historic city centre
near the imposing Olde Hova tower.
£££

GRONINGEN

De Doele
36 Grote Markt,
9711 LV Groningen
Tel: 050-312 7041
Fax: 050-314 6112.
This hotel is in a 200-year old
building in the city centre not far
from the train station. A typical
Dutch breakfast is included with the
room price. **£££**

Youth Hostels

There are more than 45 official
Youth Hostels in the Netherlands,
including two in Amsterdam (in
Vondelpark and on the
Kloveniersburgwal canal). If you do
not already belong to the YHA,
membership can usually be taken

Hotel Price Guide

Approximate prices for a double
room with bathroom, usually
including breakfast, are:

££££	Over f.280
£££	f.200–275
££	f.85–195
£	Under f.85

out on the spot. Most offer
dormitory accommodation but some
have private rooms. For full details,
contact the Nedelandse
Jeugdherberg Central, Professor
Tulpstraat 2, 1018 GX Amsterdam,
tel: 020-551 3155.
  In several cities, especially in
Amsterdam, you will find numerous
so-called "youth hostels", and you
may well be approached at the
station by touts looking for likely
customers. Some of these hostels
are well-run establishments offering
clean, basic accommodation –
though you should expect to have to
share rooms and bathrooms.
Others are fleapits and may be
located over a noisy all-night bar.
  Do not pay until you are satisfied
with the room on offer, and never
leave valuables unattended.

Camping

Dutch campsites are numerous and
well equipped. Some sites offer
trekkershutten – cabin
accommodation, with basic
furniture – for up to four people, for
around f.50 a night. The
Netherlands Board of Tourism (*see
Planning the Trip: Tourist Offices*)
publishes a free list of sites and
facilities. Cabins are best booked in
advance through The Netherlands
Reservation Centre (*see
Reservations at the start of this
section*).

Where to Eat

What to Eat

When it comes to dining out in the Netherlands, one may choose from the simplest fare in an "eetcafe" or the more costly, formal environs of a top level restaurant. In between, you can select from one of the many ethnic restaurants, which are especially predominant in larger cities like Amsterdam, Utrecht, Rotterdam, Maastricht or The Hague.

Eetcafés are a kind of informal local eatery, offering a daily changing menu with a choice of fish, meat or vegetarian main course. They are popular because they are reasonably priced but don't dine too late or the menu will be sold out.

Broodjes, filled sandwiches with cheese, meat or fish are the fare when it comes to lunch, and generally you need to consume a couple of them to fill you up. Soup and salads also predominate café menus these days.

As the dining out tradition continues to evolve, more and more influences from other European cities, and also from America, show up on the menus. Bagels, focaccia, *insalata caprese* (mozzarella and tomato salad) and basic bacon, lettuce and tomato club sandwiches crop up on many menus, and salad bars are an increasingly common sight in restaurants.

Home Cooking
When it comes to Dutch cooking, you will find restaurants that serve a traditional *hutspot*, featuring red cabbage, sauerkaut or endive. Vegetarians should be cautioned that these hearty stews are usually cooked with sausage chunks and

bits of bacon. This also goes for the winter soups like *erwten* (green pea soup) or *bruinenbonen* (brown bean). If you want a snack late at night, most bars/cafés serve *tostis*, a basic grilled cheese sandwich, often topped off with ham. Pancakes are a very Dutch tradition, and these are plate-sized versions which you can eat with a sweet topping of fruits or liqueurs, or savoury toasted sandwiches with ham, mushrooms, cheese or tomato ragout. *Poffertjes* are mini-pancakes topped with powdered sugar. For snacking on the run, stop at one of the herring wagons located in prime locations around the city. If you prefer not to eat your herring raw, you can get a *broodje* filled with smoked salmon, local shrimp, eel or mackerel. Walking along Dutch beaches in spring and summer, you'll find herring wagons every few metres.

Cheap Eats and Haute Cuisine
Pizzerias are abundant in the Netherlands and serve a variety of plate-sized pizzas, salads or pastas. Chinese restaurants are also ubiquitous, and many are combined with an Indonesian kitchen. The upscale restaurants favour French cuisine, but in recent years, there has been an influence of so-called "fusion" East meets West cooking, with chefs creating their own unique flavours and dishes.

Tipping
When dining out, bear in mind that 15 percent service charge and VAT are invariably included in bills, both for restaurants and bars, and there is no compulsion to tip in addition, although an additional 10 percent is generally expected at finer restaurants. At simple cafés and bars, just leaving the remaining change from your bill is quite acceptable.

Restaurant Listings

The following is a selective list of restaurants in the major cities and towns covered by this guide, listed alphabetically by region.

Restaurants in Amsterdam are listed in three price categories. See also the hotel listings for recommended hotel restaurants open to non-guests.

Price Guide

Price for a three-course meal for two, including two glasses of wine and service:

£££	More than f.250
££	f.150–250
£	Less than f.100

AMSTERDAM

Expensive
Amstel Hotel
1 Professor Tulpplein
Tel: 020-622 6060
Elaborate French cuisine in this intimate and elegant hotel restaurant. Formal, faultless service. Robert Kranenbourg was the first chef in Holland to earn two Michelin stars. **£££**

Yamazato
Okura Hotel
Ferdinand Bolstraat 333
Tel: 020-678 8351
Its reputation for having the best Japanese food in Holland is deserved, not only for the usual offerings like sushi and tempura, but also for its changing theme menus, which feature lobster and game when in season. Afterwards go up to the 23rd floor for a drink with a view. **£££**

Yam Yam
90 Frederik Hendrikstraat
Tel: 020-681 5097
In Amsterdam West, accessible by Tram 3, this modern trattoria features a wood-burning oven for making gourmet pizzas, imaginative pastas and salads, as well as daily fish and meat offerings. Casual and friendly. **££–£££**

Moderate
Chez Georges
3 Herenstraat
Tel: 020-626 3332
Belgian speciality restaurant with a seasonal menu. Intimate dining in

the heart of the chic grachtengordel quarter. **££**

D' Theeboom
210 Singel
Tel: 020-623 8420
A charming French bistro in an old warehouse along the canal. Imaginative, delicious cooking and friendly service. **££**

Dorrius
5 Nieuwezijds Voorburgwal
Tel: 020-420 2224
This is an institution of authentic Dutch cooking. Soups and *hutspots* abound and, depending on the season, you can enjoy them with duck, deer or even lamb sausages. In October, sauerkraut is featured in many varieties, from soup to a tart. Original furnishings from the 17th century complete the ambience. Dorrius also has a non-smoking room. **££**

Grekas Traiterie
311 Singel
Tel: 020-620 3590
What started as a Greek takeout has become a no-frills taverna with extremely authentic food. A vegetarian's delight, with a variety of *mezes* and salads, as well as a place for those who love a good *gyros* pita and a moussaka with bite. **£–££**

Lucius Seafood Restaurant
247 Spuisstraat
Tel: 020-624 1831
Fresh shellfish platters and a diverse selection of daily market produce. Bistro atmosphere and good wine list. Central location in the small restaurant row leading to Spui square. **££**

Morita-Ya
18 Zeedijk
Tel: 020-638 0756
Reasonably priced Japanese restaurant with good, simple fare on the edge of the Red Light district. Excellent sushi. If they are not too busy they will show you how to make your own. Order the razor thin beef which you cook at the table. Try to get the one table with the canal view. Closed: Wednesday. **££**

Pier 10
10 De Ruyterkade Steigers
Tel: 020-624 8276

Located behind Centraal Station with its own landing, this waterside restaurant requires reservations. In fact, the glass dining room with waterfront view of the IJ has two seatings per evening. The menu changes seasonally and the chef does wonderful things with fish and game. **££**

Price Guide

Price for a three-course meal for two, including two glasses of wine and service:

£££	More than f.250
££	f.150–250
£	Less than f.100

Cheap Eats

Bojo
Lange Leidsedwarsstraat 51
Tel: 020-622 7434
Good value Indonesian food just off Leidseplein. Open all night so it attracts the party crowd. **$**

Centra
29 Lange Niezel
Tel: 020-622 3050
Take a walk on the wild side when you dine at this wonderful Spanish tapas "dive", which also serves a mean paella or *zarzuela*. Share a table with locals, enjoy the Rioja, flamenco music and reasonable prices. This is a taste of Spain in the heart of the Red Light district. **$**

De Blauwe Hollander
Leidsekruisstraat 28
Tel: 020-623 3014
Straightforward wholesome Dutch food in a cosy setting. Spare ribs are a favourite, and so too is the variety of *hutspots*. **$**

Golden Chopsticks
1 Oude Doelenstraat
Tel: 020-620 7040
This hole-in-the-wall in the Red Light district offers delectable Chinese fare like steamed oysters in black bean sauce, Peking duck or whole fish with vegetables and tofu. If you prefer a more upmarket ambience, go upstairs to their sister restaurant Oriental City. Both attract a loyal crowd of Chinese customers. **$**

Golden Temple Vegetarian Restaurant
126 Utrechtsestraat
Tel: 020-626 8560
Some people come just for the salad buffet, but the main courses feature Indian, Mexican and vegetarian cuisine. **$**

La Brasa Steak Restaurant
16 Harlemmerdijk
Tel: 020-625 4438
Choose from a variety of tender steaks or a leg of lamb in this serious meat-eating environment, which uses a charcoal method of grilling. For non-red meat fans, a tender half chicken is another option. Fresh vegetables, salad and baked potatoes are included. Wines from Argentina and Chile complement the meal. Reasonably priced and friendly service. **$**

The Pancake Bakery
191 Prisengracht
Tel: 020-625 1333
This is the place to try oversized Dutch pancakes, savoury or sweet. A cosy atmosphere in a 17th-century warehouse cellar on a canal. **$**

poentjak Pas
366 Nassaukade
Tel: 020-618 0906
Like dining in the home of an Indonesian aunt. Delicious, reasonable and a warm atmosphere. Order one *rijstaffel* for two and supplement it with some side dishes like spicy lamb in coconut sauce or the omelette stuffed with chicken and vegetables. **$**

De Portugees
39A Zeedijk
Tel: 020-427 2005
Authentic Portuguese fare and wine in a modern ambience. Try the pork and clams cooked in a *cataplana*. The owners have just opened a tapas café across the street. **$**

Speciaal
142 Nieuwe Leliestraat
Tel: 020-624 9706
Off the beaten path in the Jordaan district, but good Indonesian food, including *rijsttafel*, in a semi-tropical setting. The restaurant attracts a loyal local clientele among the tourists. **$**

Witteveen
256 Ceintuurbaan
Tel: 020-662 4368
This elegant Old World restaurant takes you back in time. A simple menu of classics like filet of sole and *entrecôte* is offered. Oyster platters when in season. **$**

DELFT

Le Vieux Jean
3 Heilige Geestkerkhof
Tel: 015-213 0433
This charming restaurant celebrated its 25th anniversary in 1999. The menu is classic French with a modern touch and changes seasonally. The house speciality, sweetbreads with lobster sauce, is available year-round. **£££**

HAARLEM

Lezer
37 Spaarne
Tel: 023-533 5525
Just across from the Teylers Museum with a waterfront view, this restaurant is the pride of owner Ron Lezer. His imaginative menu has vegetarian offerings, as well as fish and meat, and there is a very impressive wine list. **£££**

Ma Brown's
31–33 Nieuwe Groenmarkt
Tel: 023-531 5829
Traditional English cooking dating back several centuries – "before the French influence," according to proprietor/chef Michael Cowley. Afternoon teas are served the first and third Sunday of the month. Reservations a must. Open Tues–Sun for dinner. **£££**

De Oude Florijn £££
28 Lange Kerkstraat
Tel: 023-531 1502
A traditional brown café, close to the Grote Kerk, with a devoted crowd of locals who come to drink draft beer or jenever in the Old Dutch atmosphere that pervades the place.

Café de Roemer
17 Botermarkt
Tel: 023-532 5267

A popular *eetcafé* on the Botermarkt square, featuring simple, inexpensive fare for lunch and a daily changing menu for dinner. **££**

THE HAGUE

Corona Hotel £££
39–42 Buitenhof
Tel: 070-363 7930
Fax: 070-361 5785
Sophisticated French cuisine in an elegant ambience.

Djawa
12a Mallemolen
Tel: 070-363 5763
The Hague boasts some of the best Indonesian restaurants in Europe and Djawa is considered one of the best restaurants in The Hague. Try some of the special dishes from Middle Java, Bali and Sumatra. Not all of the dishes are spicy, but do brave *Rendang Padang*, a piquant beef dish with coconut and spices, or the *Pete Ketjap*, chicken with Indonesian beans. Also recommended is the mixed satay – five kinds of grilled meats. The *Ikan Bali* or *Ikan Mangoot* are two spicy fish dishes.
And remember that beer or tea go better with Indonesian food than wine. **$**

It Rains Fishes
123 Noordeinde
Tel: 070-365 2598
The first address in The Hague to feature fusion cuisine with the emphasis on Thai-French. Begin with the house apéritif, Champagne with ginger liqueur, then the spicy coconut soup served with lobster and chicken. If you like it hot, choose from courses marked with one, two or three peppers. There are also less piquant choices.Try the whole fish or shellfish, served with three types of curry sauce. Between courses, a pot of warm chicken broth is served to aid digestion. **££**

Kandinsky
Kurhaus Hotel
30 Gevers Deynootplein,
Scheveningen
Tel: 070-416 2636

Fax: 070-416 2646
Innovative classic cuisine in an elegant setting which attracts locals as well as hotel guests. Menu changes with the seasons. **£££**

Le Bistroquet
98 Lange Voorhout
Tel: 070-360 1170
Diplomats and the theatre-going crowd love to lunch or dine at this cosy bistro, which features blinis with house-smoked salmon and Zeeland oysters. Extensive wine list with half bottles. Terrace dining in summer. **££**

Le Haricot Vert
9a Molenstraat
Tel: 070-365 2278
Family-run French bistro with "old Paree" atmosphere in a stylish shopping street in the city centre. Start with the "indulgence platter" (*verwen plateau*) which features a little taste of house appetisers like country paté, smoked salmon, small Dutch shrimps and Parma ham. Although fish soup is the house speciality, the mustard soup is not to be missed. **££**

Mero
50 Schokkerweg,
Scheveningen
Tel: 070-352 3600
This "seafood shack" on the site of

Drinking Notes

The most popular drinks are fresh coffee and lager. Holland is the world's number one producer of beer and the local lager is served in cafés and restaurants throughout the country, usually in 25cl measures. Heineken is the most popular. Foreign brands are available at much higher prices. The native gin is *jenever*, drunk neat (and traditionally knocked back in one) or with a beer chaser. Various varieties include *oude* (old), which is the sweeter, and *jonge* (young), the more powerful. The place to try out the local spirits and liqueurs is a *proeflokaal* or tasting house, the best known being De Drie Fleschjes in Amsterdam (see *Nightlife*).

a canning factory in Scheveningen's old harbour attracts an upmarket crowd for its fresh assortment from calamari to caviar. House specialities include fried *calamari bottarga* and dover sole wrapped in seaweed. The laid-back owner will make you feel welcome, especially if you order a fish soup or a platter of oysters. Great wine selection also. **££**

LEIDEN

Jill's
6–9 Morsstraat
Tel: 071-514 3722
This brasserie/restaurant, situated in the heart of the city, offers different menus in adjoining facilities for either a quick lunch or a more leisurely three-course meal. Friendly service and a pleasant ambience. **££**

ROTTERDAM

Blauwe Vis
33 Weena-zuid
Tel: 010-213 4243
This is a late night dinner and dancing spot in a former pedestrian

Cafés

Every Dutch town has a choice of cafés, invariably serving good coffee – often with apple tart or spicy biscuits. A typical brown café is an intimate, semi-bohemian bar with nicotine-stained walls (hence the name), rugs on tables, sawdust on the floor and newspapers to peruse. These are usually frequented by the locals (as well as tourists) and are places where you can often get good quality food at reasonable prices or linger over a drink and a book on a rainy afternoon.

Cafés displaying a marijuana plant or a green and white placard sell soft drugs as well as coffee. See the Nightlife section for café and bar listings.

Price Guide

Price for a three-course meal for two, including two glasses of wine and service:

£££	More than f.250
££	f.150–250
£	Less than f.100

tunnel – one of Rotterdam's unique nightspots. **££**
Brasserie Boompjes
701 Boompjes
Tel: 010-413 6070
Built overlooking the Meuse river, with wonderful views and a lively bistro ambience. **££**
Café Restaurant Loos
1 Westplein
Tel: 010-411 7723
In the maritime quarter, this restaurant attracts an artistic crowd. Dine simply or extravagantly in a post-modern ambience. **££**
Chalet Suisse
31 Kievitslaan
Tel: 010-436 5062
Located in the park in the maritime quarter, by the Euromast. Swiss/Dutch kitchen. **££**
Dewi Sri
20 Westerkade
Tel: 010-436 0263
Colonial atmosphere and regal *rijsttafels* (and prices). **££**
Estaminet Het Gelagh
40B Witte de Withstraat
Tel: 010-240 0333
Charming *eetcafé* with Belgian influence. Try some mussels or *witlof* (endive) and quaff a beer from the tap. If there are no tables available, go across the street to their filial restaurant Van Popering at No.51. **££**
Kantjil en de Tijger
76 Haringvliet
Tel: 010-213 1760
The name comes from an Indonesian fairy tale. The cuisine is typically Indonesian from the recipes of the owner's grandmother. Modern interior inhabited by a lively crowd who have adopted the newest location of this popular restaurant chain. Others are in The Hague and Amsterdam. **££**

Old Dutch
20 Rochussenstraat
Tel: 010-436 0344
Heavy beams create a good atmosphere for the traditional Dutch food. **£££**
Oma
136b 's-Gravendijkwal
Tel: 010-436 3114
This charming brown café pays homage to grandmothers (*omas*) with prints and old photographs lining the walls. The simple, inexpensive fare has a Spanish influence, so it is no surprise to find a paella on the menu next to an entrecote. Visit their other restaurant Opa ("grandfather") which has live music once a month and a vibrant atmosphere – it's at 49a Witte de Withstraat. **££**
Parkheuvel
21 Heuvellaan,
Tel: 010-436 0530
This is a Bauhaus-style building situated in the park overlooking the port, with terrace dining in the summer. **£££**

UTRECHT

Polman's Café-Restaurant
Corner Jansdam and Keistraat
Tel: 030-231 3368
Whether you come for lunch, dinner of a cup of coffee, this elegant 19th-century monument offers a unique atmosphere of days gone by. **££**
Pomo
22 Wittevrouwenstraat
Tel: 030-231 9272
This is a chance to try the exotic taste of the Surinam kitchen. A bit of soul cooking with some similarity to the Indian kitchen. Spicy peanut soup, *pom*, a kind of mashed sweet potato served with spicy chicken or lamb and roti bread. Reasonably priced, friendly service and pleasant ambience. **££**

Culture

Museums

There are more than 600 museums in Holland, with 440 of them listed in the *Attractions* booklet (f.1) from vvv offices. The entry price varies; some museums are free. A Museum Year Card gives free admission to all of them – see the box overleaf.

Most museums are open from Tues–Sun 10am–5pm. On public holidays they are normally open Sunday hours.

Performing Arts

Amsterdam, The Hague and Rotterdam take pride in their cultural centres: Het Muziektheater on Waterlooplein, the Anton Philips Zaal and De Doelen, respectively. The national opera, ballet and theatre companies are all based in Amsterdam, while The Hague and Rotterdam have their own resident orchestras and dance companies.

In Amsterdam, over the last weekend in August, theatre, dance and music companies from all over the Netherlands perform extracts from their year's forthcoming programme in the streets and squares of the city (the Uitmarkt). In June, an ambitious month-long arts programme called "Holland Festival", takes place in cultural centres in Amsterdam, featuring national and international artists.

Most performances are in Dutch but during the Holland Festival foreign companies also perform in different languages. For details contact: Holland Festival, Kleine Gastmanplantsoen 21, 1017 RP Amsterdam, or the Uitburo on the Leidseplein. There is also a new plan in Amsterdam to promote more English-speaking events for international guests year-round, and the vvv publishes brochures promoting these Amsterdam Arts Adventures in summer and winter months.

See *Festivals* for details of other special events in the arts.

The Top Art Galleries

● **Amsterdam:**
Rijksmuseum
42 Stadhouderskade
Tel: 020-6732121
The National Gallery of The Netherlands. Stupendous collection ranging from old Dutch Masters (Rembrandt's *Night Watch*) to Asiatic art and doll's houses. Open: daily 10am–5pm. Closed 1 January. (Tram: 1, 2, 5, 6, 7, 10, 16, 24, 25.)
Stedelijk Museum of Modern Art
13 Paulus Potterstraat
Tel: 020-573 2737
Continually changing displays of modern art. Open: Monday–Sunday 11am–5pm. (Tram: 2, 5, 20.)
Van Gogh Museum
7 Paulus Potterstraat
Tel: 020-570 5200
After a complete renovation the museum will reopen June 1999 with a new wing for exhibition space designed by Kisho Kurokawa. Outstanding collection of paintings and drawings of Vincent van Gogh and his contemporaries. Open: Tuesday–Saturday 10am–5pm, Sunday and public holidays 10am–6pm. (Tram: 2, 5, 16.)

● **The Hague:**
Mauritshuis
8 Korte Vijverberg
Tel: 070-302 3456
A Dutch Renaissance mansion which houses paintings by Rubens, Vermeer, Rembrandt and more – the Royal Collection of Old Masters. Open: Tuesday–Saturday 10am– 5pm, Sunday from 11am.
Museum Mesdag
Laan van Meerdervoort 7f
Tel: 070-362 1434
Hague and Barbizon school art, including Delacroix, Mauve and Breitner. Open: Tuesday–Sunday 12–5pm.
Schilderijengalerie Prins Willem V
Buitenhof 35
Tel: 070-318 2486
The country's first ever art gallery. Open: Tuesday–Sunday 11am–4pm.

● **Leiden:**
Stedelijk Museum De Lakenhal
(Municipal Museum)
28–32 Oude Singel
Tel: 0715-165360
Paintings by Rembrandt, Jan Steen, Lucas van Leyden and Gerard Dou.

Sculptures, decorative glass and silver from the 17th century; rooms in the styles of the 17th to 19th century. Open: Tuesday–Friday 10am–5pm, Saturday, Sunday and public holidays 12–5pm.

● **Otterlo (near Arnhem):**
Kröller-Müller Museum
Hoge Veluwe National Park
Tel: 0318-591041.
One of Europe's finest art museums. 276 Van Gogh paintings and others by Seurat, Mondrian, Braque, Gris. Modern sculptures in the garden include works by Moore and Maillol and Jean Dubuffet's *Jardin d'Email*. Open: Tuesday–Sunday 10am–5pm. (Bus 12 from Arnhem station.)

● **Rotterdam:**
Boijmans van Beuningen Museum:
Museum Park 18–20
Tel: 010-441 9400
From Old Masters to Surrealism and modern art. They will be renovating extensively in 1999, and some of the galleries will be closed during this time. Open: Tuesday–Saturday 10am–5pm, Sunday from 11am.

MUSIC

The Netherlands has several symphony orchestras of international repute. The Amsterdam Concertgebouw Orchestra achieved world-wide fame under the baton of Bernard Haitink, and in recent years under the able direction of Riccardo Chailly. The Netherlands Radio Philharmonic Orchestra is in residence at the Beurs van Berlage, Amsterdam's former stock exchange. The Rotterdam Philharmonic and the Residentie Orchestra of The Hague are also well known, with Rotterdam's leadership in the talented hands of conductor/musician Valery Gergiev. Small ensembles including the Eighteenth-Century Orchestra, the Amsterdam Baroque Orchestra and the Schonberg Ensemble are very successful.

Ticket Offices

● **Amsterdam:**
For most of the annual 12,000 concerts, theatre, ballet and opera performances in Amsterdam, seats can be booked in advance at one of the **vvv theatre booking offices** situated in the information offices at Stationsplein, Leidseplein and inside Centraal Station. Open: Monday–Saturday, 10am–4pm. No bookings by telephone. The monthly programme is available in "What's on in Amsterdam," f.3.50 from the **vvv**.

Tickets can also be booked at the **Amsterdam Uit Buro (AUB)** at 26 Leidseplein/corner. Marnixstraat, 1017 PT Amsterdam, tel: 020-621 1211. Open daily 10am–6pm.

● Reservations can be made from abroad via the **National Reservations Centre (NRC)**, P.O. Box 404, 2260 AK Leidschendam, tel: 070-419 5500, fax: 070-419 5519.

There is a wide range of jazz and improvised music; Willem Breuker, Louis Andriessen and Misha Mengelberg are among the leading names with an international reputation. A small venue for contemporary music is the Ijsbreker Café along the Amstel at 23 Weesperzijde.

OPERA AND MUSICALS

The main opera companies are: The Netherlands Opera Company, which stages about 10 productions a year, mainly in Amsterdam and The Hague; and the Forum Opera Company, which performs mostly in the east and south. Visiting companies often perform at the RAI congress centre. In recent years, The Netherlands Opera has achieved international prestige under the inspired direction of Pierre Audi.

Musicals are popular in the Netherlands. Several companies tour the country with Dutch productions and adaptations from foreign musicals, which are presented mainly at the elegant century-old Carr, on the Amstel.

BALLET

The Amsterdam-based National Ballet Company performs traditional, classical and romantic ballets. The Netherlands Dance Theatre in The Hague specialises in modern dance. The Scapino Ballet performs narrative ballets mainly for young people.

Many internationally respected dance companies with choreographers like William Forsythe and Pina Bausch visit Holland throughout the year.

Cinema

The Netherlands not only shows imported films in the original language with Dutch subtitles, but is also acquiring an international reputation for its own home-produced films. The Rotterdam Film

Festival (January/February) and the Utrecht Film Festival (September) provide a chance to see the past year's production of Dutch films. In late November the International Documentary Film Festival takes place in Amsterdam.

For Free Admission...

The **Museum Year Card** allows free entry to all museums in the Netherlands. The card costs f.55 for people aged 19 to 64; those aged 18 or under pay f.25, and those aged 65 or more pay f.45. It is valid for one calendar year.

The Museum Card can be obtained at **vvv** Tourist Information offices and many museums. A passport photo is required when purchasing the card. Special exhibitions with a separate admission charge may not be covered by the Museum Card.

Nightlife

After dark in Amsterdam, entertainment focuses on three main areas: Leidseplein, for lively discos and nightclubs; Rembrandtplein for clubs, cabarets and strip shows pandering to older tastes; and the Red Light District, notorious for scantily dressed females sitting in windows and notice-boards saying "room to hire".

Strip shows, porn videos and sex shops centre on the main canals of Oude Zijds Voorburgwal and Oude Zijds Achterburgwal. The smaller, sleazier streets leading off these two canals are best avoided, and you are advised never to take photographs.

On an entirely different note, you could spend the evening on a candle-lit canal cruiser, with wine and cheese or full dinner provided. On-board theatre is sometimes provided as an added attraction.

In any case, try out one of the numerous brown cafés (*see Where to Eat: cafés*), a classic grand café with a reading table and more of a modern ambience, or, alternatively, one of the new-wave bars, with cool, whitewashed and mirrored walls, an abundance of greenery and a long list of cocktails. Some cafés and bars have live music, often jazz or blues. They usually post notices in the windows announcing events.

Here is a selection of recommended nightspots, including cafés, bars, clubs and music/dance venues:

Americain
American Hotel, Leidseplein 28
Splendid Art Nouveau café

overlooking Leidseplein; very popular amongst fashionable locals. Mata Hari had her wedding reception here.

Arena
51 's-Gravesandsestraat
This former convent houses a budget hotel, restaurant, café and popular disco which is open Thursday, Friday and Saturday nights until 4am. On the east side of town outside the centre, with parking on premises.

Bamboo Bar
Lange Leidsedwarsstraat 66
Live jazz and blues in an exotic setting.

BIMhuis
Oudeschans 73
The "in place" for jazz, especially modern and improvisational.

Boom Chicago
Leidseplein
Tel: 020-423 0101
An improvisational comedy club which performs in English at a renovated theatre.

De Drie Fleschjes
Gravenstraat 18
Traditional proeflokaal just off the Dam where you can sample local spirits and liqueurs.

Escape
11 Rembrandtplein
A cavernous disco with a variety of music, and a lively, mixed crowd.

Eylders
Korte Leidsedwarsstraat
Former haunt of the literati, just by Leidseplein. Occasional modern art exhibitions.

Havana
Reguliersdwarsstraat 17–19
Up-market gay bar with yuppie clientele and super-cool atmosphere – starting bar for later drinking and dancing at the Exit disco at No 42.

Het Hok
Lange Leidsedwarsstraat 134 café specialising in chess, backgammon and draughts.

Hoppe
Spui 20
Smoke-filled and crowded bar, unremarkable except for the fact that the locals all love it. Crowds usually spill out on to the street. (Hoppe has been closed since

Summer 99 for drug violations; it may reopen in 2000)

Amstelstraat 24
Music is a mix of all the new sounds, something for everyone, and special theme evenings make this one of the city's top discos.

Melkweg
Lijnbaansgracht 234a
Off-beat arts centre-cum-club near Leidseplein, with concert hall, café, disco, experimental plays (some in English) and art exhibitions. Dope and space cakes for sale.

The Ministry
12 Reguliersdwaarsstraat
This has attracted many of the nightclubbers who used to frequent the Roxy before it burned down. Something for everyone in terms of music and ambience.

Odeon
Singel 460
Elegant 17th-century house, converted into disco and café, with suitably smart clientele.

Paradiso
Weteringschans 6–8
Just off Leidseplein. The hot spot for rock, reggae and live pop concerts.

Schiller
Rembrandtplein 26
This café is worth visiting for the splendid Art Deco interior and interesting after-theatre crowd.

Sinners in Heaven
Wagenstraat 3
The hip, "upmarket" crowd comes here to dance and mingle.

Soul Kitchen
Amstelstraat 32
The name says it all – good dance venue.

Look for the free listings magazine *Den Haag Day by Day* at hotels and the **VVV**.

Nightlife revolves around the music bars and late-night cafés, such as **Jazz Café Le Musicien**, Van Bylandstraat 191 (live bands Wednesdays and Fridays), and **La Valetts**, Nieuwe Schoolstraat 13a. The casino by the Kurhaus Hotel, **Scheveningen**, is open daily 2pm–2am.

Rotterdam

Look for the local listings magazine *Rotterdam This Month*, free from hotels and the **vvv**. A popular jazz venue is the **Jazzcafé Dizzy**, s'Gravendijkwal 129. **Rotown**, 19 Nieuve Binnenweg, hosts local and well-known bands during the week, or visit Holland Casino's **The Gambler** at 624 Weena for another kind of action. At the Hilton Hotel, **Weena 10**, the disco, attracts a cosmopolitan crowd and the hotel's casino is open 2pm–2am. **De Après Skihut**, 29 Stadhuisplein, is a lively spot modelled on a skihut, with dancing and entertainment.

Utrecht

Look for the free English-language directory in *'n out Utrecht*, "a guide to eating, drinking, going out and sleeping." Utrecht has a lively scene around the Oude Gracht, where cafés and restaurants line the lower level of the tree-lined canals. You can dine on Indian, Italian and other international food, or enjoy a Dutch pancake.

Festivals

January

Leiden, 14–21 January: a lively jazz week in this university town.
Rotterdam, 25 January–4 February: International Film Festival.

February

Big pre-Lent carnivals take place all over the country, especially in the southern provinces of Noord Brabant and Limburg, but with parades in Amsterdam and The Hague as well. Forget about Rio; temperatures are low here in February, so don't expect scanty costumes. Floats are wittily decorated, and there is always lots of beer.
Rotterdam, 26 February–4 March: The Dutch ABN Bank hosts its International Tennis Tournament which brings world-class stars to Rotterdam.

March

Amsterdam, 1–3 March: the Antiquarian Book Fair; Good Friday: the dramatic and emotional St Matthews Passion is performed by the Concertgebouw Orchestra.
Amsterdam, Maastricht, 9–17 March: the European Fine Art Fair brings hundreds of antique and fine art dealers together and attracts thousands of visitors.
Lisse: 29 March–24 May: this is the month the world-famous tulip park, De Keukenhof, opens for the bulb season.

April

Amsterdam, 1 April–31 October: the city switches on its

illuminations, turning the canals into a fairyland.
Alkmaar, 13 April–14 September: the traditional cheese market opens with porters wearing their historic guild uniforms. There are usually demonstrations of old crafts during the very colourful market that is held every Friday.
The Hague, 15 April–21 October: the International Rose Exhibition featuring 20,000 roses and some 350 varieties, opens in Westbroekpark.

May

Amsterdam, every Sunday, May–October: Antique Markets on the Waterlooplein.
The Hague, May and June: the beautiful Japanese Gardens at Clingendael Park are open; 3 May–30 September: the city's Antique Market, along the elegant Lange Voorhout, opens every Thursday (until 9pm) and Sunday (until 6pm).
Scheveningen: the wonderfully colourful Vlaggetjesdag at Scheveningen Harbour marks the opening of the herring season. All the fishing boats are decorated with flags, there is a traditional market and, of course, lots of fish to eat.
  The Dutch have a way of eating herring which will either delight or repel you. They first dip the raw, salted fish into a dish of chopped onion, raise it by the tail above their tilted head and then slowly lower the fish into open mouths. At this point you either swallow or gag.

June

This is Holland Festival month, with various events taking place around the country.
Amsterdam: International rowing competition, the Bosbaan; 3 June–2 September: the summer-long Open-Air Theatre season begins in Vondelpark, where it has all been happening since the 1960s.
Scheveningen, 2 June: a wonderfully exhilarating Air Show with stunt flying demonstrations;

16–24 June: fly your kite, it's great fun, at the International Fokker Kite Festival, with kite fliers from as far as Japan coming to fly their often strange-looking but always wonderfully colourful kites on the beaches of Scheveningen.

The Hague, 9 and 10 June: horse-lovers flock for the grand equestrian event, called Paardendag. Two days of events, again on the lovely Lange Voorhout.

Rotterdam, 16–23 June: Poetry International. Draws poets and poetry lovers from around the world.

Assen: the big, and very noisy, International Netherlands Motorcycling T.T. Grand Prix. Big bikes, newest in fashion leathers, lots of fun, bring your own earplugs.

July

Amsterdam: International Chess Tournament, with many well-known Masters. International Ballet Festival at the Muziektheater.

The Hague, 13–15 July: the North Sea Jazz Festival with all the big names in jazz at the Congress Centre. A must for jazz lovers.

Zandvoort, 26–29 July: the KLM Golf Open Championship.

Scheveningen: street parades, with jazz and dixieland concerts, take place along the main boulevard.

August

Rotterdam, 15–19 August: the year's major horse show.

Leersum, 18 August: a wonderfully colourful Flower Parade.

Yerseke, 18 August: this is the month to eat mussels and the fishing village of Yerseke is the place to eat them, especially on Mussel Day, the first of the new season.

Amsterdam, last weekend in August:Uitmarkt Festival, when previews of the next year's artistic events are performed in the city streets and squares.

Scheveningen, last weekend in August: major fireworks display for the International Firework Festival.

Zandvoort, 26 August: the International Motor Races start, with Formula 1 drivers competing for the Zandvoort Grand Prix.

September

Taking place countrywide (date varies each year) is the Monument Preservation Day, when listed buildings around the country are opened to the public.

Amsterdam, 3–9 September: the famous Gaudeamus Music Week.

The Hague, third Tuesday in September: the State Opening of Parliament by Her Majesty Queen Beatrix. Colourful parade along Lange Voorhout to the Binnenhof (Parliament Square), with the Queen sitting in the traditional Golden Coach.

October

Delft, 11–25 October: the major Art and Antiques Fair.

Scheveningen, 19–21 October: Pall Mall Export's International Wind-surfing Event. The event that launched a thousand cigarette ads; 28 October: International Beach Motorcycle Races.

November

Amsterdam, 1–4 November: "Jumping Amsterdam", the international horse show at the RAI complex.Countrywide, 17 November (or nearest weekend): this is the time for children, when St Nicholas arrives in the country from his home in Spain. At all major harbours a traditional steam boat pulls in, complete with St Nicholas, riding on his white stallion and accompanied by his Moorish assistant known as Black Pete.

December

Gouda, 15–25 December: beautiful scenes in this old town where the historical town square is lit by candles. The lighting of the Christmas Tree, accompanied by singing and a carillon concert, is a major crowd-puller.

Excursions

Boat Trips & Charter

Water is everywhere in Holland and there are always boats for hire and local tours. Most trips have multi-lingual guides. Some of the main tourist attractions are listed below.

NOORD-HOLLAND

Amsterdam

Viewing Amsterdam's canal-side mansions from a glass-topped canal cruiser gives you a different perspective on the city. There are several cruise companies and a detailed leaflet may be obtained from the **VVV**, which will also handle bookings. All cruisers have toilets. Arrangements may be made for groups; there may be dining facilities and music on board.

Most cruises run every 15 minutes in summer and every 30 minutes in winter. The different trips take 60, 75 or 90 minutes. Seeing the city by night on the candlelight and wine cruise, which

The Museum Boat

Many Amsterdam museums lie on or near the canals. Two boats run every 45 minutes from jetties all over town. On each boat a guide gives details about the different museums. A day ticket costs f.12 and entitles you to discounts on museum entrance charges. A combi-ticket gives free entrance to three museums of your own choice. Tickets may be bought from the **VVV** tourist office.

runs daily in summer at 9.30pm, except 2 May, will take 2 hours.

Departure points
Rederij Amsterdam: opposite Heineken Brouwerij, 1a Nicolaas Witsenkade, 1017 ZS, tel: 020-626 5636 (75 mins/f.15).
Holland International: opposite Central Station, 33a Prins Hendrikkade 1012 TK, tel: 020-622 7788 (60 mins/f.15).
Rederij P Kooy BV: near Spui, 125 Rokin, 1012 KK, tel: 020-623 3810 (60 mins/f.13).
Rederij Lovers BV: Prins Hendrikkade 25, 1000 AV, tel: 020-622 2181 (facilities for disabled/60 mins/f.15).
Meyers Rondvaarten: Damrak, jetty 4–5, 1012 LG, tel: 020-623 4208 (60 mins/f.12).
Algemene A-Dam Rederij Noord-Zuid: Stadhouderskade 25, opposite Parkhotel, 1071 ZD, tel: 020-679 1370 (75 mins/f.17.50).

OUTSIDE THE CITY

For excursions along the picturesque river Vecht or the Loosdrechtse waterway (in Het 'Gooiland) from May to September, contact Wolfrat Rondvaarten, Oud Loosdrechtsedijk 165, 1231 LV, Loosdrecht, tel: 035-5823309.
Rederij Naco, just behind Amsterdam's Centraal Station at Landing 7, has daily excursions to Ijmuiden's old harbour where one can enjoy a fresh fish meal at local restaurants like Henk Schorl or the more upmarket Imko's. In summer, they also offer excursions to the fort island of Pampus, which includes a visit to Muiderslot Castle. For more information, tel: 020-626 2466.

ZUID-HOLLAND

A *leede* is a watercourse, so the name of **Leiden** may be interpreted as "a town on the watercourses". During the summer season there are boat trips on the Leiden canals. Departures from Beestenmarkt and Hoogstraat. In the afternoons and evenings there are boat trips to the Kagerplassen lakes (windmill cruise). Information: Rederij Rembrandt, tel: 071-513 4938. Rowing boats are for hire in the summer at the bridge, Rembrandtburg, tel: 071-514 9790.

ZEELAND

This area is popular with those who enjoy boating. Sailing schools and boat hire companies abound, with one in virtually every harbour. A special attraction lies in the traditional old sailing vessels of Zeeland. These can be hired, with skipper, from Zeilvloot "De Zeeuwse Stromen", Nieuwe
Bogerdstraat 7 4301 CV, Zierikzee, tel: 0111-415 830.

NOORD-BRABANT

At **Lage Zwaluwe**, Biesboschtours, 7 Biesboschweg, offer boat trips in magnificent scenery. Easter Sunday–June and September, Sundays and public holidays; July and August daily.

LIMBURG

In **Maastricht**, contact Rederij Stiphout Bordertour, 27 Maaspromenade, tel: 043-3254 151. Several boat trips on the Maas. January–March 2pm and 4pm; 15 April–29 September daily on the hour 10am–5pm. Trips take 1–3 hours (including caves); adults f.8–13.50, children f.4.75–7.75.

GRONINGEN & FRIESLAND

Around the **IJsselmeer** and in the northern provinces of Groningen and Friesland, boat rental agencies offer a range of craft, some of which have living accommodation. Especially recommended are the week-long or weekend trips aboard the many antique sailing ships moored in **Harlingen**. For more information, write to: Rederij Vooruit Holland, Geeuwkade 9, 8651 AA IJlst, tel: 0515-531 485. Day boat trips and sailing boat (with skipper) rentals can also be arranged through Zeilvloot Harlingen, Noorderhaven 17, 8861 AJ, tel: 0517-417 101.

Coach Tours

These may be booked through any **VVV** office. All depart from Amsterdam.

City Sightseeing
Duration 2–3 hours. Summer, 10am daily. Winter, 2.30pm daily. A drive through Amsterdam which takes in an open-air market, a windmill, the Royal Palace and a visit to a diamond-cutting workshop. Plus, in winter, a ticket for a canal ride.

Marken and Volendam
Summer, 10am and 2.30pm daily. Winter, 10am daily and 2.30pm Sunday only. Duration approx 3 hours. A chance to see the traditional costumes still worn by many residents in these old fishing villages. Also included is a visit to "De Jacobs Hoeve" cheese farm at Volendam or to the cheesemaker "De Catharina Hoeve" at the Zaanse Schans, plus windmills.

Grand Holland Tour
Summer 10am daily. Winter 10am Tues, Thurs and Sun. Duration 8 hours. Lunch not included. First to

Steam Trains

● **Hoorn-Medemblik** (Noord-Holland): historic steam train ride through characteristic landscape and attractive villages. Open: May to beginning of September (except Monday).
● **Goes-Oudelande** (Zeeland): steam train ride through the typical South Beveland landscape with fields divided by hedges. Open: mid-May to beginning September and Christmas holiday.

the flower market at Aalsmeer (or to a clog factory on Saturday and Sunday), on to a porcelain factory in Delft, Rotterdam and then The Hague, including, in summer, the miniature village of Madurodam.

Tulip fields and Keukenhof flower exhibition

10am and 2.30pm daily. 25 March–14 May. Duration 3 hours. A drive through the colourful flower-growing region with a visit to a bulbgrower and the Keukenhof flower exhibition.

Alkmaar Cheese Market and Windmills

9am departures every Friday from 21 April–15 September. Duration 4 hours. Alkmaar on Fridays shows the traditional market life of old Holland. Porters in ancient dress carry cradles heaped with yellow cheeses. Then to de Zaanse Schans to visit a windmill.

Note: For suggested cycle tours, see the *Getting Around* section.

Shopping

Opening Times

Shops are generally open 9am–6pm or 6.30pm Tues– Fri, 1–6pm or 6.30pm Mon (closed am), and 9am–5pm Sat. On Sunday it is almost impossible to shop, although you may find some grocery stores open in the larger cities. All shops must close for one half-day a week by law, but all of them display their opening times in the door or window. Shops open late (until 9pm) one day a week in big cities: Thursday in Amsterdam and The Hague; Friday in Rotterdam and Delft.

Amsterdam

Bargains are a rarity but browsing is fun, particularly in the markets and the small specialist shops. For general shopping the main streets are Kalverstraat and Nieuwendijk, for exclusive boutiques try P.C. Hooftstraat and for the more off-beat shops, head to the Jordaan northwest of centre where many of the local artists live. Two unusual shopping centres are worth a visit: Magna Plaza opposite the Royal Palace and Kalvetoren on Kalverstraat.

The **VVV** Tourist Office produces brochures on shopping for antiques and diamonds. These give maps, route descriptions, places of interest and a list of addresses and shop specialities.

ANTIQUES

Nieuwe Spiegelstraat (starting opposite the Rijksmuseum) is lined with small and immaculate antique shops. Look out for old Dutch tiles,

copper and brass, glass, pewter, snuff boxes, clocks and dolls; and look for the names of respected dealers like Frides Lameris, Ines Stodel, Frans Leidelmeijer and Jaap Polak. In markets, beware of imitation antique copper and brass, made in Tunisia.

ART & PRINTS

The major museums and art galleries have excellent reproductions of paintings in their collections, particularly the Rijksmuseum and the Stedelijk. There are numerous small commercial galleries selling original oil paintings, watercolours, drawings, engravings and sculpture. For old prints and engravings, try Antiek-markt de Looier, Elandsgracht 109.

BOOKS

The city has an exceptionally large choice of books, both new and second-hand. For second-hand English-language books, try Book Traffic, Leliegracht 50 (near the Anne Frank House). Allert de Lange, Damrak 62, is strong on literature, travel and art; the Athenaeum Boekhandel & Nieuwscentrum, Spui 14–16, has a superb selection of literature and academic books and very helpful staff. Spui also has a weekly book market.

CLOTHES

The major department stores are concentrated along Kalverstraat and Nieuwendijk, but the biggest and most prestigious is De Bijenkorf, Dam 1. For designer labels, try P.C. Hooftstraat, Rokin, Van Baerlestraat and Leidsestraat; for less conventional boutiques, the Jordaan or the side streets between the canals are the places to go. Also visit Magna Plaza shopping complex opposite the Royal Palace or Kalvertoren on the Kalverstraat by the Muntplein.

JEWELLERY

Jewellery shops all over town have eyecatching displays of modern and traditional pieces, some original and designed on the spot. Note: the fact that Amsterdam is a major diamond-cutting centre doesn't mean you'll get them cheap. For modern jewellery designs, visit Hans Appenzeller at 1 Grimburgwal or Anneke Schat at 20 Spiegelgracht.

PORCELAIN

Cheap imitations of the familiar blue Delftware are sold all over town. The genuine article, always with a capital "D", is sold at Royal Delft's official retail branch, De Porceleyne Fles, Muntplein 12. You can watch painting demonstrations in their showrooms.

Focke & Meltzer, with branches at P.C. Hooftstraat 65–69 and the Okura Hotel, have a good choice of porcelain and glass, and some

Value Added Tax

Tourists from non-European Union countries are entitled to claim back the 20 percent local Value Added Tax (BTW) on any goods purchased with a value of over f.300. Upon purchasing the item the shopkeeper has to fill in a certificate of export (form OB90). When leaving the Netherlands the form is handed to Dutch customs. The returned certificates of export are sent back to the shops and the BTW will then be forwarded by cheque or postal order.

Some shops are affiliated to "Holland Tax Free" shopping which caters for the repayment of this tax, but administration and service charges are deducted from the amount of tax refunded. For further details, obtain the leaflet, "Tax Free for Tourists" from Schiphol airport or VVV offices.

attractive reproduction Delft tiles. For a huge range of antique tiles, try Eduard Kramer, Nieuwe Spiegelstraat 64.

OTHER GIFTS

Tulips and bulbs are always popular. If you fail to get them at the flower market (*see below*) you can buy them at higher prices at Schiphol Airport. Other things typically Dutch are: cigars (the best known shop is Hajenius, Rokin 92) and chocolates made by Van Houten, Verkade or Droste (Pompadour at Huidensstraat 12 has a superb selection, as does Jordino, who also makes exquisite Italian ice cream at 25 Harlemmerdijk). There's always Edam and Gouda cheeses and clogs for those who love to garden. Excursions to Volendam, Marken or Zaanse Schans usually take in a cheese farm and a visit to a craftsman making clogs – one pair can take as little as five minutes to make.

SCHIPHOL AIRPORT

If there are any guilders left you will no doubt be tempted by the enormous range of goods at Schiphol Airport. Despite the changes in duty-free laws, there is an excellent food section, selling smoked Dutch eel and cheeses, and shops specialising in bulbs and seeds, flowers, Delftware, clothes and souvenirs. There are also clothing shops with brands like Mexx, Esprit, Inwear and Benetton, as well as some speciality shops where you can find some unusual and affordable gifts.

MARKETS

Amsterdam's street markets are a source of amusement and interest.

Flower market: Singel. Monday–Friday 9am–6pm, Saturday 9am–5pm. Probably Amsterdam's most famous market, housed in

boats and bright with colours and perfumes even in the depths of winter. Prices are reasonable and quality is excellent.
Flea market: Waterlooplein. Monday–Saturday 10am–5pm. Lively and fun.
Farm produce: Noordermarkt or Oudemanhuispoort. Saturday 10am–4pm.
Book market: Oudemanhuispoort. Monday–Saturday 10am–4pm. Unusual books and prints. Far more interesting is the extensive antiquarian book market, held every Friday 10am–6pm at the Spuiplein and during the summer one Sunday each month at Dam Square or next to the Muziektheater.
Stamp market: NZ Voorburgwal. Wednesday and Saturday 1–4pm. Stamps and coins.
Open-air antique market: Nieuwmarkt. Daily 9am–5pm May–September.
Antiques, curiosities and junk: "De Looier", 109 Elandsgracht. Saturday–Thursday 11am–5pm Indoor market.
Flea and Textile market: Noordermarkt/ Westerstraat. Monday 9am–1pm. An interesting mix of people and junk. Have a cup of coffee and a piece of *appletaart* at the corner Winkel Café – some say it is the best in the city.
Bird market: Noordermarkt. Saturday 8am–1pm.
Art market: Thorbeckeplein. April–October, Sunday 10.30am–6pm. Artists sell their own drawings and paintings – some of the work is very good.
General markets: Albert Cuypstraat: Monday–Saturday 9.30am–5pm; Westerstraat: Monday 9am–1pm.

The Hague

The main shopping street is Grote Marktstraat. Here you will find the department store De Bijenkorf, notable for its fine architecture and interiors. Behind is a network of covered arcades lined with small and characterful shops. For art, antiques and cafés, go to Noordeinde. On Thursdays, there is a book market near the square by the American embassy.

Rotterdam

In Rotterdam the better shops are concentrated around Lijnbaan and Binnenweigplein. Antiques, art and crafts can be found in the market on Mariniersweg, in the old port, on Tuesday and Saturday 9am–5pm and also in the museum quarter on side streets.

Sport

Participant Sports

Canoeing
For all information contact The Netherlands Canoe Association, Postbus 1160, 3800 BD, Amersfoort, tel: 033-4622341, fax: 033-4612714.

Cycling
The leaflet *Cycling in Holland*, available from The Netherlands Board of Tourism (see *Planning the Trip: Tourist Offices*) contains information on long-distance routes and special holidays. See also *Getting Around: Cycling*.

Fishing
Holland – The Ideal Angling Country contains information on licences, angling centres, fishing excursions and the hire of equipment and can be had from The Netherlands Board of Tourism (see *Planning the Trip: Tourist Offices*) or contact the NNVS, Postbus 288, 3800 AG Amersfoort, tel: 033-46 3 4924.

Golf
For information on courses open to non-members, contact the Dutch Golf Federation, Postbus 221, 3454 ZL, De Meern, tel: 030-662188, fax: 030-662 1177.

Horse Riding
For details of facilities ask The Netherlands Tourist Board for its *Horseriding* brochure or contact the NHS, Postbus 456, 3740 AL Baarn, tel: 035-548 3600, fax: 035-541 1563.

Sailing
For an introduction to the multitude of options, with practical advice and suggested itineraries, ask for the brochure *Holland: Watersports Paradise*, which is available from The Netherlands Board of Tourism. The NBT also has brochures on *Traditional Sailing, Boat Hire* and *Sailing Schools*. See also *Excursions: Boat Trips & Charter*.

Watersports
Apart from the brochure mentioned above, information on windsurfing, skiing, motor-boating, etc can be obtained from Koninklijk Nederlands Watersport Verbond, Postbus 53034, 1007 RA Amsterdam.

Spectator Sports

Football
Amsterdam's Ajax is one of the top European clubs and tickets for games, played at the Ajax Stadium, 3 Arena Boulevard, in southeast Amsterdam, can be booked in advance through the **vvv** or travel agents, or bought at the gate. The Ajax Museum is also worth visiting, though it is closed on game days. Take the Metro to the Strandvliet exit.

Many cities in the Netherlands have clubs of world class (e.g. Rotterdam's Feyenoord FC; The Hague's FC Den Haag; PSV Eindhoven). The local **vvv** can supply details.

Golf
The Open Dutch Championship Golf Tournament is held in Hilversum every July.

Motor Racing
National and international events are held at the Circuit Park Zandvoort#. The big event of the year is the Zandvoort Grand Prix, which is held at the end of August. Assen is the place to be in June for the International Netherlands Motorcycling T.T. Grand Prix.

Tennis
The International Tennis Tournament, held in Rotterdam in late February/early March, brings world-class players to the Netherlands. The Dutch Open Championships are held in Amsterdam every July.

Language

Useful Words

Almost every Dutch person speaks English, but it is useful to recognise some words and phrases in timetables and menus. You will also gain more respect if you try to speak the language, however hesitantly.

Days of the Week
Monday *Maandag*
Tuesday *Dinsdag*
Wednesday *Woensdag*
Thursday *Donderdag*
Friday *Vrijdag*
Saturday *Zaterdag*
Sunday *Zondag*

Greetings and Pleasantries
hello/goodbye *dag (pronounced "dach")*
good morning *goedenmorgen*
good afternoon *goedenmiddag*

Numbers

One *Een*
Two *Twee*
Three *Drie*
Four *Vier*
Five *Vijf*
Six *Zes*
Seven *Zeven*
Eight *Acht*
Nine *Negen*
Ten *Tien*
Twenty *Twintig*
Thirty *Dertig*
Forty *Veertig*
Fifty *Vijftig*
Sixty *Zestig*
Seventy *Zeventig*
Eighty *Tachtig*
Ninety *Negentig*
Hundred *Honderd*

good evening *goedenavond*
goodbye *tot ziens*
see you later *tot straks*
thank you very much *dank u wel*
please *als't u blieft*
I am sorry, pardon *neemt u mij niet kwalijk*
yes *ja*
no *nee*

Out and About
open *open*
closed *gesloten*
entrance *ingang*
exit *uitgang*
admission free *vrije toegang*
left *links*
right *rechts*
church *kerk*
theatre *theater*
cinema *bioscoop*

Street Signs
no entry *verboden toegang*
through traffic *doorgaand verkeer*
no parking *niet parkeren*
hospital *ziekenhuis*
police *politie*
fire brigade *brandweer*

Bars and Cafés
bottle *fles*
glass *glas*
cup *kop*
lager *bier*
Dutch gin *jenever*
coffee, wine, liqueur *koffie, wijn, likeur*
no smoking *verboden te roken*

Newsagents and Post Offices
newspaper *krant*
magazines *tijdschriften*
how much does it cost? *wat kost dit?*
airmail *uchtpost*
ordinary mail *gewone post*
registered *aangetekend*
stamp *postzegel*

Further Reading

General

The British and the Dutch by K.H.D. Haley, George Philip, London (1988).
Political and cultural relations through the ages. A clear and exciting study of the love-hate relationship between the countries.
The Dutch Revolt by Geoffrey Parker, Peregrine Books (Penguin Group), London (1988).
A brilliant picture of the character of the Dutch in their revolt against the Spanish overlords during the Eighty Years War (1568–1648).
Dutch Art and Architecture 1600–1800 by Jakob Rosenberg et al, Penguin, London (1988).
A standard work, first published in 1966, rewritten by popular demand, with new insights especially into the works of Frans Hals and Rembrandt. Richly illustrated but in monochrome.
Dutch Painting by R.H. Fuchs Oxford University Press (1978; now reprinted).
A condensed though comprehensive overview of Dutch painting from the Middle Ages to the present, written by the current director of the Stedelijk Museum of Contemporary Art in Amsterdam.
The Story of Amsterdam by Anthony Vanderheiden, Rootveldt Boeken, Amsterdam (1987).
All the clichés about the Dutch capital in one volume of colour photographs and colourful prose.
The Embarrassment of Riches by Simon Schama, University of California Press (1988).
An academic but very readable insight into Golden Age culture.
The Low Sky: Understanding the Dutch by Han Vander Horst, Scriptum/Nuffic Books, The Hague (1996).
This thoughtful book investigates below the surface, into modern Holland's dilemmas and taboos.

The Undutchables by Colin White and Laurie Boucke, White & Boucke Publishing (1995).
An irreverent, often accurate, though cliché-ridden, observation of the Dutch and their habits.
The Tulip by Anna Pavord, Bloomsbury (1999).
Not just a horticultural examination of an extraordinary flower, but also a fantastic piece of sociological and historical research, revealing the tulip's turbulent past.
Rembrandt's Eyes by Simon Schama, Allen Lane (1999).
A fitting tribute to the artist who could turn the most formal portrait into what Schama terms "a statement of intimacy". Schama recreates not only the socio-political circumstances of Rembrandt's world but also its sights, sounds and smells.
Amsterdam – A Brief Life in the City by Geert Mak, Harvill Press (1999).
Part history, part imaginative travel guide, Mak's book traces the city's progress from a little town of merchants and fishermen into a thriving metropolis.

Other Insight Guides

The Insight Guides series, with 200 titles, plus 120 Insight Pocket Guides (with pull-out map) and 120 Insight Compact Guides, cover every significant travel destination.

Insight Guide: Amsterdam combines observant text and vivid photojournalism to give real insight into this youthful and permissive city where anything goes. The book begins with a vivid history section and a series of incisive essays designed to shed light on what it's like to live and work in the city. It then gives a complete run-down, with maps, on the sights worth seeing.

Insight Compact Guide: Holland is an intensely practical guide to an intensely practical country. A comprehensive yet portable read.
Insight Compact Guide: Amsterdam unveils the elegance of this canal-laced city; possibly Europe's most tolerant and embracingly pleasurable capital.

ART & PHOTO CREDITS

AKG London 26, 27, 29, 36, 46
Amsterdam Historical Museum
Back cover centre, 22/23, 25, 28, 43, 48, 104
Amsterdam Rijksmuseum 32, 39, 40, 41, 42, 134, 184
Axiom Photographic Agency 1, 307
Bram van Biezen/Foto Natura 162/163
Bodo Bondzio Back cover bottom, Back cover top right, 37, 69, 77, 82, 83, 86, 174, 177, 187, 281
Bogaard/Hollandse Hoogte 19
Hans van den Bos/Foto Natura 316
The Bridgeman Art Library 93, 94
Dirk Buwalda Back cover centre right, 6/7, 8/9, 14, 16, 17, 20, 58, 64/65, 66/67, 76, 101, 158, 201, 216, 238, 244, 256, 257, 261, 301, 309
Jan Castricum/Foto Natura 287
Cephas Picture Library 103, 108, 109, 113, 156, 159, 167, 205T, 206, 259T
theartarchive 45
Toon Fey/Foto Natura 317
Foster/Apa Photo Agency 60, 243
Lee Foster 149
Frans Hals Museum, Haarlem 33, 167T, 168
Robert Fried 140, 143T, 146, 176T, 179, 185T, 192, 193, 220, 224, 225T, 228
Guglielmo Galvin/Apa 133T, 141L, 152
Blaine Harrington Back cover main picture, 105, 114/115, 120, 148, 161, 165, 169T, 172T, 175, 181, 190, 191, 194, 197, 198, 198T, 199, 203T, 205, 273, 285, 302
Han Hartzuiker Back flap top, Front flap top, 96, 116/117, 131, 227, 236, 245, 246, 259
Sharon Hartzuiker 118/119
Hans Höfer 30
Michael Jenner 129
Martin Kers 230, 231, 234, 276, 278R, 314, 315, 319
Niels Kooyman/Foto Natura 293
Lyle Lawson Back flap bottom, 38, 80, 99, 170, 172

Hans Leijnse/Foto Natura 95
Eddy Marissen/Foto Natura 266
Wil Meinderts/Foto Natura 318
Dene Moedt/Foto Natura 311
Bert Muller/Foto Natura 98, 110, 111, 133, 135, 144, 144T, 157
Nealeman/Hollandse Hoogte 250
Netherlands Board of Tourism 180R, 185, 208/209
Flip de Nooyer/Foto Natura 268T, 269
Christine Osborne 100, 189, 229, 235
The Picture Box 49, 90/91, 164, 182, 186, 225, 271, 280, 285T, 298, 304/305, 313
Lesley Player 106, 112, 130, 138, 139T, 141R, 153, 160, 320
Eddy Posthuma de Boer Front flap bottom, 2/3, 2B, 34, 44, 68, 70, 71, 73, 78, 79, 81, 107, 137, 143, 148T, 150, 180L, 195, 200, 203, 207, 213, 215, 239, 240, 247, 248L, 248R, 249, 264/265, 267, 275, 277, 292, 299, 303, 306, 312T
Rex Features 62, 63, 75
Paul van Riel 10/11, 21, 74, 92, 97, 132, 139, 147, 151, 221, 226, 241, 242, 260
Aad Schenk/Foto Natura 312
Gordon Singer 87, 130T, 145, 151T, 188
Spaarnestad Fotoarchief 18, 50, 51, 52, 53, 54, 55, 56, 57, 59, 61, 142, 270
S T/Foto Natura 253
Thermae 2000 251
Topham Picturepoint 218
G. Veld/Foto Natura 290/291

D. van Veldhuizen/Foto Natura 310
Jan Vermeer/Foto Natura 284, 296/297
Wallrafen/Hollandse Hoogte 210
Bill Wassman/Apa 84, 85, 102, 128, 136, 171, 173, 183T, 199T, 204, 211, 214, 217, 217T, 233T, 237, 239T, 242T, 252, 254, 255T, 258, 272, 273T, 274, 278L, 279, 279T, 282, 283, 286, 295, 296T, 300, 308
George Wright 12/13, 72, 126/127

Picture Spreads

Pages 88–89 *Top row, left to right*: Lesley Player, Cephas/M J Kielty, Martin Kers, Cephas/M J Kielty. *Centre row*: Martin Kers, Picture Box. *Bottom row*: Cephas/ M J Kielty, Picture Box, Lesley Player.
Pages 154–155 *Top row, left to right*: Eddy Posthuma de Boer, Eduard Bergman, George Wright, Lesley Player. *Bottom row*: Lesley Player, Cephas/M J Kielty, Michael Jenner.
Pages 262–263 *Top row, left to right*: Picture Box, Jan Vermeer/Foto Natura, Picture Box. *Centre row*: both Picture Box. *Bottom row*: Eddy Posthuma de Boer, Picture Box, Eddy Posthuma de Boer.
Pages 288–289 *Top row, left to right*: C Castelijns/Foto Natura, Martin Kers, Martin Kers, Fred Hazelhoff/Foto Natura. *Centre row*: Flip de Nooyer/Foto Natura, Flip de Nooyer/Foto Natura. *Bottom row*: Dietmar Nill/Foto Natura, Hans Bos/Foto Natura, Flip de Nooyer/Foto Natura, Gerhard Schulz/Foto Natura.

INSIGHT GUIDE **NETHERLANDS**

Cartographic Editor **Zoë Goodwin**
Production **Stuart A Everitt**
Design Consultants
Carlotta Junger, Graham Mitchener
Picture Research **Hilary Genin**

Map Production Gar Bowes Design
© 2000 Apa Publications GmbH & Co.
Verlag KG (Singapore branch)

Index

*Numbers in italics refer
to photographs*

Amsterdam Transport

R40572